Lecture Notes in Computer Science 14251

The series Lecture Notes in Computer Science (LNCS), including its subseries Lecture Notes in Artificial Intelligence (LNAI) and Lecture Notes in Bioinformatics (LNBI), has established itself as a medium for the publication of new developments in computer science and information technology research, teaching, and education.

LNCS enjoys close cooperation with the computer science R & D community, the series counts many renowned academics among its volume editors and paper authors, and collaborates with prestigious societies. Its mission is to serve this international community by providing an invaluable service, mainly focused on the publication of conference and workshop proceedings and postproceedings. LNCS commenced publication in 1973.

Francesca Palumbo · Georgios Keramidas ·
Nikolaos Voros · Pedro C. Diniz
Editors

Applied Reconfigurable Computing

Architectures, Tools, and Applications

19th International Symposium, ARC 2023
Cottbus, Germany, September 27–29, 2023
Proceedings

 Springer

Editors
Francesca Palumbo
Università degli Studi di Sassari
Sassari, Italy

Georgios Keramidas
Aristotle University of Thessaloniki
Thessaloniki, Greece

Nikolaos Voros
University of Peloponnese
Patras, Greece

Pedro C. Diniz
University of Porto
Porto, Portugal

ISSN 0302-9743   ISSN 1611-3349 (electronic)
Lecture Notes in Computer Science
ISBN 978-3-031-42920-0   ISBN 978-3-031-42921-7 (eBook)
https://doi.org/10.1007/978-3-031-42921-7

This Springer imprint is published by the registered company Springer Nature Switzerland AG
The registered company address is: Gewerbestrasse 11, 6330 Cham, Switzerland

Paper in this product is recyclable.

Preface

The 19th International Symposium on Applied Reconfigurable Computing (ARC 2023) was organized by the Brandenburgische Technische Universität Cottbus-Senftenberg, Germany, from September 27–29, 2023.

As with previous years, the ARC 2023 edition covered a broad spectrum of applications of reconfigurable computing, from driving assistance, data and graph processing acceleration, and computer security to the societally relevant topic of supporting early diagnosis of Covid infectious conditions.

This year's symposium program included 18 regular and 4 short PhD papers selected from 33 submissions. The selection process was very competitive with each submission having three or four reviews. The symposium also included two special sessions, one session devoted to *Near and In-Memory Computing* and another to *Collaborative EU-funded Research Projects*.

This year's successful program was made possible by the contribution of many talented individuals. First, and foremost, we would like to thank all submission authors who responded to our call for papers, the members of the program committee and the additional external reviewers who, with their opinions and expertise, ensured a program of the highest quality.

Thank you all.

July 2023

Francesca Palumbo
Georgios Keramidas
Nikolaos Voros
Pedro C. Diniz

Organization

General Chairs

Marc Reichenbach   Brandenburg University of Technology
                                              Cottbus-Senftenberg, Germany
Diana Goehringer   TU Dresden, Germany

Program Committee Chairs

Francesca Palumbo   University of Sassari, Italy
Georgios Keramidas   Aristotle University of Thessaloniki, Greece
Nikolaos Voros   University of the Peloponnese, Greece

Steering Committee

Hideharu Amano   Keio University, Japan
Jürgen Becker   Karlsruhe Institute of Technology, Germany
Mladen Berekovic   Lübeck University, Germany
Koen Bertels   QBee.EU, Belgium
João M. P. Cardoso   University of Porto, Portugal
Katherine (Compton) Morrow   University of Wisconsin-Madison, USA
George Constantinides   Imperial College London, UK
Pedro C. Diniz   University of Porto, Portugal
Philip H. W. Leong   University of Sydney, Australia
Walid Najjar   University of California Riverside, USA
Roger Woods   Queen's University Belfast, UK

Program Committee

Hideharu Amano   Keio University, Japan
Christos Antonopoulos   University of the Peloponnese, Greece
Zachary Baker   Los Alamos National Laboratory, USA
João Bispo   University of Porto, Portugal
Vanderlei Bonato   University of São Paulo, Brazil
Marcelo Brandalero   Infineon Technologies, Germany

Christos Bouganis	Imperial College London, UK
João Canas Ferreira	University of Porto, Portugal
João M. P. Cardoso	University of Porto, Portugal
Luigi Carro	Universidade Federal do Rio Grande do Sul, Brazil
Ray Cheung	City University of Hong Kong, China
Daniel Chillet	University of Rennes 1 - IRISA/Inria, France
Steven Derrien	University of Rennes 1 - IRISA/Inria, France
Pedro C. Diniz	University of Porto, Portugal
Giorgos Dimitrakopoulos	Democritus University of Thrace, Greece
António Ferrari	University of Aveiro, Portugal
Ricardo Ferreira	Universidade Federal de Viçosa, Brasil
Mohammad Ghasemzadeh	Apple Inc, USA
Roberto Giorgi	University of Siena, Italy
Diana Goehringer	TU Dresden, Germany
Marek Gorgon	AGH University of Science and Technology, Poland
Frank Hannig	Friedrich-Alexander University Erlangen-Nürnberg, Germany
Jim Harkin	University of Ulster, UK
Christian Hochberger	TU Darmstadt, Germany
Michael Huebner	Brandenburg University of Technology Cottbus-Senftenberg, Germany
Lester Kalms	TU Dresden, Germany
Kimon Karras	Think Silicon S.A., Greece
Krzysztof Kepa	GE Global Research, USA
Georgios Keramidas	Aristotle University of Thessaloniki, Greece
Paraskevas Kitsos	University of the Peloponnese, Greece
Andreas Koch	TU Darmstadt, Germany
Angeliki Kritikakou	University of Rennes 1 - IRISA/Inria, France
Tomasz Kryjak	AGH University of Science and Technology, Poland
Konstantinos Masselos	University of the Peloponnese, Greece
Cathal McCabe	Xilinx, UK
Antonio Miele	Politecnico di Milano, Italy
Takefumi Miyoshi	e-trees.Japan, Inc., Japan
Horácio Neto	University of Lisbon, Portugal
Dimitris Nikolos	University of Patras, Greece
Andrés Otero	Universidad Politécnica de Madrid, Spain
Kyprianos Papadimitriou	Technical University of Crete, Greece
Monica Pereira	Universidade Federal do Rio Grande do Norte, Brazil

Nikolaos Petrels	University of the Peloponnese, Greece
Thilo Pionteck	Otto-von-Guericke Universität Magdeburg, Germany
Marco Platzner	University of Paderborn, Germany
Mihalis Psarakis	University of Piraeus, Greece
Fernando Rincón	Universidad de Castilla-La Mancha, Spain
Yukinori Sato	Toyohashi University of Technology, Japan
António Carlos Schneider	Universidade Federal do Rio Grande do Sul, Brazil
Olivier Sentieys	University of Rennes 1 - IRISA/Inria, France
Yuichiro Shibata	Nagasaki University, Japan
Hayden Kwok-Hay So	University of Hong Kong, China
Dimitrios Soudris	National Technical University of Athens, Greece
George Souliotis	University of the Peloponnese, Greece
George Theodoridis	University of Patras, Greece
Chao Wang	University of Science and Technology of China, China

Additional Reviewers

Aqib Javed
Marco Procaccini
Ricardo G. Aguiar
Nidhin Thandassery Sumithran
David Simpson
Daniele Passaretti

Contents

Architectures

Special Session: Near and In-Memory Computing

PhD Forum Papers

Design Methods and Tools

High-Level Synthesis of Memory Systems for Decoupled Data Orchestration

Masayuki Usui[✉] and Shinya Takamaeda-Yamazaki

The University of Tokyo, Tokyo, Japan
{mu2519,shinya}@is.s.u-tokyo.ac.jp

Abstract. With the end of Dennard scaling and the slowdown in Moore's law, domain-specific hardware accelerators are increasingly popular. Although accelerators achieve high performance and energy efficiency, their design requires considerable effort. To increase the productivity of accelerator design, high-level synthesis (HLS) generates hardware from high-level descriptions, raising the level of abstraction. The efficiency of memory systems in accelerators significantly impacts performance. However, the design of such memory systems can be cumbersome because high-performance accelerators often require explicit decoupled data orchestration (EDDO). EDDO is suited to accelerators because explicit control over data movement allows exploiting domain knowledge to improve performance, and decoupled hardware modules for data movement enable the overlapping of computation and data transfers between on- and off-chip memories. To facilitate the design of accelerators with high-performance EDDO memory systems, we propose a high-level synthesis method for generating optimized memory systems based on decoupled data orchestration. Our method splits high-level source code into computation and communication parts and synthesizes each part into hardware using HLS. In addition, we incorporate synchronization mechanisms in data structures to synchronize decoupled hardware modules. To support complex memory access patterns such as data-dependent indirect accesses, we also propose partially decoupled data orchestration based on the fork-join model. To automate partial decoupling, our method automatically determines the points to fork and join at by hierarchically testing whether decoupling is possible. We implemented the proposed method on top of the HLS tool Veriloggen. We evaluated the performance of accelerators for GeMM and SpMM synthesized using the proposed method. Experiments show that the accelerators achieved at most 2x performance.

Keywords: High-level synthesis (HLS) · Accelerator · Memory system · Explicit decoupled data orchestration (EDDO)

1 Introduction

With the end of Dennard scaling and the slowdown in Moore's law, performance benefits can no longer be derived solely from the evolution of semiconductor

© The Author(s), under exclusive license to Springer Nature Switzerland AG 2023
F. Palumbo et al. (Eds.): ARC 2023, LNCS 14251, pp. 3–18, 2023.
https://doi.org/10.1007/978-3-031-42921-7_1

technology, necessitating enhancing computer architecture. One promising approach is to design hardware optimized for specific applications, called accelerators [8,11]. Although accelerators achieve high performance and energy efficiency, their design requires considerable effort. Hardware description languages (HDLs), such as Verilog HDL and VHDL, are traditionally used for accelerator design; however, they require low-level specifications. To increase the productivity of accelerator design, high-level synthesis (HLS) raises the level of abstraction by converting behavioral specifications described using high-level programming languages, such as C/C++ and Python, into structural specifications described using HDLs. Various HLS tools have been developed [3,4,7,13]. Among them, Veriloggen [3,13] is an open-source HLS tool that converts Python code into Verilog HDL code, and our implementation is based on it, as will be mentioned later.

A memory system is a critical component of an accelerator. Buffets [12] discuss data orchestration, the organization of a memory system, and point out that explicit decoupled data orchestration (EDDO) is suited for accelerators. In EDDO, data movement is explicitly controlled, allowing leveraging domain knowledge to improve performance. In addition, a separate hardware module handles data movement in EDDO; thus, computation and communication (data transfers between on- and off-chip memories) are overlapped, improving performance.

Although EDDO enhances performance, it complicates accelerator design because it requires decoupling the hardware module for communication from the one for computation and adding mechanisms for synchronization between the decoupled modules. In this paper, we propose a method to automate these procedures, thereby facilitating the development of accelerators with EDDO. Figure 1 illustrates the proposed method. First, our method splits source code into computation and communication parts and synthesizes each part into hardware using HLS. The hardware synthesized without our method (the left side of Fig. 1) cannot overlap computation and communication because the same module both computes and communicates. By contrast, the hardware synthesized with our method (the right side of Fig. 1) can overlap computation and communication because separate modules compute and communicate, working in parallel. Second, we incorporate synchronization mechanisms in data structures to synchronize decoupled hardware modules. We propose two data structures for this purpose: PIPO and BuffetLike. PIPO, derived from a ping-pong buffer, materializes double buffering. BuffetLike, a variant of a buffet [12], enables fine-grained synchronization.

In applications with complex memory access patterns, communication cannot be perfectly decoupled from computation. A typical example of such applications is sparse linear algebra with indirect memory accesses. To support these applications, we introduce partial decoupling based on the fork-join model. To automate the partial decoupling, our method automatically determines the points to fork and join at. The proposed method recursively traverses an abstract syntax tree and hierarchically tests whether decoupling is possible.

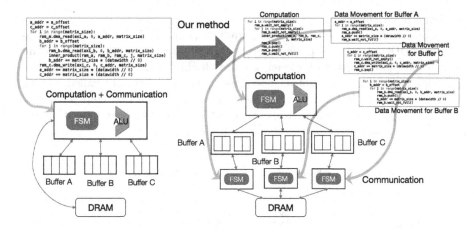

Fig. 1. The illustration of the proposed method. Source code is split into computation and communication parts, each synthesized into hardware using HLS. A gray arrow represents the relation that a program is synthesized into a hardware module. Separate finite-state machines (FSMs) within hardware modules indicate that the modules operate independently.

We implemented the proposed method on top of the HLS tool Veriloggen [3, 13]. We implemented accelerators for GeMM and SpMM on an FPGA to evaluate the proposed method. Decoupled data orchestration synthesized using PIPO reduces execution time by almost half. Performance improvement by decoupled data orchestration synthesized using BuffetLike is less than that by decoupled data orchestration synthesized using PIPO; however, BuffetLike consumes fewer resources than PIPO.

2 Background and Related Work

2.1 Taxonomy of Data Orchestration

Buffets [12] classify data orchestration, the organization of a memory system, along two axes: implicit versus explicit and coupled versus decoupled. Buffets advocate that explicit decoupled data orchestration (EDDO) is best suited to accelerators.

In implicit data orchestration (the left side of Fig. 2), a cache handles data movement between on- and off-chip memories; the programmer is uninvolved. In explicit data orchestration (the right side of Fig. 2), on the other hand, the programmer or architect explicitly controls data movement between on- and off-chip memories. The advantage of explicit data orchestration is that explicit control over data movement allows leveraging domain knowledge to improve performance. For example, it is possible to streamline data movement in matrix multiplication by tiling matrices so that they fit in local buffers and swapping data tile by tile. Because of this advantage, explicit data orchestration is often employed in accelerators.

Among explicit data orchestration paradigms, explicit decoupled data orchestration (EDDO) improves performance by overlapping computation and communication (data transfers between on- and off-chip memories). In EDDO (the right side of Fig. 3), a decoupled, independent hardware module, called a DMA engine, is responsible for data movement between on- and off-chip memories. The DMA engine operates in parallel with the datapath; thus, computation and communication are overlapped, increasing performance.

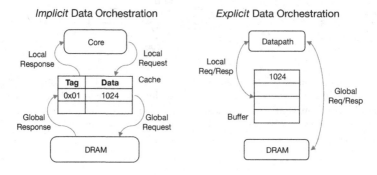

Fig. 2. Implicit data orchestration versus explicit data orchestration.

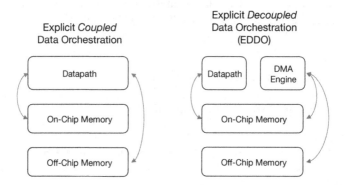

Fig. 3. Explicit coupled data orchestration versus explicit decoupled data orchestration (EDDO).

2.2 Storage Idioms

Many studies have proposed various storage idioms (effective usages of memories). Furthermore, some studies present compilation frameworks to utilize storage idioms.

LEAP Scratchpads [6] divide monolithic off-chip memory into multiple scratchpads. Each client has its own scratchpad interface, and the scratchpad controller handles arbitration between clients.

CoRAM [9] decouples data transfers between SRAMs and a DRAM from computation. The user logic interacts with an external memory only through specific SRAMs called CoRAMs. Control threads, which are essentially FSMs, handle data movement between CoRAMs and an external memory. Although data orchestration is decoupled in the CoRAM architecture, the user must manually decouple it. C-to-CoRAM [14] compiles C source code into the CoRAM abstraction but only supports fixed-bound perfectly-nested loops. On the contrary, our work supports arbitrary programs and decouples data orchestration.

DeSC [10] decouples memory accesses from computation. The Supplier Device (SuppD) computes addresses and accesses memory, whereas the Computation Device (CompD) computes values. The DeSC compiler splits source code into the communication slice, executed by the SuppD, and the computation slice, executed by the CompD. While DeSC achieves the overlapping of computation and communication through decoupling memory accesses from computation, they use caches for data reuse, potentially leading to suboptimal performance for accelerators. In contrast, our method adopts explicit data orchestration and has the potential to improve performance by leveraging domain knowledge.

Buffets [12] introduce a storage idiom with fine-grained synchronization for EDDO, discussed in Sect. 2.1. Buffets allow hierarchical composition and support multicast.

3 PIPO: An Data Structure for Decoupled Data Orchestration

We introduce a data structure to synchronize decoupled hardware modules in synthesizing memory systems for decoupled data orchestration, and refer to the data structure as PIPO (derived from a ping-pong buffer). PIPO realizes double buffering in effect. Although double buffering is frequently employed, the concept of double buffering is merely swapping buffers and is abstract. We propose concrete structure and operations to apply double buffering on the high-level synthesis of memory systems for decoupled data orchestration.

3.1 Definition of PIPO

Because PIPO is similar to FIFO, we explain PIPO by comparing it with FIFO. We refer to the entity generating data as the producer and the one using data as the consumer. Figure 4 shows the structure of FIFO and PIPO. FIFO is

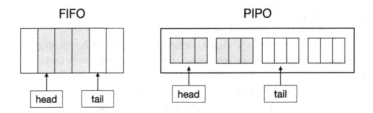

Fig. 4. Structure of FIFO and PIPO.

implemented with one RAM, and an element of FIFO is an element of a RAM. On the other hand, PIPO is implemented with multiple RAMs, and an element of PIPO is an entire RAM. PIPO can be viewed as FIFO whose element is a whole RAM. In FIFO, the head register points to the location from which the consumer reads data, whereas the tail register points to the location to which the producer writes data. In PIPO, the head register points to the location that the consumer reads data from or writes data to, whereas the tail register points to the location that the producer reads data from or writes data to.

```
class FIFO:                        def push(self, data):                       def pop(self):
    def __init__(self, size):          while self.occupancy == self.size:          while self.occupancy == 0:
        self.ram = RAM(size)               pass                                        pass
        self.size = size               self.ram[self.tail] = data                  data = self.ram[self.head]
        self.head = 0                  self.tail = (self.tail + 1) % self.size     self.head = (self.head + 1) % self.size
        self.tail = 0                  self.occupancy += 1                         self.occupancy -= 1
        self.occupancy = 0                                                         return data
```

Fig. 5. Python-like pseudocode for FIFO implementation.

```
class PIPO:                                    def push(self):
    def __init__(self, size, length):              self.tail = (self.tail + 1) % self.length
        self.rams = [RAM(size)                     self.occupancy += 1
                     for i in range(length)]   def pop(self):
        self.length = length                       self.head = (self.head + 1) % self.length
        self.head = 0                              self.occupancy -= 1
        self.tail = 0                          def read_producer(self, addr):
        self.occupancy = 0                         return self.rams[self.tail][addr]
    def wait_not_full(self):                   def write_producer(self, addr, data):
        while self.occupancy == self.length:       self.rams[self.tail][addr] = data
            pass                               def read_consumer(self, addr):
    def wait_not_empty(self):                      return self.rams[self.head][addr]
        while self.occupancy == 0:             def write_consumer(self, addr, data):
            pass                                   self.rams[self.head][addr] = data
```

Fig. 6. Python-like pseudocode for PIPO implementation.

Figure 5 and 6 show pseudocode for operations in FIFO and PIPO, respectively. In FIFO, the push operation writes data and increments the head register, whereas the pop operation reads data and increments the tail register. In PIPO, on the other hand, the push operation only increments the head register, whereas the pop operation only increments the tail register. This difference stems from the fact that data elements are added to or removed from FIFO one by one, and double buffering switches the entire RAM at once. Therefore, separate read and write operations are provided in PIPO.

FIFO and PIPO are used for communication and synchronization between the producer and consumer. Blocking is necessary to prevent reading from or writing to an invalid location because the producer and consumer operate independently in this settings. It is reasonable to integrate blocking into the push and pop operations in FIFO because data elements are added and removed one by one. Accordingly, the push and pop methods in Fig. 5 include the while loops for blocking. In contrast, it is suboptimal to integrate blocking into the read and write operations in PIPO because an entire RAM is switched at once. The producer and consumer read from and write to the same RAM many times before they eventually swap RAMs. As such, checking fullness or emptiness only once before reading or writing multiple times is possible. To this end, separate blocking operations for synchronization are provided in PIPO. The wait_not_full and wait_not_empty methods in Fig. 6 correspond to those operations.

3.2 Automatic Insertion of API Calls

While FIFO only requires the user to call the push and pop functions, PIPO requires the user to properly call many functions: push, pop, wait_not_full, wait_not_empty, read, and write. To facilitate development, we propose an algorithm to automatically insert these functions except read and write. The read and write functions are closely tied to the algorithm described by the user, and it is impossible to insert them automatically.

The algorithm splits an input program into the producer and consumer parts and inserts appropriate API calls into the boundary between these parts. Specifically, it inserts the push and wait_not_empty calls into the location corresponding to the transition from the producer part to the consumer part, and inserts the pop and wait_not_full calls into the location corresponding to the transition from the consumer part to the producer part.

Figure 7 shows an example of automatic insertion of API calls. The region from line 3 to line 5 is the producer part because it transfers data from the main memory to the local buffer. The region from line 6 to line 7 is the consumer part because it reads the transferred data. The algorithm inserts the push and wait_not_empty calls between line 5 and 6 because the producer part ends at line 5 and the consumer part starts at line 6. The algorithm inserts the pop and wait_not_full calls into just after line 7 because the consumer part ends at line 7 and the producer part starts at line 3 if we unroll the for loop or suppose that one end of the loop connects to the other end of the same loop.

4 Automatic Decoupling of Data Orchestration

4.1 RAM-Wise Decoupling

We must decouple data orchestration RAM by RAM because data structures for decoupled data orchestration have blocking operations, including the push

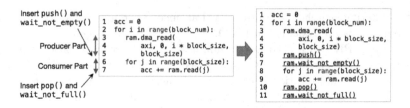

Fig. 7. An example of automatic insertion of API calls.

and `pop` operations of the FIFO and the `wait_not_full` and `wait_not_empty` operations of the PIPO. If we implement data orchestration mechanisms for multiple RAMs as a single thread or FSM, the thread or FSM will be blocked by one RAM while other RAMs can be accessed.

4.2 Decoupling Algorithm

We decouple data orchestration by the following algorithm:

1. – DMA engine: Extract function calls for DMA (`dma_read`, `push`, and `wait_not_full` for DMA read; `dma_write`, `pop`, and `wait_not_empty` for DMA write)
    – Datapath: Extract function calls with side effects except ones for DMA.
2. Extract variables appearing in the arguments of the extracted function calls.
3. Construct a dependence graph whose nodes are variables.
4. Collect variables reachable from the extracted variables in the graph.
5. The resulting code is the extracted function calls plus the assignment statements whose destination variables are contained in the collected variables.

4.3 Compilation Example

Figure 8 illustrates compilation steps. The input code (shown at the top left of the figure) performs matrix multiplication $AB = C$. It contains RAM A, B, and C, corresponding to matrix A, B, and C, respectively. The algorithm presented in the preceding section inserts API calls for each RAM, generating the code shown at the top right of the figure. The algorithm presented in this section decouples data orchestration, generating the code shown at the bottom left of the figure.

5   Automatic Partial Decoupling

5.1   Partial Decoupling Based on the Fork-Join Model

By the method described above, communication cannot be decoupled from computation in applications with complex memory access patterns. Examples

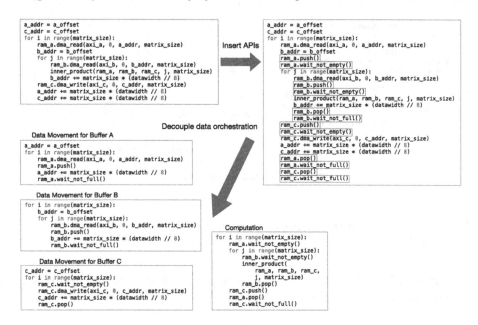

Fig. 8. Example of compilation process. Red frames indicate inserted API calls. (Color figure online)

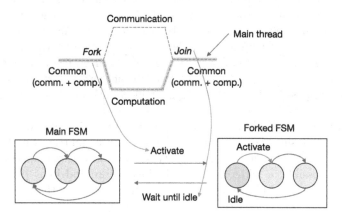

Fig. 9. The fork-join model and its implementation. At the fork point, the main FSM forces the forked FSM to transition from the idle state to another state. At the join point, the main FSM waits until the forked FSM is in the idle state.

include sparse workloads, including SpMM, where dependencies caused by indirect accesses hinder decoupling. Specifically, data orchestration for each RAM cannot be separated because the address computation for one RAM requires data from another RAM. To support these applications, we propose partial decoupling of data orchestration based on the fork-join model. Figure 9 illustrates the partial decoupling and its implementation. When forking, the main FSM activates

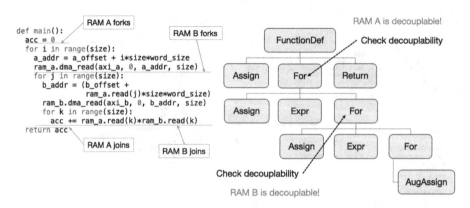

Fig. 10. Example of automatic partial decoupling. Source code is shown on the left side. A corresponding abstract syntax tree is shown on the right side.

the forked FSM by forcing it to transition from the idle state to another. When joining, the main FSM waits until the forked FSM is in the idle state.

5.2   Automatically Determining the Fork and Join Points

To automate partial decoupling, we must automatically determine the points to fork and join at. Our approach is to hierarchically test whether decoupling is possible. We recursively traverse an abstract syntax tree (AST) and try to fork just before and join just after the node when we encounter a node of specific types such as If, For, and While. Because we visit from the root node to leaf nodes, as wide a range as possible is selected. In these procedures, we judge that decoupling is impossible for a DMA engine if any RAM read by the DMA engine is written.

Figure 10 illustrates automatic partial decoupling. Our method recursively traverses the AST shown on the right side of the figure and tests whether decoupling is possible when a node of specific types (For in this example) is visited. If judged as possible, a DMA engine forks just before and joins just after the node. Consequently, DMA engines fork and join as shown on the left side of the figure.

6   BuffetLike: Another Data Structure for Decoupled Data Orchestration

Double buffering enables the overlapping of computation and communication, thereby improving performance. However, it is inefficient in resource utilization because it requires twice as many resources as the original RAM. Buffets [12] improve performance without requiring extra resources through fine-grained synchronization. Based on a buffet [12], we propose a resource-efficient data structure to synthesize memory systems for decoupled data orchestration. We call it BuffetLike.

Figure 11 shows the structure of BuffetLike. The `head` and `tail` registers manage the region accessed by the datapath. The datapath can access the range from `head` (inclusive) to `tail` (exclusive). The `base` register serves as a base address for data accesses. If the datapath wants to access data whose index is `index`, it accesses the location whose address is `base + index`. The `limit` register determines the limit of indices. If the datapath tries to access data whose index is `index` such that `index >= limit`, it is blocked until `index < limit` holds. Note that `(base + limit) % size == tail` holds, where `size` denotes the size of the underlying RAM.

Figure 12 shows the implementation of BuffetLike. BuffetLike is implemented as either the fill or drain version. The datapath accesses data via the `read` or `write` operation. The datapath is blocked if the data is unavailable, as noted above. The `release` operation frees elements and advances `head` one by one. Accordingly, we must make `base` follow `head` at some point. The `rebase` operation does this by making the `base` register equal to the `head` register. In the fill version, the DMA engine reads data from off-chip memory and writes it to the freed location through the `fill` operation. In the drain version, the DMA engine reads data from the freed location through the `drain` operation and writes it to off-chip memory.

BuffetLike has one essential difference from a buffet [12]: the register used as a base address for data accesses (the `base` register in BuffetLike) and the register used to manage the front of the region accessed by the datapath (the `head` register in BuffetLike) are distinct. If they are identical, the datapath must modify indices to access data whenever it frees a location. This is inconvenient for high-level synthesis and complicates address generation.

In our method, the algorithm presented in the previous sections decouples data orchestration, as in PIPO.

7   Evaluation

7.1   Experimental Setup

We selected general matrix multiplication (GeMM) from dense workloads and sparse-matrix dense-matrix multiplication (SpMM) from sparse workloads. We designed accelerators for these workloads. We implemented the accelerators on an FPGA. We used the Ultra96-V2 [2] as an FPGA board and Vivado 2022.2 [5]

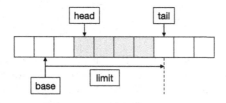

Fig. 11. Structure of BuffetLike.

```
class BuffetLikeBase:                           class BuffetLikeFill(BuffetLikeBase):
    def __init__(self, size):                       def __init__(self, size):
        self.ram = RAM(size)                            super().__init__(size)
        self.size = size                                self.occupancy = 0
        self.head = 0                                   self.limit = 0
        self.tail = 0                               def fill(self, data):
        self.base = 0                                   while self.occupancy == self.size:
    def read(self, index):                                  pass
        while index >= self.limit:                      self.ram[self.tail] = data
            pass                                        self.tail = (self.tail + 1) % self.size
        addr = (self.base + index) % self.size          self.occupancy += 1
        return self.ram[addr]                           self.limit += 1
    def write(self, index, data):
        while index >= self.limit:              class BuffetLikeDrain(BuffetLikeBase):
            pass                                    def __init__(self, size):
        addr = (self.base + index) % self.size          super().__init__(size)
        self.ram[addr] = data                           self.occupancy = size
    def release(self):                                  self.limit = size
        self.head = (self.head + 1) % self.size     def drain(self):
        self.occupancy -= 1                             while self.occupancy == self.size:
    def rebase(self):                                       pass
        self.base = self.head                           data = self.ram[self.tail]
        self.limit = self.occupancy                     self.tail = (self.tail + 1) & self.size
                                                        self.occupancy += 1
                                                        self.limit += 1
                                                        return data
```

Fig. 12. Python-like pseudocode for BuffetLike implementation. `BuffetLikeBase` is a base class. `BuffetLikeFill` is the fill version. `BuffetLikeDrain` is the drain version.

as an EDA tool. We utilized PYNQ [1] to control the FPGA from the CPU in a SoC FPGA. We set the clock frequency to 300 MHz.

We modified the source code of Veriloggen [3,13] to implement the proposed method. Accelerators synthesized by the modified version of Veriloggen are compared to the baseline accelerators synthesized by the original version of Veriloggen.

7.2 Execution Time

Figure 13 compares the execution time of accelerators. Our method reduces execution time by almost half. Our method (using PIPO) almost fully overlaps computation and communication because the execution time of accelerators with our method (using PIPO) is almost equal to the longer of computation and communication parts of the execution time of baseline accelerators (the computation

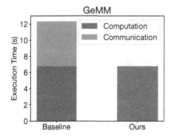
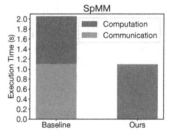

Fig. 13. Execution time of accelerators. Baseline is an accelerator without decoupled data orchestration. Ours is an accelerator with decoupled data orchestration synthesized by our method (using PIPO). The breakdown of execution time is shown for baseline. For ease of comparison between baseline and ours, computation and communication parts are piled in different orders for GeMM and SpMM accelerators.

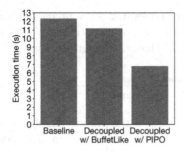

Fig. 14. Execution time of GeMM accelerators without decoupled data orchestration, with decoupled data orchestration synthesized using BuffetLike, and with decoupled data orchestration synthesized using PIPO.

part is longer than the communication one in GeMM, and it is the other way around in SpMM).

Figure 14 compares the execution time of GeMM accelerators. The execution time of the accelerator with data orchestration based on BuffetLike is shorter than that of the baseline accelerator but longer than that of the accelerator with data orchestration based on PIPO. This implies that decoupled data orchestration synthesized using BuffetLike partially overlaps computation and communication.

7.3   Resource Utilization

Table 1 compares the memory resource utilization of accelerators. The resource utilization of the accelerator with data orchestration based on PIPO is double that of the baseline accelerator because PIPO is based on double buffering. In contrast, the resource utilization of the accelerator with data orchestration based on BuffetLike is the same as that of the baseline accelerator.

Table 1. Memory resource utilization measured by the number of consumed block RAMs. Technically, the number of RAMB36 primitives is shown.

Method	GeMM	SpMM
Baseline	86.5	20
BuffetLike	86.5	N/A
PIPO	173	36

7.4   Discussion

We consider a performance model to interpret the results of the experiment. Let l_{comp} and l_{comm} be the latency of computation and communication, respectively.

The execution time of an accelerator without decoupled data orchestration is $l_{comp} + l_{comm}$. The execution time of an accelerator with decoupled data orchestration is $\max(l_{comp}, l_{comm})$. Hence, the performance gain is

$$\frac{l_{comp} + l_{comm}}{\max(l_{comp}, l_{comm})} = \frac{1}{\max(1 - r, r)} = \min\left(\frac{1}{1-r}, \frac{1}{r}\right)$$

where $r = l_{comm}/(l_{comp} + l_{comm})$ is the proportion of communication in execution time. Figure 15 shows the graph of this function. The performance gain is large if r is close to 0.5, that is, l_{comp} and l_{comm} are comparable. Furthermore, the upper bound of the performance gain is 2.

The performance gain close to the upper bound is achieved in the experiment because the latency of computation and communication is comparable (see Fig. 13). The condition of comparable latency is reasonable because the Roofline model [15] suggests that we should balance computation and communication to optimize performance. Nevertheless, the proposed method is less effective for applications inherently biased toward either computation or communication.

Decoupled data orchestration synthesized using BuffetLike improves performance without requiring additional resources, whereas decoupled data orchestration synthesized using PIPO further improves performance using more resources. BuffetLike is beneficial if memory resources are limited; otherwise, PIPO is helpful.

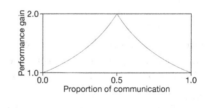

Fig. 15. Plot of performance gain when varying the proportion of communication in execution time.

8   Conclusion

We propose automatically decoupling data orchestration in explicit data orchestration. We introduce data structures for decoupled data orchestration: PIPO and BuffetLike. We present the automatic decoupling of data orchestration based on the data structures. We evaluate the proposed method with the GeMM and SpMM workloads. Decoupled data orchestration synthesized using PIPO reduces execution time by almost half. Decoupled data orchestration synthesized using BuffetLike reduces execution time without using extra resources.

Acknowledgements. This work is supported in part by JSPS KAKENHI 19H04075 and 18H05288, JST CREST JPMJCR21D2, the collaborative research with KONICA MINOLTA, and the research grant from Google.

References

1. PYNQ: Python productivity for Zynq. http://www.pynq.io/
2. Ultra96-V2.   https://www.avnet.com/wps/portal/us/products/avnet-boards/avnet-board-families/ultra96-v2/
3. Veriloggen: A Mixed-Paradigm Hardware Construction Framework. https://github.com/PyHDI/veriloggen
4. Vitis High-Level Synthesis User Guide. https://docs.xilinx.com/r/en-US/ug1399-vitis-hls
5. Vivado. https://www.xilinx.com/products/design-tools/vivado.html
6. Adler, M., Fleming, K.E., Parashar, A., Pellauer, M., Emer, J.: Leap scratchpads: automatic memory and cache management for reconfigurable logic. In: Proceedings of the 19th ACM/SIGDA International Symposium on Field Programmable Gate Arrays, FPGA 2011, pp. 25–28. Association for Computing Machinery, New York (2011). https://doi.org/10.1145/1950413.1950421
7. Canis, A., et al.: LegUp: high-level synthesis for FPGA-based processor/accelerator systems. In: Proceedings of the 19th ACM/SIGDA International Symposium on Field Programmable Gate Arrays, FPGA 2011, pp. 33–36. Association for Computing Machinery, New York (2011). https://doi.org/10.1145/1950413.1950423
8. Chen, Y.H., Krishna, T., Emer, J.S., Sze, V.: Eyeriss: an energy-efficient reconfigurable accelerator for deep convolutional neural networks. IEEE J. Solid-State Circuits **52**(1), 127–138 (2017). https://doi.org/10.1109/JSSC.2016.2616357
9. Chung, E.S., Hoe, J.C., Mai, K.: CoRAM: an in-fabric memory architecture for FPGA-based computing. In: Proceedings of the 19th ACM/SIGDA International Symposium on Field Programmable Gate Arrays, FPGA 2011, pp. 97–106. Association for Computing Machinery, New York (2011). https://doi.org/10.1145/1950413.1950435
10. Ham, T.J., Aragón, J.L., Martonosi, M.: DeSC: decoupled supply-compute communication management for heterogeneous architectures. In: Proceedings of the 48th International Symposium on Microarchitecture, MICRO-48, pp. 191–203. Association for Computing Machinery, New York (2015). https://doi.org/10.1145/2830772.2830800
11. Parashar, A., et al.: SCNN: an accelerator for compressed-sparse convolutional neural networks. In: Proceedings of the 44th Annual International Symposium on Computer Architecture, ISCA 2017, pp. 27–40. Association for Computing Machinery, New York (2017). https://doi.org/10.1145/3079856.3080254
12. Pellauer, M., et al.: Buffets: an efficient and composable storage idiom for explicit decoupled data orchestration. In: Proceedings of the Twenty-Fourth International Conference on Architectural Support for Programming Languages and Operating Systems, ASPLOS 2019, pp. 137–151. Association for Computing Machinery, New York (2019). https://doi.org/10.1145/3297858.3304025
13. Takamaeda-Yamazaki, S.: Pyverilog: a python-based hardware design processing toolkit for Verilog HDL. In: Sano, K., Soudris, D., Hübner, M., Diniz, P.C. (eds.) ARC 2015. LNCS, vol. 9040, pp. 451–460. Springer, Cham (2015). https://doi.org/10.1007/978-3-319-16214-0_42

14. Weisz, G., Hoe, J.C.: C-to-CoRAM: compiling perfect loop nests to the portable CoRAM abstraction. In: Proceedings of the ACM/SIGDA International Symposium on Field Programmable Gate Arrays, FPGA 2013, pp. 221–230. Association for Computing Machinery, New York (2013). https://doi.org/10.1145/2435264.2435302

15. Williams, S., Waterman, A., Patterson, D.: Roofline: an insightful visual performance model for multicore architectures. Commun. ACM **52**(4), 65–76 (2009). https://doi.org/10.1145/1498765.1498785

Rapid Prototyping of Complex Micro-architectures Through High-Level Synthesis

Sara Sadat Hoseininasab$^{(\boxtimes)}$ (ID), Caroline Collange, and Steven Derrien (ID)

Inria, Univ Rennes, CNRS, IRISA, Rennes, France
{sara-sadat.hoseininasab,caroline.collange}@inria.fr,
steven.derrien@irisa.fr

Abstract. Register-Transfer Level (RTL) design has been a traditional approach in hardware design for several decades. However, with the growing complexity of designs and the need for fast time-to-market, the design and verification process at the RTL level can become impractical. This has motivated for raising the abstraction level in hardware design. High-Level Synthesis (HLS) provides higher-level abstraction by automatically transforming a behavioral specification of a circuit into a low-level RTL, making it easier to design, simulate and verify complex digital systems. HLS relies on static scheduled data paths which can limit its effectiveness. This limitation makes it difficult to design the micro-architectural features of processors from an Instruction Set Architecture described in high-level languages. This work aims to demonstrate how the available features of HLS can be deployed in designing various pipelined processors micro-architecture. Our approach takes advantage of the capabilities of HLS and employs multi-threading and dynamic scheduling techniques to overcome the limitation of HLS in pipelining a processor from an Instruction Set Simulator written in C.

Keywords: High-Level Synthesis · Pipelined Micro-architecture · Multi-threading

1 Introduction

Field-programmable gate arrays (FPGAs) are flexible devices that offer numerous advantages for fast prototyping and evaluating complex designs, including CPUs and multi-cores [15]. During the hardware design process, prototyping serves as a crucial preliminary step to explore and evaluate designs before committing to the costly and time-consuming process of application-specific integrated circuit (ASIC) design. This approach enables designers to swiftly evaluate their designs on physical hardware, pinpoint any issues in the design process, and address them early on, prior to finalizing them for ASIC implementation.

Designing an FPGA-based soft-core processor using Register-Transfer Level (RTL) spans both software and hardware designs. First, the designer usually

© The Author(s), under exclusive license to Springer Nature Switzerland AG 2023
F. Palumbo et al. (Eds.): ARC 2023, LNCS 14251, pp. 19–34, 2023.
https://doi.org/10.1007/978-3-031-42921-7_2

expresses the Instruction Set Architecture (ISA) execution model using programming languages such as C/C++ to verify the functional correctness of the processor. Then they develop the processor with its micro-architectural features in Hardware Description Languages (HDLs) such as Verilog and VHDL for synthesis which requires detailed digital design knowledge at a low abstraction level. These two design steps are performed sequentially, resulting in a time-consuming and challenging design flow and verification process, particularly for individuals lacking a background in hardware engineering. However, with the advent of High-Level Synthesis (HLS), the design and verification steps can now be conducted in parallel, thereby streamlining the process and enhancing its efficiency. By increasing the abstraction level from RTL to the behavioral level in HLS, software developers can also program FPGAs by focusing on their algorithm rather than individual registers and cycle-to-cycle operations. HLS automatically translates a design written in high-level languages (e.g., C/C++) into a hardware description, making FPGA programming easier and accessible for all developers, reducing the design time, facilitating design exploration and evaluation, and simplifying debugging compared to the manual RTL [12].

The process of synthesizing a processor from a high-level programming language involves expressing the behavioral description of the ISA as an Instruction Set Simulator (ISS) model in C/C++ and utilizing the HLS tool to obtain the hardware implementation. Although HLS works well with straightforward control flows, it encounters challenges when dealing with data-dependent control flows [7]. As we will show in Sect. 2, current HLS tools cannot infer a fully pipelined micro-architecture from this ISS. Since HLS relies on static scheduled data paths, it conservatively considers dependencies on the program counter (pc) and register file for all instructions and limits the performance to the worse-case schedule data path. We will show in Sect. 4 how this work tackles the challenge of designing pipelined micro-architecture of a processor.

This study serves as a use case to demonstrate the potential of HLS for inferring the micro-architectural characteristics of processors from an ISS implemented in C, with a particular focus on the RISC-V ISA. Our contributions are outlined as follows:

- Exploiting automatic scheduling in HLS: We showcase the effective utilization of the automatic scheduling feature offered by HLS, enabling the design of a CPU without delving into the RTL implementation details.
- Designing various micro-architectures: We propose and implement various classes of micro-architectures, including dynamic single-threaded, static multi-threaded, dynamic multi-threaded, and multi-core designs.
- Performance and area evaluation: We thoroughly evaluate our designed micro-architectures in terms of both performance and area metrics. Performance assessment involves analyzing factors such as maximum clock speed (F_{max}), and Million Instruction Per Second (MIPS), while area evaluation includes the examination of resource utilization on an FPGA.

The rest of the paper is organized as follows. Section 2 provides the necessary background and the motivation of our work. We discuss related works in Sect. 3.

In Sect. 4, we dive into the details of our designs and implementations. The experimental results and concluding remarks are presented in Sects. 5 and 6, respectively.

2   Background and Motivation

A single-threaded in-order pipelined processor is a type of CPU that leverages a pipeline to improve its performance by processing multiple instructions concurrently. The pipeline is single-threaded because it can only process instructions from a single hardware thread (*hart* in RISC-V terminology). In case of two consecutive instructions are dependent or require the same hardware resource at the same time an hazard occurs, resulting in a delay or stall in the execution of subsequent instructions. Designing the micro-architecture of this processor at RTL level can be complex and challenging and requires careful attention to ensure that all pipeline stages are well-coordinated.

2.1   Different Micro-architecture Design Tools

There are various methodologies for designing digital circuits, including HDL, HLS and Hardware Construction Language (HCL). Using HDL, designers must accurately describe the behavior of digital circuits using registers, logic gates and other basic building blocks that operate on the data stored in the registers. In addition, designers must introduce many of the performance and timing constraints in the design and carefully balance the trade-offs between performance, area and power consumption. Designing process using HDL is time-consuming and error-prone as it requires extensive manual coding and testing which can lead to mistakes and delays.

On the other hand, HLS and HCL allows designers to describe the hardware design at a higher level of abstraction than HDL. HLS achieves this by enabling designers to describe hardware designs in C, C++, or SystemC, raising the level of abstraction and coping with design complexity [18]. HLS tools then automatically translate this high-level code into low-level hardware description languages, resulting in faster design time, easier verification and simplified DSE. In contrast to HLS which infers hardware from high-level software description, HCL allows designers to build complex hardware designs in a higher-level programming paradigm [3], while operating at the same level as RTL. Chisel as an HCL candidate allows designers to compose reusable components using high-level constructs like object-oriented programming for describing the functionality of a hardware [1]. However, prototyping and exploring different design alternatives using Chisel is not straightforward and can be time-consuming.

Figure 1 illustrates the anticipated pipelined schedule derived from a vector addition example. Consider two arrays, namely A and B, both containing three elements. The objective is to perform element-wise addition of Array A with the corresponding elements of Array B, storing the results in Array D. The pipeline approach enables concurrent execution of addition operations on different elements. This figure also presents the code snippets in HLS, and RTL level necessary to achieve this scheduling. To achieve the desired scheduling using HLS, the loop pipelining directive can be applied over a loop that iterates on the size of the array, performing addition on the elements of arrays A and B. The automatic pipeline scheduling feature provided by HLS facilitates the generation of the desired schedule. On the other hand, when working at RTL level, it is necessary to carefully divide the various stages of the pipeline and describe the operations that must be performed at each individual stage.

The complexity of designing vector addition at the RTL level, as shown in Fig. 1, highlights the challenges and difficulties faced in designing the micro-architecture of a processor at this level of abstraction. Although HCL provides a higher level of design methodology compared to HDL, designers still need to focus on the explicit description of micro-architecture and manage the pipeline stages in their design, resulting in complicated hazard detection and resolution.

In summary, HLS technology presents several advantages over HDL and HCL by increasing the level of abstraction. First, HLS can significantly reduce design time by eliminating the need for manual coding of hardware descriptions, resulting in rapid prototyping and simulation. Second, HLS can enable designers to explore multiple design options quickly and efficiently, allowing them to identify the optimal design solution. Third, HLS can provide a more intuitive and easier-to-understand design flow, allowing designers to focus on system-level behavior rather than implementation details [14].

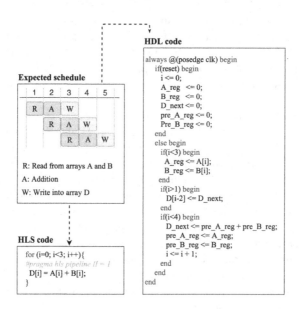

Fig. 1. The expected 3-stage pipeline schedule of vector addition.

2.2   HLS Limitation in Pipelining an Instruction Set Simulator

The code snippet displayed in Fig. 2 shows the ISS of an in-order single-threaded processor. To boost the processor's performance, a pipelined architecture can

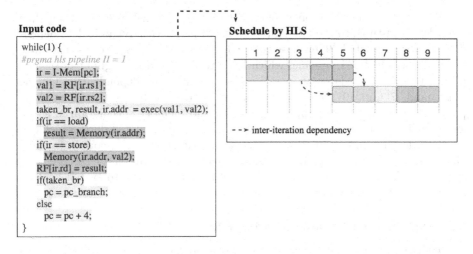

Fig. 2. Static pipelining of a single-threaded processor by HLS

be constructed by utilizing the loop pipelining directive in HLS. The schedule provided by HLS from this kernel as an input is depicted in this figure, where each stage corresponds to the line(s) in the code with the same color.

Loop pipelining is a technique that allows for the execution of different instructions to overlap, resulting in better throughput and ideally leading to a new instruction commencing execution every cycle. However, the read-after-write (RAW) dependency over the `pc` and the content of the register file presents significant obstacles for generating a pipelined micro-architecture by HLS tools. As demonstrated in the figure, HLS is unable to generate a fully pipelined micro-architecture from a single-threaded ISS because of its reliance on static scheduling and consideration of worst-case scenarios, where dependencies exist between all two instructions in a row. Therefore, HLS has to increase the Initiation Interval (II) - the number of cycles between the execution of two consecutive iterations of a loop - to 4 in order to respect these dependencies.

Over the years, pipeline hazards have emerged as a major challenge in micro-architecture design using HLS, significantly limiting the achievable throughput. This work takes advantage of dynamic scheduling and hardware multi-threading to handle the data dependencies in the pipeline.

3   Related Work

This section examines some of the approaches to tackle the challenges posed by static pipelining in HLS. Furthermore, this section also explores relevant works in dynamic multi-threading micro-architecture designs.

3.1   Deploying Speculative and Dynamic Techniques in HLS

Several recent researches focus on developing scheduling methods to address the conservatism in static scheduling of HLS. Two such methods proposed by All et al. [2] and Dai et al. [6] involve introducing a mechanism for resolving pipeline hazards at run-time, thus enabling pipelining of loops with dynamic data dependencies. Josipović et al. [9] propose generating elastic data flow circuits that allow for dynamic scheduled pipeline, which leads to increased throughput in scenarios involving variable-latency operations or dynamic data dependencies. On the other hand, [7] and [10] present works on speculative scheduling. Derrien et al. [7] propose a mechanism for supporting control and memory speculation in static loop pipelining. Their approach involves tracking all speculated data, which can be discarded if a misspeculation occurs. Josipović et al. [10] incorporate speculation into data flow circuits by allowing parts of the circuit to execute with speculated data, while also employing a rollback mechanism to switch back to correct data when needed.

3.2 Pipelined CPU Designs Using HLS

In recent years, there have been several endeavors to generate pipelined processors using HLS. Researches such as those discussed in [16] and [13] concentrate on exposing the pipeline and hazard detection unit at the C level to enhance performance, necessitating coding that directly presents the pipeline stages. Additionally, a pipelined multi-threaded processor introduced in [8] using a similar approach but it partitioned all arrays in design, such as register file, into the registers in order to achieve $II = 1$. Moreover the design's generality is limited, as it can accommodate a maximum of 8 harts, and scaling it to support a larger number of hart is a tedious task as it needs to adapt the hart scheduling unit at every stage of the pipeline. All these approaches described the pipeline stages at a programming level and forced HLS tool to adhere to this schedule, rather than relying on its automatic scheduling. Despite their use of high-level languages, they can be seen as RTL designs in disguise, with a level of complexity similar to RTL, as they require identification and handling of pipeline stages and pipeline hazards.

3.3 Dynamic Hart Scheduling in Multi-threaded CPU and GPU

Many studies focus on dynamic hart scheduling in multi-threaded CPUs. Notably, the research presented in [11] and [4] implement a dynamic hart scheduler that effectively switches to the next hart in case of long latency events, such as a cache miss.

Simty [5] and Vortex [19] are two RTL-based GPU cores that employ a dynamic scheduling methodology to effectively select a warp - a group of harts - to proceed within their architectures. The adaptive warp scheduling enables the GPU core to dynamically prioritize and schedule warps based on their readiness for execution and available resources.

4 Proposed Approach

In this section, the aim is to demonstrate the feasibility and challenges of designing an in-order pipelined processor at a higher level of abstraction by HLS.

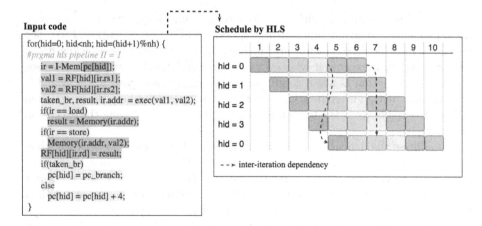

Input code

```
for(hid=0; hid<nh; hid=(hid+1)%nh) {
#prgma hls pipeline II = 1
    ir = I-Mem[pc[hid]];
    val1 = RF[hid][ir.rs1];
    val2 = RF[hid][ir.rs2];
    taken_br, result, ir.addr = exec(val1, val2);
    if(ir == load)
        result = Memory(ir.addr);
    if(ir == store)
        Memory(ir.addr, val2);
    RF[hid][ir.rd] = result;
    if(taken_br)
        pc[hid] = pc_branch;
    else
        pc[hid] = pc[hid] + 4;
}
```

Fig. 3. Instruction Set Simulator of a static multi-threaded processor with four harts

4.1 Static Multi-threaded RISC-V Core

Figure 3 represents the high-level description of a multi-threaded processor where several harts (nh) are interleaved in a round-robin fashion at left and its corresponding schedule provided by HLS tool at right. This processor architecture allows each hart to have a unique identifier (hid), as well as a private pc and register file, which can support hardware multi-threading.

The round-robin scheduling of the harts means that switching to a different hart at each cycle, eliminating the need for dependency checking on the register file and branch prediction logic. Additionally, since the number of harts within the core is greater or equal the pipeline's depth, the processor does not fetch an instruction from the same hart until all control and data dependencies are resolved. This method offers a significant benefit by enabling the processor to mask the latency involved in accessing off-chip memory, a potential bottleneck that can limit the performance of high-computing applications [17]. By using a round-robin scheduling approach for multiple harts, the processor can ensure that each hart can execute its instructions without delay, even if another hart is engaged in a memory operation with high latency.

4.2 Dynamic Single-Threaded RISC-V Core

To ensure the effectiveness of static multi-threading, it is important to have an adequate number of harts within the processor. This number depends on the specific architecture of the design and the latency of the off-chip memory, and it is predetermined during the design phase. If the number of harts falls below this threshold, the performance of the processor will diminish as it is not possible to achieve $II = 1$ anymore. Hence, it is crucial to use dynamic scheduling to mitigate the impact of the dependencies and memory latency by effectively leveraging as many harts as available within a processor.

To pipeline a processor with a single hart, a specific sequence of actions must be implemented to ensure efficient instruction fetching and execution. First, the processor must be forced to initiate the instruction fetching process when its pc is ready, and then execute it whenever its source registers are available. In cases where an instruction is not a conditional branch, the next pc will be available after the instruction is fetched. On the other hand, in cases where the instruction is a conditional branch, the branch pc will only be available during the execution stage.

To address the dependency on pc, a scoreboard is utilized to determine when the pc will become available. During each cycle, the processor first checks the scoreboard to verify if the pc is ready. If the pc is not yet ready, the processor must wait before proceeding with instruction fetching. On the other hand, if the pc is available, the processor can proceed with fetching the instruction. The processor utilizes a similar mechanism to tackle the dependency on the register file: when an instruction depends on the result of a load instruction, the processor must wait until the write back stage is completed. However, if the dependency is on a non-load instruction, the forwarding path comes into play, and the value from the previous execution stages is forwarded to the current execute stage.

4.3   Dynamic Multi-threaded RISC-V Core

In a dynamic single-threaded environment, CPU experiences idle cycles while awaiting the valid pc or write back of the previous instructions in case of the dependency on register file. Therefore, it is important to find ways to maximize CPU usage and minimize idle cycles. One effective approach is to engage the CPU in productive tasks rather than waiting for dependency resolution. This can be achieved by initiating execution from another hart that is ready at a given cycle. By making the most of idle cycles and leveraging multiple harts, it's possible to achieve significant improvements in overall efficiency and processing speed.

The Input code in Fig. 4 provides an illustration of an efficient approach to pipeline the execution of instructions from two harts by dynamically interleaving them. This algorithm involves a few key steps that enable the processor to operate efficiently. The first step is to select a single hart from a pool of available harts. In this case, the pool contains two harts. Once a hart is selected, the processor can proceed with the fetch of an instruction from the selected hart and subsequently execute it. This allows for the processor to take full advantage of the available harts and execute instructions in a parallel and efficient manner. However, in the event that no hart is chosen (*idle_state*), the processor will encounter a stall in its operation.

Each individual hart in the processor is equipped with a dedicated scoreboard that displays the readiness of the private pc to initiate the retrieval of an instruction, as well as the anticipated readiness of the source registers. This allows for efficient execution of instructions in a parallel fashion. In cases where the previous load instruction has yet to commit its result to the register file, this scoreboard serves as an indicator of potential dependencies. The scoreboard

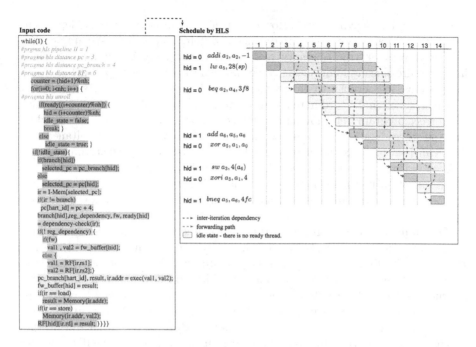

Fig. 4. Instruction Set Simulator of a dynamic multi-threaded processor with two harts

helps to identify potential data hazards that may occur during the execution of instructions. By examining the scoreboard, the processor can determine whether the instruction can proceed or if it needs to wait until the dependent instruction commits its result (*reg_dependency*). By detecting these hazards early, the processor can take corrective actions to ensure that the execution of instructions proceeds smoothly without any stalls. Additionally, each hart features a forwarding buffer that retains the outcomes of executed ALU instructions. The length of this buffer is correlated with the maximum number of preceding instructions on which the current instruction has dependency on based on the register file content and influenced by off-chip memory latency. The forwarding buffer is crucial in reducing the latency of dependent instructions. In cases where an instruction requires a value that has not yet been written to the register file, the processor executes a thorough examination of the forwarding buffer. Subsequently, the required value is forwarded to the instruction, thereby circumventing the need to wait for the instructions to write their results into the register file. This reduces the delay caused by the need to access the register file and improves the overall performance of the processor.

4.4 Thread Synchronization

In the previous sections, we have explored the possibility of hiding the dependency between two instructions from the same hart by either statically or dynamically interleaving harts. However, when it comes to memory dependencies between harts, we need to consider a different approach. Assuming that all harts access distinct memory regions, as done in [8], is not realistic since harts require sharing information at certain points. In modern parallel computing systems, it is crucial to ensure that multiple processors or harts operate in a synchronized and coordinated manner to avoid race conditions and guarantee correct program behavior. In parallel computing, data races can occur when multiple threads attempt to access the same memory location simultaneously. This can lead to unexpected program behavior, such as incorrect values being read or written, or even crashes. To prevent such issues, it is important to use synchronization mechanisms to ensure that different harts access shared memory locations in a coordinated way and they are operating on consistent memory states.

One approach to synchronize harts, as proposed in this work, is to introduce a new instruction called *Barrier* to the processor. When a hart reaches the *Barrier* instruction, it will enter a sleep state, waiting for the other harts to arrive. The idea is to pause execution until all harts have reached the *Barrier* instruction. Once all harts have reached the *Barrier*, they can then be woken up one by one in sequence, ensuring that all harts proceed from the synchronization point together in a consistent manner. It is important to note that during this synchronization process, any hart in a sleep mode must not be included in the scheduling process. This ensures that the harts have already hit the *Barrier* are waiting for other harts to arrive, preventing any potential data races or incorrect program behavior. The *Barrier* instruction provides a way for harts to coordinate their actions and ensure that they are operating on consistent memory states. This is particularly important in parallel computing, where harts can execute in a non-deterministic order, leading to potential data races and incorrect program behavior.

From the software perspective, developers can easily integrate the *Barrier* instruction into their code using inline assembly where it is needed. Doing so, all executing threads are forced to pause and wait until all other threads reach the same point in the program before continuing.

4.5   Shared-Memory RISC-V Multi-core

The multi-threaded multi-core processor offers an efficient solution for handling different program instructions simultaneously. Each core in this processor has its own Instruction memory (*I-Mem*) and Data Scratchpad Memory (*D-SPM*), while sharing a single Data memory (*D-Mem*) with all other cores. The ability to perform multiple tasks at the same time significantly boosts the overall processing power of the system, making it a desirable option for various applications.

Designing such a multi-core processor in HLS can be achieved by using two nested loops, as described in Input code in Fig. 5. The outer loop iterates on the number of harts interleaved within a core, while the inner loop iterates on the number of cores (*nc*). Unrolling the inner loops by the factor of the number of cores will instantiate *nc* cores, and by pipelining the outer loop, one hart of

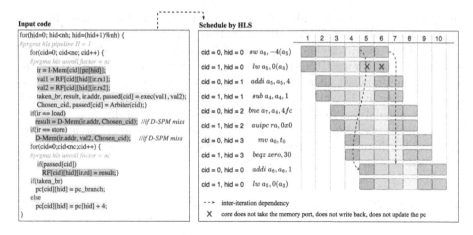

Fig. 5. Instruction Set Simulator of a Shared-memory multi-core system with two cores, each core has four harts

all cores starts execution at each cycle. However, designing such a processor in HLS can be challenging, because the HLS tool has no prior knowledge about the different instructions from different cores until run-time, it expects nc memory instructions at the same cycle. This leads to resource conflicts on the shared memory, II bigger than one, and poor performance.

To overcome the challenge of multiple cores accessing a shared port, an arbiter unit has been designed. The arbiter unit employs a round-robin algorithm to ensure that each core has an equal opportunity to access the port at each cycle. In addition, the pipeline is decomposed to separate the memory and write back stages from other stages, thereby ensuring that there is no more than one memory transaction at any given cycle. If multiple memory requests are received at the same cycle, the core that is granted access to the port (*Chosen_cid*) can proceed with its execution, while the other cores will have to wait until their turn comes up. Ultimately, only the cores that execute non-memory instructions or manage to acquire the port for the memory transaction (*passed*) will write back the results to their register file and update their pc. This approach allows designing the multi-threaded multi-core processor using HLS tools to handle multiple program instructions simultaneously in a highly efficient and effective manner.

5   Experimental Validation

In this section, we present an experimental study aimed at evaluating the performance and area utilization of our proposed micro-architecture designs. To conduct these experiments, we utilize the Vitis HLS 2022.2 tool, targeting a Kintex7 XQ7K410TRF9002L FPGA board. It is important to note that the data memory is considered off-chip and is accessed through an M-AXI port with a latency of 8 cycles. To assess the performance of our designs, we employ the matrix multiplication benchmark, which offers a comprehensive workload for evaluating computational efficiency. The entire evaluation process, encompassing C simulation, C synthesis, RTL simulation, and RTL synthesis, is seamlessly executed using a single tool, Vitis HLS, streamlining the workflow. To measure the performance of the proposed micro-architectures, we record the maximum frequency achieved during RTL synthesis and the total number of clock cycles obtained from RTL simulation. Additionally, we evaluate the area utilization based on RTL synthesis, providing a comprehensive assessment of the micro-architectures' efficiency. Furthermore, as a baseline for comparison, we synthesize the RV32I configuration of the Comet processor [16].

Table 1. Area and performance evaluation: Comparison of proposed multi-threaded micro-architectures and Comet using matrix multiplication benchmark

Approach	nh	II	F_{max} (MHz)	MIPS	LUTs	FFs	SRLs	BRAMs
Comet [16]	1	1	134	48	$2k$	$1.1k$	0	2
Fully Dynamic	2	1	113	52	$10k$	$5.8k$	132	2
	4	1	98	92	$16k$	$7.2k$	133	2
	8	1	78	75	$21.4k$	$8.6k$	134	10
Hybrid	4	1	109	103	$11.1k$	$2.2k$	131	2
	8	1	103	85	$15.3k$	$3k$	142	3
Fully Static	16	1	203	186	$2.2k$	$1.4k$	297	6

Table 1 presents the experimental results for our multi-threaded processor with different numbers of harts, indicated by the *nh* column. We consider various approaches, including Fully Dynamic, Hybrid, and Fully Static. When using 2 harts in the processor, dynamic scheduling is the only option to hide dependencies. However, when the processor has at least 4 harts, we have the choice to schedule them either dynamically or statically. In the static scheduling approach, we can hide the dependency on pc, leaving only the dependency on the register file. This allows us to dynamically resolve the register file dependency. In this approach which is referred as Hybrid in the table, harts are scheduled using a round-robin scheduling technique, which ensures fairness and balanced utilization. Before the execution of each hart, a thorough verification of the scoreboard is performed to ascertain the readiness of the source registers. In the event of identifying a dependency, the scheduled hart is required to forfeit its turn, resulting in a temporary halt in processor activity. Upon the subsequent arrival of the hart's turn, the same instruction must be reissued.

The data presented in Table 1 clearly demonstrates that the proposed multi-threaded micro-architectures exhibit superior performance in terms of MIPS when compared to the Comet architecture. By employing multiple harts in the processor, we are able to achieve a remarkable increase in MIPS, surpassing Comet by at least 8%. Notably, the Fully static micro-architecture with 16 harts demonstrates significantly better performance while occupying a comparable area to Comet.

In our experimental evaluation, we observe that in the Fully Dynamic and Hybrid approaches, the forwarding unit is in the critical path of the design and becomes a limiting factor in terms of performance. This characteristic explains why increasing the number of harts from 4 to 8 does not yield performance benefits, despite increasing the utilized area. In the Fully Dynamic approach, the scheduling unit is essential for resolving dependencies and ensuring proper execution order, resulting in increased area usage. However, by adopting the Hybrid approach, we are able to eliminate the scheduling unit, thereby reducing the area overhead while achieving better performance compared to the Fully Dynamic approach. To visualize the trade-offs between performance and area utilization, a scatter plot is generated (see Fig. 6). The scatter plot represents the Hybrid and Fully Dynamic approaches with 4 and 8 harts. The Pareto front showcases the designs that offer the best compromise between performance and area utilization. Upon examining the plot, it becomes evident that the Hybrid approach with 4 harts (4H) occupies a position on the Pareto front. This positioning indicates that the Hybrid approach with 4 harts is a superior design choice, as it achieves a desirable balance between performance and area utilization compared to the other approaches.

In our investigation, we examine the impact of increasing the number of harts to 16 on our micro-architecture. This expansion enables us to adopt a Fully Static execution scheme, eliminating the need for scheduling, hazard detection, and forwarding units. By statically interleaving multiple harts, we successfully conceal dependencies on both pc and register file. Through coordination of instruction execution in a predetermined order, we achieve static scheduling and hazard resolution. This approach significantly reduces the complexity of the design and the required area for these units, leading to increased performance. While the configuration with 8 harts using Fully Dynamic approach is found to be inefficient, we can utilize either 4 harts with a Hybrid approach or 16 harts with a Fully Static approach instead. Our study demonstrates how different micro-architectures and configurations, considering various numbers of harts and approaches, can be designed to determine the optimal design based on silicon budget and desired performance.

Figure 7 illustrates the scatter plot for proposed multi-core processor, where each data point is labeled with the corresponding number of cores ranging from 1 to 8. It is important to note that each core in our design supports 16 harts, implemented using the Fully Static approach. This configuration allows for increased parallelism and enhanced performance within each core. The plot provides a visual representation of the performance and area trade-offs associated with different core counts. It enables us to observe how the number of cores impacts both performance and area utilization. A noticeable trend observed in the plot is the linear increase in the used area as the number of cores is increased. This observation aligns with our expectations, as each additional core contributes to an incremental area overhead. However, it is essential to highlight that the performance does not scale linearly with the number of cores, as anticipated. Notably, by utilizing our design, researchers and developers have the opportunity to rapidly prototype various multi-core micro-architectures with different core counts, tailored to their specific parallelism requirements and workloads. The linear increase in the used area as the number of cores expands demonstrates the flexibility of our design in accommodating diverse multi-core configurations. By swiftly iterating through different core counts, designers can explore and evaluate the performance and area trade-offs for their particular applications, allowing for quick experimentation and optimization of the micro-architecture. This capability to rapidly prototype different multi-core configurations empowers designers to fine-tune their designs according to the specific demands of their workloads, harnessing the potential benefits of parallel processing while considering the limitations imposed by sequential portions of the program.

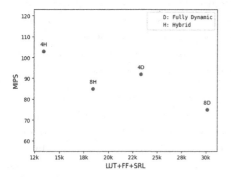
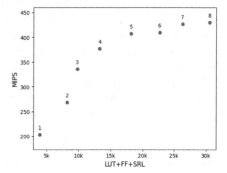

Fig. 6. Relationship between performance and area utilization for different approaches in multi-threaded processor with 4 and 8 harts

Fig. 7. Relationship between performance and area utilization for different number of cores in multi-core processor

6   Conclusion

This study demonstrates the benefits of using automatic scheduling in HLS for rapid prototyping of CPU architectures. We identify limitations of existing HLS tools in inferring fully pipelined micro-architectures with dynamic data dependency. Additionally, we showcase the successful design of complex micro-architectures, such as static multi-threaded CPU, dynamic multi-threaded CPU, and multi-core systems. These results emphasize the effectiveness of leveraging HLS for advanced architectures.

Future work involves exploring GPU micro-architecture design using HLS to uncover potential challenges and limitations.

Acknowledgements. This study is partially funded by the French National Research Agency (ANR) as part of the project DYVE (ANR-19-CE25-0004-01).

References

1. Chisel Homepage. https://www.chisel-lang.org
2. Alle, M., Morvan, A., Derrien, S.: Runtime dependency analysis for loop pipelining in high-level synthesis. In: Proceedings of the 50th Annual Design Automation Conference, pp. 1–10 (2013)
3. Bachrach, J., et al.: Chisel: constructing hardware in a scala embedded language. In: Proceedings of the 49th Annual Design Automation Conference, pp. 1216–1225 (2012)
4. Borkenhagen, J.M., Eickemeyer, R.J., Kalla, R.N., Kunkel, S.R.: A multithreaded powerPC processor for commercial servers. IBM J. Res. Dev. **44**(6), 885–898 (2000)
5. Collange, C.: Simty: generalized SIMT execution on RISC-V. In: CARRV 2017–1st Workshop on Computer Architecture Research with RISC-V, vol. 6, p. 6 (2017)
6. Dai, S., et al.: Dynamic hazard resolution for pipelining irregular loops in high-level synthesis. In: Proceedings of the 2017 ACM/SIGDA International Symposium on Field-Programmable Gate Arrays, pp. 189–194 (2017)
7. Derrien, S., Marty, T., Rokicki, S., Yuki, T.: Toward speculative loop pipelining for high-level synthesis. IEEE Trans. Comput. Aided Des. Integr. Circuits Syst. **39**(11), 4229–4239 (2020)
8. Goossens, B.: Guide to Computer Processor Architecture: A RISC-V Approach, with High-level Synthesis. Springer, Cham (2023). https://doi.org/10.1007/978-3-031-18023-1
9. Josipović, L., Ghosal, R., Ienne, P.: Dynamically scheduled high-level synthesis. In: Proceedings of the 2018 ACM/SIGDA International Symposium on Field-Programmable Gate Arrays, pp. 127–136 (2018)
10. Josipovic, L., Guerrieri, A., Ienne, P.: Speculative dataflow circuits. In: Proceedings of the 2019 ACM/SIGDA International Symposium on Field-Programmable Gate Arrays, pp. 162–171 (2019)
11. Kvatinsky, S., Nacson, Y.H., Etsion, Y., Friedman, E.G., Kolodny, A., Weiser, U.C.: Memristor-based multithreading. IEEE Comput. Archit. Lett. **13**(1), 41–44 (2013)
12. Liu, S., Lau, F.C., Schafer, B.C.: Accelerating FPGA prototyping through predictive model-based HLS design space exploration. In: Proceedings of the 56th Annual Design Automation Conference 2019, pp. 1–6 (2019)
13. Mantovani, P., Margelli, R., Giri, D., Carloni, L.P.: HL5: a 32-bit RISC-V processor designed with high-level synthesis. In: 2020 IEEE Custom Integrated Circuits Conference (CICC), pp. 1–8. IEEE (2020)
14. Meeus, W., Van Beeck, K., Goedemé, T., Meel, J., Stroobandt, D.: An overview of today's high-level synthesis tools. Des. Autom. Embed. Syst. **16**, 31–51 (2012)
15. Ravindran, K., Satish, N., Jin, Y., Keutzer, K.: An FPGA-based soft multiprocessor system for IPv4 packet forwarding. In: International Conference on Field Programmable Logic and Applications, pp. 487–492. IEEE (2005)
16. Rokicki, S., Pala, D., Paturel, J., Sentieys, O.: What you simulate is what you synthesize: designing a processor core from C++ specifications. In: 2019 IEEE/ACM International Conference on Computer-Aided Design (ICCAD), pp. 1–8. IEEE (2019)

17. Smith, B.J.: Architecture and applications of the HEP multiprocessor computer system. In: Real-Time Signal Processing IV, vol. 298, pp. 241–248. SPIE (1982)
18. Takach, A.: High-level synthesis: Status, trends, and future directions. IEEE Des. Test **33**(3), 116–124 (2016)
19. Tine, B., Yalamarthy, K.P., Elsabbagh, F., Hyesoon, K.: Vortex: extending the RISC-V ISA for GPGPU and 3D-graphics. In: MICRO-54: 54th Annual IEEE/ACM International Symposium on Microarchitecture, pp. 754–766 (2021)

NVMulator: A Configurable Open-Source Non-volatile Memory Emulator for FPGAs

Sajjad Tamimi[1]([⊠]) [iD], Arthur Bernhardt[2] [iD], Florian Stock[1] [iD], Ilia Petrov[2] [iD], and Andreas Koch[1] [iD]

[1] Embedded Systems and Applications Group, Technical University of Darmstadt, Hochschulstr. 10, 64289 Darmstadt, Germany
{tamimi,stock,koch}@esa.tu-darmstadt.de
[2] Data Management Lab, Reutlingen University, Alteburgstr. 150, 72762 Reutlingen, Germany
{arthur.bernhardt,ilia.petrov}@reutlingen-university.de

Abstract. Near-Data Processing (NDP) is a key computing paradigm for reducing the ever growing time and energy costs of data transport versus computations. With their flexibility, FPGAs are an especially suitable compute element for NDP scenarios. Even more promising is the exploitation of novel and future *non-volatile memory* (NVM) technologies for NDP, which aim to achieve DRAM-like latencies and throughputs, while providing large capacity non-volatile storage.

Experimentation in using FPGAs in such NVM-NDP scenarios has been hindered, though, by the fact that the NVM devices/FPGA boards are still very rare and/or expensive. It thus becomes useful to *emulate* the access characteristics of current and future NVMs using off-the-shelf DRAMs. If such emulation is sufficiently accurate, the resulting FPGA-based NDP computing elements can be used for actual full-stack hardware/software benchmarking, e.g., when employed to accelerate a database.

For this use, we present *NVMulator* [7], an open-source easy-to-use hardware emulation module that can be seamlessly inserted between the NDP processing elements on the FPGA and a conventional DRAM-based memory system. We demonstrate that, with suitable parametrization, the emulated NVM can come very close to the performance characteristics of *actual* NVM technologies, specifically Intel Optane. We achieve 0.62% and 1.7% accuracy for cache line sized accesses for read and write operations, while utilizing only 0.54% of LUT logic resources on a Xilinx/AMD AU280 UltraScale+ FPGA board. We consider both file-system as well as database access patterns, examining the operation of the RocksDB database when running on real or emulated Optane-technology memories.

Keywords: FPGA · Non-volatile memory · Emulator

F. Palumbo et al. (Eds.): ARC 2023, LNCS 14251, pp. 35–50, 2023.
https://doi.org/10.1007/978-3-031-42921-7_3

1   Introduction

With the ever-growing volume of data generated due to the success of the Internet, Near-Data Processing (NDP) offers a promising solution to improve overall system performance and optimize bandwidth usage. NDP achieves this by facilitating more direct access to the actual storage devices for suitable compute elements, enabling both greater throughput as well as shorter latencies. FPGAs serve as an ideal compute element for NDP applications for two primary factors. First, they can offer wide I/Os for direct connections to DRAM banks and maintain a high level of fine-grained parallelism to manage multiple in-flight requests from various Flash banks. Second, their inherent flexibility allows users to readily implement their ideas and adapt to evolving requirements. Moreover, the efficacy of NDP is more promising by the potential integration of cutting-edge non-volatile memory (NVM) technologies. These innovative solutions offer high-density storage, DRAM-comparable performance, and significant capacity for persistent storage. As a result, the utilization of NDP in conjunction with advanced NVM technologies holds significant promise for addressing the challenges posed by ever-increasing data generation.

Utilizing FPGAs in NDP-capable systems based on NVM remains a challenge, though, as NVM devices themselves or suitably equipped FPGA boards are still very rare and/or expensive. To address this challenge, prior research has proposed either software simulation or hardware emulation environments. Software-based approaches utilize standalone simulators or those integrated with DDR systems to model NVM behavior, facilitating the assessment of software-based solutions [3,19]. On the other hand, hardware-based techniques propose the emulation of NVM characteristics by leveraging commercially available DDR on FPGAs. These methods introduce additional latency between read and write accesses during the request handshake process [14] or alter the memory parameters of the memory controller [16]. Despite their potential, these solutions necessitate specialized devices that are also rare or expensive. Moreover, existing research lacks a user-friendly NVM emulation environment that is compatible with various FPGA platforms.

To allow research to push ahead here, we propose an open-source, user-friendly Non-Volatile-Memory emulator (referred to as NVMulator) that can accurately replicate the access characteristics of present and future NVM technologies utilizing commercially available DRAM components. The NVMulator is designed as a hardware emulation module that can be seamlessly integrated between the NDP processing unit on an FPGA and conventional DRAM-based memory system. We demonstrate the application of the NVMulator within the context of the reconfigurable computing framework Task Parallel System Composer (TaPaSCo), which is an open-source platform offering both hardware and software stacks for FPGAs for users, aimed at users without specialized knowledge in the field. The objective of this work is to provide NVM access latencies by creating a fully-functional and *easily usable* emulator.

In order to assess the efficiency of the proposed approach, we conducted a comparative analysis with existing NVM technologies, specifically Intel Optane, utilizing a Xilinx/AMD AU280 UltraScale+ FPGA board. Our evaluation was carried out through two distinct methods. Initially, we employed a file-system benchmarking tool (i.e., the FIO tool) to demonstrate the accuracy of the emulator in the context of real-world workloads. Subsequently, we implemented on the FPGAs an emulated non-volatile persistent storage for a host running RocksDB. The findings indicate that not only can the emulator successfully emulate Intel Optane within real-world applications, but it can also be seamlessly deployed as emulated persistent storage with minimal effort. Note that our emulation only considers timing behavior. Lower level characteristics such as reliability (wear) and error rates are not covered, as they were out-of-scope for our use-cases.

In the remaining of the paper, first we give an overview of off-the-shelf NVM technology as well as a discussion of related work in Sect. 2. Then, we present NVMulator in Sect. 3.1 and we show how it is integrated in the TaPaSCo platform in Sect. 3.2. Afterwards we evaluate the accuracy of the proposed approach by comparison to OptaneDC memory in Sect. 4. We close with a conclusion in Sect. 5.

2 Storage Technologies and Related Work

In this section we begin with an overview of NVM storage technologies and the proposed NDP compute units. Afterwards, we discuss previous studies that have aimed to emulate the characteristics of NVM.

2.1 NVM Storage Technologies

Due to their inherent characteristic, exploiting NVM as a storage system has been often proposed by previous research in different domains, ranging from embedded applications to data-centric applications. The properties of newer NVM differ from those of conventional storage technologies such as Flash or DRAM in the following ways:

Byte-Addressability. Newer NVM technologies are byte-addressable, similar to DRAM, and do not rely on page-block accesses like Flash. This characteristic presents new opportunities for NDP approaches that wish to utilize it, however, current algorithmic approaches have not yet succeeded in fully utilizing byte-level reads/writes on NVM.

Read/Write Latency. NVM technologies have higher access latency compared to DRAM. For instance, Phase-Change Memory (PCM) has higher read/write latency than DDR (though still comparable) but significantly lower latency than NAND [6]. Additionally, read and write latency in NVM exhibit asymmetry, characterized by low-latency read operations and slower write operations.

Non-volatile. Modern NVM technologies such as PCM and Spin-Transfer Torque Memory (STT-RAM) are non-volatile. This means that data is preserved intact even when the memory is powered off or in the event of memory or power failure.

Endurance. NVM technologies are wear-prone and face endurance challenges. While NVMs have higher endurance compared to NAND Flash [6,9], implementing wear-leveling strategies is essential to enhance their longevity.

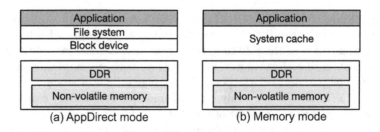

Fig. 1. OptaneDC in (a) AppDirect and (b) Memory modes [18].

Intel Optane DC. Intel® Optane™ DC Persistent Memory module (short: OptaneDC) is an innovative and widely recognized technology developed by Intel Corporation that has captured the attention of users. The OptaneDC technology offers two configuration modes: Memory mode (cached) and AppDirect mode (uncached) [18]. In Memory mode, users can extend the system memory capacity, effectively increasing the overall performance and efficiency of the system. On the other hand, AppDirect mode enables users to leverage the module as persistent storage. Figure 1 shows the integration process of the OptaneDC memory module into a system in these two modes. The primary objective of this study is to examine and replicate the access latency of NVM when employed as persistent storage.

NDP Compute Units. Prior research has explored various types of compute units for Near-Data Processing (NDP) that can be classified into several categories. In the first category, studies such as [4,12] have proposed using existing embedded hard-core processors, such as multi-core ARM processors, for query processing on Samsung's smart-SSD devices. These processors are typically employed for controlling storage modules and managing wear-leveling to enhance flash endurance.

In the second category, researchers have suggested FPGAs as NDP compute units. [20] introduced an approach that connects an FPGA to the NVMe flash via a PCIe interface, allowing for data processing in close proximity to the storage. However, this method is limited by the bandwidth of the PCIe connection and only enables processing close to, rather than near, the storage. [22] proposed offloading operations from the query engine in the host to an embedded ARM core and FPGA on the COSMOS+ board [17]. However, the underlying storage in these approaches relies on NAND Flash. Generally, FPGA boards with NVM devices scarce (often just prototypes) and/or expensive, posing challenges for wider use.

2.2 Related Work

Prior research efforts to emulate NVM behavior can be classified into two categories: software-based and hardware-based solutions. In the following, we will examine both of these categories.

Software-Based Solution. In the first category of research, prior studies have explored the utilization of software to emulate the behavior of NVM as either a standalone simulator or in conjunction with DDR systems. NVMain [19] is a cycle-accurate main memory software simulator that effectively models NVM architectural behavior, including aspects such as power consumption and performance. The simulator facilitates seamless integration with the gem5 simulator, providing a familiar user interface and simplifying the overall experimentation process. HMMSim [5] is an NVM software simulator that incorporates hybrid main memory, comprising both NVM and DDR, to emulate various memory architectures, such as NVM. By offering an Application Programming Interface (API), this work facilitates the evaluation of software solutions for managing hybrid main memory systems. HME [5] is an NVM emulator that simulates remote NVM on Non-Uniform Memory Access (NUMA) nodes by introducing software delays to remote memory accesses. However, these solutions are solely software-based and do not provide users with the ability to employ them as persistent storage. Moreover, the execution time of these software emulations is considerably longer compared to actual hardware implementations.

Hardware-Based Solution. In the second category of related research, prior studies have focused on emulating NVM on FPGAs. TUNA [14] proposed adding a module between the memory controller and processing element within the design, which would enable NVM behavior emulation over existing off-chip DDR memory on FPGA devices. This proposed module introduces additional latency to handshake signals by applying a fixed delay for read and writes accesses. While this approach is suitable for handling large data chunks, it lacks accuracy due to its disregard for memory bank parallelism in the overlaid DDR and NVM systems. To address this limitation, authors in [15] [16] proposed introducing fine-grained latency to memory parameters, such as tRCD or tRP, to more accurately mimic the underlying memory controller. However, modifying the memory controller proves to be a challenging undertaking, particularly as it often involves working with proprietary technology like the Memory Interface Generator (MIG) IP provided by AMD/Xilinx.

While the existing body of research offers a foundation for further exploration, to the best of our knowledge, no current solutions enable designers to easily utilize NVM emulators across various FPGA platforms without the need for specialized hardware. While internal FPGA prototype boards using actual NVMs, such as PCM coupled to an AMD/Xilinx Virtex 7 FPGA, do exist, they are not available to most researchers and often have hardware limitations that make them unsuitable as a general-purpose platform.

3   Proposed Approach

We start by introducing the NVMulator micro-architecture and discussing the proposed approach for emulating NVM characteristics. Then, we show the integration process of the NVMulator within the TaPaSCo FPGA computing framework. By integrating the NVMulator into a framework, instead of just providing

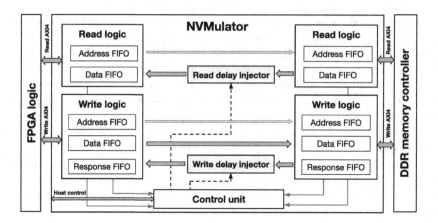

Fig. 2. NVMulator!t micro-architecture.

a stand-alone hardware module as has been done in prior work, we can leverage all of the existing TaPaSCo functionality and design automation to enable
productive research into NDP with NVM more quickly.

3.1 NVMulator Micro-Architecture

Figure 2 shows the micro-architecture of NVMulator, which is designed to emulate
read/write access latencies. This module is equipped with an AXI4-Slave interface that receives read/write requests from the FPGA logic, an AXI4-Master
interface that forwards these requests to the DDR memory controller, and a
controlling interface. For read requests, the module injects latency into the
read response, in accordance with the host-specified latency. Similarly, for write
requests, the module adds an additional delay to the write response, as determined by the host. The controlling interface allows the host to manage the NVMulator functionalities during operation without requiring the stop of execution or
re-synthesis of the design for simple timing parameter changes. The NVMulator
enables the emulation of access latency for emerging NVM technologies, such as
PCM and Spin-Transfer Torque Memory (STT-RAM).

Timing Model. Equation 1 shows the timing model employed in the NVMulator. Upon receiving a read/write request (r/w) on the address channels, the
NVMulator module forwards this request to the DDR memory controller and
records the request receipt ($Time_{received}$). Once the response from the DDR
is obtained, NVMulator logs the completion time of the request($Time_{completed}$).
Subsequently, the control unit computes the expected latency for the request,
taking into consideration the burst size (Burst_size) and the host-specified
delays per beat for read and write requests ($Delay_{beat}$). Then, the control
unit determines the delay to inject ($Delay_{inject}$), which represents the differ-

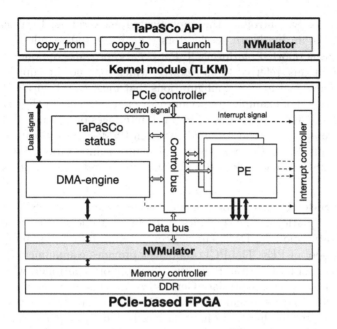

Fig. 3. Integration of NVMulator module into the software and hardware stacks of the TaPaSCo framework

ence between the expected time for the request and the actual response time from the DDR memory.

$$\text{Delay}_{\text{NVM}}(r/w) = \text{Burst\_size}(r/w) + \text{Delay}_{\text{beat}}(r/w)$$
$$\text{Delay}_{\text{DDR}}(r/w) = \text{Time}_{\text{completed}}(r/w) - \text{Time}_{\text{received}}(r/w) \quad (1)$$
$$\text{Delay}_{\text{inject}}(r/w) = \text{Delay}_{\text{NVM}}(r/w) - \text{Delay}_{\text{DDR}}(r/w)$$

3.2 TaPaSCo Integration

TaPaSCo is an open-source hardware/software framework [13] that facilitates the integration of FPGA-based accelerators into heterogeneous computing systems. The goal of TaPaSCo is to provide a flexible and scalable framework for both expert and non-expert FPGA users. It supports a wide range of FPGA platforms, including high-performance PCIe-based platforms with large FPGA devices, such as data center AU280 and AU250 FPGA or Versal cards, small embedded Zynq platforms like Xilinx ZC702 and ZC706, and Amazon AWS F1 instances with FPGA accelerators.

TaPaSCo comprises an automated System-on-Chip (SoC) design generator and an Application Programming Interface (API). The SoC design generator enables the construction of a pool of Processing Elements (PE) with the peripheral module to interface with user applications. The API provides a software interface for easily controlling the implemented accelerators. Users can implement their custom hardware accelerators (i.e., PEs) and seamlessly use them across various supported platforms. TaPaSCo also provides optional functionality through plugins, referred to as *features*, which may not be supported by all platforms. These features are configurations that must be set during the design-building process. For example, users can easily enable the use of High Bandwidth Memory (HBM) RAM interfaces or network interfaces on supported devices. In this work, we aim to extend TaPaSCo with an NVMulator as a feature in PCIe-based platforms. In the following, we will explain the integration of the emulator into the TaPaSCo framework in both the hardware and software stack.

Hardware-Side. Figure 3 shows the SoC architecture of TaPaSCo on a PCIe-based FPGA platform that includes a PCIe controller, memory controller, TaPaSCo status module, DMA-engine, control and data buses, interrupt controller, and pool of PEs. The PCIe controller provides communication between the hardware and host via the PCIe bus. The memory controller, which utilizes the AMD/Xilinx Memory Interface Generator (MIG) IP core, provides an interface to the off-chip device memory, such as DDR. The TaPaSCo status module is responsible for storing hardware information, including mapped addresses, and the DMA-engine manages PCIe-DMA transfers between the host memory and device memory. The control bus enables the host to control FPGA modules and the data bus enables PEs and DMA-engine to access device memory. The interrupt handler collects signals raised by the hardware modules and forwards them to the host API of TaPaSCo. PEs are custom hardware accelerators, which can be implemented in either Hardware Description Language (HDL) or by High-Level Synthesis (HLS), and are responsible for executing applications on the hardware. It is essential to design and implement PEs with a so-called *T-shape* architecture compatible with TaPaSCo, featuring three interfaces: control, interrupt, and data interfaces. The control and interrupt interfaces enable the host to manage the PE, while the data interface provides PE access to off-chip memory. As shown in Fig. 3, the NVMulator has been integrated into the TaPaSCo SoC. To provide runtime control of the NVMulator by the host, the module's controlling interface is connected to the control bus, which allows the host to manage it via the software interface of TaPaSCo. To enable the module within the design, it is necessary to include --features 'NVMmulator enable: true' flag during the TaPaSCo building process as follows:

```
tapasco compose [PE x 1] @ 100MHz
                    --platforms AU280
                    --features "NVMulator {enable: true}"
```

Software-Side. The TaPaSCo software interface consists of an API and kernel module. The API is based on a task-parallel model, which involves decomposing computations into discrete tasks that can be independently executed on hardware accelerators. The kernel module, known as the TaPaSCo Loadable Kernel Module (TLKM), communicates with the device using ioctl commands. As shown in Fig. 3, the nvMulator function has been integrated into the software layer hierarchy. When the API call invokes this function, it triggers the corresponding functions in the kernel, allowing users to modify the control registers of the NVMulator in the hardware. This approach enables on-the-fly configuration of the NVMulator, eliminating the need for design alterations to accommodate various types of NVM during experimentation. Figure 4 presents a C++ example utilizing the nvMulator() function call within the user program. This function call requires three parameters: read_latency and write_latency in a number of clock cycles, and an NVM_mode that accepts values of either 0 or 1 to disable or enable the NVMulator functionality.

```
1  #include <tapasco.hpp>
2
3  #define PE_ID        7
4  #define READ_DELAY   100    // in clock cycles
5  #define WRITE_DELAY  200    // in clock cycles
6  #define NVM_MODE     1      // enable NVM emulation mode
7
8  int main() {
9      tapasco::Tapasco tapasco;
10
11     tapasco.nvMulator(READ_DELAY, WRITE_DELAY, NVM_MODE);
12
13     auto job = tapasco.launch(PE_ID, reg1, reg2, ...);
14     job();
15
16     return 0;
17 }
```

Fig. 4. Example of using the nvMulator() function call in the C++ API of TaPaSCo

4   Experimental Setup and Evaluation

To evaluate the accuracy of the emulator, we built a TaPaSCo design on an AMD/Xilinx Alveo U280 FPGA card, which is connected to a host through a PCIe Gen3 interface with 16x lanes. The host is an ARM Neoverse N1 System Development Platform (N1-SDP). Furthermore, we have developed a rudimentary block device driver to facilitate the utilization of the FPGA as a storage device. Throughout the experiments conducted in this study, we have compared the measured latency and throughput values to the reported values for OptaneDC, as presented in [11].

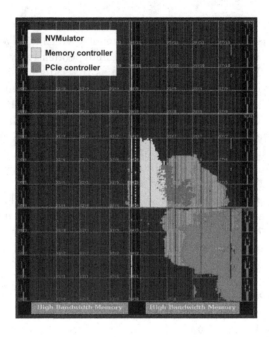

Fig. 5. Layout of the NVM storage built on the AU280.

Figure 5 shows the floorplan of the AU280, which includes the PCIe controller, MIG, TaPaSCo related modules, and NVMulator. This design is synthesized using Xilinx Vitis 2022.2. As reported in Table 1, the NVMulator occupies less than 0.6% of the available resources and logic resources. Thus, the remaining portion of the design provides ample space for the integration of the actual NDP processing units.

In the following, we evaluate the effectiveness of the proposed methodology by measuring the on-device latency and its performance as a persistent storage when executing real-world applications. As actual Optane devices are no longer commercially available, we gauge the accuracy of our emulation by using the measurements reported in [11], on an Intel server platform, as a reference baseline. For simple I/O-dominant benchmarks (latency, throughput), our emulation can be quite accurate. For more complex benchmarks (e.g., database workloads), the differences in the underlying host machines become more apparent, but our emulator stills stays within 2x of the original.

4.1 Latency

In the first experiment, our objective was to assess the random read and write latency of single cache-line sized (64B) accesses to the emulated NVM. To this end, we employed a custom hardware module to generate such accesses and an Integrated Logic Analyzer (ILA) [10] to accurately measure each access latency. The measured read and write latencies for the NVM emulator, and

Table 1. Resource utilization of the NVM storage on AU280

Module name	LUTs	Registers	BRAM
Available resources	1303680	2607360	2016
NVMulator	0.54%	0.19%	0.42%
Memory controller	1.54%	0.93%	1.26%
DMA-engine	0.88%	0.68%	0.74%
PCIe controller	3.09%	1.7%	3.13%

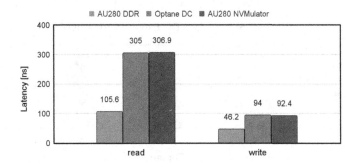

Fig. 6. Cache line sized (64B) read and write latency comparison between the OptaneDC [11] and NVMulator

the OptaneDC are illustrated in Fig. 6. The results reveal that the NVMulator is capable of emulating the read access latency of the OptaneDC with a precision of 0.62% of the target latency (i.e., 305 ns [11]). Similarly, the NVMulator emulates the write access latency with an accuracy of 1.7% of the target latency (i.e., 94 ns [11]). These findings indicate that our proposed approach effectively emulates access latency in close proximity to the intended objective.

4.2   FIO Bandwidth

In this experiment, we aimed to assess NVMulator when used as storage for filesystem-managed data by using the well-known Flexible I/O (FIO) tool [1] for benchmarking. This tool enables us to generate practical I/O traffic on the storage device. To achieve this, we configured the FIO tool to create workloads using the sync ioengine for random read and write accesses. The generated workload comprised a 512 MB file size per thread and a block size of 4KB. We ran this experiment by varying the number of active threads between one and four, and executed fsync() following each write request to the storage, ensuring that the written data was not delayed. For the underlying file system, we employed Ext4, which is a widely used Linux file system.

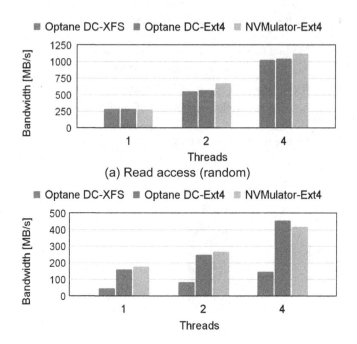

Fig. 7. A FIO 4 KB random read and write bandwidth comparison between the OptaneDC [11] and NVMulator

Figure 7 shows the results of this experiment in comparison to the OptaneDC for random read and write operations. As expected, the NVMulator effectively emulates the OptaneDC under practical I/O traffic generation conditions. We further extended this experiment for sequential read and write operations. To this end, we expanded our block device driver to support *memory coalescing*, enabling the combination of sequential accesses into a single, larger transaction. The outcomes of this experiment are shown in Fig. 8. As expected, the NVMulator effectively emulates both sequential and random access operations.

4.3 Database Application

One of the key advantages of the proposed methodology is its capacity to facilitate easy and seamless integration of emulated NVM into a given system, thereby allowing users to execute applications on it. NVM has demonstrated benefits in database applications, serving as both persistent and computational storage capable of managing database operations through NDP [2,21,22]. To demonstrate the ease of integrating NVMulator for this use-case, we will examine the usage of the emulated NVM as persistent storage for a popular key-value database system. The database system employed here is RocksDB [8], which is an embedded key-value store designed by Facebook/Meta. In order to assess the

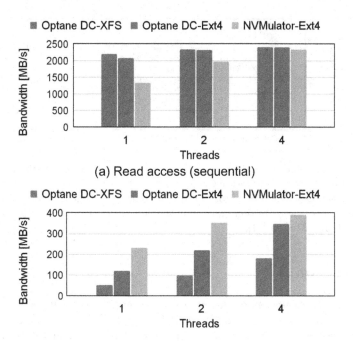

Fig. 8. A FIO 4 KB sequential read and write bandwidth comparison between the OptaneDC [11] and NVMulator

performance of the suggested methodology, we conduct an experiment utilizing the db_bench tool. This involves executing the fillrandom command with a key and value size of 20B and 100M, respectively, while processing 10 million records on RocksDB V5.4.

Figure 9 shows the measured throughput of the number of operations while executing db_bench benchmark for the Ext4 file system. The NVMulator, as demonstrated in the figure, effectively manages read-and-write accesses to the storage device with a similar behaviour as the OptaneDC modules. It is important to acknowledge that the block device driver employed in this research is a simplified version, lacking the comprehensive buffering and caching functionalities present in existing drivers, such as the NVMe block device driver and that the server used for the AU280 and the ones used by the authors of [11] are quite different (e.g. 24 cores compared to 4). However, the raw performance of the block driver is only secondary for this experiment, which aims at accurate emulation of NVM timing behavior, specifically for OptaneDC. As shown here, that can be achieved even without optimizing the block driver further.

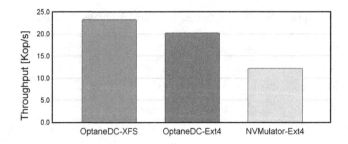

Fig. 9. A comparison of RocksDB throughput while executing db_bench on emulated NVM and OptaneDC. Note that the Optane and AU280 measurements were performed on two different host machines. For this more complex workload, the differences in host machines become more dominant, but the emulation still stays within 2x of the measurements reported in [11].

5   Conclusion

We introduce NVMulator, an open-source easy-to-use NVM emulator for FPGAs, which has been integrated into the TaPaSCo framework to enable the emulation of NVM access latencies using off-the-shelf DRAM memories. Our approach enables users to effortlessly emulate various types of NVM, including PCM and STT, while also incorporating their accelerators into FPGA designs. Furthermore, the NVMulator module can be easily configured through the TaPaSCo API, providing users with the flexibility to modify the emulator's configuration and switch between different NVM types without requiring a complete redesign and re-synthesis of the system. Our evaluation examines both file-system and database access patterns and shows tight accuracy of our emulation for I/O-dominant benchmarks, with the emulator staying within 2x of accuracy even for more complex database workloads. It is thus suitable to support further work on NVM-based Near Data Processing architectures.

Acknowledgment. The authors would like to thank the anonymous reviewers for their valuable comments. This research was funded by the German Research Foundation (DFG) as project #419942270 *neoDBMS*.

References

1. Axboe, J.: Fio tool source code. https://github.com/axboe/fio. Accessed 16 Dec 2021
2. Bernhardt, A., Tamimi, S., Stock, F., Vinçon, T., Koch, A., Petrov, I.: Cache-coherent shared locking for transactionally consistent updates in near-data processing DBMS on smart storage. In: EDBT, pp. 2–424 (2022)

3. Bock, S., Childers, B.R., Melhem, R., Mosse, D.: Hmmsim: a simulator for hardware-software co-design of hybrid main memory. In: 2015 IEEE Non-Volatile Memory System and Applications Symposium (NVMSA), pp. 1–6 (2015)
4. Do, J., Kee, Y.S., Patel, J.M., Park, C., Park, K., DeWitt, D.J.: Query processing on smart SSDs: opportunities and challenges. In: Proceedings of SIGMOD, p. 1221 (2013)
5. Duan, Z., Liu, H., Liao, X., Jin, H.: HME: a lightweight emulator for hybrid memory. In: 2018 Design, Automation & Test in Europe Conference & Exhibition (DATE), pp. 1375–1380. IEEE (2018)
6. Eilert, S., Leinwander, M., Crisenza, G.: Phase change memory (PCM): a new memory technology to enable new memory usage models (2011)
7. Embedded Systems and Applications Group, TU Darmstadt: Tapasco on Github. https://github.com/esa-tu-darmstadt/tapasco
8. Facebook: Rocksdb (2017). http://rocksdb.org
9. Hoefflinger, B.: ITRS: the international technology roadmap for semiconductors. In: Hoefflinger, B. (ed.) Chips 2020, pp. 161–174. Springer, Heidelberg (2011). https://doi.org/10.1007/978-3-642-23096-7_7
10. Xilinx Inc.: Vivado design suite user guide: programming and debugging (UG908). Technical report, Xilinx Inc. (2021). https://docs.xilinx.com/r/en-US/ug908-vivado-programming-debugging/ILA
11. Izraelevitz, J., et al.: Basic performance measurements of the intel optane DC persistent memory module. arXiv preprint arXiv:1903.05714 (2019)
12. Kim, S., Oh, H., Park, C., Cho, S., Lee, S.W., Moon, B.: In-storage processing of database scans and joins. Inf. Sci. **327**, 183–200 (2016)
13. Korinth, J., Hofmann, J., Heinz, C., Koch, A.: The TaPaSCo open-source toolflow for the automated composition of task-based parallel reconfigurable computing systems. In: Applied Reconfigurable Computing (2019)
14. Lee, T., Kim, D., Park, H., Yoo, S., Lee, S.: FPGA-based prototyping systems for emerging memory technologies. In: 2014 25nd IEEE International Symposium on Rapid System Prototyping, pp. 115–120 (2014)
15. Lee, T., Yoo, S.: An FPGA-based platform for non volatile memory emulation. In: 2017 IEEE 6th Non-Volatile Memory Systems and Applications Symposium (NVMSA), pp. 1–4 (2017)
16. Omori, Y., Kimura, K.: Performance evaluation on NVMM emulator employing fine-grain delay injection. In: 2019 IEEE Non-Volatile Memory Systems and Applications Symposium (NVMSA), pp. 1–6 (2019)
17. OpenSSD Project: COSMOS Project Documentation (2019). http://www.openssd-project.org/wiki/Cosmos_OpenSSD_Technical_Resources
18. Peng, I.B., Gokhale, M.B., Green, E.W.: System evaluation of the intel optane byte-addressable NVM. In: Proceedings of the International Symposium on Memory Systems, pp. 304–315 (2019)
19. Poremba, M., Xie, Y.: NVMain: an architectural-level main memory simulator for emerging non-volatile memories. In: 2012 IEEE Computer Society Annual Symposium on VLSI, pp. 392–397 (2012)
20. Salamat, S., Haj Aboutalebi, A., Khaleghi, B., Lee, J.H., Ki, Y.S., Rosing, T.: Nascent: near-storage acceleration of database sort on SmartSSD, FPGA 2021, pp. 262–272. Association for Computing Machinery, New York (2021). https://doi.org/10.1145/3431920.3439298

21. Tamimi, S., Stock, F., Koch, A., Bernhardt, A., Petrov, I.: An evaluation of using CCIX for cache-coherent host-FPGA interfacing. In: 2022 IEEE 30th Annual International Symposium on Field-Programmable Custom Computing Machines (FCCM), pp. 1–9 (2022)
22. Vinçon, T., et al.: Near-data processing in database systems on native computational storage under HTAP workloads. Proc. VLDB Endow. **15**(10), 1991–2004 (2022). https://doi.org/10.14778/3547305.3547307

On the OpenCL Support for Streaming Fixed-Function Accelerators on Embedded SoC FPGAs

Panagiotis Mousouliotis[1]([✉]), Topi Leppänen[2], Pekka Jääskeläinen[2],
Nikos Petrellis[1], Panagiotis Christakos[1], Georgios Keramidas[1],
Christos Antonopoulos[1], and Nikolaos Voros[1]

[1] University of Peloponnese, Patra, Greece
{p.mousouliotis,p.christakos,g.keramidas,
ch.antonop,voros}@esdalab.ece.uop.gr, npetrellis@uop.gr
[2] Tampere University, Tampere, Finland
{topi.leppanen,pekka.jaaskelainen}@tuni.fi

Abstract. OpenCL is used in contemporary FPGA High-level Synthesis (HLS) design tools for the development of the host-side code which controls the data transfer between the processing system and the FPGA design. High performance FPGA designs in embedded SoC FPGAs often make use of data movers with streaming capabilities for the direct data transfer between the host's main memory and the local memory of the FPGA accelerator. Unfortunately, the OpenCL memory model does not currently support streaming data movement between the host system and the FPGA accelerator. Earlier work has shown up to 8x latency improvement in data transfer when streaming data movement is used. To emphasize on this important issue, this work extends the Portable Computing Language (PoCL) OpenCL framework to support direct streaming data movement between the host's main memory and the accelerator's local memory. Furthermore, this work uses the CNN-Grinder workflow to map the execution of a traffic sign recognition Convolutional Neural Network (CNN) on the SqueezeJet-3 FPGA accelerator in order to showcase the details of controlling the SqueezeJet-3 streaming accelerator from a PoCL application. Results show that it is possible to achieve high performance accelerator execution and efficiently control an FPGA streaming accelerator on an embedded SoC FPGA using OpenCL augmented with direct streaming data transfer capabilities between the host and the kernel.

Keywords: OpenCL · FPGA · CNN Accelerator · High-Level Synthesis

1 Introduction

Today's HLS FPGA design tools [2, 11] from major vendors, such as AMD Xilinx and Intel, make use of the OpenCL language [9] in the host side for setting-up the required data transfers between the host and the kernel, and for controlling the kernel execution. A typical OpenCL program which issues an FPGA kernel

F. Palumbo et al. (Eds.): ARC 2023, LNCS 14251, pp. 51–65, 2023.
https://doi.org/10.1007/978-3-031-42921-7_4

execution using an in-order OpenCL command queue consists of the following steps: (1) the required data are transferred from the host memory to the global memory, where both the host and the kernel have access, (2) the kernel execution is issued and the results are written back to the global memory, and (3) the kernel results are transferred from the global memory back to the host memory. If in the same program the FPGA kernel execution is issued more than once, the aforementioned steps will repeat. Figure 1 depicts the OpenCL memory model as it is applied for (a) the case of the data-center and (b) the embedded SoC FPGAs. The OpenCL execution model is tightly associated with the OpenCL memory model.

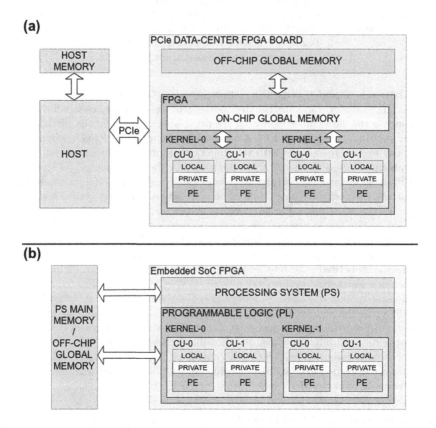

Fig. 1. The OpenCL memory model for (a) the data-center and (b) the embedded SoC FPGAs.

In the above OpenCL FPGA kernel execution model, two overheads are introduced: (1) the OpenCL API overhead for enqueueing the kernel (e.g. enqueueing commands for kernel argument transfer and kernel execution), and (2) the data movement overhead. For minimizing the effect of the first overhead, the HLS FPGA design tool vendors propose designing a small number of large task-level

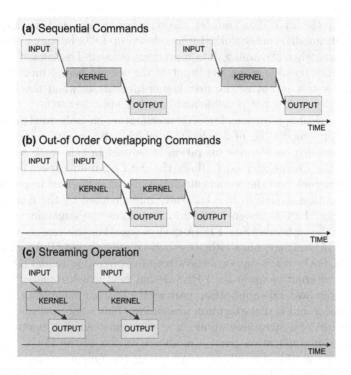

Fig. 2. The kernel execution timelines for **(a)** the OpenCL in-order execution queue, **(b)** the OpenCL out-of-order execution queue, and **(c)**, the streaming operation. In **(c)**, the kernel execution overlaps with both input consumption and output production leading to significant latency improvements.

computational kernels which will require fewer invocations than multiple small computational kernels. For the minimization of the second overhead, the tool vendors propose the scheduling of the data transfers and the kernel executions in a way that allows to overlap the data transfer for a next kernel execution with the current kernel execution, assuming that the application requires multiple sequential kernel invocations. The proposed host-side OpenCL solution for overcoming the data transfer overhead is not supported by the FPGA design tool vendors for the case of embedded SoC FPGAs; only the data-center type of SoC FPGAs is supported. In embedded SoC FPGAs, the FPGA on-chip memory size is limited and overcoming the data transfer overhead by overlapping data communication and kernel computation is not possible (by using techniques such as double or ping-pong buffering).

Figure 2 shows kernel execution timelines for **(a)** the OpenCL in-order execution queue, **(b)** the OpenCL out-of-order execution queue, and **(c)**, the streaming operation. As can be seen from Fig. 2, case **(c)** requires only a fraction of the time required by the **(a)** and **(b)** cases; the main reason is that in streaming operation the latency overlap of the following operations is possible in each kernel invocation: the input data transfer, the kernel execution, and the output data transfer. Additionally, earlier work [13] has shown up to 8x latency improvement in data transfer when streaming data movement is used. The latency overlap of case **(b)** is only possible when the input of the second kernel invocation does not depend on the output of the first kernel invocation; when there is such a dependency, case **(b)** is not possible and case **(a)** must be used.

Latency critical applications for CNN acceleration on embedded SoC FPGAs require the implementation of accelerators which support streaming operation [16]. The streaming accelerator operation is defined in this work as the operation where the execution model allows the data communication between the host and the kernel, and the kernel calculation, to be performed in parallel. The OpenCL execution model, as it is currently implemented by the contemporary commercial SoC FPGA design tools, does not allow the streaming accelerator operation for the embedded SoC FPGA devices case. For this reason, the embedded SoC FPGA designers must either use non-OpenCL based HLS tools, such as the Xilinx SDSoC, which supports the streaming operation model [18], or they must use an alternative lower-level HLS design flow which replaces the use of OpenCL for the host-side application part with a custom made solution for kernel data transfer and kernel execution invocation. This work presents the design flow for the use of a streaming accelerator where instead of a custom solution for the host-side application part, a modified version of the PoCL framework [7] is used; this modified PoCL version extends the OpenCL execution model to support streaming FPGA accelerator execution. The advantage of using the modified PoCL version over a custom host-side solution is that PoCL, as an OpenCL framework, provides additional opportunities for heterogeneous computing, e.g. scheduling the concurrent execution of computational kernels on several supported devices, such as CPUs, GPUs, and FPGAs. Additionally, the advantage of using the modified PoCL solution over the Xilinx Vitis tool is that Vitis supports the use of OpenCL for offloading computation only on Xilinx FPGA devices; it does not support the computation offloading to other system hosted devices such as GPUs. Finally, in contrast to the proposed modified PoCL solution, the Xilinx Vitis tool does not support the streaming kernel operation model on embedded SoC FPGAs.

To evaluate the effectiveness of the proposed OpenCL streaming accelerator execution model, a PoCL fixed-function FPGA accelerator application is developed for performing the traffic sign recognition task. For the purposes of the traffic sign recognition task, a custom CNN architecture is developed, the GTSRB-NET, for achieving high accuracy on the German Traffic Sign Recognition Benchmark (GTSRB) [17]. For the development of this application, the CNN-Grinder workflow [16] is used along with the SqueezeJet-3 CNN FPGA accelerator [15].

In the following, Sect. 2 presents the related work, Sect. 3 exposes the methodology regarding the PoCL extension to support streaming fixed-function accelerators, Sect. 4 describes the PoCL CNN application development, Sect. 5 presents and compares the results of the PoCL and the Xilinx SDSoC CNN application implementations, and, finally, Sect. 6 concludes this paper and proposes future work.

2   Related Work

This section presents works related to the OpenCL host-to-kernel (and vice versa) data transfer methods that enable streaming kernel operation on FPGAs.

In the AMD Xilinx Vitis tool, the OpenCL language is used for scheduling data transfers and invoking kernel executions from the host-side [1]. By using double buffering, an out-of-order OpenCL command queue, and by careful usage of OpenCL events, it is possible to use OpenCL to enable the overlapping of the data transfers and the kernel executions for the data-center type of SoC FPGAs. This operation mode is possible due to the PCIe full-duplex interconnect property, which allows to transfer data to and from the FPGA simultaneously. In this way, the PCIe interconnect allows the concurrent data transfer for the next kernel invocation and the write-back of the data of the previous kernel invocation, while the kernel operates on a current set of data. Additionally, the Vitis tool supports the host-to-kernel dataflow operation mode where again the data transfers can be overlapped with the kernel execution; this operation mode is not supported for embedded SoC FPGAs. For enabling the host-to-kernel dataflow operation mode the kernel must be designed to process the input data in stages. In this case, the low-level Xilinx Runtime (XRT) library restarts the kernel with a new set of data while the kernel is still processing a previous set of data in a further stage of the kernel execution pipeline.

The host-pipes extension [6,8], found in the Intel FPGA SDK for OpenCL, enables point-to-point pipe communication between a kernel and the host program; this extension mode is supported for the data-center type of SoC FPGAs such as the Intel Arria 10 GX. In the host-pipes implementation, a combination of DMAs and FIFOs along with a PCIe intellectual property (IP) are used [8]. Two host-pipes are currently supported; one for writing data from the host to the kernel and one for reading data from the kernel to the host.

Both the AMD Xilinx Vitis and the Intel FPGA SDK for OpenCL tools support direct kernel to kernel communication. In the Xilinx Vitis tool case this is possible through the use of AXI Stream interfaces [1], and in the Intel FPGA SDK for OpenCL tool case this is possible through the use of the OpenCL channels extension or the use of the OpenCL pipes [6]. In the Intel FPGA SDK for OpenCL tool, the OpenCL channels and pipes allow kernels to communicate directly with each other via FIFO buffers; unlike channels, pipes have a default non-blocking behavior.

In work [14] an extension of the PoCL AlmaIF v1 [4] hardware interface called AlmaIF v2 is presented. The AlmaIF v2 memory-mapped hardware interface supports OpenCL built-in kernels to be implemented by fixed-function hardware accelerators in the PoCL framework. A custom device driver is used for passing the kernel arguments from the host to the hardware kernel and for controlling the hardware kernel execution through the AlmaIF v2 memory-mapped hardware interface. The hardware kernel must include support functionality for interacting with the custom device driver; for this purpose HLS templates are provided for easy hardware kernel integration. In work [13], the AlmaIF v2 hardware interface is further extended to support direct memory data transfers from the host to the kernel. This is achieved by integrating the combination of a DMA IP and a FIFO IP into the hardware kernel; this makes it possible to implement streaming accelerators and control them through the OpenCL host-side code. The PoCL host to kernel direct data transfer solution can be used in both the data-center and the embedded SoC FPGA types.

In this work, we modify the PoCL custom device driver in order to control the DMA transfer setup and initiation. For this purpose, the DMA and FIFO IPs become part of a modified AlmaIF v2 interface. In this way, there is no need for the hardware kernel to setup and initialize the DMA transfers through the OpenCL arguments passed from the PoCL application code, as it is done in work [13]. In our case, the PoCL application developer is responsible for passing to the PoCL custom device driver the required data through calls for setting-up the DMA transfers. The PoCL custom device driver requires the discrimination of the registered built-in kernels to DMA capable and to non-DMA capable. Thus, there is no need for enqueueing special DMA related arguments for a DMA capable kernel execution; the only introduced requirement is the usage of the calls to the PoCL custom device driver for informing it for DMA setup and data size transfer. The PoCL custom device driver is responsible to initiate the DMA transfers when the hardware DMA capable kernel has received a related execution command. Using this PoCL OpenCL extension, support for both streaming and non-streaming OpenCL hardware kernels is possible in both the data-center and the embedded SoC FPGAs. Additionally, in the case of DMA capable kernels, the OpenCL execution model is responsible to pass only the non-DMA related arguments; the DMA related arguments are responsibility of the application developer and the PoCL custom device driver.

In the following, we describe the modifications to the PoCL custom device driver and to the AlmaIF hardware interface.

3   Methodology

In this section, the steps for developing a PoCL application which offloads computation to a DMA capable hardware kernel are described. For the support of a non-DMA capable hardware kernel, the OpenCL application developer can skip the DMA related calls to the PoCL custom device driver. In the following, a top-down approach is used for the description of our methodology. Initially, we describe the OpenCL and the extension application software required for preparing the data and invoking the streaming hardware kernel on the FPGA. Then, we present the interaction between the PoCL custom device driver and the streaming hardware kernel during the kernel execution.

3.1   Application Software

The first step in the application software development requires passing to the PoCL custom device driver the physical memory address of the host which will

```
1    // -- DMA initialization code --
2    // Set DMA physical address
3    set_dma_address(XDMA_AXI_LITE_ADDRESS);
4    // Set DMA related buffer physical addresses
5    set_dma_src_data_address(XDMA_SRC_DATA_ADDRESS);
6    set_dma_dst_data_address(XDMA_DST_DATA_ADDRESS);
7    // Memory map DMA related buffers physical to virtual addresses
8    XDMA_SRC_DATA_VIRT_ADDRESS = memmap(XDMA_MEM_AREA_BYTES, XDMA_SRC_DATA_ADDRESS);
9    XDMA_DST_DATA_VIRT_ADDRESS = memmap(XDMA_MEM_AREA_BYTES, XDMA_DST_DATA_ADDRESS);
10
11   // -- OpenCL initialization code --
12   // Pick platform
13   // Create context
14   // Query the set of devices attached to the context
15   // Build program
16   // Create command queue
17
18   // -- Kernel initialization code --
19   // Create OpenCL buffer for kernel scalar arguments
20   // Get the kernel object from the program
21
22   // -- Kernel invocation code --
23   // Set DMA related buffer values
24   set_dma_src_array_val(XDMA_SRC_DATA_VIRT_ADDRESS);
25   set_dma_dst_array_val(XDMA_DST_DATA_VIRT_ADDRESS);
26   // Set DMA transfers' size in bytes for write and read channels
27   set_dma_src_data_bytes(XDMA_SRC_DATA_BYTES_NUM);
28   set_dma_dst_data_bytes(XDMA_DST_DATA_BYTES_NUM);
29   // Initialize OpenCL kernel argument values
30   // Enqueue OpenCL kernel arguments
31   // Set the kernel arguments
32   // Run the kernel
```

Fig. 3. The additional code required for issuing a DMA capable kernel in a PoCL OpenCL application.

be used for controlling the DMA IP. The next step requires passing to the custom device driver the physical addresses which will be used for the DMA data transfers. Next, follows the memory mapping of a host physical memory address space to virtual memory address space; this step is necessary since moving data from the host to the streaming FPGA kernel through DMA transfers is done using physically continuous memory address space. This address space is used for storing the host data that will be written to and read from the on-chip memory of the streaming FPGA kernel. The application developer can now use the virtual address space, which maps to the physical address space, for setting-up the buffers for the FPGA kernel input and output data. The aforementioned steps consist of the additional initialization code required for developing a PoCL OpenCL application which controls a DMA capable fixed function streaming FPGA accelerator.

In the next step, the OpenCL initialization code follows for setting up the platform, the context, and the device. An OpenCL program is selected and built from the available devices and built-in kernels. The PoCL custom device driver has been modified to use the built-in kernel descriptor for recognizing if a built-in kernel is DMA capable or not.

Next, a command queue and an OpenCL DMA capable kernel is created using the built-in kernel defined during the previous OpenCL program built statement. Then, the device OpenCL memory buffers are created. The OpenCL buffers are used for moving small-size arguments such as the scalar arguments required by the kernel; these arguments' size is limited by the size of the available FPGA on-chip memory used as an OpenCL global memory. At this point, the OpenCL memory buffers and the DMA-related data buffers are initialized. The OpenCL buffers are enqueued to be written to the device memory and are registered as kernel arguments. The only visible arguments to the OpenCL kernel are the ones passed to the kernel using the OpenCL buffers; the DMA-related buffers are transparent to the OpenCL execution model, but are visible to the kernel as it is implemented in the FPGA. The OpenCL kernel is now ready to be enqueued for execution; the kernel is enqueued for execution using global and local workgroup sizes equal to one. After the OpenCL queue commands execution, the result of the kernel execution is found in the DMA-related buffer associated with the output of the FPGA kernel. Figure 3 shows the additional code required for issuing a DMA capable kernel in a PoCL OpenCL application; the actual OpenCL code is replaced by descriptive comments in order to showcase the small code overhead for the support of DMA capable kernels.

3.2   Custom Device Driver and Kernel Interaction

The PoCL custom device driver is responsible for implementing the lower level of the OpenCL software calls related to the data transfers and the execution of the FPGA kernel. The AlmaIF hardware interface [4,14] is used by the custom device driver for communicating data transfer and execution commands from the host to the FPGA kernel. In this work, an extended version of both the custom device driver and the AlmaIF v2 hardware interface [14] are developed and used.

The AlmaIF hardware interface consists of a host memory-mapped FPGA on-chip memory which is split into four parts; the control, the program, the data, and the parameter memory parts. The control memory part is used for controlling the PoCL fixed-function accelerator execution and for defining the accelerator's address space. The program memory part can be used for configuring the FPGA, but currently the FPGA configuration is performed during the embedded SoC FPGA boot. The data memory is used for storing an Heterogeneous System Architecture (HSA) queue [5] whose indexes are exposed to the control memory part. The HSA queue is implemented as a ring buffer of Architected Queue Language (AQL) packets. These packets carry information related to the execution of a specific kernel and its arguments. The parameter memory part is used for storing kernel argument buffers as well as kernel completion signals. In this work, the AlmaIF v2 hardware interface is extended to support DMA data transfers. This is implemented by using a DMA IP and two FIFO IPs; one FIFO for the DMA write channel, used for host-to-kernel direct data movement, and one FIFO for the DMA read channel, used for kernel-to-host direct data movement. Both the AlmaIF hardware interface and the DMA IP are configured and managed by the custom device driver. Figure 4 shows both the hardware and the software stack used for running a PoCL application which supports a DMA capable kernel.

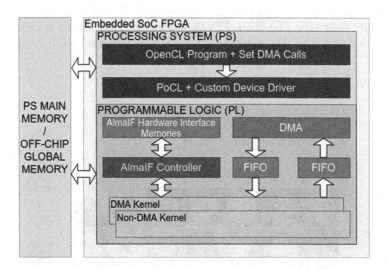

Fig. 4. The hardware and the software stack used for running a PoCL application which supports a DMA capable kernel.

The PoCL FPGA kernel interacts with the host through the AlmaIF hardware interface using an AlmaIF controller. The AlmaIF controller has access to the AlmaIF memory parts and uses them for controlling the FPGA kernel's operation. Execution control information is found in the AlmaIF control memory part. OpenCL execution commands and pointers to the OpenCL kernel arguments' data are found in the AQL packets which are stored in the AlmaIF data memory part; the actual OpenCL kernel's argument data is stored in the parameter AlmaIF memory part. The custom device driver prepares and uses the data found in the AlmaIF hardware interface memory in order to orchestrate the OpenCL kernel's execution on the FPGA. The FPGA kernel interacts with the custom device driver by reading and modifying the data in the AlmaIF hardware interface memory through the operation of the AlmaIF controller.

A PoCL FPGA accelerator is implemented as a free running accelerator in which the AlmaIF controller constantly checks for valid AQL packets in the AlmaIF data memory part. When an OpenCL PoCL application enqueues kernel data transfer and kernel execution commands, the kernel's argument data are stored in the AlmaIF parameter memory part, and a valid AQL packet, used for kernel execution, is prepared and stored in the AlmaIF data memory part. The AlmaIF controller unpacks the valid AQL packet and prepares the data, which consists of the kernel ID and the pointers to the kernel's argument data, to be used for execution by the FPGA kernel which supports the specific kernel ID.

In the current work, the PoCL FPGA accelerator interface includes one memory interface, used for communicating with the AlmaIF hardware interface, and two streaming ports; one for data input and one for data output. These streaming ports are connected to the FIFOs of the extended AlmaIF hardware interface. A PoCL FPGA accelerator can support multiple OpenCL built-in kernels which are identified by their IDs. The PoCL FPGA accelerator used in this work supports the execution of both DMA capable and non-DMA capable FPGA kernels.

4   CNN Application

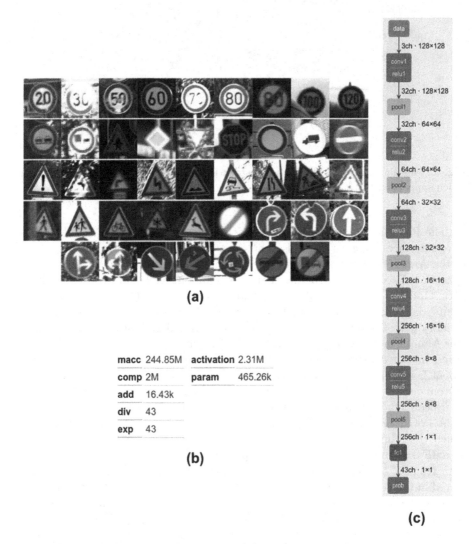

Fig. 5. (a) GTSRB dataset sample images, (b) the developed CNN specifications, and (c), the GTSRB-NET CNN architecture.

For the evaluation of our method we have developed a CNN algorithm, the GTSRB-NET CNN, and trained it on the GTSRB dataset[1]. The GTSRB dataset includes traffic sign images; each image belongs to a single class. Totally, the dataset includes 43 traffic sign classes and more than 50000 images in total. Using a fixed input image size of 128 × 128 pixels and training the GTSRB-NET CNN on the GTSRB dataset using the Adam optimizer [10] we achieve a top-1 accuracy of 96.35% and a top-5 accuracy of 99.44%. The Caffe deep learning framework and a GeForce GTX 1080 Ti GPU are used for the CNN training. Figure 5 shows (a) GTSRB dataset sample images, (b) the developed CNN specifications, and (c), the GTSRB-NET CNN architecture.

HLS templates provided by the PoCL framework [14] are used for the development of the PoCL FPGA accelerator. The SqueezeJet-3 accelerator [15,16] is modified to include one streaming input port interface, used for CNN parameter and input activation data transfer, and one streaming output port interface, used for output activation data transfer. The CNN-Grinder workflow [16] is used for mapping the GTSRB-NET CNN on the FPGA using the modified SqueezeJet-3 accelerator. The GTSRB-NET CNN mapping on the FPGA includes a CNN quantization step, using the Ristretto Caffe extension [3], and a convolutional layer splitting to sub-layers step, in order for the CNN parameters to fit in the on-chip memory of the embedded SoC FPGA. The quantized version of the GTSRB-NET at 8 bits achieves a top-1 accuracy of 96.14%, 0.21% top-1 accuracy drop compared to the floating-point implementation, and a top-5 accuracy of 99.27%; this quantized version of the GTSRB-NET CNN is used for acceleration by the modified SqueezeJet-3 accelerator. The modified SqueezeJet-3 accelerator is used as a DMA capable kernel in the HLS design of the PoCL FPGA accelerator. The resulting PoCL HLS accelerator is exported as an IP, using the Xilinx Vivado HLS tool. The PoCL FPGA accelerator IP is used by a Xilinx Vivado tool template which implements the modified AlmaIF hardware interface; the modified AlmaIF interface includes support for both DMA and non-DMA capable kernels. Figure 6 shows an interface view of the PoCL accelerator Xilinx Vivado design implementation for DMA capable kernel support.

Since the SqueezeJet-3 accelerator executes the combination of a convolutional layer followed by a maxpool layer, the PoCL GTSRB-NET application executes the CNN layer-by-layer. For this purpose, for each combination of a convolutional layer followed by a maxpool layer, the PoCL application prepares and schedules the input/output activation arguments to be transferred using the DMA IP, and the layer's scalar arguments (filter size, stride, etc.) to be transferred using the OpenCL buffers. As soon as the SqueezeJet-3 FPGA kernel receives the scalar arguments, the overlapped operation of the following takes place: (1) the input activation data transfer, (2) the kernel execution, and (3) the output activation data transfer.

---

[1] https://benchmark.ini.rub.de/gtsrb_dataset.html.

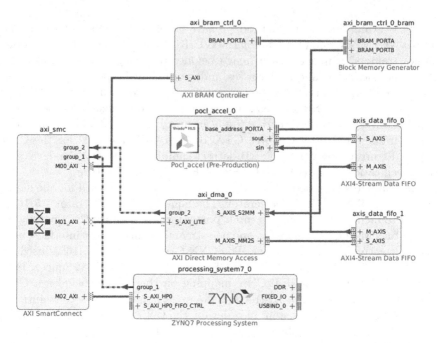

Fig. 6. The PoCL accelerator Xilinx Vivado design implementation for DMA capable kernel support.

5   Results and Discussion

In this section we evaluate the efficiency of our methodology using the acceleration of the GTSRB-NET as a benchmark. Specifically, we develop the GTSRB-NET application using both the PoCL workflow and the Xilinx SDSoC tool; both development methods support the execution of streaming accelerators. We compare the results of these two toolflows in terms of performance and resources usage.

Table 1 shows the on-board measured GTSRB-NET Convolution+MaxPool (CMP) latency results in ms for the ARM A9 software implementation operating at 666 MHz, the Xilinx SDSoC FPGA accelerator implementation operating at 100 MHz, and the PoCL FPGA accelerator implementation operating at 100 MHz; the Zedboard featuring a XC7Z020 Zynq SoC FPGA was used for these measurements. The combination of the CMP accelerated layers can be seen in **(c)** of Fig. 5; CMP layers number 4 of Fig. 5 have been split into 2 sub-layers in order for the convolution parameters to fit into the on-chip memory of the XC7Z020 Zynq SoC FPGA; these layers are denoted as CMP04_1 and CMP04_2 in Table 1. From the **TOTAL** row of Table 1, it is clear that the PoCL accelerator solution is really close in terms of performance to the optimized Xilinx SDSoC standalone solution. The small difference in the performance can be attributed to the OpenCL API calls and the usage of the AlmaIF HW interface for passing the scalar arguments.

Table 1. Convolution+MaxPool (CMP) latency results in ms for the ARM A9 at 666 MHz software implementation, the Xilinx SDSoC FPGA implementation at 100 MHz, and the PoCL FPGA accelerator implementation at 100 MHz.

CNN LAYER	ARM A9	SDSoC	PoCL
CMP01	193.09	12.13	13.75
CMP02	407.73	7.07	7.31
CMP03	467.77	4.79	5.11
CMP04_1	234.97	2.25	2.53
CMP04_2	235.13	2.24	2.56
CMP05	27.52	0.46	0.79
TOTAL	**1566.20**	**28.94**	**32.05**

Table 2 shows the resources usage of the Xilinx SDSoC and the PoCL accelerator implementations. From the **Diff** column, it can be seen that the PoCL implementation uses around 8.5–15% more XC7Z020 FPGA resources compared to the Xilinx SDSoC implementation, with the exception of the DSP resources. This can be attributed to the implementation of the AlmaIF HW interface, the AlmaIF controller, and the custom size selection of the FIFOs used for the implementation of the modified AlmaIF hardware interface which provides DMA capable kernel support.

Compared to commercial design tools such as the Xilinx SDSoC and the Xilinx Vitis, the presented PoCL method offers additional opportunities for heterogeneous computing, such as the simultaneous offloading of the computational workload to CPUs, GPUs, and FPGAs [12]; the contemporary SoC FPGA design tools lack this kind of heterogeneous computing support even though they offer OpenCL support for host-side code development. Finally, compared to the Xilinx Vitis tool, our PoCL-based methodology offers support for using OpenCL to control streaming kernels in embedded SoC FPGAs; this is not currently supported by the Xilinx Vitis tool. Using the Vitis tool for the acceleration of the GTSRB-NET would result to a much slower implementation in terms of latency because there is no latency overlap for data transfers and kernel execu-

Table 2. FPGA resources usage percentage of the Xilinx SDSoC and the PoCL accelerator implementations on the XC7Z020 Zynq SoC FPGA.

RESOURCE	SDSoC	PoCL	Diff
LUT	57.52 %	72.50 %	14.98 %
LUTRAM	21.44 %	30.35 %	8.91 %
FF	18.50 %	27.08 %	8.58 %
BRAM	73.21 %	86.79 %	13.57 %
DSP	100.00 %	100.00 %	0 %

tion. Specifically, since the input of a subsequent kernel invocation depends on the output of the previous kernel invocation in the GTSRB-NET application, Vitis can only support the operation mode shown in case **(a)** of Fig. 2.

6   Conclusion and Future Work

This work has presented a modified PoCL software and hardware interface for the support of DMA capable kernels which operate in a streaming manner. Evaluation of the developed method in the acceleration of a CNN application revealed that our method produces results that perform on par with the commercial SoC FPGA design tools using OpenCL for kernel execution control. The small FPGA resources usage overhead introduced by our modified PoCL method can be alleviated by the additional opportunities offered for heterogeneous computing which are missing by contemporary FPGA design tools; Xilinx SDSoC and Xilinx Vitis can offload computation only on a Xilinx FPGA device even though other devices, such as GPUs, can be present in the system. Additionally, the Xilinx Vitis tool does not support the streaming kernel operation model for embedded SoC FPGAs, and cannot be used for the implementation and the control of the execution of the SqueezeJet-3 accelerator.

Future work could introduce improvements in our method in terms of both software and hardware. The custom device driver modifications and the application API could be redesigned to be OpenCL standard compliant, and our AlmaIF hardware templates could be improved both in terms of performance and resources usage. Finally, a more heterogeneous computing oriented application could be implemented which would take advantage of the full OpenCL potential of the PoCL framework by offloading concurrently the workload to different device types such as CPUs, GPUs, and FPGAs.

Acknowledgments. This work has received funding from the European Union's Horizon 2020 research and innovation program under Grant Agreement No 872614 - SMART4ALL: Selfsustained CrossBorder Customized Cyberphysical System Experiments for Capacity Building among European Stakeholders.

References

1. AMD Xilinx: Vitis Unified Software Platform Documentation, Application Acceleration Development, UG1393 (v2022.2), 7 December 2022. https://docs.xilinx.com/viewer/book-attachment/aJhJw9uEf3GPMuRNo0jveg/5jCMHSlRPIRfufLlzZMsOQ. Accessed 31 Mar 2023
2. Cong, J., et al.: FPGA HLS today: successes, challenges, and opportunities. ACM Trans. Reconfigurable Technol. Syst. (TRETS) **15**(4), 1–42 (2022)
3. Gysel, P., Pimentel, J., Motamedi, M., Ghiasi, S.: Ristretto: a framework for empirical study of resource-efficient inference in convolutional neural networks. IEEE Trans. Neural Networks Learn. Syst. **29**(11), 5784–5789 (2018)
4. Hoozemans, J., Van Straten, J., Viitanen, T., Tervo, A., Kadlec, J., Al-Ars, Z.: ALMARVI execution platform: heterogeneous video processing SoC platform on FPGA. J. Sig. Process. Syst. **91**, 61–73 (2019)

5. HSA™ Foundation: HSA Platform System Architecture Specification v1.2. http://hsa.glossner.org/wp-content/uploads/2021/02/HSA-SysArch-1.2.pdf. Accessed 31 Mar 2023
6. Intel: Intel® FPGA SDK for OpenCL™ Pro Edition: Programming Guide. https://cdrdv2.intel.com/v1/dl/getContent/749418?fileName=aocl_programming_guide-683846-749418.pdf. Accessed 31 Mar 2023
7. Jääskeläinen, P., Sanchez de La Lama, C., Schnetter, E., Raiskila, K., Takala, J., Berg, H.: pocl: a performance-portable OpenCL implementation. Int. J. Parallel Program. **43**(5), 752–785 (2015)
8. Kang, K., Yiannacouras, P.: Host pipes: direct streaming interface between OpenCL host and Kernel. In: Proceedings of the 5th International Workshop on OpenCL, pp. 1–2 (2017)
9. Khronos® OpenCL Working Group: The OpenCL™ Specification. https://www.khronos.org/registry/OpenCL/specs/3.0-unified/pdf/OpenCL_API.pdf. Accessed 31 Mar 2023
10. Kingma, D.P., Ba, J.: Adam: a method for stochastic optimization. arXiv preprint arXiv:1412.6980 (2014)
11. Lahti, S., Sjövall, P., Vanne, J., Hämäläinen, T.D.: Are we there yet? A study on the state of high-level synthesis. IEEE Trans. Comput. Aided Des. Integr. Circuits Syst. **38**(5), 898–911 (2018)
12. Leppänen, T., Lotvonen, A., Jääskeläinen, P.: Cross-vendor programming abstraction for diverse heterogeneous platforms. Frontiers Comput. Sci. **4** (2022)
13. Leppänen, T., Lotvonen, A., Mousouliotis, P., Multanen, J., Keramidas, G., Jääskeläinen, P.: Efficient OpenCL system integration of non-blocking FPGA accelerators. Microprocess. Microsyst., 104772 (2023)
14. Leppänen, T., Mousouliotis, P., Keramidas, G., Multanen, J., Jääskeläinen, P.: Unified OpenCL integration methodology for FPGA designs. In: 2021 IEEE Nordic Circuits and Systems Conference (NorCAS), pp. 1–7. IEEE (2021)
15. Mousouliotis, P., Tampouratzis, N., Papaefstathiou, I.: SqueezeJet-3: an HLS-based accelerator for edge CNN applications on SoC FPGAs. In: 2023 XXIX International Conference on Information, Communication and Automation Technologies (ICAT), pp. 1–6. IEEE (2023)
16. Mousouliotis, P.G., Petrou, L.P.: CNN-grinder: from algorithmic to high-level synthesis descriptions of CNNs for low-end-low-cost FPGA SoCs. Microprocess. Microsyst. **73**, 102990 (2020). https://doi.org/10.1016/j.micpro.2020.102990
17. Stallkamp, J., Schlipsing, M., Salmen, J., Igel, C.: The German traffic sign recognition benchmark: a multi-class classification competition. In: The 2011 International Joint Conference on Neural Networks, pp. 1453–1460. IEEE (2011)
18. Xilinx: SDSoC Profiling and Optimization Guide. https://www.xilinx.com/support/documents/sw_manuals/xilinx2019_1/ug1235-sdsoc-optimization-guide.pdf. Accessed 31 Mar 2023

Design Space Exploration of Application Specific Number Formats Targeting an FPGA Implementation of SPICE

Jonas Gehrunger$^{(\boxtimes)}$ (ID) and Christian Hochberger (ID)

Computer Systems Group, Technische Universität Darmstadt,
Merckstr. 25, 64283 Darmstadt, Germany
{gehrunger,hochberger}@rs.tu-darmstadt.de

Abstract. Most scientific computations use double precision floating point numbers. Recently, posits as an additional alternative have been established and are subject to ongoing research. In FPGA implementations arbitrary combinations of mantissa and exponent widths are possible. For some applications the required precision can be determined analytically without knowledge of the input data. Thus, in these cases a lower bound for the hardware effort can be given. Other applications may be more resilient to the precision of the chosen number representation. One example of such application is SPICE for circuit simulation. SPICE exhibits kind of self-healing behavior, since it detects the accumulated error and if the error gets too large, it can take recovery measures. In this case, more iterations are required, leading to more operations in total. This allows us an additional degree of freedom: We can trade lower precision and thus smaller area against the increased calculation effort. This paper develops a methodology to use these different options to find an optimal solution for each specific SPICE application scenario. It turns out that for regular IEEE-754 floating point formats a number format between single and double precision delivers the best trade off between operator size and computation time. Surprisingly, using posit based representations does not improve the overall runtime of simulations.

Keywords: FPGA · Posits · Floating Point Numbers · SPICE Circuit Simulation · Design Space Exploration

1 Introduction

Simulations of electronic circuits are carried out using SPICE. This simulation software can model arbitrary elements like resistors, capacitors, inductors and also active components like MOS-Fets or diodes or bipolar transistors. In our case, we want to simulate memristors [1]. To develop read/write electronics for arrays of memristors, we have to simulate many thousands of such devices in one circuit. This can easily lead to hours of simulation times [2]. Thus, it is desirable to run parallelized versions of SPICE which speed up the execution. One potential execution platform could be field programmable gate arrays (FPGA). Unfortunately, SPICE – like many other scientific computations – uses double floating point numbers internally. These double numbers are not well suited for FPGA implementation. At the same time, SPICE seems to be relatively robust against errors during calculations. It carries out calculations until it reaches a convergence. Thus, one could use other number formats and thereby achieve faster/smaller operators on the FPGA. We can either change the number of bits used in mantissa and exponent or we can change to more modern data types like unums [9] or posit numbers [10] (which are a special case of unums). One might think that fixed point numbers are an even better choice, but unfortunately, the high dynamic range of values in SPICE prevents their usage.

This new degree of freedom calls for a more elaborate design space exploration. We have to analyze the consequences of different number formats (in terms of total calculations that a simulation needs) and have to relate this number to the speed and size of the respective operator implementations. Overall, we are looking for the fastest possible implementation of a generic simulator optimized for a set of specific circuits for a given FPGA device.

In this paper we focus on the mentioned design space exploration and present the following contributions:

- A sample evaluation of different number formats for a given application.
- An analysis of SPICE with respect to its resilience against imprecise calculations.
- A linear programming model to find the best performing combination of number format and bit width to minimize the overall calculation time.

The remainder of this paper is structured as follows: Section 2 gives an overview on the technical background and related work. It is followed by an analysis of SPICE behavior for large circuits using a spectrum of number formats in Sect. 3. Then, we analyze the technical features of operator implementations on FPGAs for the chosen number formats in Sect. 4. The trade-offs for the whole application are presented in Sect. 5. Finally, we give a conclusion and an outlook onto future work.

2   Background

2.1   Related Work

SPICE (Simulation Program with Integrated Circuit Emphasis) itself is a historic development from the early 70s [19]. As it was the first publicly available circuit simulator for analog and digital (or mixed signal) circuits, it represents a historic landmark for circuit simulation. In this work we use ngspice [20], which is a descendant of the original Berkeley SPICE version »3f5«. It is published as open source and thus is an ideal starting point for our own investigations.

SPICE simulations can easily run for hours. Thus, accelerations of the original approach seem to be quite natural. Graphics Processing Units (GPU) have become a major way to speed up scientific computations. Thus, a GPU based version of ngspice has been published [17]. Unfortunately, the mathematical problem solved in SPICE does not seem to be a good fit for GPUs, as they achieve only very moderate speed-ups of up to 3. Limiting factor is the complexity of the device models. Higher speed-ups for commercial software of up to 10 for some circuits have been reported [6]. It is likely that this high speed-up can only be achieved for very specific circuits.

Other researchers have already changed underlying data type for SPICE simulations. In [14], the authors experiment with single precision floating point numbers. Yet, it should be noted that they only run a small part of the SPICE workload (i.e. the model evaluation) using this data type.

Since precision requirements within SPICE simulations heavily depend on utilized device models and the input circuit combined with the large number of supported device types, analytical approaches to determine a minimum precision like [4] can not be effectively utilized. Likewise, there is no clear cut-off on what can be considered to be sufficient precision prior to running the simulation. Investigations into the effects of adjusting the precision have been successfully done before for other problems, such as Model Predictive Control [22].

Individual parts of SPICE have been implemented using FPGAs before [13, 15]. Yet, these researchers never fully integrated the individual parts into one design. In contrast, we are targeting a full FPGA implementation of SPICE so we can explore the benefits of arbitrary number formats.

In order to implement the required operations with arbitrary mantissa and exponent width, we rely on FloPoCo [7]. After specifying the bit width of the operations and giving a target clock frequency, it automatically generates FPGA optimized implementations of all operators. To obtain similar operators for Posit number formats, we use PACoGen [12], a parametric verilog implementation.

Recently, FloPoCo has been extended to support Posit numbers as well. Unfortunately, the source is not yet complete and it does not support dividers. Thus, we could not make use of this more efficient implementation.

2.2 Posit Numbers

The author of [9], Gustafson, first proposed a universal number system (unum) in 2015. Designed as a possible replacement for IEEE 754 floating point numbers, it aims to resolve some existing deficiencies of floating point representations - mainly rounding errors (as overflows are rounded up to infinity), the lack of associativity (results of calculations differ depending on their order), subnormal numbers and a large unused value range in the exponent (mostly reserved for representing the Not-A-Number flag NaN). Unums have a variable width to represent numbers exactly and can specify their exponent and fraction size at runtime however needed. Due to their dynamic size, unums are not suitable for hardware implementations. This gap is filled by the type-3 unums introduced in [10], which are called posits.

Compared to IEEE 754 floating point numbers of the same size, posits have a higher precision around 1 and a much wider dynamic range and do not over-/underflow. The format uses a fixed total width and can have up to n_{es} exponent-bits. The exact distribution of bits within any given number varies at runtime, only the total width is fixed. In theory, this allows for a smaller hardware implementation and in combination with the much larger dynamic range leads to much attention in the science community.

2.3   Principle of Circuit Simulation with SPICE

The foundation of circuit simulation with SPICE is the Modified Nodal Analysis [11], which allows to generate a linear equation system for the entire circuit by looking at the contributions of each circuit component to the nodes it is connected to. These contributions are independent from each other and follow the same pattern for each component type, allowing to make use of predefined so-called *stamps* to create the circuit matrix G. The linear equation system (1)

$$G * \boldsymbol{V} = \boldsymbol{I} \qquad (1)$$

consisting of the matrix G, a vector of node voltages V and a vector of currents I on the right hand side yields all voltages in the circuit as well as currents through voltage sources. While this works well for linear components, non-linear devices require a more complex approach.

The basic principle for the (transient) simulation of non-linear devices in SPICE is shown in Fig. 1 and based on the iterative Newton-Raphson (NR) algorithm. An initial operating point for the circuit is chosen (usually using the DC operating point if available or zeros if not) and all non-linear devices are linearized around that point. Using these linearized approximations, the circuit matrix is filled and the resulting equation system solved.

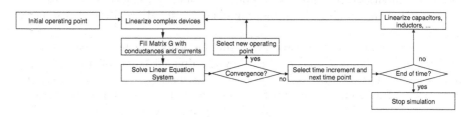

Fig. 1. Flowchart of Newton-Raphson-based simulation of non-linear circuit elements

For the result, a convergence test is executed. Only when the difference in voltage to the previous NR-iteration is smaller than a threshold, convergence is assumed. Otherwise, a new trial operating point is selected based on the current state and a new NR-iteration started. Once convergence is reached, the next timestep is selected and the simulation continues. Through dynamically adjusting the increments between timesteps based on the observed convergence behavior and through discarding non-converging operating points, this method exhibits a strong resilience against numerical errors and thus is a prerequisite for the analysis done in this work.

3   Analysis of Number Formats in SPICE

The version of SPICE evaluated in this work is the open-source package ngspice [20] in version 35 written in C. For calculations during the circuit simulation, *ngspice* uses almost exclusively double precision floating point numbers. To support arbitrary number formats, the software was first adapted to C++ and then all `double` declarations were replaced using a C++-class with overloaded operators. The replacement class needs to have the same size as the native double type to preserve compatibility with state memory allocations.

To substitute the default double precision format, the library *floatX* [8] is used for floating point numbers. *floatX* supports arbitrary floating point formats, though with both exponent and mantissa limited to at most the equivalent size of double precision. Elementary functions such as *sqrt*, *exp* and *sinh* are passed through to the C++ standard library and their results are rounded to the appropriate number format. Similarly, *universal* [21] is used to provide support for posit number formats with arbitrary width and exponent size.

Additionally, instrumentation is added to count calculations like additions, multiplications and divisions for each Newton-Raphson iteration, for each timestep and for the entire simulation run.

The modified version of *ngspice* is verified using the integration test cases provided by the project itself and by comparing the simulation results of the circuit benchmark suites *ISCAS'85* [5] and *ACM/SIGDA CircuitSim90* [3] against an unmodified *ngspice-35* build. As the employed MOS models have a complexity comparable to memristor models, they are a well suited base for our work. To indicate the floating point format used, the notation $bits_{exponent}\_bits_{mantissa}$ will be used, e.g. 10_40 refers to a floating point format with 10 bit exponent and 40 bit mantissa. In graphs with both posit and floating point formats, the total width of the number representation is used instead, with the chosen posit exponent size indicated as $< size_{exponent} >$.

The benchmarks used for evaluation in this work can be coarsely divided into two groups, analog and digital. They are divided based on the structure and behavior. For digital circuits, generally less precision is required as both input and output signals have much higher error tolerance compared to analog circuits even though they are simulated the same way as analog devices. The collection of digital circuits consists of schmitt triggers, latches and basic logic gates, multiplexers and different RAM cells. The collection of analog circuits included in the benchmark suites contains voltage regulators, wideband amplifiers, different operation amplifier topologies and rectifiers. In total 10 analog and 20 digital circuits are evaluated, excluding the *mos2large* collection of the CircuitSim90 suite due to excessive runtime combined with small numerical differences compared to the *mos2* collection.

3.1   Distribution of Operations

Figure 2 shows the relative number of each type of calculation that was measured. Additions and multiplications account for a combined 90% of all calculations with 53% of number operations being additions and 37% multiplications. Elementary functions, such as *sin*, *exp* and *sqrt*, are not split up further since they can be replaced by approximations or table lookups in practice.

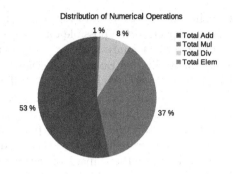

Fig. 2. Averaged distribution of numerical operations

For any given circuit, the relative percentages of this distribution stay within ±0.5% when varying the number format and within ±2% when comparing benchmark circuits. Variations between circuits can be explained by different device models being used and differing ratios of device types to each other. This stability allows to determine a more generalized distribution of hardware resources between operators.

One source of the large number of additions is rooted in *SPICE* employing Modified-Nodal-Analysis (MNA) for building up the circuit equation system: In each iteration, the contribution of each device to a given node is added onto the corresponding matrix entries. Resistors and (DC) voltage sources, to name one example, perform only additions after their initial setup.

Signal Values. When observing the measured range of exponents, certain large numbers appear repeatedly across different circuits. One example for this is the number $1.0e^{99}$, which appears in most of the benchmark circuits making use of BJT, resistor or capacitor device models. Investigating their origin in the *ngspice* code identifies this number as a hard-coded default value.

Following the flow of this value and similar instances throughout the simulation shows that the actual value is not relevant for the simulation result and is instead used as a *signal value* to indicate either infinity or that the current value is still a default. Since these signal values are intentionally chosen to be higher than any reasonable parameter value, replacing them with either an additional bit in the number format or encoding them as specific exponent/mantissa combination like it is done for NaN or Inf in floating point formats would allow a further reduction of the required exponent width.

Excluding this signal value leads to a much reduced maximum exponent value during the benchmarks. Limiting factor preventing a further width reduction is the negative exponent required to represent very small numbers. If these can be limited, making a fixed point implementation of SPICE would be feasible.

3.2 Impact on Convergence and Output Error

Reducing the precision and range of the number format used for simulation has a direct impact on the possible output error and the convergence of simulation.

The transient analysis is the analysis type most susceptible to convergence failure due to limited range or precision. This is due to the distance to the next step Δ_t being calculated based on the differences of voltages and states compared to the previous timestep. Accumulating errors can lead to shrinking step sizes and when reaching the minimum (by default $10^{-11} * \Delta_{t,max}$), ultimately termination of the simulation. Other analysis types such as DC or AC sweeps are more stable since each of their discrete steps is started with a clean slate.

To investigate the impact of varying the number format on convergence, the size of exponent and mantissa are swept separately. For the floating point exponent, reducing the size down to 8 bit has no measurable impact on circuit convergence, as the full required value range can still be represented. Reducing the exponent size below 8 bit leads to non-convergence of all benchmark circuits.

Figure 3 shows the number of circuits for each format that successfully converged without modification to their parameters. Shown are both floating point formats with fixed exponent size of 8 bit and five posit configurations, with exponent sizes from 0 to 4 bit. Starting from the right, as width of the representation is progressively reduced, the number of successful benchmark drops. Reducing the size of the mantissa (or total format width in the case of posits) has a gradual effect that is notably not perfectly monotonic - Some circuits fail to reach convergence for certain higher precision formats but are successfully simulated at lower precision. Since this behavior follows no clear pattern and is not reliably predictable, circuits are assumed to be failing for the current precision if they failed for a higher precision as well. There are three relevant vertical ranges in the graph: Below 15 circuits, between 15 and 25 as well as above 25 passing circuits. Device models fail at different precisions. High level transistor and MOSFET models, such as *BSIM4v7* through *HiSIM2*, fail first, as they cannot model their internal parameters (e.g. parasitic capacitance values) properly and fail internal parameter consistency checks with lower precision.

As we aim to simulate memristor models together with their driver circuitry, for practical applications there is a flexibility to choose less extensive MOSFET and transistor models - Making the second plateau most interesting for the purpose of this research. Here, 15 to 25 benchmark circuits still pass, allowing a trade-off between device model accuracy and required resources. When reducing width of the representations further, the number of converging benchmark circuits drops rapidly, making these formats unsuitable for practical applications. In the range below 15 passing benchmarks, only analog circuits remain.

At first glance, Fig. 3 indicates that any precision below 44 bit width for floating point is not suitable to simulate all circuits and thus cannot be used. Fortunately, this is not the case as SPICE provides many tools to approach convergence issues. The easiest option is to increase the convergence threshold and the allowed current error tolerance (exposed as parameter `abstol`). Increasing the convergence threshold, which defaults to $1 * 10^{-12}$, allows a larger output

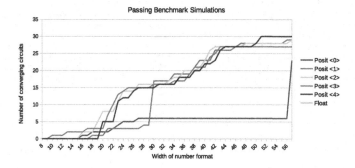

Fig. 3. Convergence of benchmark circuit simulations

error but makes convergence much easier to reach. This is not an uncommon approach to improve convergence, for 11 of the benchmark circuits this is done anyway to aid convergence in the unmodified version of SPICE and would just require further tweaking of the selected value. Additionally, SPICE can fall back onto *gmin-stepping* and *source stepping*, the former of which adding progressively larger conductances in parallel to active devices in the circuit to aid convergence. Their default values are optimized for double precision and need to be tweaked to match the format in question.

Besides these options and the mentioned limiting influence of certain high complexity device models, a significant part of convergence behavior is down to the equation system solver, which was not functionally modified for this work. Conditioning of the circuit matrix can greatly influence the resulting numerical stability. Alternative solvers with more options for scaling and conditioning exist and one, KLU [16], is already implemented in ngspice. Unfortunately, KLU is only available on an experimental branch of ngspice and associated options for increasing numerical stability are not employed.

If convergence is reached, the output error is small across all benchmark circuits. For evaluation of the output error, relative error is used and calculated as $e_{rel} = \frac{v_{orig} - v_{modified}}{v_{orig}}$. For the floating point format 10_27, a worst case relative error of $8 * 10^{-7}$ for analog and $4 * 10^{-5}$ for digital circuits is reached. Posit implementations exhibit a larger range of errors, with the average error being lower than for an equivalent width floating point, but the relative error in the worst case reaching up to $7 * 10^{-5}$ for analog and $3 * 10^{-3}$ for digital circuits for a posit format with 37 bits width. This points towards a greater importance of mantissa precision than available dynamic range for the resulting error, putting posit formats at a disadvantage.

The greatest error occurs for voltage swings with the simulation recovering during relatively small changes in output. The root cause for this behavior can be traced to a loss of precision in the calculation of time derivatives for non-linear devices. As a result, the observed behavior differs between digital and analog circuits, as the former type has large voltage swings followed by periods of small changes and the latter frequently exhibits continuously changing node voltages.

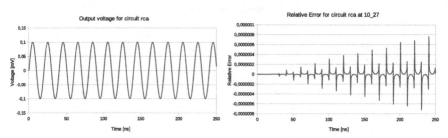

(a) Output voltage of analog amplifier circuit rca

(b) Resulting relative output error for rca with format 10_27

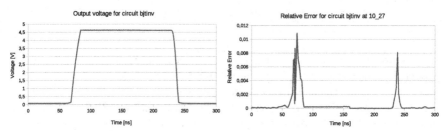

(c) Output voltage of inverter circuit bjtinv

(d) Resulting relative output error for bjtinv with format 10_27

Fig. 4. Output error for different circuit types

This can lead to amplification of output errors over the course of the simulation and accompanying risk of convergence failure. An example for each type is provided in Fig. 4. Circuit rca is an analog wideband amplifier and is simulated with a small amplitude sinusoidal voltage, exhibiting close to the largest relative error observed for analog circuits in the benchmark suite. Most analog circuits evaluated in this work don't exhibit this error amplification, thus rca can be considered as a worst case example.

3.3   Impact on Simulation Runtime

Due to the ability of SPICE to reject infeasible time points and NR-iterations, the resulting deviation of the simulation output from the reference curve stays relatively small. At the same time, with lower precision more iterations are discarded and thus, a larger number of total calculations is observed, an effect that holds true across the different analysis types supported by *ngspice*. While this neglects the effects of memory accesses, it is a good indicator for the influence on simulation runtime.

This can be illustrated by comparing the total number calculations for a single circuit over the range of investigated number formats and is shown in Fig. 5. The increase in required calculations (and iterations) stays moderate for high precision and starts to grow exponentially when approaching the minimum

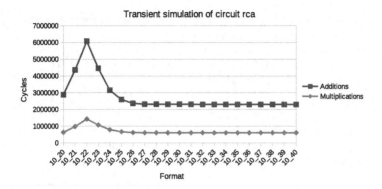

Fig. 5. Total number of multiplications and additions for transient analysis of circuit rca

precision needed to simulate this circuit. When the format is further reduced below 10_22, the required number of calculations drops down rapidly, but the simulation no longer converges and no valid result is produced. This holds true for both floating point and posit number formats.

4 Operator Implementation

To determine the resource requirements of the numerical operators for a specific number format, the toolkit *flopoco* is used. For each format, floating point adders, multipliers, dividers and comparator implementations are generated. To obtain a realistic result, a target frequency of 200 MHz is provided to the tool. Posit operators are generated with PACoGen. As PACoGen only provides combinatorial implementations, it was manually pipelined to reach the same target frequency. Source code for these modifications is publicly available in [18].

Each format is wrapped into an individual top level design and synthesis run in Xilinx Vivado targeting the Ultrascale+ VCU118 board. To prevent optimizations merging different operators together, synthesis attributes are used. For the resulting implementations, resource usage and timing details are extracted.

Looking at the synthesis results in Fig. 6, a near linear relationship between number format and the required resources is observed for LUTs, more so for posits than for floating point formats. Integer multiplications contained in the multipliers were automatically synthesized using dedicated Digital Signal Processing (DSP) blocks, the corresponding resource usage increases in discrete steps. Area needs for comparators are negligible and omitted here for posits. Varying exponent size has a small influence of less than 1% over all investigated formats and as such is not shown here. Compared to floating point implementations, the posit operators consume a much larger area for the same format width and twice the DSP slices.

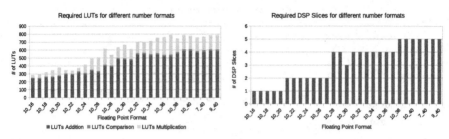

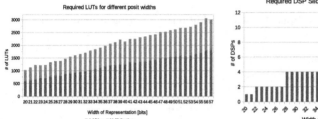

(a) Required LUTs for Floating Point Adders and Multipliers

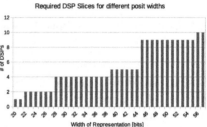

(b) Required DSP Slices for Floating Point Multipliers

(c) Required LUTs for Posit Adders and Multipliers

(d) Required DSP Slices for Posit Multipliers

Fig. 6. Resource requirements for different number formats

5   Whole Application Analysis

The runtime variance shown in Sect. 3 and the resource requirements for implementing a given numerical format discussed in Sect. 4 show a contrary trend: Increasing precision leads to a smaller total number of calculations while at the same time reducing the possible parallelism in hardware since resources on the target FPGA are limited. Finding the ideal number format for a given circuit can be formulated as a linear optimization problem.

For this purpose, data dependencies are disregarded and the assumption is made that during any clock cycle each operator can start a single operation (as all generated operators are fully pipelined). To further simplify the problem, only adders and multipliers are considered as they make up the majority of calculations during simulation of the benchmarks. For brevity, modeling the resource usage is limited to Lookup-Tables (LUTs) and DSP-slices, since they are the most restricted in the target device. Given these simplifications, the resource usage can be expressed as in (2) and (3):

$$lut_{add} * n_{add} + lut_{mult} * n_{mult} \leq lut_{device} \tag{2}$$
$$dsp_{add} * n_{add} + dsp_{mult} * n_{mult} \leq dsp_{device} \tag{3}$$

The inverse of the required time to execute all calculations can be determined using the total number of operations through (4):

$$\frac{1}{t} < \frac{1}{operations_{add}} * n_{add}; \frac{1}{t} < \frac{1}{operations_{mult}} * n_{mult} \tag{4}$$

Finally, using the following constraints, the problem can be solved by optimizing for the minimum t (or maximum $\frac{1}{t}$):

$$0 < \frac{1}{t} < 1 \quad ; \quad n_{add} > 0 \quad ; \quad n_{mult} > 0 \tag{5}$$

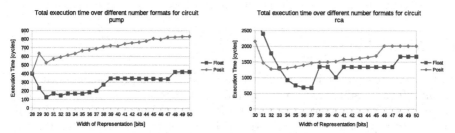

(a) Execution Time in cycles for bench-   (b) Execution Time in cycles for benchmark circuit *pump*   mark circuit *rca*

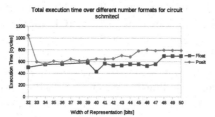

(c) Execution Time in cycles for benchmark circuit *schmitecl*

Fig. 7. Optimization problem solved for three circuits

This linear optimization problem yields the ideal number of adders and multipliers to implement within a given resource limit and the theoretical execution time for the circuit simulation, ignoring data dependencies.

When solving this equation system for each number format considered in Sects. 3 and 4, the results show a clear sweet spot for each circuit. The results reveal three distinct types of relative behavior between posit and floating point, each represented by a circuit as an illustrative example in Fig. 7.

The first circuit, *pump*, has a fairly low numerical complexity and its execution time decreases until the floating point format 8_21 (width of 30 bits) is reached. Below this precision, the required execution time increases exponentially and no further convergences can be reached. Interestingly the sweet spot for posit formats is at the same width for this circuit, though for this circuit a more than twice as large execution time is required if a posit implementation is employed. This is due to the much larger area requirement of the posit operators.

The second circuit, *rca* shows a clear sweet spot for floating point formats for a format width of 37 bits (8 bit exponent, 28 bits of mantissa) with an increase in execution time for further reduction in precision. For posits, the sweet spot is at a smaller format with a width of 32 bit, but even though the difference in execution time is smaller, floating point formats yield significantly better results.

For the third circuit, the influence of varying the representation width on runtime is small and posit and floating points achieve similar execution times. This represents a best case for posit implementations over the benchmark circuits investigated for this work. For all three circuits, a posit exponent width of 3 had the best convergence behavior over the analyzed exponent range.

6   Conclusion

In this contribution, we have analyzed how SPICE works with different number formats. It is possible to use floating point numbers with arbitrary bit widths for mantissa and exponent, if we use an FPGA as our implementation platform. Similarly, it is possible to vary the overall bit width for posit numbers and within these numbers, we can select different exponent widths.

We have shown that SPICE can operate with both number representations and a wide variety of bit widths and still simulates the given circuit with the required accuracy. This is achieved by the SPICE intrinsic feature of running certain steps until a convergence is reached. This feature can be regarded as kind of »self-healing«. Nevertheless, it has an impact on the number of iterations and therefore on the number of operations to carry out a whole simulation.

We also showed that both, floating point and posit operators require varying resources according to the selected bit width. For floating point operators, the wider the mantissa, the more resources are required. For posit numbers, the overall bit width is closely related to the amount of resources. Thus, the bit width can be regarded as tuning parameter and in turn it defines how many operators can be implemented concurrently in the FPGA.

For each bit width, we can now calculate a lower bound for the wall clock time as an indication of the whole application performance (which we will most likely not achieve). It turns out that for a specific type of circuit, a sweet spot for the number format can be found. Surprisingly, this is a floating point format with unconventional mantissa and exponent width in most cases (and not a posit format!). It is smaller than double precision and wider than single precision. By this optimization, we can cut down the computation time by a factor of two. Circuits with similar device model compositions can be simulated on the same simulator implementation without resynthesis and for large simulations the possible speed-up can outweigh the time required for FPGA synthesis.

One reason, why posits are not performing as most people expect, lies in the relatively early stage of HW development for posit operators. We can expect that when posits have reached the same level of maturity as floating point implementations, they might be a superior choice to custom floating point formats.

We are currently working on a tunable Chisel implementation of all steps of SPICE, which allows us to generate HW implementations of SPICE with an arbitrary degree of parallelism such that we optimally use the available resources.

Acknowledgments. The authors acknowledge the financial support provided by Merck KGaA, Darmstadt, Germany, in the framework of the joint research platform by the company and TU Darmstadt called "Sustainability Hub".

References

1. Aguirre, F.L., Suñé, J., Miranda, E.: SPICE implementation of the dynamic memdiode model for bipolar resistive switching devices. Micromachines **13**(2), 330 (2022)
2. Aguirre, F.L., et al.: Application of the quasi-static memdiode model in cross-point arrays for large dataset pattern recognition. IEEE Access **8**, 202174–202193 (2020)
3. Barby, J.A., Guindi, R.: CircuitSim93: a circuit simulator benchmarking methodology case study. In: Sixth Annual IEEE International ASIC Conference and Exhibit, pp. 531–535 (1993)
4. Boland, D., Constantinides, G.A.: A scalable approach for automated precision analysis. In: Proceedings of the ACM/SIGDA International Symposium on Field Programmable Gate Arrays, FPGA 2012. Association for Computing Machinery, Monterey, California, USA, pp. 185–194 (2012). https://doi.org/10.1145/2145694. 2145726
5. Bryan, D.: The ISCAS 85 benchmark circuits and netlist format. North Carolina State Univ. **25**, 39 (1985)
6. Customer Spotlight: Synopsys PrimeSim Circuit Simulation Improvements with NVIDIA A100 GPUs. https://blogs.synopsys.com/from-silicon-to-software/2022/02/09/nvidia-gpu-circuit-simulation/
7. de Dinechin, F., Pasca, B.: Designing custom arithmetic data paths with FloPoCo. IEEE Des. Test Comput. **28**(4), 18–27 (2011)
8. Flegar, G., et al.: FloatX: a C++ library for customized floating- point arithmetic. ACM Trans. Math. Softw. (TOMS) **45**(4) (2019). ISSN: 0098-3500. https://doi.org/10.1145/3368086
9. Gustafson, J.L.: The End of Error: Unum Computing. Chapman and Hall/CRC (2015). https://doi.org/10.1201/9781315161532
10. Gustafson, J.L., Yonemoto, I.T.: Beating floating point at its own game: posit arithmetic. Supercomput. Frontiers Innov. **4**(2), 71–86 (2017). https://doi.org/10.14529/jsfi170206
11. Ho, C.-W., Ruehli, A., Brennan, P.: The modified nodal approach to network analysis. IEEE Trans. Circuits Syst. **22**(6), 504–509 (1975)
12. Jaiswal, M.K., So, H.K.-H.: PACoGen: a hardware posit arithmetic core generator. IEEE Access **7**, 74586–74601 (2019). https://doi.org/10.1109/ACCESS.2019.2920936
13. Kapre, N., DeHon, A.: Parallelizing sparse matrix solve for SPICE circuit simulation using FPGAs. In: 2009 International Conference on Field-Programmable Technology, pp. 190–198 (2009)

14. Kapre, N., DeHon, A.: Performance comparison of single-precision SPICE model-evaluation on FPGA, GPU, Cell, and multi-core processors. In: 2009 International Conference on Field Programmable Logic and Applications, pp. 65–72 (2009)

15. Kapre, N.G.: SPICE2: a spatial, parallel architecture for accelerating the spice circuit simulator. Ph.D. thesis. California Institute of Technology (2011)

16. Lannutti, F., Nenzi, P., Olivieri, M.: KLU sparse direct linear solver implementation into NGSPICE. In: Proceedings of the 19th International Conference Mixed Design of Integrated Circuits and Systems - MIXDES 2012, pp. 69–73 (2012)

17. Lanutti, F., Menichelli, F., Olivieri, M.: 12th MOSAK ESSDERC/ESSCIRC Workshop, Venice, 26 September 2014. https://mos-ak.org/venice_2014/publications/T_2_Lannutti_MOS-AK_2014.pdf

18. Modified version of PACoGen with pipelining. https://gitlab.rs.e-technik.tu-darmstadt.de/rs/pacogen

19. Nagel, L.W., Pederson, D.O.: SPICE (Simulation Program with Integrated Circuit Emphasis). Technical report, UCB/ERL M382. EECS Department, University of California, Berkeley, April 1973

20. Ngspice, the Open Source Spice Circuit simulator. https://ngspice.sourceforge.io/

21. Theodore, E., Omtzigt, L., et al.: Universal numbers library: design and implementation of a high-performance reproducible number systems library. arXiv:2012.11011 (2020)

22. Roldao-Lopes, A., et al.: More flops or more precision? Accuracy parameterizable linear equation solvers for model predictive control. In: 2009 17th IEEE Symposium on Field Programmable Custom Computing Machines, pp. 209–216 (2009). https://doi.org/10.1109/FCCM.2009.19

Memory-Aware Scheduling for a Resource-Elastic FPGA Operating System

Shaden Alismail[1,2](✉) and Dirk Koch[1,3]

[1] The University of Manchester, Manchester, UK
shaden.alismail@manchester.ac.uk, dirk.koch@ziti.uni-heidelberg.de
[2] Imam Mohammad Ibn Saud Islamic University, Riyadh, Kingdom of Saudi Arabia
[3] Heidelberg University, Heidelberg, Germany

Abstract. The memory subsystem is often the main performance bottleneck in an FPGA acceleration system. This paper presents two memory-aware runtime schedulers that decide the order of running tasks to improve the system's performance: memory model-aware (MMA) and memory access pattern-aware (MAPA) schedulers. The proposed approaches consider memory characteristics in scheduling decisions to alleviate the memory overhead and enhance the system's performance. MMA considers the accessed memory regions when scheduling the tasks in a way that reduces the memory page miss rates. On the other hand, MAPA alleviates the pressure on the memory subsystem by scheduling the tasks mainly based on their memory intensity and access patterns. The proposed runtime schedulers are evaluated and implemented on an Ultra96 FPGA board. The presented approaches show (on average) approximately 10%, 22%, 12%, and 9% improvements in memory throughput, task execution time, makespan time, and job throughput, respectively, over an existing state-of-the-art memory-agnostic scheduler.

Keywords: FPGA · memory subsystem · DRAM · scheduling · memory-aware scheduling · operating system · multidimensional bin packing

1 Introduction

Most modern processing systems are computation oriented with high parallel computation capabilities. The more parallel processing elements that integrate into a single hardware chip, the more load the memory subsystem will bear. In compute-oriented systems, the memory subsystem can hit performance, especially in memory-bound applications. Most of the related research focuses on improving memory performance in software systems by reducing the data movements [1,2] or by considering the memory intensities of the tasks [3]. However, memory-aware scheduling for FPGA acceleration in dynamically reconfigurable systems has yet to be explored. Moreover, FPGA acceleration can introduce excessive pressure on the memory subsystem (e.g., due to the absence of caches).

© The Author(s), under exclusive license to Springer Nature Switzerland AG 2023
F. Palumbo et al. (Eds.): ARC 2023, LNCS 14251, pp. 81–96, 2023.
https://doi.org/10.1007/978-3-031-42921-7_6

CPUs commonly use caches to absorb most memory requests from hitting the relatively slow main memory. FPGA accelerators, however, usually use scratch-pad memories, and there is no data sharing among multiple cores[1]. Thus, FPGA accelerators can induce dramatically more pressure on the external DRAM than multicore CPU systems alone, which has a corresponding impact on performance and power consumption.

The following motivation example illustrates the effectiveness of memory-aware scheduling in reducing DRAM active time (t_{Active}) and increasing throughput, as compared to memory-agnostic scheduling; based on Eq. (1) and Eq. (2) respectively. These equations are discussed in Sect. 3. Figure 1 shows the memory requests from FPGA accelerators that their acceleration requests are scheduled in a memory-agnostic way. However, the memory controller reschedules these requests to improve throughput while considering their age. For the memory-agnostic scheduler in this figure, with LPDDR4, the DRAM active time is 129 clock cycles, and the memory throughput per t_{Active} is 1.11 Byte/clock cycle. On the other hand, Fig. 2 shows an example of memory-aware scheduling, which results in a higher page-hit rate due to the scheduler's consideration of memory characteristics. With this, we observe a 26% increase in memory throughput and a 23% decrease in t_{Active} for the memory-aware scheduler compared to the agnostic schedule resulting in 1.5 Byte/clock cycle and 99 clock cycles, respectively.

$$t_{Active} = MAX \Big[\Big\lceil \tfrac{\lambda_{\#ofPageMiss}}{4} \times tFAW \Big\rceil,$$
$$\lambda_{\#ofPageMiss} \times MAX(tRC, tRP + tRCD + tBurst)] + \qquad (1)$$
$$\lambda_{\#ofPageHit} \times tCAS + \lambda_{\#ofDQ\_swt} \times tWTR$$

$$Throughput_{Mem} = \sum_{i=1}^{\alpha_B} \sum_{j=1}^{\lambda_{\#ofMemReq\_in\_i}} \frac{tBurst \times \alpha_{\#of\_data\_rates}}{t_{Active_i}} \qquad (2)$$

Fig. 1. Memory-agnostic scheduling.   **Fig. 2.** Memory-aware scheduling scheme.

Therefore, this paper investigates memory-aware runtime schedulers that enhance system performance by considering the memory characteristics of

---

[1] The ARM SoCs found in recent Intel and AMD FPGAs support coherent memory usage of the last-level cache. However, that feature is mainly used for synchronization rather than acceleration data sharing to prevent cache-trashing effects..

accelerators when scheduling. We propose two different scheduling strategies to alleviate memory pressure: Memory Model-Aware (MMA) and Memory Access Pattern-Aware (MAPA) scheduling. The suggested schedulers are described in Sect. 3.

We base our research on the open-source FPGA Operating System – FOS [4]. FOS is a virtualized resource-elastic FPGA operating system that greedily utilizes the FPGA resources in the scheduling process. The FOS scheduler works efficiently with compute-bound jobs but not for memory-bound jobs. We found that FOS intends to overload the memory subsystem (e.g., by causing row-buffer pollution effects in DRAMs), which can cause performance degradation.

Our proposed memory-aware schedulers alleviate the memory overhead by considering the memory locality and characteristics of the requested jobs (i.e., FOS acceleration services). Improving the memory subsystem in a multi-tenant environment is challenging due to the shared random memory regions and often unpredictable access patterns among users. The scheduling problem investigated in this paper is NP-hard and states a multidimensional bin packing problem [5, 6] that considers the memory bandwidth, DRAM resources, memory access patterns, FPGA reconfigurable regions (slots), and I/O resources.

The main contributions of this paper include the following:

1. Identifying the performance bottlenecks in parallel processing systems and surveying the related memory performance factors (Sect. 2).
2. Introducing two memory-aware runtime scheduling approaches for a multi-tenant FPGA OS (Sect. 3).
3. Designing a demonstration framework to evaluate the performance of the proposed heuristics (Sect. 4).

In addition, Sect. 3 presents the proposed memory-aware schedulers, and Sect. 5 concludes the paper.

2   Background and Related Work

This section provides background and an overview of the techniques utilized to enhance memory subsystem performance. An overview of DRAM performance parameters related to this research are explained in Sect. 2.1. Afterward, related research is discussed in 2.2.

2.1   DRAM Performance

Accelerators and other parts of a system usually operate on data stored in DRAM memory. Due to the DRAM organization, accessing various regions in DRAM usually results in varying overheads. Generally, DRAM access delay depends on the status of the row buffer (which is fed from the DRAM memory arrays' sense-amplifier), and it falls into three situations: page-empty, page-hit, and page-miss.

The page-empty case occurs in the first read on an idle bank. In this case, the whole row containing the requested data is activated (row buffered) before the requested data can be retrieved. The page-empty latency includes the Column Access Strobe time $tCAS$ and RAS to CAS Delay $tRCD$.

A page hit happens when data in an active row is consecutively accessed. This request is the best case since the data can be retrieved in only $tCAS$ time because the row is already active. In the page-miss case, the requested data exists in an inactive row in an active bank. In this case, the DRAM will precharge the previously buffered row (tRP) and then buffer the new row of the requested data, resulting in a higher latency than the page-empty and the page-hit. The repeated row-buffer misses significantly degrade the DRAM performance, which is called "row buffer pollution."

Another DRAM performance key factor is the order of read and write commands. Switching between read and store modes on the data bus causes an expensive penalty known as turnaround delay ($tWTR$). Consequently, frequent bus turnarounds hit the bandwidth. Table 1 lists the DRAM timing parameters. The values of these timing parameters are relative to the DRAM model and differ from one DRAM to another.

Table 1. DRAM parameters.

Abbr.	Description	Abbr.	Description
tRCD	RAS to CAS delay	**BL**	Burst Length
tRAS	Row Address Strobe time	**tCAS**	Column Address Strobe
tRP	Row Precharge delay	**tWTR**	Turnaround delay between write and read
tRL	The request latency. The access latency depends on the status of the row buffer.		
tFAW	The length of a rolling window allows up to four rows of activation commands.		

2.2 Related Work

Various research was conducted to improve the performance of the memory subsystem. Some studies focus on the hardware aspects [7,8], and others concentrate on enhancing task scheduling [1,3,9,10]. Most of the related software research aims to reduce the data movements by performing as many tasks as possible with the data at hand [1,2] or by considering the memory contentions [3,11].

Gonthire and Marchal et al., in [1], proposed a software approach for partitioning and ordering tasks that have shared input data to balance the load on GPUs and reduce the data movements between GPUs. The applied data eviction technique is based on Belady's rule [1,12]. The proposed policy in [2] aims to reduce the number of active memory nodes accessed by VMs, by scheduling the VMs that request the same data to run simultaneously.

Ma M. proposed a memory-aware scheduling framework for streaming applications in [9]. The problem is represented by Synchronous Dataflow Graphs (SDFG). An SDFG is passed through multi-scheduling steps that aim to reduce the memory usage for SDFGs on multicore systems considering the communication overhead. Merkel and Bellosa proposed scheduling and frequency heuristics for a Linux kernel running on the CPU [3]. The proposed scheduling policy sorts the tasks in each core's run queue by their memory intensity to co-schedule memory-bound with compute-bound tasks to reduce memory contention. Further, a heuristic is applied that lowers the frequency in the CPU when running memory-bound tasks only. In that research, the resource contentions are studied at the CPU caches and memory bandwidth levels [3].

Dooley et al. proposed memory-aware scheduling in message-driven parallel programs where a dynamic memory threshold is used by measuring the memory consumption across all processors to schedule tasks [13]. Sbîrlea D. et al. proposed a Bounded Memory Scheduling (BMS) approach for parallel programs modeled as dynamic task graphs. Before running a task, BMS provides dynamic task analysis, transformations, and optimizations based on the task graph.

In such software scenarios, most memory accesses are absorbed by caches, and tasks usually interact frequently with the OS. This provides such systems with better opportunities for making good scheduling decisions than the here-considered FPGA scenario where accelerators directly access DRAM and may run longer without any OS interaction.

Memory-aware scheduling is commonly bound to static acceleration systems (offline scheduling problems) for FPGA systems comprising multiple concurrently running accelerators. However, real online systems require a dynamic run-time system. The scheduler in dynamic FPGA acceleration systems should be resilient to dynamic changes in the underlying hardware. In other words, the dynamic FPGA scheduler must consider configuration overheads and latencies to deal with internal states, a minor concern in CPU/GPU systems. Further, the lower levels of the FPGA layered stack should be considered in the dynamic FPGA scheduler, which makes the problem much more complicated than the ones to be considered with traditional instruction-based architectures.

3   The Proposed Approach

The here proposed memory-aware MMA and MAPA schedulers are efficiently orchestrating the running of FPGA accelerations in a way that increases the page-hit rates by parallel running acceleration services. The suggested heuristics address the multidimensional dynamic knapsack problem, which involves allocating a set of n tasks $T := t_1, t_2, ..., t_n$ from m users to a set of k FPGA slots $PR := pr_1, pr_2, ..., pr_k$ using a variety of finite resources, such as memory size, aggregated memory bandwidth, memory controller queues, banks, and memory clock cycles. Note that we express system hardware parameters using α and task requirement parameters using λ. Additionally, we use the words "job" and "task" to describe a request for an accelerated service. The finite resources are:

FPGA resource slots: the running accelerations should not exceed the total capacity of the FPGA slots $\alpha_{pr_{max}}$, at time i. If we must overload the slots, the system will fall back to time-division multiplexing (which requires extra cost for configuration but prevents the system from denying service or even crashing).

DRAM memory: the memory has limited banks α_B and capacity $\alpha_{mem_{max}}$. The total allocated task memory cannot exceed the total DRAM capacity.

Aggregated memory bandwidth: the available bandwidth α_{BW} to read/store data from/into the memory, which includes: the number and width of data buses α_{DQ_w}, ports $\alpha_{AXI_{max}}$, buffers, command/address buses, command/control buffers, address buffers, and number of memory devices $\alpha_{\#of\_devices}$ and channels per device $\alpha_{\#of\_channels}$. The theoretical peak bandwidth $\alpha_{BW_{max}}$ is the total channel width α_{DQ_w} multiplied by the memory/bus clock frequency α_{freq}. A tasks' bandwidth λ_{bw_j} is deducted from the peak memory bandwidth $\alpha_{BW_{max}}$, and the total concurrent task bandwidth cannot transcend $\alpha_{BW_{max}}$, as in Eq. (3) and Eq. (4).

$$\alpha_{BW_{max}} = \alpha_{\#of\_devices} \times \alpha_{\#of\_channels} \times \alpha_{DQ\_w} \times \alpha_{freq} \tag{3}$$

$$\sum_{j=1}^{n} \lambda_{bw_j} \leq \alpha_{BW_{max}} \tag{4}$$

Memory controller queues: the amount of waiting memory commands is limited by the depth of the read and write queues in the memory controller. Full command queues can slow the port buffers flow and, consequently, stall accelerators.

Banks: the number of banks and their organization affects the system performance. The bank bin is hardest to obey by the schedulers since the state of the bank usage can change rapidly when multiple accelerators operate concurrently on memory regions because it depends on the access pattern and the physical memory mapping/allocation if bank collisions occur.

Memory clock cycles: DRAM has constraint timing parameters for memory requests. The DRAM timing parameters are presented in Table 1. Only four active commands are allowed during $tFAW$ time. Thus, just four page-miss requests can access the DRAM in each $tFAW$ period. A high DRAM access latency is evident when the number of page miss requests increases, costing a $tFAW$ penalty for every 4 of page miss accesses. However, a rise in page hit requests will cause a linear ($tCAS$) increase in latency to serve outstanding memory commands.

The **objective** of the scheduling problem is to speed up the acceleration services execution and maximize their throughput by implicitly reducing the DRAM row-pollution effects. In more detail, our scheduling problem aims to minimize the average makespan of the running tasks (Eq. (5)), the DRAM active time t_{Active} (Eq. (1)), and maximize the DRAM throughput per t_{Active} (Eq. (2)). The makespan of a task consists of the task processing delay (t_{exec}), configuration/reconfiguration delay (t_{config}), and memory stall time (t_{stall}). t_{Active} to serve n tasks is determined by the nature of the memory requests and their order. Since DRAM serves parallel requests, its active time will be the required time to process the page misses memory requests $\lambda_{\#ofPageMiss}$ (restricted by $tFAW$) and the page hit requests plus the $tWTR\times$ number of read/write switches $\lambda_{\#ofDQ\_swt}$.

$$Minimize, \sum_{i=1}^{m}\sum_{j=1}^{n_i} \frac{(t_{exec,i,j} + t_{config,i,j} + t_{stall,i,j})}{n_i} \tag{5}$$

$$subject\ to,$$
$$\sum_{i=1}^{m}\sum_{j=1}^{n_i}\lambda_{pr_{ij}} \leq \alpha_{pr_{max}}$$
$$\sum_{i=1}^{m}\sum_{j=1}^{n_i}\lambda_{mem_{ij}} \leq \alpha_{mem_{max}} \tag{6}$$
$$\sum_{i=1}^{m}\sum_{j=1}^{n_i}\lambda_{A\_bw_{ij}} \leq \alpha_{BW_{max}}$$

Our proposed MMA and MAPA schedulers run on the top of the driver layer of the implemented layered FPGA operating system, as shown in Fig. 4. Further, the schedulers manage the partially reconfigurable slots that host the hardware accelerators.

The remaining sections are structured as follows. Section 3.1 briefly describes the roofline model used in this paper to characterize task memory and compute intensities. Then, the proposed MMA and MAPA schedulers are presented in Sect. 3.2 and Sect. 3.3, respectively.

3.1 Task's Memory Characteristics

The kernel performance is determined by complex combinations of factors (i.e., source code, compiler, and memory traffic). The roofline model visualizes the performance in a plot against operational intensity, the work rate, and the memory bandwidth [14]. Figure 3 illustrates the Roofline model. A given task or kernel is characterized by a point given by its arithmetic intensity (AI) on the x-axis. The AI of a task shows how much work is delivered per Byte of data accessed, as shown in Eq. (7), and indicates whether the task is bounded by the memory performance or the peak processing performance.

$$AI = Operations/Byte \tag{7}$$

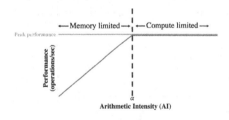

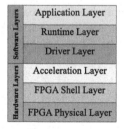

Fig. 3. Roofline model.

Fig. 4. Our FPGA operating system architecture.

Following the roofline model, a task is memory-bound if it saturates the memory with requests: $AI \geq \alpha_{RL\_thr}$. Otherwise, the task is considered compute-bound. α_{RL_thr} is calculated as an aggregated memory bandwidth saturation threshold based on Little's law [15].

Due to the DRAM structure, different memory access behaviors cause variant latency. Sequential access patterns are favorable and can gain around 92.5% of the theoretical memory peak throughput [16]. On the other hand, random access patterns to memory require activating a row for each requested burst. According to [16], random memory accesses reduce memory throughput to just 30% of the peak DDR throughput, which we want to reduce with our schedulers. In this paper, **Ran-jobs** refers to tasks that randomly access the memory regions, while **Seq-jobs** are tasks that sequentially access the memory regions. Further, **RM**, **RC**, **SM**, and **SC** refer to memory-bounded Ran-jobs, compute-bounded Ran-jobs, memory-bounded Seq-jobs, and compute-bounded Seq-jobs, respectively.

3.2   Memory Model-Aware (MMA) Scheduling

MMA scheduler requires a global view of the system memory model and, therefore, the locality of the accessed task data. The main idea of MMA is to reduce the parallel execution of tasks that intensively and sequentially access the same bank to alleviate bank conflicts.

This technique characterizes the requested tasks by their memory intensity, the locality of their data, and the memory access pattern. The locality of the task data gives a hint about the memory banks that will be accessed and, therefore, the used row buffers. Thus, each task is characterized by its accessed banks to reduce parallel bank accesses.

The MMA passes the requested accelerator tasks from different tenants/processes to a job manager component. Next, the job manager adds each tenant's requests into a separate dependency-based Directed Acyclic Graph (DAG). For tenant i, the DAG $G_i = \{V_i, E_i\}$ is partitioned into I_i tasks, where the nodes $V_i = \{v_{i,x} | x = 1, 2, ..., I_i\}$ denote the acceleration tasks and the edges $E_i = \{e_{v_{i,x}, v_{i,y}} | (x, y) \in \{1, 2, ..., I_i\} \times \{1, 2, ..., I\}\}$ represent the dependencies between tasks such that task $v_{i,x}$ must be completed before task $v_{i,y}$ can begin. G_i has many head vertexes v_i that represent the independent/satisfied acceleration tasks, see Fig. 5, which keeps a list of ready-to-run tasks (RTR list) that are sorted based on arriving/inserting times.

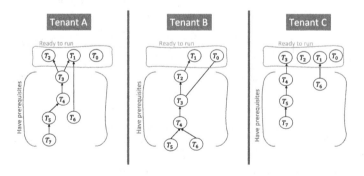

Fig. 5. DAG structure used in the MMA scheduler.

This scheduler has different tiers of scheduling policies, as present in Algorithm 1 and discussed below:

1. Providing fairness between users.
2. Avoiding any bank conflict with memory-bounded Seq-job (SM). Since the sequential memory access patterns reduce the memory overhead, this policy can break the fairness policy.
3. Reducing the bank conflicts for different users without affecting the fairness between users. This policy is achieved by selecting the first ready task that does not access an open bank by another user. If no request by this user satisfies this policy, then the MMA selector will choose the first ready task that satisfies policy 1 and policy 2.
4. Serve each user's tasks in the First Ready First Serve manner in the case of equality in the policies (1), (2), and (3).

Algorithm 1 presents the MMA scheduler. MMA serves the users in a round-robin manner with the best effort fairness. In each user's turn, MMA selects the first job request that accesses a closed bank from the scheduler view (not in the OB list). However, if the user's RTR list has no request to a closed bank, the scheduler chooses and runs the first request that satisfies policy 2. Though, if the user also has no request that satisfies the policy 2, the scheduler will select the following user and repeat the same process.

Algorithm 1: MMA scheduler selector.

List OB ;   //a list containing the status of all opened memory banks used by the currently running jobs.
Job $nomi\_job$;   //a nominated job that satisfies policies (1.) and (2.).
while *has free FPGA slot & has waiting jobs* **do**
  foreach *user* **do**
    foreach *job in user's RTR list* **do**
      if *job can run on the available system resources* **then**
        if *job.accessedBanks* $\cap$ *OB* $= \emptyset$ **then**
          Run job on a free FPGA slot;
          break foreach loops;
        else if *nomi_job is not founded && MAP of (job.accessedBanks $\cap$ OB) is not memory-bounded sequential pattern* **then**
          //MAP: memory access pattern.
          $nomi\_job$ = job;
        else
          Go to next job;
        end
      end
    end
    if *nomi_job is founded* **then**
      Run nomi_job on a free FPGA slot;
    else
      Go to next user;
    end
  end
end

3.3 Memory Access Pattern-Aware (MAPA) Scheduling

The proposed MAPA scheduler aims to enhance memory throughput by reducing the row-pollution effects and $tWTR$ penalty through running different memory access patterns and types in variant time slots.

The MAPA scheduler behaves like MMA scheduling by inserting user requests into DAG modeling dependencies. However, to take a view of all of the memory access patterns of RTR tasks at runtime efficiently, the RTR tasks in MAPA are sorted into five aging-based priority queues per user, one queue for each of the considered memory characteristics (instead of one RTR list as in MMA), which are:

1. Write-intensive jobs (**w jobs**): have high write request intensity (>50%), such as logging tasks.
2. Read-intensive jobs (**r job**): non-w jobs, which are classified as SM, SC, RM, and RC jobs, are described in Sect. 3.1.

Each queue is sorted based on an aging-based priority, which considers the task's age (i.e., the time from a task's arrival time), the number of dependent tasks, and the average age of dependent tasks. The priority (Pr) of job $v_{i,x}$ is calculated as in Eq. (8). The applied aging-based priority helps to enhance the fairness between users/tasks and avoids starvation.

$$Pr(v_{i,x}) = Age(v_{i,x}) + |E_i, x| \times \sum_{j=0}^{|E_{i,x}|} \frac{Age(v_{i,j})}{|E_{i,x}|}, v_{i,j} \in E_{i,x} \qquad (8)$$

Generally, the MAPA scheduler runs different time slots called modes and phases. This scheduler runs sequentially in two modes: Write and Read. During the Write mode, the scheduler selects the highest priority w jobs and executes them on the available FPGA slots. On the other hand, the Read mode works with the r jobs. By running these modes separately, we can reduce the costly read/write memory switching penalty $tWTR$. The r mode is also run sequentially in two phases, one for the Seq-jobs and the other for the Ran-jobs. Therefore, the Seq-jobs can sustain the high page-hit benefits from sequential access patterns without overlapping the Ran-jobs. Figure 6 presents the modes and phases in MAPA.

During each mode and phase, the scheduler selector elects the highest priority task that matches the memory access pattern of the running phase to run on the FPGA. The compute and memory-bounded tasks are co-scheduled together, similar to [3], to reduce resource contentions. While this policy does not provide fairness between users, it will provide a faster execution for acceleration service requests that sequentially access the memory, reducing the average waiting time of queued jobs.

To alleviate the overhead on the memory subsystem, MAPA applies a memory overhead reduction policy by preventing the memory-bound accelerations from utilizing more than α_{slots_thr} of the FPGA processing elements; this threshold is calculated based on the peak flow of the ports that saturate the memory subsystem and its value can vary from system to system. In this situation, we will under-utilize the FPGA slots to gain a shorter makespan. Unused slots are not necessarily wasted as they may be used to prefetch configurations (in order to hide configuration latency).

Note that, like FOS, our schedulers are based on a fine-grained cooperative scheduling model where tasks are decomposed into smaller run-to-completion pieces (e.g., workgroups in the case of OpenCL tasks). The partial reconfiguration overheads are reduced by allowing the scheduler to reuse accelerators already available on-chip. Otherwise, reconfiguration is mandatory.

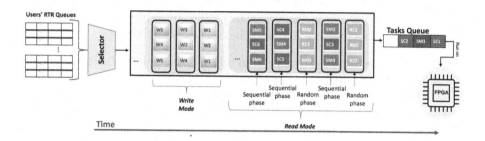

Fig. 6. MAPA scheduler.

4 Evaluation

This section evaluates and compares the proposed schedulers against FOS [4], the most established existing academic scheduler. Section 4.1 presents the evaluation setup, and Sect. 4.2 analyses and discusses the results.

4.1 Evaluation Design

This evaluation examines the proposed memory-aware schedulers on an Ultra96 Zynq Ultrascale+ FPGA board running Linux Ubuntu 16.04.5 LTS. To compare against FOS, we use the ZUCL shell infrastructure [17] with a High-Performance 128-bit wide AXI port (AXI4) serving three hardware accelerator slots. The Ultra96 board provides 2 GB LPDDR4 memory. The memory allocation for acceleration services is managed by u-dma-buffer [18] for all schedulers. The accelerators in ZUCL operate on pinned physical memory. Based on this architecture, a single slot can access memory via a 128-bit wide AXI port, and at an FPGA clock frequency of 1/5th the memory frequency of 533 MHz, a single port can cause $\simeq 51$ Byte/ cycle throughput and two slots ($\alpha_{slots\_thr} = 2$) are sufficient to saturate the memory thoroughly.

The proposed MAPA and MMA schedulers are compared with a memory-agnostic scheduler, FOS [4]. Four performance metrics were measured to evaluate the proposed schedulers: makespan, execution time, acceleration throughput, and memory throughput. The memory throughput is captured in Bytes every $10ms$ using Xilinx AXI Performance Monitor [19].

The proposed MMA/MAPA are evaluated on top of the ZUCL shell [17] (shown in Fig. 7). Five OpenCL modules (acceleration services) with different synthesized memory characteristics are implemented to evaluate the performance of the proposed scheduler; each module is segmented into three work groups. These modules are categorized to write and read-intensive modules. An example of a physical implementation of a partially reconfigurable module is presented in Fig. 8.

The write-intensive module (w) has a constant time complexity and works similarly to logging software. Since the proposed schedulers consider the memory access pattern of the read-intensive acceleration services, four read-intensive modules (r) with different memory characteristics are used in the evaluation. The r acceleration services are described below:

- *Sequential access pattern, Memory-bounded (SM):* a sequential search module for n elements with linear time and space complexity $O(n)$.
- *Sequential access pattern, Compute-bounded (SC):* an RSA-like encryption with a linear space complexity $O(n)$ (like SM) but with $O(n^3)$ compute complexity.
- *Random access pattern, Memory-bounded (RM):* a binary search module on n sorted elements accessing memory randomly with $O(\log n)$ time and space complexities.
- *Random access pattern, Compute-bounded (RC):* a Fast Fourier-like Transform on a Binary Tree with n^3 memory I/O and $O(n^3 \log n)$ compute complexity [20].

Since this research considers different dimensions of memory characteristics, we evaluate the schedulers under variant memory characteristics, levels of parallelism, and workloads. In r-class experiments, the parallelism is doubled until it reaches the highest allowed concurrency. Then, we saturated the memory by increasing the r and w workload by $\times 10$ to raise the memory overhead to the maximum provided load by the u-dma-buffer. After that, we doubled the w modules. Each module is evaluated with different loads. The workload details for w and r modules are presented in Table 2. The first letter in each module abbreviation indicates its size; small (s), medium (m), and large (l).

Two scenarios were evaluated: read-intensive acceleration services scenarios and read-with-write-intensive acceleration services (rw). The evaluation scenarios detail is presented in Table 2.

Table 2. The evaluation scenarios.

	Parallel acceleration services		Accessed memory	Workload increment
	Workloads	Acceleration services		
r jobs	2 Small r	1 sRC × 1 sSM	78 KB [1]	-
	4 Small r	1 sRC × 1 sRM × 1 sSC × 1 sSM	156 KB	× 2R
	8 Small r	2 sRC × 2 sRM × 2 sSC × 2 sSM	312 KB	× 2R [2]
	8 Medium r	2 mRC × 2 mRM × 2 mSC × 2 mSM	3.12 MB	× 10
rw jobs	5 Small rw	1 sw × 4 sr[3]	168 KB	-
	5 Medium rw	1 mw × 4 mr	1.68 MB	× 10
	5 Large rw	1 lw × 4 lr	16.8 MB	× 10
	6 Large rw	2 lw × 4 lr [4]	18 MB	× 2W

[1]For more accurate memory access pattern emulation, the mapped memory for all random modules is much larger than the accessed ($\simeq$ ×4).
[2]The largest number of parallel modules, 8 modules.
[3] 4 r = 1 RC × 1 RM × 1 SC × 1 SM.
[4]The largest number of large modules that can run on the system

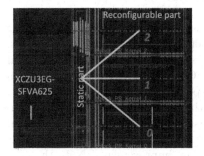

Fig. 7. ZUCL shell implementation for Ultra96 [17].

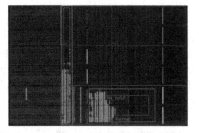

Fig. 8. Physical implementation of the sequential search module.

4.2 Results and Discussion

Figure 9-(A), Fig. 9-(B), Fig. 10-(A), and Fig. 10-(B) depict the evaluation results of the average memory throughput, the execution time of acceleration services, the acceleration services throughput, and the makespan time, respectively. The proposed MMA and MAPA have almost outperformed the memory-agnostic scheduler across all performance matrices. These improvements are mainly gained from alleviating memory pressure.

Figure. 9-(A) shows the average memory throughput in MMA, MAPA, and FOS. Unexpectedly, the proposed schedulers have shown a slight enhancement in the memory throughput despite being faster on the same problem (as in Fig. 9-(B)) compared to FOS. This result means that the system is memory bound, and the speed-up in the execution time has raised the memory contention.

Generally, all schedulers have utilized around half of the theoretical bandwidth in most experiments. However, when increasing the w workloads, MMA and MAPA improvement rates have increased up to 31% and 27%, regarding memory performance as compared to FOS; our schedulers have utilized 49% of the theoretical bandwidth, while FOS memory performance has dropped to 38% of the theoretical bandwidth. Thus, considering the memory characteristics in the scheduling leads to better memory efficiency, which has widened the system's performance bottleneck. Further, we also found that MAPA had an average of 3% higher memory throughput than MMA due to the MAPA's $tWTR$ penalty consideration.

The mean execution time of the acceleration services in all algorithms is illustrated in Fig. 9-(B). The MMA and MAPA have shown, on average, 15% and 28% faster execution time than FOS. The enhanced memory throughput is reflected in the improvements by our schedulers in execution time.

All schedulers have slowed down when increasing the w modules; however, MAPA is the faster among them. In the smallest rw experiments, FOS and MMA have shown a slower execution time compared to their performance in most small r experiments; while MAPA has exhibited comparable execution times. This slowdown occurred in FOS and MMA due to the $tWTR$ penalty by running the write-intensive jobs.

All schedulers in the extensive rw jobs experiments have shown an enormous increase in the jobs' execution times by over 300% compared to the medium jobs. This steep increase in the execution time has significantly slowed the makespan time and reduced the jobs' throughput. ZUCL's limited memory bandwidth causes these significant delay increments in response to large acceleration services.

Figure 10-(A) shows the mean makespan time in our schedulers and FOS. In most experiments, MAPA and MAMA have shown enhancements in makespan time compared to FOS, with, on average, around 6% and 17%, respectively. This had been reflected by their jobs' execution time improvements. Note that the reported makespan times include the scheduling overhead, and the results show that it is worth investing in better scheduling decisions. Further, MAPA has outperformed MMA performance by around 15% on average in terms of makespan time. Hence, the makespan time performance gained from the scheduling based on the memory access patterns of the acceleration services surpassed the scheduling based on the accessed banks by the acceleration services in bank interleaving DRAM access mapping.

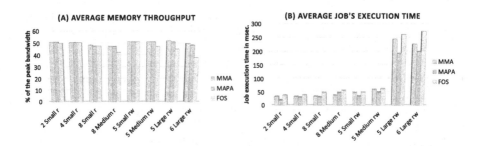

Fig. 9. Average memory throughput and execution time for MMA, MAPA, and FOS schedulers.

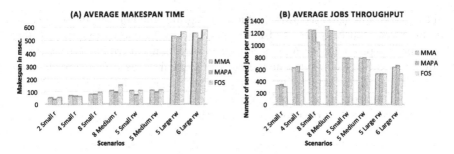

Fig. 10. Average makespan time and acceleration throughput for MMA, MAPA, and FOS schedulers.

The acceleration services throughput is depicted in Fig. 10-(B). The proposed memory-aware schedulers have generally increased the job throughput compared to FOS. The enhancements in the proposed schedulers' throughput are derived from their makespan time enhancement.

MAPA, as expected, has shown job throughput enhancement in small r job experiments compared to MMA; due to its enhanced makespan and job execution times. However, MMA outperformed MAPA on job throughput in medium r experiments due to the different fairness policies in MMA and MAPA scheduling.

In summary, the proposed memory-aware schedulers intend to outperform state-of-the-art FOS in all performance matrices. The advantage gets more prominent at high loads w and large problem sizes, making systems more performance resilient. MAPA has almost always outperformed MMA in most evaluation scenarios and performance matrices.

5   Conclusion

This research proposed memory-aware schedulers, MMA and MAPA, to enhance the system performance by speeding the memory performance in multi-tenant FPGA environments. The acceleration service requests are scheduled in MMA and MAPA according to the memory model and the memory access patterns of the jobs. Our experiments showed that MMA and MAPA improved the memory throughput in bandwidth-limited situations and showed more improvements at higher bandwidth (up to 31%) compared to the most recent memory-agnostic FPGA scheduler, FOS. We conclude from the results that running the proposed schedulers is profitable on both bank interleaving and (lightly loaded) sequential access mapping DRAMs.

As future work, MMA and MAPA will be enhanced to multi-priority services on compute-bounded systems at the software level by considering the service's priorities within the memory characteristics. Moreover, all system components share the memory subsystem, and the background system operations affect its performance. Therefore, considering the memory characteristics of more heterogeneous systems will be necessary for future work.

This work demonstrated that traffic shaping and memory-aware scheduling could be transparently applied to FPGA acceleration systems through a runtime. This improves productivity and performance and can generally boost a wider deployment of FPGAs. Our scheduling is implemented as a software daemon that can be easily integrated into other software stacks than the used ZUCL runtime. Our schedulers are available under:
https://github.com/FPGA-Research-Manchester.

Acknowledgment. This work is supported by the UK EPSRC Programme Grant FORTE (agreement EP/R024642/1) and Carl-Zeiss-Stiftung (Germany).

References

1. Gonthier, M., et al.: Memory-aware scheduling of tasks sharing data on multiple GPUs with dynamic runtime systems. In: 36th IPDPS (2022)
2. Alqudah, M.A.: Energy reduction through memory aware real-time scheduling on virtual machine in multi-cores server. IEEE Access **9**, 55436–55447 (2021)
3. Merkel, A., Bellosa, F.: Memory-aware scheduling for energy efficiency on multicore processors. HotPower **8**, 123–130 (2008)
4. Vaishnav, A., et al.: FOS: a modular FPGA operating system for dynamic workloads. ACM TRETS **13**(4), 1–28 (2020)
5. Chen, Z.-L.: Parallel machine scheduling with time dependent processing times. Discrete Appl. Math. **70**(1), 81–93 (1996)
6. Pisinger, D.: Algorithms for Knapsack problems (1995)
7. Gandhi, J.: Efficient memory virtualization. The University of Wisconsin-Madison (2016)
8. Farshchi, F., et al.: Bru: bandwidth regulation unit for real-time multicore processors. In: IEEE RTAS, pp. 364–375 (2020)
9. Ma, M.: A Memory-Aware Scheduling Framework for Streaming Applications on Multicore Systems. The University of Manchester (2019)
10. Ding, B., et al.: Memory-aware partitioning, scheduling, and floorplanning for partially dynamically reconfigurable systems. ACM Trans. Des. Autom. Electron. Syst. **28**(1), 1–21 (2023)
11. Brilli, G., et al.: Understanding and mitigating memory interference in FPGA-based HeSoCs. In: DATE, pp. 1335–1340 (2022)
12. Belady, L.A.: A study of replacement algorithms for a virtual-storage computer. IBM Syst. J. **5**(2), 78–101 (1966)
13. Dooley, I., et al.: A study of memory-aware scheduling in message driven parallel programs. In: IEEE HPC. IEEE (2010)
14. Ofenbeck, G., et al.: Applying the roofline model. In: IEEE ISPASS (2014)
15. Little, J.D.C.: A proof for the queuing formula: L = w. Oper. Res. **9**(3), 383–387 (1961)
16. Manev, K., et al.: Unexpected diversity: quantitative memory analysis for ZYNQ UltraScale+ systems. In: ICFPT, pp. 179–187. IEEE (2019)
17. Pham, K.D., et al.: ZUCL 2.0: virtualised memory and communication for ZYNQ UltraScale+ FPGAs. In: 6th FSP Workshop. VDE (2019)
18. KAWAZOME Ichiro. -u-DMA-buffer (2017). https://github.com/ikwzm/udmabuf
19. XILINX (2019)
20. Xu, Z.: Two matlab functions for understanding how fast Fourier transform works. riptsize (2013). https://www.mathworks.ca/matlabcentral/fileexchange/

ArcvaVX: OpenVX Framework for Adaptive Reconfigurable Computer Vision Architectures

Lester Kalms[1,2]([✉]) [iD], Matthias Nickel[1] [iD], and Diana Göhringer[1,2] [iD]

[1] Technische Universität Dresden, Dresden, Germany
{lester.kalms,matthias.nickel,diana.goehringer}@tu-dresden.de
[2] Center for Scalable Data Analytics and Artificial Intelligence (ScaDS.AI)
Dresden/Leipzig, Leipzig, Germany

Abstract. The field of computer vision is steadily growing in its complexity and application areas. FPGAs have shown that they can meet the growing demands for performance and energy efficiency. However, their programmability is a major challenge for software programmers. With OpenVX a standard for cross platform acceleration of computer vision applications exists. Existing OpenVX FPGA frameworks often contain non-standard constructs and consider either fixed processor architectures or specialized non-adaptive accelerators. Therefore, we propose ArcvaVX, a framework that generates a runtime-adaptive vision architecture from OpenVX applications, which is performant and flexible. It (1) verifies the user implemented OpenVX applications, partitions them into task graphs and creates their meta-data (2) maps these tasks to physical nodes, creates a schedule, and clusters and places the nodes within a partition-based topology (3) creates the hardware architecture, including additional components required to generate a runtime-adaptive system. These components contain runtime configurable network adapters that can prevent deadlocks, a controller for direct memory access, and a manager that configures both and maintains the schedule. The architecture is designed for applications with high data rates and low synchronization overhead. The evaluation shows a low latency overhead of 0.006% added by the architecture, while resource consumption is more than halved compared to a design consisting only of accelerators.

Keywords: OpenVX · Computer Vision · FPGA · HLS · Framework

1 Introduction

Many application areas, such as medical x-ray imaging, advanced driver assistance or unmanned aerial vehicles, require computer vision [3]. However, the application areas and their requirements are becoming more and more complex. The implementations require increasingly powerful computing systems to meet demands. At the same time, energy plays an important role in both embedded

© The Author(s), under exclusive license to Springer Nature Switzerland AG 2023
F. Palumbo et al. (Eds.): ARC 2023, LNCS 14251, pp. 97–112, 2023.
https://doi.org/10.1007/978-3-031-42921-7_7

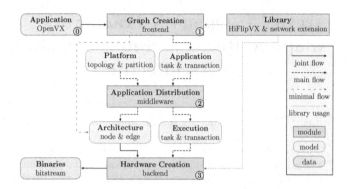

Fig. 1. Overview and flow of the ArcvaVX framework.

systems and large computing clusters. To counteract this, FPGA-based heterogeneous systems provide an excellent solution in terms of energy efficiency, flexibility, and performance [9]. Especially in the field of computer vision, these systems can show their strengths and benefits compared to acceleration on CPU or GPU [12]. E.g., through their streaming capability, which enables large parallelism with little external memory access.

However, efficient programming is becoming increasingly challenging. Thus, developers need a comprehensive framework with efficient automation, good usability, reasonable abstraction, and seamless integration of different tools and libraries. It should provide an easy entry point for users, and reduce the effort required to learn new concepts, programming languages and tools. Libraries should be well integrated and easy to use, but complex enough to cover many use cases. This allows users to focus on developing new applications without having to deal with the underlying details. The framework needs efficient algorithms to execute applications on heterogeneous architectures with maximum performance. These algorithms should be able to distribute applications across various heterogeneous nodes with low fragmentation and communication overhead. The applications need to be optimizable based on various objectives such as performance or resource utilization. Ideally, an application-specific architecture can be created from a set of applications using design time optimizations.

This work proposes a framework (Fig. 1) that creates an application specific architecture out of an OpenVX [1] program. (1) The frontend takes an OpenVX implementation, checks its validity and creates an application model. It integrates a highly parameterizable High-Level Synthesis (HLS) library, while abstracting its hardware details. The advantage of this abstraction is that, regardless of the target platform, the user does not have to learn new concepts and input languages, or deal with the underlying hardware architecture and vendor tools. (2) The application distribution algorithm takes the application model to design an application-specific hardware architecture inside of a partition-based and mesh-like topology (Fig. 2). This infrastructure enables the reusability of vision functions in multiple applications to improve resource

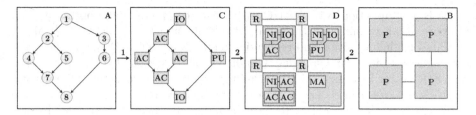

Fig. 2. Application distribution model. Application task graph (A) is mapped & scheduled (1) to a node graph (C), which is clustered & placed (2) into platform model (B) to create final architecture (D) containing additional components. Accelerator (AC), Input/Output (I/O), Processing Unit (PU), Network Adapter (NA), Manager (MA), R (Router), P (Partition).

efficiency. Additionally, it eases using techniques like Dynamic Partial Reconfiguration (DPR) that need defined interfaces, enables the communication between multiple FPGAs in a cluster, or maintains a high-frequency when using chiplets. We can show that including a communication infrastructure only has a negligible effect on the performance. One key-feature of the low latency overhead are the proposed components. (a) Network Adapters (NAs) can connect multiple nodes to a router and schedule the various transactions that originate from them. Additionally, they synchronize communicating nodes, avoids deadlocks by preventing buffer overflows, and can be configured with a new application flow at runtime. (b) Direct Memory Access (DMA) controllers give nodes a direct access to main memory. (c) The Manager (MA) stores the OpenVX graphs to execute and orchestrate the applications in the system. (3) The backend generates all hardware components needed for the scalable communication infrastructure and generates the streaming-optimized architecture. It generates the parametrizable NA with the network information and number of needed ports and stores the Openvx graphs in the internal memory of the MA.

2   Related Work

OpenVX [1] eases the integration of libraries from various vendors and developers. Because of its graph-based approach and memory management, it is much more than just a library. Several researchers proposed OpenVX based frameworks to facilitate the development process of computer vision applications for different systems [2], but only a few for FPGAs. Tagliavini et al. [14] proposed ADRENALINE, which contains techniques based on graph analysis and image tiling to accelerate image processing applications represented as OpenVX graphs. Its architecture contains RISC-based Processing Units (PUs) that share multi-banked data memory, and are connected by a logarithmic interconnection. It uses OpenCL as low-level API and its system is evaluated using the STHORM architecture connected to a XILINX Zynq system that uses an FPGA as interconnection to bridge to the ARM CPU. Omidian et al. [10] presents JANUS, which is a compilation system for OpenVX that can analyze and optimize the compute graph to find area/throughput trade-offs and map to FPGAs. It also combines module selection and replication methods as well as changing tile size with node combining and splitting. Omidian et al. [10] expanded this approach for a Soft Vector Processor (SVP), including a runtime environment, a library of OpenVX C/C++ kernels and a library of prebuilt vector custom instructions. The user selects the vector size (SIMD width), the scratchpad size, and the size of the Partial Reconfigurable Region (PRR). Taheri et al. [15] presented the AFFIX framework for turning a high-level OpenVX graph specification into an FPGA implementation. AFFIX receives an algorithm representative Directed Acyclic Graph (DAG) in a textual format developed by a user including the desired vector size. It outputs an implementation of the vision algorithm using Intel's OpenCL SDK. It adds high and low-level optimization methods to improve the efficiency. While HIPA^{CC} [7] allows portability and efficient generation of high-performance accelerator code, application scheduling is left to the programmer. HIPA^{CC}VX [11] aims to fuse the graph-based approach and execution model of OpenVX with the code generation implemented in HIPA^{CC}. They extended the OpenVX specification such that programmers can register HIPA^{CC} kernels as custom nodes to OpenVX programs. They generate device specific code for a target platform using the HIPA^{CC} code generation. They list 53 OpenVX functions. 9 of these are implemented as OpenCV kernels since they cannot be described with HIPA^{CC}.

ArcvaVX, JANUS, AFFIX, and HIPA^{CC}VX provide the best computation time since they use optimized Accelerators (ACs) rather than generic PUs. They are less bandwidth constrained than other approaches since they stream data between ACs. Using the Canny edge detector [6] as example application, ADRENALINE achieves 109 Mpx s^{-1} running on 16 cores at 433MHz, and JANUS SVP achieves 21Mpx s^{-1}. On the contrary, ArcvaVX and AFFIX can achieve about 2Gpx s^{-1} by increasing the vector size to 8 and the bandwidth of the communication infrastructure. JANUS SVP seems to be a good option for software programmers, since almost no hardware knowledge is needed. HIPA^{CC}VX and ArcvaVX have the advantage of using an OpenVX compliant interface. In contrast, AFFIX requires the user to use OpenCL constructs and channels. HIPA^{CC}VX, AFFIX and ArcvaVX provide a large set of image processing functions available as an open-source library. However, ArcvaVX contains most functions, also support CNNs and feature detection. It enables numerous optimization and tuning possibilities through its high number of parameters. In addition, the library has been used for large applications such as MobileNets [4] and AKAZE [8] with up to 163 IP-cores. Of all the approaches, JANUS SVP is the only one considering PRRs. However, the architecture of ArcvaVX provides the opportunity for PRRs, due to the definition of our platform model (Fig. 2) and clear network interfaces. In addition, ArcvaVX builds a flexible communication infrastructure with a minimal runtime system. However, this flexibility does not come with the performance drawbacks of JANUS SVP or ADRENALINE.

3   Framework

Figure 1 shows the toolflow of ArcvaVX. The different modules can work independently to increase abstraction and interchangeability. Their inputs and outputs are described by the models to provide a clear interface. First, the user implements an application using the **Graph Creation module**. The module abstracts away all hardware related code and gives the user an OpenVX conform interface to implement object detection applications for FPGA-based systems. The module creates a task graph from the implemented application and verifies if it is OpenVX-compatible. It utilizes the Library module for the tasks (computer vision functions) to target FPGAs. To generate IP-cores for the final architecture from these tasks, it creates wrappers which define the parameters and interfaces. At the end, it takes the task graph and calculates all parameters for the application model. These parameters are a combination of synthesis and analytical estimates.

The **Application model** (Fig. 2.A) describes a task (data-flow) graph containing tasks and transactions. *Tasks* are functions of an input application that are executed on Compute Units (CUs). They can have input & output data streams and internal buffers. *Transactions* are messages sent between two tasks. They can contain a single variable or a complete image. The **Platform model** (Fig. 2.B) describes a 2D mesh-like topology consisting of partitions. The model should on the one hand provide a minimum structure to generate a scalable architecture and on the other hand be as flexible as possible. Partitions should represent fixed regions of a physical system. These can be e.g. complete FPGAs, chiplets, or PRRs to enable DPR. The *topology* can be heterogeneous since different types of links and partitions are possible. They could differ, e.g., in their available resources and bandwidth. Additionally, irregular (not rectangular) 2D mesh-like topologies are supported A limitation is that no empty spaces are allowed within a row or column of partitions, to allow easy routing of data between partitions.

The **Library module** contains several components to enable the creation of a runtime-adaptive and flexible architecture inside of the platform model: (1) Routers, for the communication between different partitions (based on RAR-NOC [13]). (2) NAs to connect routers with physical nodes. (3) ACs to execute computer vision tasks (based on HiFlipVX [6]). (4) DMA controllers for direct access of global memory by physical nodes. (5) MAs to orchestrate task flow and configure components, like NAs and DMA controllers.

The **Application Distribution module** (based on [5]) distributes the application model onto the platform model. First, it maps the task graphs of the application model to physical nodes (Fig. 2.C) and creates a schedule. The physical nodes are clustered and placed into the partitions of the predefined platform model specified by the user. The algorithm uses load balancing techniques to find initial solutions within a predictable and scalable amount of time. The algorithm optimizes the solutions using various heuristics. Simulated Annealing allows solutions to get worse up to a certain value, which decreases from time to time. Tabu Search uses a multilevel history to prevent the algorithm from calculating the same solutions. The constraints and objectives are the FPGA resource utilization, network bandwidth consumption, and network hop count. Multiple physical nodes can be placed in one partition, depending on the available resources. The algorithm uses a multithreaded approach and divides the solution space into a grid to prevent threads from calculating same solutions.

The **Architecture model** (Fig. 2.D) consists of physical nodes and edges. It determines the placement of these nodes inside the mesh-like topology and how they are interconnected. *Nodes* are IP-cores (MA, CU, NA, router or DMA controller). Wormhole Routers transfer all data between different partitions via packet in a streams manner. CUs are placed on partitions and can run multiple tasks in sequential order. Programmable NAs can connect multiple CUs to a router. They send and receive data streams between CUs via the routers using a round robin scheduler. They create the routing information of packets and synchronize between each other to avoid deadlocks. MAs orchestrate & schedule the execution of the applications. They configure NAs by sending messages through the network that contain the destination of transactions, which is send by a task executed on a CU. DMA controllers are configured by the MAs via messages to give CUs direct access to main memory. *Edges* are physical connections between nodes and transfer transactions. Links are specific edges that connect routers, are full duplex, and can be off-chip. The **Execution model** describes the application flow, with respect to the architecture, and is stored on the MA. It includes applications, tasks, transactions and memory access.

The **Hardware Creation module** creates the final architecture from the distribution results and generates the bitstream. The entire architecture is designed for computer vision applications with high data rates and low synchronization overhead. An advantage of the approach is the reusability of ACs and Input/Outputs (I/Os) in different application scenarios, while preserving the performance of pure AC designs. Alternatively, the Hardware Creation module can directly create a pure AC design, which only consist of ACs that directly stream data between each other, from the results of the Graph Creation module.

The **Configuration** has some non-mandatory options to provide the user with a more granular control of the architecture: A max buffer size for FIFO units used to connect CUs. CU types can be predefined for PUs and I/Os. CUs can be predefined, and certain tasks can be bound to them. CUs can be bound to specific partitions. Partitions can be blocked for CUs that are not bound to them. It can be useful if the user wants I/Os to be placed on certain partitions or connect fixed architecture to the remaining system via the network.

3.1   Library Module

As shown in Fig. 3, additional components are needed to create a runtime-adaptive system. These components communicate with each other via control messages (Fig. 4): to synchronize, to maintain the schedule, and to avoid deadlocks. Each message begins with a header flit containing the x and y coordinates of the router and the output port of the RX unit, which is part of the NA. The bit-widths of the different fields in the flit are parameterizable. They

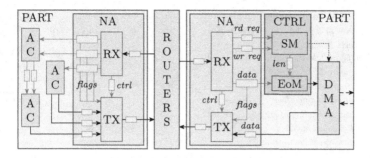

Fig. 3. Two partitions of an architecture using Network Adapters (NAs) and DMA controller (CTRL). Accelerator (AC), EndofMessage (EoM), State-Machine (SM).

depend on the bit-width of the routers, its max size in x and y direction, and the max number of ports of the RX and TX units. Most units send data using the AXI4-stream protocol represented by the solid lines in Fig. 3. The `last` signal of the protocol (optional), determines the end of a packet if it is connected to a router, otherwise the end of a message. The signal is excluded if not needed (gray solid lines). The AXI4-lite protocol (dotted lines) is needed to configure registers within IP-cores. The MA can be configured from outside and the DMA by its controller. The DMA is connected to the DDR controller using the AXI4-full protocol, which enables burst reads and writes (dashed lines).

Manager: On system setup the MA sends an `init` message to all TX units. It contains the MA coordinates and the max packet size for data transfer via routers. The TX unit splits larger messages into multiple packets to avoid high response latencies. The MA contains lists for coordinates (NAs & MA) and implemented applications. Each application points to its first and last element in a task list. A task stores its number of transactions, ID and predecessor/-successor tasks. Each task points to its first element in a transaction list. A transaction stores its receiver coordinates and transmitter port. It can point to an element in a memory access list. A memory access stores address and length of a transaction, connected RX port, and transfer type (read/write). The user starts an application by sending its ID and a `start` bit to the MA via its AXI4-lite port. Then the MA iterates through the list of tasks until it reaches a barrier. A barrier is reached if a task needs to wait until its predecessor on the same CU is finished. Tasks mapped to different CUs can be executed in parallel. Since all CUs stream data, they start processing a task as soon as data is available. For each task, the MA sends a message to the corresponding TX unit containing the `strt` flits of its transactions. They store the destination coordinates (x, y, rx_{port}) the source port (tx_{port}) and $task_{id}$ of a transaction. The TX unit sends a `stop` message to the MA for each transaction that has finished. The MA sets a `done` bit to inform the user that the application is finished.

Network Adapter. When receiving a packet, the RX unit takes the header flit to configure the destination port for the following data flits. Control flits will

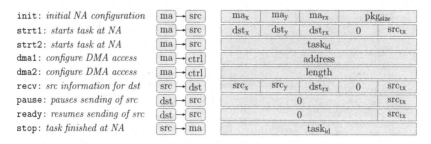

Fig. 4. Control flits transferred between MA, TX and CTRL. src/dst (source/destination of transaction), x/y (router coordinate), rx/tx (receive/transmit port number of NA), ctrl (DMA controller), pkt_{size} (max packet size send by TX unit).

be sent to the TX unit. The RX unit is connected to CUs via BRAM-based FIFO units to maximize throughput. All other buffers only need small LUT-based FIFO units to maintain data-flow. Data-width conversion units are used for down-conversion after a FIFO or for up-conversion before a FIFO. This is the opposite for the TX unit, since it receives data. The TX unit transmits transaction data and sends/receives control messages. For transmission it generates a header-flit and sets a `last` bit for the tail of a packet. It stores the destination of each input port a job was assigned to. After receiving the `strt` flits for a transaction, it sends a `recv` message to its receiver for synchronization purpose. The TX unit iterates over all input ports connected CUs in a round robin manner. It selects a port if data is available and a job was assigned to it and sends a packet of max pkt_{size} data flits. A packet can be smaller if it receives a `last` bit indicating the end of a message. The TX unit monitors the programmable almost empty ($empty_a$) and almost full ($full_a$) flags of the BRAM-based FIFO units. If a $full_a$ flag is set, a `pause` message will be sent to its sender. The sender will then pause the corresponding job until it gets a `ready` message, which is send after the FIFO $empty_a$ flag is set. The `pause` and `ready` messages are used to prevent deadlocks occuring due to a high congestion within the network.

DMA Controller: If a transaction requires memory access, a message is sent from MA to DMA controller containing its start address and length in bytes. The controller has separate ports for read and write requests, because the DMA can send and receive data in parallel. Based on the length of a write request, the EndofMessage (EoM) unit sets the `last` bit so that the DMA can accept a new request. This unit is needed, since the `last` bit is used for the individual packets of a message. The state machine of the controller can accept read and write requests in parallel. After getting a request it reads the corresponding control registers of the DMA. If the DMA is ready for a new request, its control registers are written. In addition, the length flit is sent to the EoM unit for write requests.

Discussion: The proposed architecture focuses on streaming applications with large data transfers and heavy loads. The multiport NA approach can achieve a high throughput. The buffers and `pause`/`ready` messages can reduce synchronization overhead. The MA overhead is low, since it only maintains the schedule, by starting transactions, configuring memory access, and being notified when finished. One advantage is that ACs can easily be reused by different applications and send data to different locations. There are possibilities for redundancy, since the responsible MA of a NA can be updated at runtime. Larger networks can use several MAs for multiple applications. Depending on the network load, the MA can change the max packet size of the individual NAs.

3.2   Graph Creation Module

The Graph Creation module implements an interface which is compliant with the OpenVX standard. The user implements an algorithm in C++ and inserts images (edges) and nodes (vision functions). A `vx_context` contains the overall structure of the implemented OpenVX program. It contains one or more `vx_graph` objects, each expressing the data flow of an application.

Nodes and Images: A `vx_node` object is an instantiation of a vision function using its default parameters, which can be changed before execution. Specified parameters are automatically verified. Library functions or parameters which are not part of the standard have been incorporated. The `vx_image` object stores image information, such as the resolution, format, and vector size (SIMD width). When changing vector size or format, the resolution does not need to be adjusted by the user as it is managed internally. For example, the 24bit `RGB` image format is internally interleaved to 32bit data types. Virtual images must have a source and do not need to specify their parameters. Vision functions consisting of multiple functions, like the Canny edge detector, are split into their sub-functions. Each sub-function is added as node to the graph and additional images are created. This enables a more fine-granular application distribution and reduces fragmentation when placing IP-cores into PRRs. It also reduces synthesis time, since the IP-cores are generated in parallel.

Verification and Scheduling: The `vx-VerifyGraph` function creates a graph and verifies if it satisfies the OpenVX 1.2.1 standard. A graph must be a DAG and bipartite, but not all nodes must be connected. It must not contain cycles, and each virtual image must be preceded by nodes with a real image as input. The verification process checks various attributes required by the vision functions. This ensures that functions call images with correct sizes and data types, but also that attributes of function output are applied to virtual images. However, there are functions that do not allow virtual output parameters, e.g., when changing image format. Due to the nature of FPGAs, there are deviations to the standard in the `vxScheduleGraph` function. It generates an IP-core for each node, extracts synthesis results, and creates an application model.

Timing: Latencies and offsets of transactions and tasks are needed to estimate time behavior, e.g., to calculate bandwidth usage between routers. The estimation of the different latencies is very accurate if functions are not memory-bound. Some information is extracted from synthesis estimates to calculate the parameters of the application model. One parameters is the task latency (L_{task}), which is the sum of all non-concurrent loops (N) of a task. Some functions, like the histogram, consist of more than one loop executed in a sequential manner. The latency of each loop can be calculated by its trip count (T_C), pipeline interval (P_I) and pipeline depth (P_D). The trip count (T_{C_i}) of a single loop can be calculated from the image columns (I_C), image rows (I_R), kernel radius (K_R) and vector size (V_S). (K_R) is calculated from the scaled (σ) kernel size ($K_R = \left\lfloor \frac{(K_S-1)\cdot\sigma+1}{2} \right\rfloor$). The memory access pattern of the library functions is quite similar, as they are all streaming-capable. Reading from input starts at the beginning of a pipeline and writing to output at the end. In addition, the start of the writing process is delayed by the time it needs to initially fill internal line buffers and sliding window (B_j). Based on L_{task}, the latency of a transaction (L_{trans_j}), and its offset (Rd_j, Wr_j) compared to the start of the associated tasks, can be calculated. Here, j refers to the observed loop of a transaction an i to all previous loops. There are two types of functions that have an additional influence on transaction latency and offset. Scatter functions influence the sender, and gather functions the receiver. In block mode the latency is divided by the scatter/gather factor (L_{trans_j}/SG). The associated offset is shifted depending on the index (sg) of the function (($L_{trans_j}/SG)\cdot sg$). In cyclic mode, the latency is reduced by ($sg - 1$) and the offset is shifted by ($sg - 1$).

$$L_{task} \approx \sum_{i=0}^{i<N} (T_{C_i} \cdot P_{I_i} + P_{D_i}), \quad T_{C_i} \approx (I_{R_i} + K_{R_i}) \cdot \left(\frac{I_{C_i}}{V_{S_i}} + \left\lceil \frac{K_{R_i}}{V_{S_i}} \right\rceil \right)$$

$$L_{trans_j} \approx I_{R_i} \cdot \left(\frac{I_{C_i}}{V_{S_i}} + \left\lceil \frac{K_{R_j}}{V_{S_j}} \right\rceil \right) \cdot P_{I_i}, \quad Rd_j \approx \sum_{i=0}^{i<j} (T_{C_i} \cdot P_{I_i} + P_{D_i}) + 1,$$

$$Wr_j \approx \sum_{i=0}^{i<j} (T_{C_i} \cdot P_{I_i} + P_{D_i}) + P_{D_j} + B_j, \quad B_j = K_{R_j} \cdot \left(\frac{I_{C_j}}{V_{S_j}} + \left\lceil \frac{K_{R_j}}{V_{S_j}} \right\rceil \right) \cdot P_{I_j}$$

Buffers: It is also possible to generate a pure AC design. For this, the minimum buffer size between the ACs is calculated to avoid deadlocks and optimize throughput. Therefore, an As-Soon-As-Possible (ASAP) schedule is created using the latencies and offsets to calculate the time stamps of the transactions. Transactions between tasks are synchronized to update their timestamps. The buffer size results from the number of elements of a transaction, written by the sender before the receiver starts reading. This imbalance can occur, e.g., if a node operates on two input images, but one arrives earlier. In this case, a deadlock occurs without a larger enough buffer. The synchronization between two nodes can have an influence on the start time of transactions and thus on the buffer size. This includes scatter/gather functions and functions consisting of more than one loop. For edges with no successor/predecessor, a DMA is created and connected. Its buffer size needs to be large enough for bursts transfers.

Synthesis: A C++ wrapper is created to instantiate a library function and create synthesis results. It sets the template parameters and adds directives to

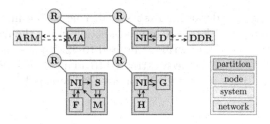

Fig. 5. Example architecture. Router (R), Manager (MA), Network Adapter (NA), D (DMA), G (Gaussian), S (Sobel), M (Magnitude), F (Fast), H (Hysteresis).

create an AXI4-stream interface. No control port is needed, since global memory will be accessed through DMA. The IP-cores are synthesized in parallel using a Tool Command Language (TCL) script using Vivado HLS. Open MultiProcessing (OpenMP) directives were used for parallel synthesis of different IP-cores (`schedule(dynamic, 1)`). The system configuration file specifies the FPGA part number, targeted clock period and max packet size.

3.3 Hardware Creation Module

This module creates the final architecture and FPGA bitstream. It takes the execution model, architecture model and system configuration as input. It currently supports two types of XILINX platforms (Zynq-7000 System-on-Chip (SoC) and Zynq Ultrascale+ Multiprocessor System-on-Chip (MPSoC)). Identifiers and interface names have been extracted to simplify the incorporation of further platforms. Due to the DMA controller, the architecture itself is not bound to SoC designs. There is only one AXI4-lite connection between ARM and MA. This can be exchanged by three signals: (1) app ID, (2) start bit and (3) ready bit. The only other external links are the signals for clock, reset, and DDR memory. A flag can be set to create a simulation design to debug the architecture. It replaces the connection between the ARM and MA with the three mentioned signals. It relocates the clock and reset signals and adds a simple testbench. It uses BRAM and a BRAM controller instead of DDR memory.

The first step creates the HLS-based components needed for the architecture, if its not a pure AC-based design. These components are the RX and TX units, the MA, and DMA controller. To generate IP-cores, wrapper functions are created in which the parameters and interfaces are specified. The various IP-cores are synthesized in parallel using a TCL script. When creating the MA, its program memory containing the execution model is added. It contains the lists for the MA/NA coordinates, applications, tasks, transactions and memory accesses. Depending on the size of each list, LUT or BRAM-based memory is selected. Based on the architecture model, a TCL script is generated that creates a Vivado project. It loads all repositories and adds the HLS-based IP-cores. If necessary, it adds data-width converters and buffers to connect components. If needed, it sets buffer sizes, buffer types (BRAM, LUT), flags (programmable empty & full), packet mode and a `last` signal. Due to the limited number of ports of DDR memory and XILINX interconnection units, the number of DMA units, which can both read and write, is limited to 32. Names and version numbers of all vendor IP-cores have been extracted to adapt to new IP-core versions. Finally, the address space is set and the bitstream is created.

4 Evaluation

The total computation time of the toolchain mainly depends on synthesis time of the IP-cores in the HLS tool and final bitstream generation. Therefore, all modules use OpenMP with dynamic scheduling to generate their IP-cores in parallel, which significantly speeds up the design process. E.g., the tool needed only one minute to synthesize the 19 HLS IP-cores of the ORB [6] feature detector on an AMD 3900X CPU. The same design took four minutes when synthesizing it in a single IP-core containing all vision functions in a large region using the `dataflow` directive. For the parallel synthesis of the IP-cores and the creation of the entire block design, including the automatic connection of the cores in Vivado, the design of AKAZE [8] feature detector took about 32/43 minutes for 95/163 IP-cores. Packing all vision functions of AKAZE in one IP-core using the HLS `dataflow` directive took more than 1 day. In general, an exponential increase in synthesis time was observed with an increasing number of functions when using the `dataflow` directive instead. It was also observed that in some cases the achieved latencies deteriorated when using the `dataflow` directive.

Figure 5 shows an example that demonstrates the benefits of the proposed architecture. It contains a 5×5 Gaussian (G), a 3×3 Sobel (S), a magnitude (M), a 7×7 segment test detector (F) and a 3×3 hysteresis (H) function. F detects the corners of the FAST corner detector [6] and outputs an image of response values. H is part of the Canny edge detector [6]. The output value of an input pixel is true if the value is above an upper threshold (strong), or above a lower threshold (weak) and a strong pixel is in the neighborhood. The architecture implements five different applications that share the mentioned functions: smoothing filter (G), segment test detector (F), smoothed gradient magnitude $(G+S+M)$, edge detector $(S+M+H)$, corner detector $(F+H)$. The evaluation is done on a Zynq Ultrascale+ ZCU104 and the following configuration: FPGA frequency (100MHz), image dimension (1920×1080x8 bit), node vector size (1), max number of data flits per packet (8), router bit-width (32).

Table 1. Runtime overhead of architecture in Fig. 5 compared to a pure AC design.

	extra cycles	overhead [%]
simulation (w.o. CPU, DMA, DMA ctrl)	133	0.006
on device (w.o. DMA ctrl)	426	0.020
on device	320	0.011

Table 1 evaluates latency overhead of the proposed architecture against a pure AC design. Both designs were created using ArcvaVX. The first test runs both architectures in the Vivado simulator without DMA and DMA controller. Time measurement starts when the MA receives a start signal and ends when receiving a stop signal. The proposed architecture increases latency between 107 and 168 clock cycles (0.006% overhead on avg.). The first reason for the increase is the configuration of the NAs by the MA. The second one is the increased pipeline depth, since a pixel must pass through various routers and NAs. The second test executes the proposed architecture in a real system setup, where the ARM CPU controls MA & DMA units and measures time. Time measurement starts before the CPU sets the MA start signal and configures the DMA units. It ends after it has detected the stop signal using a busy wait routine. The system runs all applications 100 times and selects the fastest execution of each application to minimize CPU impact. The latency increases by an additional 280 to 304 clock cycles compared to the simulated design (0.014% overhead on avg.). The result shows that there is no additional interference to the architecture in a real system setup. The additional latency is due to CPU and main memory access times, and configuration time of the DMA units. The third test adds the DMA controller. It saves an avg. of 106 clock cycles, compared to the system without controller. Another advantage of the controller is that the system becomes more independent of the CPU, which eases pure FPGA designs.

Table 2 compares the resource usage of the example architecture of Fig. 5. It includes the NAs, routers, MA, DMA controller, and additional buffers and converters. The application nodes run the OpenVX-based vision functions. They have a low resource consumption due to the efficiency of the utilized library. For bigger applications the benefits of this architecture get more visible. Since each vision function is used in two different applications, the architecture saves about 50% resources. The system part contains the interconnection networks required for DMA and peripherals, and the reset signal. The proposed architecture gives the opportunity to reuse DMA units for different applications, which saves a lot of resources. One reason for the higher resource consumption of the DMA controller is the AXI4 interface generated with the HLS tool. The interface consumes 554 FFs, 628 LUTs, and 1 BRAM.

In the AC design, applications do not share nodes or DMA units. The high additional resource consumption of the system is mainly due to the many interconnection networks and additional DMA units. There is one peripheral interconnect to control all DMA units, four smart interconnects to connect to the memory controller, and five DMA units for the ten application nodes. Due to the 128bit memory interface of the ZCU104, the DMA units consume a relatively large amount of BRAM. Both systems have their advantages. On the one hand, the pure AC design could run all applications in parallel, if memory bandwidth is sufficient. On the other hand, the proposed design requires significantly fewer resources. The MA and DMA controllers simplify the start of individual applications, since the user only needs to send the application ID and start bit. An advantage of Graph Creation module is that it requires only 25 lines of code for both designs. Twelve lines of code for the five different applications and their configuration, seven lines for the edges, and six lines for the rest of OpenVX.

Table 2. Resource utilization of the implemented design for the example architecture of Fig. 5 (left) and a pure AC design offering the same applications (right).

	LUT	FF	BRAM	DSP	LUT	FF	BRAM	DSP
routers	1205	626	0	0				
manager	263	275	0	0				
RX/TX units	1029	1794	0	0				
DMA controller	803	1788	1	0				
buffers/converters	1972	3305	4	0	2295	5273	0	0
application nodes	2649	1689	7	1	5279	3358	14	2
system	5542	8215	5	0	22802	18717	0	0
total	13463	17692	17	1	30380	43671	39	2

The next test increased the frequency of the proposed design to 300MHz to evaluate the impact on execution time and resource consumption. At 3 times the frequency, the execution time increased by a factor of 2.9998. The reason for the small difference is that the frequency of the CPU and the DDR memory have not changed. The entire architecture needed only two additional LUTs compared to the 100MHz design. The last test evaluates the maximum router throughput by changing the data width of the application to 16bit increasing transmitted data by a factor of two. The execution time of the applications increased by at least 50% (64% on avg.) compared to the 8% application. This is because the router sends data at most every two clock cycles and has an additional overhead for sending the header flit and creating the route. Changing the data width of the application had no significant impact on the resource utilization of the architecture. Increasing the packet size minimizes the overhead by increasing maximum throughput, but decreases response time. Increasing it from 8 to 16 (32) increased the execution time by 32% (16%) on avg. and 25% (12%) on minimum compared to the 8bit application. The minimum occurs when using an application with only one function, since the communication is less.

5   Conclusion

This work proposes a framework that creates an application-specific runtime-adaptive architecture from an OpenVX-compliant implementation. The Graph Creation module provides users with an easy-to-use interface without learning new concepts and languages or understand underlying hardware and implementation. It checks the application graph and its parameters detecting user errors at an early stage. Image properties are propagated through the application graph to ease development. Larger vision functions are divided into their sub-functions to reduce fragmentation when distributing applications. An application model is generated from synthesis and analytical estimates. A schedule is created to determine exact buffer sizes between nodes to avoid deadlocks and increase throughput. The Application Distribution module distributes the application model onto the partition-based mesh-like platform model, thus generating the architecture. It is optimized for streaming, efficient in terms of resource consumption, flexible, and capable of running different applications. The Hardware Creation module automatically creates the final design for the selected FPGA. Synthesis of individual IP-cores is parallelized to achieve a significantly faster flow. Generic HLS-based components have been developed for the architecture: (1) A runtime configurable NA, which connects multiple CUs to a router, receives, sends, or creates packets, and integrates mechanisms to prevent deadlocks. (2) A DMA controller that allows different CUs to directly access shared DMA units. (3) A MA, which orchestrates the execution and configures the NA and DMA controller for a specific application flow. In future, we will work on automatic parameter tuning of the vision functions to more efficiently utilize the FPGA resources and make it open source.

Acknowledgements. This work was partially supported by the German Federal Ministry of Education and Research by funding the competence center for Big Data and AI "ScaDS.AI Dresden/Leipzig" and partially funded by the German Federal Ministry of Education and Research BMBF as part of the PARIS project under grant agreement number 16ES0657.

References

1. Giduthuri, R., Pulli, K.: OpenVX: a framework for accelerating computer vision. In: Conference on Computer Graphics and Interactive Techniques (SIGGRAPH) (2016)
2. Hascoë, J., de Dinechin, B.D., Desnos, K., et al.: A distributed framework for low-latency OpenVX over the RDMA NoC of a clustered manycore. In: High Performance Extreme Computing Conference (HPEC), pp. 1–7 (2018)
3. Kalb, T., Kalms, L., Göhringer, D., et al.: Tulipp: towards ubiquitous low-power image processing platforms. In: International Conference on Embedded Computer Systems: Architectures, Modeling and Simulation (SAMOS) (2016)
4. Kalms, L., Amini Rad, P., Ali, M., et al.: A parametrizable high-level synthesis library for accelerating neural networks on fpgas. Journal of Signal Processing Systems (JSPS) (2021)
5. Kalms, L., Göhringer, D.: Scalable clustering and mapping algorithm for application distribution on heterogeneous and irregular FPGA clusters. J. Parallel Distrib. Comput. (JPDC) **133**, 367–376 (2019)
6. Kalms, L., Göhringer, D.: Accelerated high-level synthesis feature detection for FPGAs using HiFlipVX. In: Jahre, M., Göhringer, D., Millet, P. (eds.) Towards Ubiquitous Low-power Image Processing Platforms, pp. 115–135. Springer, Cham (2021). https://doi.org/10.1007/978-3-030-53532-2_7

7. Membarth, R., Reiche, O., Hannig, F., et al.: HIPAcc: a domain-specific language and compiler for image processing. Trans. Parallel Distrib. Syst. (TPDS) **27**, 210–224 (2016)

8. Nickel, M., Kalms, L., Häring, T., et al.: High-performance AKAZE implementation including parametrizable and generic HLS modules. In: International Conference on Application-specific Systems, Architectures and Processors (ASAP) (2022)

9. Nurvitadhi, E., Venkatesh, G., Sim, J., et al.: Can FPGAs beat GPUs in accelerating next-generation deep neural networks? In: International Symposium on Field-Programmable Gate Arrays (FPGA) (2017)

10. Omidian, H., Ivanov, N., Lemieux, G.G.F.: An accelerated OpenVX overlay for pure software programmers. In: Conference on Field-Programmable Technology (FPT) (2018)

11. Özkan, M.A., Ok, B., Qiao, B., et al.: HipaccVX: wedding of OpenVX and DSL-based code generation. J. Real Time Image Process. (JRTIP) **18**, 765–777 (2021)

12. Qasaimeh, M., Denolf, K., Lo, J., et al.: Comparing energy efficiency of CPU, GPU and FPGA implementations for vision kernels. In: International Conference on Embedded Software and Systems (ICESS) (2019)

13. Rettkowski, J., Göhringer, D.: RAR-NOC: a reconfigurable and adaptive routable network-on-chip for FPGA-based multiprocessor systems. In: International Conference on ReConFigurable Computing and FPGAs (ReConFig) (2014)

14. Tagliavini, G., Haugou, G., Marongiu, A., et al.: Optimizing memory bandwidth exploitation for OpenVX applications on embedded many-core accelerators. J. Real Time Image Process. (JRTIP) **15**, 73–92 (2018)

15. Taheri, S., Behnam, P., Bozorgzadeh, E., et al.: AFFIX: automatic acceleration framework for FPGA implementation of OpenVX vision algorithms. In: International Symposium on Field-Programmable Gate Arrays (FPGA) (2019)

Applications

FPGA-Integrated Bag of Little Bootstraps Accelerator for Approximate Database Query Processing

V. Burtsev$^{(\boxtimes)}$ (iD), M. Wilhelm(iD), A. Drewes(iD), B. Gurumurthy, D. Broneske, T. Pionteck, and G. Saake

Die Otto-von-Guericke-Universität Magdeburg, Universitätsplatz 2, 39104 Magdeburg, Germany
vitalii.burtsev@ovgu.de
https://www.ovgu.de/

Abstract. We propose a novel approach to an FPGA-based approximate query processing accelerator using the Bag of Little Bootstraps (BLB) algorithm. The BLB algorithm is a statistical approximate computing method, allowing for efficient parallelization. We enhanced the BLB algorithm with a streaming mode to neglect data storage and memory transfer overhead. This allows us to take full advantage of the hardware capabilities of FPGAs. We supersede resampling with multiple passes over the dataset with a method based on Poisson bootstrapping using resampling coefficients. We show that our approach implemented on a Xilinx Zynq7000 FPGA with clock frequency at 125 MHz outperforms an optimized, multithreaded CPU implementation on an Intel i7-6850K with 4 GHz by factor 4 without and factor 2 with data transfer time for one million entries. This improvement increases with the amount of data to be processed. Implementing the BLB algorithm on an FPGA as an approximate query processing accelerator offers a promising approach for improving database query processing.

Keywords: Co-processor acceleration · FPGA data stream processing · Approximate query processing · Database query acceleration

1 Introduction

The ability to quickly evaluate large amounts of data is essential for modern decision processes, affecting not only decisions in science but also business processes and even governmental policy. Since data analysis is an interactive, iterative process, exact query processing is often not feasible for big data sets. Processing data sets of several terabytes can take hours to even a few days, depending on the query's complexity.

Due to these limitations of exact query processing, Online aggregation (OLA) [12] based on Approximate Query Processing (AQP) has become a central technique for data-driven decision problems, such as hypothesis testing, visualization

F. Palumbo et al. (Eds.): ARC 2023, LNCS 14251, pp. 115–130, 2023.
https://doi.org/10.1007/978-3-031-42921-7_8

of big data, and survey analysis. AQP offers a trade-off between the quality of the result and a faster response time. It produces a partial result along with an error margin estimate, allowing the user to either accept the result or further refine the query. Consequently, a higher performance of the AQP system leads to a higher result quality. In this work, we aim to improve the performance of OLA systems using an FPGA-based hardware accelerator.

Sampling-based approaches are currently state-of-the-art in AQP research. Here, the query is applied to a previously created *synopsis*, i.e., a small representation of the complete data set. They generally fall into two categories. Online sampling-based methods create samples during query execution and aggregate them into a synopsis. In contrast, offline sampling-based methods take advantage of the fact that query workloads can be partially or fully predictable because one can know prevalent query patterns in advance. Both approaches significantly reduce the data transfer and processing time. However, the pre-generated synopsis-based method has the drawback that the source database must be fully processed at least once. Hence, updating the original database requires an additional modification of the synopses or even a complete reconstruction. On the contrary, online methods are generally less accurate.

A well-known statistical algorithm that can be used for assessing the accuracy of online sampling-based methods is the bootstrapping method [8], where a set of resamples is generated from given subsamples of the original data set by repeated sampling with replacement. The resamples used in bootstrapping are of the same order of magnitude as the assessed sample, leading to a high computational load due to the resampling. The Bag of Little Bootstraps (BLB) algorithm [15] avoids this problem by resampling based on small subsamples of the original sample. This significantly reduces the amount of distinct data points in each resample and the number of computations. By this, it is not only more efficient than regular bootstrapping for assessing the accuracy of sampling-based methods but also enables us to use the algorithm itself for approximately answering queries through execution on the entire database.

Fig. 1. Traditional accelerator approach (left) vs. streaming (right).

Hardware acceleration of database queries on an FPGA generally suffers from high data transfer times in relation to the complexity of the query operations. In the traditional approach [4,33], data is copied to the onboard DRAM before being processed in the accelerator, as shown in the left part of Fig. 1. In this work, we dramatically reduce the data transfer cost by introducing *Streaming BLB*, a fully streamable implementation of the BLB algorithm, and therefore avoid any onboard data storage, as shown in the right part of the figure. Furthermore, by separating the data-heavy sampling process of bootstrapping from the computationally intensive resampling step, we aim to maximize the computation-to-data transfer ratio. Our solution can work as a stand-alone solution as well as a plugin into an existing FPGA-accelerated database system [33].

To summarize, the main contributions of this publication are as follows:

- We show how the BLB algorithm can be used for approximate query processing.
- We show how the BLB algorithm can be modified to work on FPGAs and develop an optimized streaming resampler based on Poisson bootstrapping to maximize throughput.
- We create a hardware architecture to accelerate approximate query processing in large databases and provide a prototype accelerator implementation.
- We point out the shortcomings of AQP on the CPU leading to reduced performance for the high amount of processing data.

The rest of this article is organized as follows. We shortly describe the existing AQP solutions in Sect. 2. In Sect. 3, we present an adaptation of the BLB algorithm for AQP, describe the idea of the Streaming BLB algorithm, and present the architecture for an FPGA design. Section 4 describes the implementation of our test system on an FPGA. In Sect. 5, we evaluate the results of the algorithm execution in terms of multi-threaded performance on the processor and on the FPGA, together with their resource utilization.

2   Related Work

This section will review the available work on current approximate data processing solutions as well as FPGA-accelerated query processors.

Many existing software systems use AQP for query execution acceleration with varying sampling techniques. For example, BlinkDB [2] and VerdictDB [22] use stratified sampling [23] to sample data. But stratified sampling isn't helpful for non-exhaustively partitioned groups in data. DeepDB [13] uses Sketches [6] to construct synopses, whereas DBEst [18] uses pre-compiled synopses based on regression models and probability density estimators constructed using deep learning. Acharya et al. [1] propose a solution that utilizes the Central Limit Theorem (CLT) approach for approximate query processing.

Existing solutions have also used bootstrapping for AQP accuracy assessment. For example, Peng et al. use bootstrapping as part of the AQP++ framework [24], which estimates error margins based on either bootstrapping or the CLT, depending on the query. While more computationally intensive, bootstrapping has more general applicability than the CLT-based approach for the development of data estimators due to its simulation-based nature [5,14,25].

There is considerable research on the potential of FPGAs as database query accelerators in modern architectures. FPGAs are either placed near the data, e.g. AxleDB [27], ReProVide [21], or used as a traditional co-processor with DDRAM data copying as in DoppioDB [33], Broneske et al. [4], Fang et al. [9]. However, these solutions only focus on exact but not approximate query execution and therefore are too computationally intensive to be suitable for online aggregation.

Overall, AQP techniques are mainly run on CPUs. Zhao et al. use bootstrapping to compute error estimations on GPUs [32]. To the best of our knowledge, no FPGA-based accelerators for AQP exist. Hence, with this work, we aim to open a new research branch in the application and acceleration of approximate query processing using FPGAs.

3   Architecture and Optimizations

In this section, we will describe the BLB algorithm and general optimizations applied to improve performance on the FPGA.

3.1   Bag of Little Bootstraps for AQP

The main idea of bootstrapping is to pick a number of observations from the original data set with replacement (resampling) to obtain a single resample and then to estimate a population distribution using this resample as the empirical distribution. After sufficient resamples have been received, several calculated statistical values are combined to form an approximate sampling distribution called bootstrap distribution. The resampling process leads to a high computational load. Hence, the applications in which bootstrapping is used are quite limited.

Kleiner et al. [15] show that the main drawback of bootstrapping, i.e., the large number of samples that have to be taken, can be avoided by using small subsamples for the resampling process and scaling the result up to the size n of the original data set, leading to the Bag of Little Bootstraps (BLB) algorithm. After resampling to the original size of the data set, the database query is applied to this sample to obtain a bootstrap estimate for one subsample. Results for all resampling instances are averaged to obtain an approximate answer to the query. The authors show that to get a query answer with a confidence level of 95%, it is sufficient to pass in subsamples of the size of b elements, where $b = n^\gamma$, and $\gamma \sim 0.6 \ldots 0.9$. According to their evaluation, values of γ between 0.6 and 0.7 are the most efficient in terms of the balance between accuracy and the amount of data transmitted. That is, if the size of the original data array is 10^6 of values, the subsample size would be $4 \cdot 10^3$, and if the original array is 10^9, the subsample size would be $2.5 \cdot 10^5$. Hence, even with relatively small overall data size, the amount of data that has to be processed decreases by three orders of magnitude compared to the original bootstrapping algorithm.

Algorithm 1 shows our approach based on the original BLB algorithm for query approximation. Here, $\hat{\theta}$ corresponds to the approximation of the answer to the aggregating database query, ξ is an estimate of the answer uncertainty, b is the size of the subsample from the database, s is the number of subsamples and r is the number of resampling iterations for each subsample.

In the outer loop of the algorithm, subsamples $\mathbb{S}_j$ are created from the database. In the inner loop, each subsample is used to create r resamples $\mathbb{R}_k$

Algorithm 1: BLB for Query Processing

Variables:
$\mathbb{S}_j$: Subsample j for $j = 1, ..., s$
$\mathbb{R}_k$: Resample k for $k = 1, ..., r$
$\hat{\theta}$: Estimator of interest: Query answer
ξ: Estimator of quality assessment: $\sigma(\hat{\theta})$

for $j \leftarrow 1$ **to** s **do**
 Randomly draw b elements out of n from the original data set $\mathbb{X}$ without
 replacement to get $\mathbb{S}_j$
 for $k \leftarrow 1$ **to** r **do**
  Sample $\mathbb{S}_j \sim$ Multinomial $(n, \mathbf{1}_b/b)$ to get $\mathbb{R}_k$
  $\hat{\theta}_{j,k} \leftarrow \mathbb{Q}(\mathbb{R}_k)$
 end
 $\hat{\theta}_j \leftarrow r^{-1} \sum_{k=1}^{r} \hat{\theta}_{j,k}$
end
$\hat{\theta} \leftarrow s^{-1} \sum_{j=1}^{s} \hat{\theta}_j$
$\xi \leftarrow \sqrt{s^{-1} \sum_{j=1}^{s} (\hat{\theta}_j - \hat{\theta})^2}$
return $\hat{\theta}, \xi$

---

of size n by picking a value from $\mathbb{S}$ with equal probability n times. Afterward, the query $\mathbb{Q}$ is executed on the generated resample. The bootstrap answer of one subsample is computed by averaging over all answers of the generated resamples. We average the results over the bootstrap answers of all subsamples to approximate the query over the whole data set. Along with the answer, a quality estimator will be computed for the obtained values from all subsamples.

The main advantage of the algorithm with respect to hardware acceleration is that the resampling of one data set can be done independently for all resampling blocks. In the same way, the processing of a subsample of the original data set is entirely independent of the processing of each other subsample. This allows for a scalable and granular implementation of the BLB algorithm, without changing its structure, in distributed computing systems or, in our case, on an FPGA.

3.2 Streaming BLB

Several improvements to the original bootstrapping algorithm have been developed to bring new features like stream and pipeline data processing ability. For example, Poisson bootstrapping [10,26] is more efficient when applied to data streaming and reduces data transfer. In this method, the multiple selections of a random element from the subsample are replaced by resampling $k \approx 0.63n$ distinct values and multiplying each value in the subsample by a resampling coefficient, which indicates the estimated number of occurrences of that record in the resample. The coefficient itself has a Poisson distribution with $\lambda = N$. Empirical studies of the Poisson bootstrap show that it performs equally well to the original bootstrap algorithm [28].

A promising combination occurs if the idea of Poisson Bootstrapping is combined with the BLB algorithm. While in the original Poisson Bootstrapping, a large subsample of the original data has to be taken, the BLB algorithm already operates on small subsamples which can be fully utilized for resampling coefficients. Conversely, the n-fold resampling procedure for each sample in the original BLB algorithm can be replaced by a b-fold computation of resampling coefficients, where b is the subsample size. Since $b = n^{0.6...0.7}$, this dramatically reduces the number of memory accesses and data transfers required, replacing them with calculations. We call this method *Streaming BLB*.

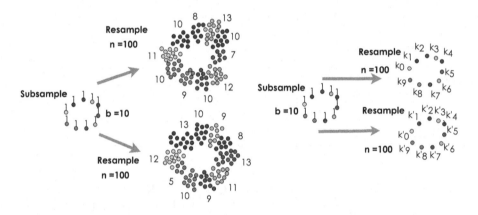

Fig. 2. Naive bootstrapping vs. Streaming BLB

Figure 2 shows a graphical explanation of the Streaming BLB approach. The left-hand part of the picture explains the naive BLB. To obtain a single resample, we need to n times randomly pick one entry from a subsample of size b. To build one resample using this approach, n memory accesses are necessary. We can conclude that every entry from the subsample is represented in the resample with a certain amount of occurrences. The number next to each element group indicates how often this entry is repeated in the resample, i.e., it shows the actual resampling coefficient. Note that it is different for the same entry in different resamples. In the right-hand part of Fig. 2 the Streaming BLB approach is shown, where, instead of resampling, the resampling coefficient k_i is computed based on a distribution function. While the actual distribution of the resample coefficients is multinomial, the distribution can be reasonably approximated by a Poisson distribution with $\lambda = n/b$. In that case, generating b random numbers with a Poisson distribution and multiplying them by the corresponding subsample entry will be sufficient. Furthermore, in the Streaming BLB we are not limited to integer resample coefficients. For large λ, the Poisson distribution can be approximated by the normal distribution with parameters $\mu = \lambda$ and $\sigma = \sqrt{\mu}$, which is often much easier to compute than a discrete distribution. Regardless of the distribution function, the data must be normalized afterwards to ensure that the sum of all resampling coefficients is equal to the original data size n.

The primary point to note about the original BLB algorithm is the lack of streamability. Using this coefficient-based Bootstrapping approach, we can ideally stream data from the subsample through the resampling IP-core and obtain resample data in b clock cycles. However, this method requires the generation of a random variable with an appropriate probability distribution in every clock cycle to achieve maximum performance.

3.3   Gauss Random Number Generator (GRNG)

Implementing random number generation on an FPGA is challenging. Various options [3, 16, 29] that differ in performance and resource consumption. The MultiHat algorithm [20] provides a compact and efficient method for streaming resampling, which generates a random number every clock cycle. The multi-hat method is based on the idea that the probability density of a uniformly distributed random sequence can be changed using additional bits and multiplexers. By a few bit changes, it generates a probability distribution function that resembles a Gaussian distribution with a tail accuracy of up to 8σ. Note that, in the Streaming BLB method, there is no need for true random numbers as long as the resampling rate approximately matches the probability distribution.

3.4   BLB Block Design

The block design presented in this section unites all ideas we introduced before to build a complete system. The BLB algorithm requires building subsamples first. Many subsampling methods offer different efficiencies and processing performance [17, 19]. However, their evaluation and implementation are beyond the scope of this publication. Instead, we focus exclusively on accelerating the resampling step of the BLB algorithm. Hence, each BLB Core shown in Fig. 3 is assigned to one subsample and roughly corresponds to the execution of the inner loop in Algorithm 1. Consequently, The number of the subsamples s corresponds to the number of BLB cores, and the number of resampling iterations r is equivalent to the number of Streaming BLB instances in each core.

We split database queries into a *preprocessing* step and an *aggregation* step to reduce the computational workload further. The query is applied to each data point during preprocessing, i.e., the data points are filtered and transformed. During aggregation, the results of all data points are aggregated into a final query result. We expect the subsamples to be preprocessed before entering the accelerator and return partially aggregated data, i.e., the query results of the resamples. The preprocessing can be done on the CPU or in a dedicated IP core outside of the architecture.

In the following, we describe how the algorithm is partitioned, with functional blocks connected using the AXI4-Stream interface. Registers are used to store the parameters that are unchangeable during the execution of the algorithm and have to be defined as parameters prior to execution.

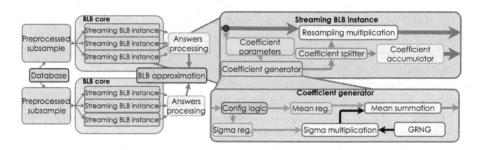

Fig. 3. BLB block design explanation. Red arrows represent query data streams. Green arrows show configuration data streams. The blue arrows correspond to the streams of resampling coefficients. The black one refers to random variables. (Color figure online)

In the left part of Fig. 3, the connection of the processing kernels with data streams to execute the BLB algorithm is shown. First, in each BLB core, the data of the associated subsample is delivered to every Streaming BLB instance, which in return creates a resample of this subsample. The bootstrap distribution parameters are constructed from the subsample data and passed down to the Streaming BLB instance. The construction of the final query answer takes place on the CPU since it needs to process a negligible amount of data, equal to the product of the number of resampling blocks and the number of subsamples, and, as we will see below, this number is of the order of a few dozens.

The right-upper part of Fig. 3 explains the design of the Streaming BLB instance. The input of this block is connected to the data stream, which provides configuration values and the subsample query data that should be resampled. The coefficient generator produces a random output value every single clock cycle. Afterward, the coefficient is split into two blocks. The first stream is connected to the multiplicator of the query data with the resampling coefficient, which is then sent to the answer processing logic via the data stream. The second block stores the sum of the coefficients to normalize the output value. Bootstrapping assumes that the sum of all resampling coefficients should equal the number of entries in the original data set because picking one value from the subsample is done n times, where n is the number of entries in the original data set. Random variables are generated without reference to this requirement, so following normalization is necessary.

The right-bottom part of Fig. 3 explains the structure of the resampling coefficient generator. It generates a standard Gauss distributed value x and transforms it as $x' = \sigma x + \mu$ to fit the expected mean and variance. To achieve maximum performance, the Multihat Gauss random number generator (GRNG) produces a random number every clock cycle. However, due to the modular structure, the random number generator can be replaced with any other random number generator if necessary. This module receives configuration values with the first data packets from the data stream. These values are used to set up the parameters for the resampling coefficient. Both coefficients are saved to the corresponding registers. The GRNG produces the first argument used in the multiplication unit. The second argument is fixed and comes from the register. After the multiplication, the result is forwarded to the summation unit along with the mean value from the register. Here we get the end of the conversion of random values with standard Gauss distribution to the resampling coefficients. This coefficient is then passed via a stream interface to the Streaming BLB instance for the following multiplication with the database query answer.

4   Test Setup for Evaluation

In this chapter, we describe the test setup implementation. We evaluate the system based on query 6 of the TPC-H benchmark [30].

4.1   Hardware Platform

The FPGA acceleration system is implemented on a Xilinx Zynq-7000 SoC ZC706 Evaluation Kit, clocked at 125 MHz. For the comparison, two different CPUs are used, an I7-6800k with 12 threads and 4 GHz clock speed and a Ryzen 7-5800X with 16 threads and 3.6 GHz clock speed. The data set is stored on a Patriot Burst SATA III 2.5 SSD.

4.2   Test System Structure

In the test system, we create subsamples from the database on the host side and preprocess the subsamples using a designated IP core on the FPGA that forwards the results directly to the BLB instances. Figure 4 shows the structure of a single core of the algorithm connected to the external interfaces via additional query processing logic. The data stream received from the host machine passes through the query stream execution core. Then, the data are broadcasted and forwarded to the Streaming BLB instances. The subsample data entries are multiplied with a resampling coefficient in each resampler. The resampled entries are then aggregated in the output accumulators in the answer aggregation block. The output data is ready to be sent to the host machine once the whole subsample is processed. The output data consists of the BLB approximation answers and the sum of all coefficients for the final calculation of the BLB approximation. The amount of output data is directly proportional to the number of BLB stream instances per BLB core.

The Xilinx® DMA/Bridge Subsystem for PCI Express® is responsible for the data transfer over the PCIe interface. The ZC706 accelerator board FPGA has two duplex AXI4-Stream channels. Thus the maximum number of BLB cores is two, whereas the number of resampling threads is limited only by the available FPGA resources. In the current implementation, the maximum number of threads tested is 32.

The TPC-H benchmark using query 6 requires additional mathematical operations in the FPGA, such as comparison, addition, and multiplication of numbers. Using 32-bit floating point numbers increases the accuracy and extends the

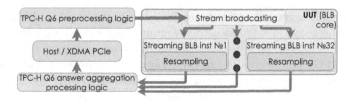

Fig. 4. Test system structure.

possibility of further optimization. Our implementation of the query processing core uses the LOGIcore Floating point v7.1 [31] IP core, providing all the necessary functions for data processing in a streaming fashion on the AXI4-Stream interface.

While we use a designated IP core for query execution, this is not central to our system. The query execution block can be replaced by another or be absent. In the latter case, the query can be executed by a CPU or a GPU on the host machine, leaving only the BLB acceleration to be performed on the FPGA.

The result processing logic is a multiplexer that uses the data from each resampling stream from the answer accumulators and normalization coefficients to create a data packet which will then be sent via PCI express DMA to the host machine for final processing and answer construction.

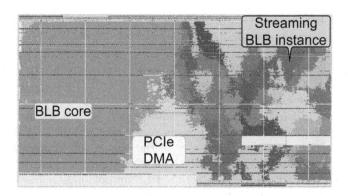

Fig. 5. FPGA floorplan for densest placement using ZC706 board.

Figure 5 shows the placement of the logical blocks of Streaming BLB instances. Each core consists of 32 Streaming BLB instances. The left part shows one entire BLB core in green. The second core is shown on the right, divided into 32 Streaming BLB instances. Each color corresponds to one Streaming BLB instance, such as the pink area in the upper right part. The TPC-H query 6 processing logic is located at the top of the yellow PCIe DMA block. The system under test can have a maximum of 32 Streaming BLB instances per core due to the limited resources of the FPGA used for testing.

4.3   CPU Implementation

The reference algorithm on the CPU is implemented in C++ with GCC v11.3.0 on Ubuntu 22.04. The execution time of the algorithm on the CPU is strongly influenced by the used Gaussian random number generator. To reflect this, we provide both implementations with the GRNG of the standard C++ library and the Ziggurat algorithm from the GNU scientific library [11]. Parallel processing on the CPU is performed using the OpenMP v4.5 library [7].

5   Evaluation

In this section, we compare and evaluate the results of the approximate processing of the test query using the Streaming BLB algorithm on both FPGA and CPU.

The resampling time measurements for a single given subsample are illustrated in Fig. 6. The CPU filtering (query execution) time is presented separately. It is only performed once for the entire subsample and is independent of the resampling time, which occurs multiple times on the processed data. On an FPGA, the filtering and resampling of data are done together in a streaming pipeline.

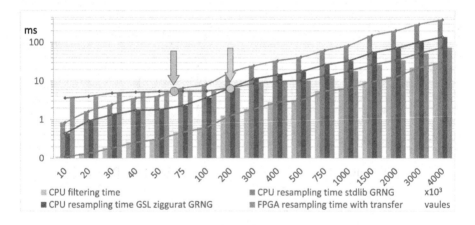

Fig. 6. Execution time in log scale

The CPU implementation on i7-6850K consists of one BLB core and eight Streaming BLB instances assigned to individual CPU cores. For direct comparison, we implemented the BLB algorithm on an FPGA with a single BLB core and eight Streaming BLB instances, even though a higher number of BLB cores and Streaming BLB instances can be easily achieved on the FPGA with virtually no overhead. The time measurement shown for FPGA processing includes data transfer overhead via the PCIe interface. The test results show a clear trend:

with small subsample sizes, resampling on the CPU is faster, but as the amount of data for resampling increases, the FPGA starts to be faster than the CPU. When using the standard C++ library for generating random values, this happens at around 60 thousand entries, as indicated by the green arrow and dot in the figure. The way the light blue trend overtakes the orange trend demonstrates the superior resampling performance of the FPGA. Most of the running time of the CPU implementation is required by the generation of normally distributed random numbers. For a more comprehensive comparison, the dark blue lines show an implementation using the optimized Ziggurat random number generator from the GSL library [11]. The CPU implementation gets significantly faster but is still overtaken by the FPGA implementation at around 200 thousand entries, as indicated by the yellow arrow and dot.

The results highlight that the FPGA can outperform the CPU even with relatively small subsample sizes. The generation of random numbers proves to be a bottleneck for the CPU. In contrast, on the FPGA random number can be provided on each clock cycle. Initially, the FPGA implementation suffers from a high PCIe initialization time, which amortizes with increasing data size. Afterward, the bottleneck for the FPGA becomes the low bandwidth of its interface. With 40 million entries, the FPGA implementation is twice as fast as the fastest CPU implementation (Note the logarithmic scale).

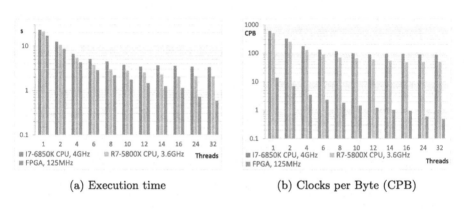

(a) Execution time   (b) Clocks per Byte (CPB)

Fig. 7. Test results with different numbers of threads

Figure 7a shows the execution time of Streaming BLB on TPC-H query 6 on a data set with 6 billion entries, which is equivalent to 1000 GB of data. We use $s = 10$ for the number of subsamples and $r = 100$ for the number of resampling iterations for each subsample. According to the hyperparameter balance selection for BLB by Kleiner et al. [15], these parameters correspond to an approximation accuracy of 95% for the answer. The resulting subsample size is equal to about one million entries (15.3 MB). The FPGA outperforms the CPU even in single-threaded execution. This balance is held for execution on the more modern R7-5800X.

Figure 7b shows the Clocks Per Byte (CPB) measurement with changing numbers of Streaming BLB instances in the execution for the same configuration as the previous measurement. By comparing the CPB, the effect of the number of Streaming BLB instances on the efficiency of the algorithm's execution can be evaluated. The CPU takes many clock cycles, which is compensated by its high frequency. As before, the random number generation drastically reduces the efficiency of the CPUs, while it does not affect the efficiency of the FPGA. The maximum efficiency of the Ryzen CPU is achieved at 16 threads with CPB $\approx$ 48. The algorithm's high level of parallelizability is evident from these figures and its performance scales directly with the number of computational threads. Using an FPGA is particularly advantageous in this scenario, as available resources only limit the number of Streaming BLB instances. With this amount of Streaming BLB instances, the FPGA is about 50 times more efficient (Note the logarithmic scale). Since the data processing is implemented with 32-bit numbers, the ideal value for the FPGA would be CPB = 0.25. In our implementation, we achieved CPB = 0.58 due to the time overhead for data transfer in the PCIe XDMA operation in the FPGA.

Table 1. FPGA resource utilisation

Resource	Utilized	Available	Utilization%	Streaming BLB instance
LUT	170 925	218 600	78.19	2 977
LUTRAM	16 841	70 400	23.92	357
FF	252 833	437 200	57.83	3 587
BRAM	36.5	545	6.69	0
DSP	580	900	64.44	9

Table 1 presents the utilization of the FPGA resources. The LUT utilization rate is at 78%. The right-hand column titled "One Streaming BLB instance" shows the resource utilization of a single Streaming BLB instance. Moderate resource consumption could make it possible to use IP core stream resampling as an add-on in any project. The number of available DSPs is a limiting factor

6   Conclusion

In this work, we created an architecture for FPGA-based hardware accelera- tion of approximate query processing. For this, we proposed a BLB variant for processing aggregation queries as well as a modification of the BLB algorithm that allows us to stream the resampling step, called *Streaming BLB*. Incorporat- ing BLB into our query processing system dramatically reduces the amount of data transfers and thereby minimizes the impact of the data transfer rate, which is usually the weakest point of any processing accelerator. With the proposed architecture, we achieve a Clocks per Byte rate < 1 in the test system. Regarding the overall execution time, the FPGA outperforms the CPU starting from medium sample sizes, even when including the data transfer time. In comparison to the CPUs, the FPGA profits considerably more from the proposed Streaming BLB algorithm, since streaming pseudo-random number generation based on the multihat algorithm allows for a high computational load to be transferred from the processor to the FPGA, earning an advantage in both execution speed and power consumption.

References

1. Acharya, S., Gibbons, P.B., Poosala, V., Ramaswamy, S., et al.: The aqua approximate query answering system. In: Proceedings of the 1999 ACM SIGMOD International Conference on Management of Data, pp 574–576. New York, NY, USA (1999). https://doi.org/10.1145/304182.304581
2. Agarwal, S., Panda, A., Mozafari, B., Madden, S., Stoica, I.: Blinkdb: queries with bounded errors and bounded response times on very large data. EuroSys 2013 (2012). https://doi.org/10.1145/2465351.2465355
3. Alimohammad, A., Fard, S.F., Cockburn, B.F., Schlegel, C.: A compact and accurate gaussian variate generator. IEEE Trans. Very Large Scale Integr. (VLSI) Syst. **16**(5), 517–527 (2008). https://doi.org/10.1109/TVLSI.2008.917552
4. Broneske, D., Drewes, A., Gurumurthy, B., Hajjar, I., Pionteck, T., Saake, G.: In-depth analysis of OLAP query performance on heterogeneous hardware. Datenbank-Spektrum **21**(2), 133–143 (2021). https://doi.org/10.1007/s13222-021-00384-w
5. Canty, A.J., Davison, A.C., et al.: Bootstrap diagnostics and remedies. Can. J. Stat. **34**(1), 5–27 (2006). https://doi.org/10.1002/cjs.5550340103
6. Cormode, G.: Sketch techniques for approximate query processing. Found. Trends Databases **4**(1-3), 1-294 (2011)
7. Dagum, L., Menon, R.: Openmp: an industry-standard API for shared-memory programming. IEEE Comput. Sci. Eng. **5**(1), 46–55 (1998). https://doi.org/10.1109/99.660313
8. Efron, B.: Bootstrap methods: another look at the jackknife. Ann. Stat. **7**(1), 1–26 (1979). https://doi.org/10.1214/aos/1176344552
9. Fang, J., Mulder, Y.T.B., Hidders, J., Lee, J., Hofstee, H.P.: In-memory database acceleration on FPGAs: a survey. VLDB J. **29**(1), 33–59 (2019). https://doi.org/10.1007/s00778-019-00581-w
10. Babu, G.J., Pathak, P.K., Rao, C.R.: Second-order correctness of the Poisson bootstrap. Ann. Stat. **27**(5), 1666–1683 (1999). https://doi.org/10.1214/aos/1017939146
11. Gough, B.: GNU scientific library reference manual. Network Theory Ltd. (2009)
12. Hellerstein, J.M., Haas, P.J., Wang, H.J.: Online aggregation. SIGMOD Rec. **26**(2), 171–182 (1997). https://doi.org/10.1145/253262.253291
13. Hilprecht, B., et al.: Deepdb: learn from data, not from queries! Proc. VLDB Endow. **13**(7), 992–1005 (2020). https://doi.org/10.14778/3384345.3384349
14. Kleiner, A., Talwalkar, A., Agarwal, S., Stoica, I., Jordan, M.: A general bootstrap performance diagnostic, pp. 419–427 (2013). https://doi.org/10.1145/2487575.2487650

15. Kleiner, Ariel, et al.: A scalable bootstrap for massive data. J. R. Stat. Soc. Ser. B (Stat. Methodol.) **76** (2011). https://doi.org/10.1111/rssb.12050

16. Li, Y., Chow, P., et al.:: Software/hardware framework for generating parallel gaussian random numbers based on the monty python method. In: 2012 International Conference on Field-Programmable Technology, pp. 190–197 (2012). https://doi.org/10.1109/FPT.2012.6412133

17. Liu, Z., Zhang, A.: A survey on sampling and profiling over big data (technical report) (2020). https://doi.org/10.48550/ARXIV.2005.05079

18. Ma, Q., Triantafillou, P.: Dbest: revisiting approximate query processing engines with machine learning models, pp. 1553–1570 (2019). https://doi.org/10.1145/3299869.3324958

19. Mahmud, M.S., Huang, J.Z., et al.: A survey of data partitioning and sampling methods to support big data analysis. Big Data Min. Anal. **3**(2), 85–101 (2020). https://doi.org/10.26599/BDMA.2019.9020015

20. Malik, J.S., Hemani, A.: Gaussian random number generation: a survey on hardware architectures. ACM Comput. Surv. **49**(3) (2016). https://doi.org/10.1145/2980052

21. Nair, L.B.G., et al.: The reprovide query-sequence optimization in a hardware-accelerated DBMs. In: Proceedings of the 16th International Workshop on Data Management on New Hardware. DaMoN 2020, Association for Computing Machinery, New York, NY, USA (2020). https://doi.org/10.1145/3399666.3399926

22. Park, Y., et al.: Verdictdb: universalizing approximate query processing, SIGMOD 2018, pp. 1461–1476. New York, NY, USA (2018). https://doi.org/10.1145/3183713.3196905

23. Parsons, V.L.: Stratified Sampling, pp. 1–11. Wiley, Hoboken (2017). https://doi.org/10.1002/9781118445112.stat05999.pub2

24. Peng, J., et al.: AQP++: Connecting approximate query processing with aggregate precomputation for interactive analytics, pp. 1477–1492. SIGMOD 2018, New York, NY, USA (2018). https://doi.org/10.1145/3183713.3183747

25. Pol, A., Jermaine, C.: Relational confidence bounds are easy with the bootstrap, pp. 587–598 (2005). https://doi.org/10.1145/1066157.1066224

26. Rao, C., Pathak, P., Koltchinskii, V.: Bootstrap by sequential resampling. J. Stat. Plan. Infer. **64**(2), 257–281 (1997). https://doi.org/10.1016/S0378-3758(97)00041-4

27. Salami, B., Gorker, et al.: Axledb: a novel programmable query processing platform on FPGA. Microprocess. Microsyst. **51**, 142–164 (2017). https://doi.org/10.1016/j.micpro.2017.04.018

28. Shoemaker, O.J., Pathak, P.K.: The sequential bootstrap: a comparison with regular bootstrap. Commun. Stat. Theor. Methods **30**(8–9), 1661–1674 (2001). https://doi.org/10.1081/STA-100105691

29. Thomas, D.B.: The table-hadamard GRNG: an area-efficient FPGA gaussian random number generator. ACM Trans. Reconfigurable Technol. Syst. **8**(4) (2015). https://doi.org/10.1145/2629607

30. TPC: Tpc-h decision support benchmark. https://www.tpc.org/tpch. Accessed 05 Aug 2022

31. Xilinx: Logicore IP product guide. https://docs.xilinx.com/v/u/en-US/pg060-floating-point (2020)

32. Zhao, H., Zhang, H., Jing, Y., Zhang, K., He, Z., Wang, X.S.: Revisiting approximate query processing and bootstrap error estimation on GPU. In: Bhattacharya, A., et al. Database Systems for Advanced Applications. DASFAA 2022. LNCS, vol. 13245, pp. 72–87. Springer, Cham (2022). https://doi.org/10.1007/978-3-031-00123-9_5

33. Ziener, D., Bauer, F., et al.: FPGA-based dynamically reconfigurable SQL query processing. ACM Trans. Reconfigurable Technol. Syst. **9**(4) (2016). https://doi.org/10.1145/2845087

Accelerating Graph Neural Networks in Pytorch with HLS and Deep Dataflows

Jose Nunez-Yanez$^{(\boxtimes)}$ (iD)

Department of Electrical Engineering, Linköping University, Linköping, Sweden
`jose.nunez-yanez@liu.se`
`https://eejlny.github.io/index.html`

Abstract. Graph neural networks (GNNs) combine sparse and dense data compute requirements that are challenging to meet in resource-constrained embedded hardware. In this paper, we investigate a dataflow of dataflows architecture that optimizes data access and processing element utilization. The architecture is described with high-level synthesis and offers multiple configuration options including varying the number of independent hardware threads, the interface data width and the number of compute units per thread. Each hardware thread uses a fine-grained dataflow to stream words with a bit-width that depends on the network precision while a coarse-grained dataflow links the thread stages streaming partially-computed matrix tiles. The accelerator is mapped to the programmable logic of a Zynq Ultrascale device whose processing system runs Pytorch extended with PYNQ overlays. Results based on the citation networks show a performance gain of up to 140x with multi-threaded hardware configurations compared with the optimized software implementation available in Pytorch. The results also show competitive performance of the embedded hardware compared with other high-performance state-of-the-art hardware accelerators.

Keywords: neural network · FPGA · sparse · HLS · GNN · Pytorch

1 Introduction

GNNs perform tasks such as graph classification, node classification, link prediction or graph clustering and have been very successful in applications such as anomaly detection, bioinformatics and cybersecurity where data can be interpreted as graphs with a non-euclidean structure. Also in natural language processing GNNs have been shown to be a generalization of the Transformer [1] that achieves state-of-the-art performance in machine translation tasks. More recently, GNNs have started to appear in domains traditionally reserved to CNNs or RNNs such as video object detection [2]. GNN processing uses both dense and sparse data representations and the resulting irregular computing and

This research was funded by the Wallenberg AI autonomous autonomous systems and software (WASP) program funded by the Knut and Alice Wallenberg Foundation.

F. Palumbo et al. (Eds.): ARC 2023, LNCS 14251, pp. 131–145, 2023.
https://doi.org/10.1007/978-3-031-42921-7_9

data access means that both inference and training of GNNs are complex. Popular machine learning frameworks like Tensorflow and Pytorch support graph neural network development. In this work, we focus on Pytorch and how its python interface can be integrated with accelerator overlays developed with Xilinx PYNQ for graph neural network processing. PYNQ is a Xilinx Python framework that runs on Ubuntu and provides a highly-productive development platform for Xilinx devices such as the Zynq family. In this paper, we present results on creating a dataflow architecture for graph neural networks using high-level-synthesis and its integration into PYNQ and Pytorch. This work focuses on a popular type of GNNs called graph convolutional networks (GCN) and the main contributions are as follows:

- We present gFADES as a graph neural network accelerator that uses a dataflow of dataflows (DoD) approach to compute the output features of the $l + 1$ layer in a GCN: $H^{(l+1)} = \sigma(\tilde{D}^{-\frac{1}{2}}\tilde{A}\tilde{D}^{-\frac{1}{2}}H^l W^l)$
  where W indicates the trainable weight matrix of layer l. H the input feature matrix for layer l and $\tilde{A}$ the normalize adjacency matrix. Each row of the input feature matrix H^0 contains attributes or features for a node of the input graph. Each row of the output feature matrix $H^{(1)}$ is the embedding of the node in a lower dimension space.
- We demonstrate how gFADES performance can be scaled to adapt to the system bandwidth and compute availability with multiple hardware threads and multiple compute units targeting resource-constrained SoC devices.
- We optimize the HLS description to handle the extreme sparsity found in graph neural networks and explore new HLS features that enable the creation of high-throughput and efficient dataflow of dataflows (DoD) architecture.
- We present performance results compared with other state-of-the-art hardware and discuss the integration flow as a Pytorch accelerator suitable for edge compute devices.
- We make our designs and framework open-source at: https://github.com/eejlny/gemm_spmm

This paper is organized as follows: Sect. 2 reviews related work and presents the current motivation. Section 3 describes the proposed DoD architecture with data access and processing optimizations for high-performance dense and sparse tensor processing that are then further refine in Sect. 4. Section 5 focuses on the details of the hardware multi-threaded extensions. Section 6 discusses the Pytorch integration while 7 performs a performance evaluation in a 2-layer GCN example network. Finally, Sect. 8 concludes this paper and proposes future work.

2   Related Work and Motivation

Over the last few years the interest on graph neural networks applications has increased significantly and the topic of hardware acceleration has started to receive widespread attention. The GNN type that has received more attention for hardware acceleration is the GCN (Graph Convolutional Network) that can be expressed as a combination of dense and sparse matrix multiplications. Other GNN models such as GAT (graph attention networks) or GIN (Graph isomorphism network) add attention mechanisms that disrupt the matrix processing [3]. The authors of [3] also consider edge features to the node features to create an accelerator for general graph neural networks but this results in a lower throughput if applied to simpler GCNs. GCN accelerators typically consider that the aggregation phase consists of sparse x dense matrix operation with an sparse adjacency matrix while the combination phase is a dense x dense operation with a dense feature matrix [4]. In [5] the authors indicate that in many applications the input features contain significant levels of sparsity and propose a sparse block strategy for these cases. The input feature matrix is encoded in CSR (Compressed Sparse Row) format with coarse-grained blocks of zeros that can be bypassed. The proposed systolic architecture allows the design to adapt the computing performance to the available input/output bandwidth. In GCNAX [6] the computation of aggregation and combination is done in two separate phases to take advantage of the sparseness of the adjacency matrix and the possible sparseness of the input features of the first layer of the GCN. The authors in [6] buffer the intermediate dense matrix resulting of the combination phase and pass it to the aggregation engine. The design employs 16 MAC array and targets an ASIC technology with performance and energy parameters estimated using a synthesised design. In GraphACT [7], a hybrid CPU-FPGA platform targeting large scale Xilinx Alveo cards equipped with HBM memory is presented focusing on the acceleration of large graph training. The hardware is based on a systolic array and the training algorithm is optimized to fit the constraints of the hardware. The paper does not provide details on logic complexity or design methodology focusing on a graph theory to improve hardware mapping. The paper reports a DSP utilization of 5632 cores and it is shown to outperform an NVIDIA tesla GPU by 10% to 30% for different datasets. Also using large Alveo cards the hardware in [8] proposes a pre-processing stage that performs graph sparsification to reduce the number of edge connections and node reordering to increase data locality. This reduces the required size of on-chip memory. The research treats the feature matrix as a dense matrix for all the layers in the network. A two mode strategy to change the order of the combination and aggregation stages (1) $(AH)W$ or (2) $A(HW)$ shows that (2) has lower computation when the next layer feature vector is shorter than the current layer. Our hardware always uses mode (2) because both A and H can be sparse and therefore both the aggregation and combination stages have the opportunity to work in sparse mode. Also, in the 2-layer GCN evaluated we have observed so far that the feature vector size decreases after the first layer. In [9] the authors also consider that feature processing consist of a dense and regular pattern and use a MLP (multi-layer-perceptron) for this stage. The hardware is described in Verilog and targets a large VCU128 equipped with HBM memory and several MBytes of device memory. They investigate an edge-level processing strategy that computes an edge a time and requires retraining and processing while our strategy processes sub-graphs as used directly in by the reference Pytorch implementation [10]. The possible workload unbalance resulting from vertices with different number of edges is dealt with by assigning bigger chunks matrices with higher sparsity to the corresponding thread. In [11] the authors also use Verilog to target a large Stratix 10 SX FPGA. They indicate that GNNs have highly unbalanced non-zero data distributions in the adjacency matrix and propose a hardware accelerator with auto-tuning that monitors the workload and balances the distribution. Similarly to our work the processing of the feature matrix precedes the adjacency matrix and it is more computationally intensive. The authors in [12] explore the potential of the latest Versal family working with graph layers that combine subgraphs with different levels of sparsity. The subgraphs with lower levels of density are processed by the VLIW-Vector multiprocessor system while subgraphs with scattered nodes are processed the FPGA fabric. A retraining strategy is used to group and reorder vertices increasing the density of the graph structure. The lack of real hardware means that the evaluation is based on simulations that indicate good energy efficiency and performance although no complexity results are available. The research done in [13] proposes a sophisticated graph reordering technique to cluster graph nodes into islands with the objective of improving data locality and reused. The system is demonstrated in a large Stratix 10 SX FPGA with 4096 PEs (Processing Units) with floating-point MAC units. Dedicated BFS (Breadth-First Search) engines are used at run-time to locate the islands that are then forwarded to idle PEs for performing its combination and aggregation jobs. The previous state-of-the-art review indicates that there is significant efforts on accelerator design for large scale FPGAs and ASICs but less focus on edge devices with limited computing and bandwidth resources. Therefore, we focus on resource constrained devices operating at the edge such as the Zynq and Zynq ultrascale family that lack high-bandwidth memory features. We also aim at integrating the accelerator as part of the Pytorch framework to facilitate ease-of-use as a drop-in replacement for the sparse/dense computation libraries available in Pytorch. The design focuses on streaming data with independent dataflow stages to optimize the limited memory bandwidth available and keep the compute units busy. We consider fine-grained sparse adjacency matrices and sparse/dense feature matrices.

3   Dataflow Description

The dataflow combines hardware engines for aggregation and combination stages that correspond to adjacency and feature matrix processing respectively. Each of these engines can instantiate a variable number of hardware threads and compute units depending on the required level of performance and available bandwidth. The dataflow of a single thread is shown in Fig. 2 and it has been fully described C with Xilinx Vitis HLS (High-Level-Synthesis) tools. In the HLS description a dataflow of dataflows (DoD) is created with a new HLS 2022 feature called *streamofblocks* that enables the selective read_lock and write_lock of the PIPO (Ping-Pong) buffers creating a inter-dataflow between aggregation and combination so that both engines can run in parallel with both single and multi-threaded hardware configurations. Internally the combination and aggregation engines use a fine-grained intra-dataflow that streams data words with bit-widths that depend on the selected data type (e.g. 16-bit half, 16-bit fixed, 32-bit float, etc.). In Fig. 2 we can see how multiple FIFOs, which total number depends on the number of compute units in each stage, join the different processing stages of the fine-grained dataflow. The coarse-grained inter-dataflow has a data granularity that consists of tiles with dimensions that depend on the number of compute units and the number of hardware threads. These tiles ensure high-throughput by keeping all stages in the dataflow active. In Fig. 2 we can see how a PIPO joins the different processing stages of the coarse-grained dataflow. Multiple PIPOs are needed in multi-threaded configurations as seen in Fig. 5. The weight matrix is always considered to be dense while the adjacency matrix is always sparse and coded in CSR format. On the other hand, the feature matrix is available in CSR sparse mode for the first layer and in dense modes for the hidden layers. Figure 1 shows how the coarse-grained dataflow enables adjacency and feature tiles to be processed in parallel and that, for the considered datasets, adjacency tiles are processed faster than feature tiles. On the other hand, the last adjacency tile execution cannot not overlap and therefore adjacency tile processing needs to be also optimized to not impact overall performance.

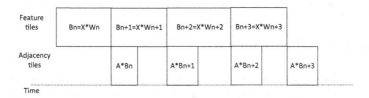

Fig. 1. Coarse-grained dataflow tiling

3.1 Combination Engine

The combination engine computes $FEA * W$ where FEA represents the feature matrix and W the weight matrix and generates a dense matrix output B in chunks (or tiles) for the aggregation engine that computes $ADJ * B$ where ADJ represents the adjacency matrix. This engine consists of two main stages that read sparse or dense feature data and compute the dot product. Sparse mode in the combination engine is generally used in the first graph layer where the size of the feature matrix is large and significantly sparse. In the second or subsequent layers the feature matrix is the output from the previous layer and dense. We have verified that this is the case even taken into account the non-linear RELU function applied to the outputs from the first layer with observed densities between 75% and 90% for the evaluated datasets. For this reason the combination engine is set to run in dense mode after the first layer. In this dense configuration the feature values port is used to read the dense input feature matrix values while the rowptr and column_index feature ports remain in idle mode.

3.2   Aggregation Engine

The aggregation engine is used always in sparse mode since the same adjacency values are used for the first and second graph layers. The aggregation engine contains read,compute, scale and write stages. The read stage is very similar to the read stage of the combination engine but it lacks the logic needed to compute in dense mode. It streams values and column indices while it internally computes the number of non-zeros present in each row using the rowptr data. All this information is streamed into FIFOs that are used by the compute stage. The compute stage has as inputs the PIPOs that are used by the combination engine to write its results and the FIFOs with the adjacency matrix data. The scaling stage is needed for low bit widths as presented in our previous work targeting Tensorflow Lite [14] and convolutional (not graphs) neural networks. In this paper we present results with a 16-bit floating-point that does not require scaling so this stage is not enabled. We leave the evaluation of other data types and scaling strategies for future work. The write stage reads the FIFOs from each compute engine and writes the results to main memory.

4   Dataflow Optimization

Figure 3 illustrates how non-zero values are broadcast to all the compute units available in the compute stage. The figure shows zeros as empty squares intermixed with sample non-zero values. The compute stage processes all non-zero data of a row in the sparse matrix before moving to the next one. The compute stage loop that processes each row achieves a initialization interval of one clock cycle (so a new iteration of the loop can be started in each clock cycle) and has a latency of four clock cycles. This latency results from the need to flush the pipeline and restart the loop after each row. This latency does not represent a significant overhead as long as the number of iterations in the loop is large (i.e. iterations $\gg$ latency) but, in graph neural networks, sparsity means that a row with thousands of elements could contain just a few non-zeros (e.g. less than 10). This extreme sparsity means that the latency overhead is significant and can result in a significant performance degradation. In addition, in the targeted Zynq family the latency of a floating point add (FADD) is larger than one and the architecture deals with this by interleaving multiple accumulations in a single MAC unit with independent accumulation registers. The efficiency of this floating point configuration also degrades if this FADD pipeline only has a few non-zero values in the row before it needs to be restarted. To address this problem we group a few rows of the sparse matrix in a single sub-block to reduce the number of row restarts. The challenge is how to distribute the results

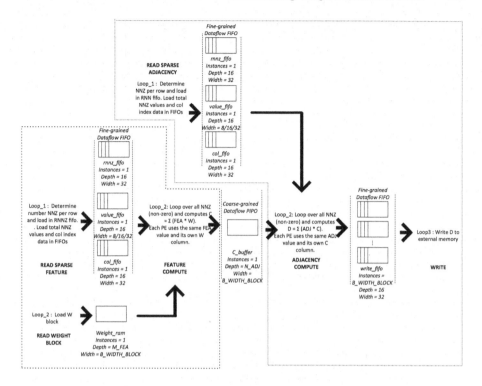

Fig. 2. Single-threaded dataflow of dataflows description

obtained from the block to the corresponding individual rows. In order to do that we create intervals accumulating the number of non-zeros in each of the rows of the sub-block. Then, the hardware can use these intervals to assign the compute loop result to the corresponding row. The FIFOs supplying the number of non-zeros in each row to the compute stage are re-organized to store these accumulations that create the intervals. The compute stage obtains multiple row results in parallel that are then assigned to the correct row result using the current iteration of the loop as an index that points to a single non-zero interval as illustrated in Fig. 4 with an example of sub-blocks formed by four rows.

Table 1. Sparse sub-block execution in ms

Dataset	sub-block1	sub-block2	sub-block4	sub-block8
citeseer	5.95	4.26	4.07	3.98
cora	4.7	2.21	2.06	1.99
pubmead	40.7	35.2	34.1	33.5

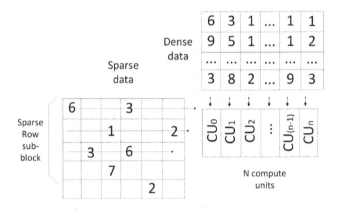

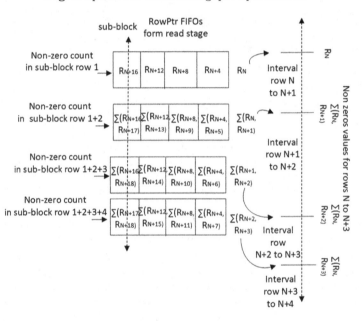

Fig. 3. Sparse sub-block throughput optimization

Fig. 4. Sparse sub-block non-zero intervals

Table 1 evaluates the effect of the proposed sparse matrix sub-blocking in execution time for the considered datasets. The dataflow is configured with 2 compute units in the feature and adjacency compute stages. Sub-block1 corresponds to a single row in the sub-block (i.e. original approach with no sub-blocking). It is clear that for all the data sets sub-blocking reduces execution time significantly and for the rest of this paper a sub-block size of 4 is selected to balance performance and complexity. Larger sub-blocks group more sparse rows together but this results in more complex interval logic needed to extract individual row results from the sub-block computation.

5   Multi-threaded Extension

To exploit the memory bandwidth and compute performance available in the Zynq ultrascale device the number of working hardware threads is configurable at compile time. Each hardware thread is assigned a number of rows of the adjacency and feature matrices while having access to the same weight data. Each hardware thread has independent ports connected to the multiple high-performance AXI ports available in the device. Figure 5 compares a base configuration with one thread for adjacency and feature processing with multi-threaded configurations with up to 4 threads per engine. The ports $column\_index, row\_-pointer$ and $values$ are used to stream the CSR matrices, w carries dense weight data and d carries the output to main memory. As seen in previous work, feature processing tends to be more compute intensive than adjacency processing so a configuration with a higher number of threads for the combination engine compared with the aggregation engine is supported as an option to better distribute the available hardware resources. The number of PIPO buffers that connect aggregation and combination stages is determined by the number of threads with a power of two relation. The figure shows how each combination thread writes the same output to a number of PIPOs equal to the number of aggregation threads. Then, each aggregation thread reads from a number of PIPOs equal to the number of combination engines. Each of these PIPOs contains different data and are needed to process all the rows involved in the adjacency tensor processing. This organization ensures that all the compute units can write and read data in parallel without dataflow stalls and overcomes the limited number of read/write ports available in the BRAMs that are used to create the PIPOs. Notice that in addition the each thread contains a number of compute units that is always a multiple of 2 to utilize efficiently the double read/write ports available in Xilinx BRAMs. Therefore the number of BRAMs present in each PIPO depends on the tile size and also the number of compute units present in each hardware thread.

Table 2 shows the memory and logic complexity for different configurations for a weight matrix size with up to 20480 rows. The configuration name is shown as $XtYtZc$ with X/Y indicating the number of threads in feature and adjacency respectively and Z the number of compute units per thread. The target device is the Zynq Ultrascale+ XCZU28DR available in the RFSoC 2x2 board and the design uses a clock frequency of 250 MHz. Notice that the maximum row count of the weight matrix is in this case limited to 20480 but this is also limited by the hardware need to allocate physically contiguous memory in main memory

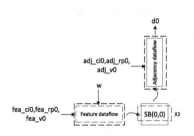

(a) 1 feature engine and 1 adjacency engine

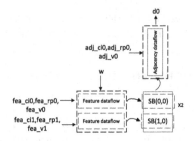

b) 2 feature engines and 1 adjacency engine

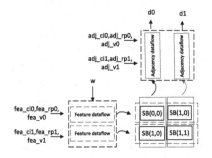

(c) 2 feature engines and 2 adjacency engines

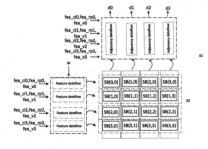

(d) 4 feature engines and 4 adjacency engines

Fig. 5. Examples of hardware multi-threaded configurations

to hold the matrix data. A way to overcome this size limitation is to introduce a new level of software tiling for large arrays using the processor to invoke the accelerator multiple times.

Table 2. configuration complexity comparison

Configuration	LUTs(K)	FFs(K)	BRAM_18Ks	DSP48Es
(1t1t2c)	22.6	29.4	109	22
(1t1c8c)	27.2	31.2	421	34
(1t1t16c)	33.7	33.6	813	50
(2t2t4c)	40.0	47.4	425	48
(2t2t8c)	48.1	50.4	841	64
(4t4t4c)	79.7	84.03	848	92
(4t2t8c)	71.5	74.2	1036	334

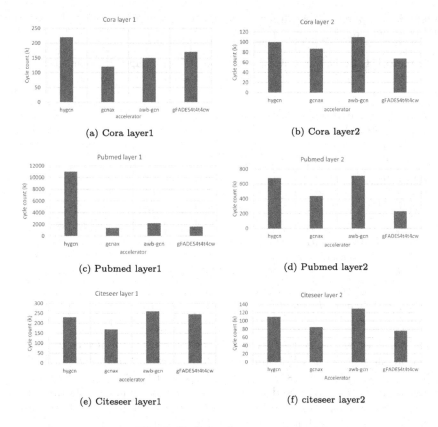

Fig. 6. Performance comparison

6   Pytorch Integration

The gFADES accelerator is implemented as a PYNQ overlay integrated in the Pytorch machine learning framework. We use a PYNQ 2.7 image running Ubuntu 22.04 and install Pytorch 1.9 on the RFSoC 2x2 board from the original sources. PYNQ enables full control of the accelerator from a python environment and it uses numpy arrays as the data buffers for the accelerator. Numpy arrays of contiguous memory are allocated in the python script to store the input and output data for the accelerator. The accelerator is then configured with the addresses of these buffers. Any additional IP control registers are also written such as those indicating dense or sparse mode and matrix sizes. Finally, a run kernel script starts the IP block by setting the AP_START bit to one and checks when the accelerator completes reading the AP_DONE bit. Pytorch uses torch tensors to store its data that in addition to the values store additional information such as $requires\_grad$ used to compute derivates automatically during the backward pass. These torch tensors are similar to numpy arrays and conversion between both data types is possible reusing the same memory without explicit data copying. This simplifies and optimizes the integration of PYNQ and Pytorch. For example:

Listing 1.1. Torch tensor and acceleerator PYNQ numpy arrays integration

```
1
2
3  from pynq import allocate
4  import torch
5  #allocate numpy array suitable for accelerator calls
6  B_buffer = allocate(shape=(P_w,M_fea),
7  dtype=np.float16)
8  #Obtain Torch tensor
9  torch_B_buffer=torch.from_numpy(B_buffer)
10 #configure IP register with numpy pointer address
11 my_ip.register_map.B_offset_1 = B_buffer.
       ↪ physical_address
12 # other register configuration and memory allocation
       ↪ omitted for clarify.
13 #run hardware kernel
14 run_kernel()
```

The obtained *torch_B_buffer* tensor and *B_buffer* numpy array can then be used in the rest of the algorithm. We perform tests of the accelerator with a GCN consisting of two layers as presented in [10] with a first layer with a fixed number of 16 hidden units and a second layer whose hidden units depend on the classification classes of the data set. The first layer runs the hardware in full sparse mode and both feature and adjacency matrix are processed in sparse mode. On the other hand, the second layer has as input the output feature matrix generated by the first layer after a *RELU* function. This second feature matrix is now dense and the accelerator uses a hybrid mode where the adjacency matrix is still sparse but the feature matrix is dense.

Listing 1.2. Pytorch acceleration with gFADES

```
1  if (acc==1):
2    print("Running gFADES")
3    self.my_ip.register_map.M_fea=self.in_features
4    self.my_ip.register_map.P_w=self.out_features
5    self.my_ip.register_map.gemm_mode=dense
6    self.my_ip.register_map.D1_offset_1 = D_buffer.
         ↪ physical_address
7    self.my_ip.register_map.values_fea1_offset_1 =
         ↪ values_fea_buffer.physical_address
8    self.my_ip.register_map.B_offset_1 = B_buffer.
         ↪ physical_address
9    self.run_kernel()
10   output_acc = D_buffer
```

```
11    output_acc = torch.from_numpy(output_acc)
12    output_acc = torch.tensor(output_acc,dtype=torch.
         ↪ float32)
13    output = output_acc
14  else:
15    print("Running CPU")
16    support = torch.mm(input, self.weight)
17    output_cpu = torch.spmm(adj, support)
18    output = output_cpu
```

7 Performance Evaluation

To evaluate the performance of the design we select the popular Cora, Citeseer
and Pubmed datasets. These datasets are designed for node classification tasks
and the objective is to predict the category of unknown publications. Table 3
summarizes the statistics of the datasets and the density of the adjacency and
feature matrix. The second layer receives as input the features output from
the first layer and the density shown in Table 3 has been measured after the
application of the RELU function.

Table 3. Dataset characteristics

Dataset	Node count	density adjacency	Feature count	density features layer1	density features layer2
cora	2708	0.18%	1433	1.27%	76.7%
citeseer	3327	0.11%	3703	0.85%	90.5%
pubmed	19717	0.028%	500	10%	84.7%

Table 4 shows the performance obtained on these dataset for the hardware
configurations presented in Table 2. The Cortex A53 CPU results are based on
Pytorch *torch.spmm/mm* sparse and general matrix as originally presented in
[10] and shown in the listing below.

Listing 1.3. GCN layer on CPU

```
1  support = torch.mm(input, self.weight)
2  output = torch.spmm(adj, support)
```

Table 4 shows that the higher hardware acceleration is obtained with the
4t4t4c configurations that outperforms the configuration 4t2c8c that sacrifices 2
adjacency threads to increase the number of compute units from 4 to 8. The hardware acceleration over the CPU version ranges from 140x to 26x for the different
data sets. As seen in Table 2 4t4t4c uses fewer memory and DSP blocks but it
requires more logic than 4t2c8c. In principle, the overlapping between adjacency
and feature processing and the lower computational complexity of the adjacency
means that having fewer adjacency threads and more compute units could be

Table 4. Layer 1/2 execution time in milliseconds

configuration	citeseer l1/l2	cora l1/l2	pubmed l1/l2
1t1t2c	4.07/0.97	2.06/0.87	34.1/3.6
2t2t2c	2.23/0.54	1.21/0.49	17.9/1.87
2t2t4c	1.43/0.53	0.92/0.48	10.06/1.83
4t2t8c	1.27/0.51	0.96/0.48	6.87/1.58
4t4t4c	0.98/0.30	0.68/0.27	6.56/0.93
CPU	158/4.29	53.5/5.1	184.6/31.8

beneficial. In the considered data sets this does not compensate the additional time required to process the final adjacency tile that does not overlap as seen in Fig. 1. Finally, Fig. 6 compares the performance of the gFADES architecture with state-of-the-art FPGA-based GNN accelerators reviewed in Sect. 2. These accelerators target high-end FPGA devices or ASICs and deploy HBM (high-bandwidth memory) that is not available in our resource constrained device. To make the comparison fairer we use the accelerator performance data taking verbatim from [6]. In [6] the architectures are normalized by using a 16 MAC array which will be equivalent to a 4t4t4c configuration or 4 hardware threads with 4 PE cores per thread stage. The results show that although gFADES targets an embedded and simpler architecture, it offers competitive performance. The explanation is that the simple and deep dataflow can exploit the limited bandwidth available in the Zynq device and that the pipeline optimizations enable up to 90% of performance of a theoretical ideal configuration where the DSP blocks never have to wait for data. In addition and compared to other architectures, the hybrid processing mode can combine dense-sparse processing in layer 2 with full fine-grained sparsity in layer1 optimally adapting to the level of sparsity present in the feature matrix.

8   Conclusions

In this paper we have presented the gFADES dataflow hardware architecture for graph convolutional networks. The gFADES architecture is highly configurable in terms of logic and bandwidth requirements and suitable for edge FPGA devices. Performance and functional results following the integration into the Pytorch machine learning framework show good acceleration both in pure sparse and in hybrid sparse-dense mode. Future work includes testing additional data sets, hardware configurations and quantization strategies for low bit-width data types. Also, we intend to streamline the integration process with Pytorch/Tensorflow and investigate how gFADES can be used in the backward pass to accelerate training in addition to the forward pass.

References

1. Chen, C., et al.: A survey on graph neural networks and graph transformers in computer vision: a task-oriented perspective (2022)
2. Han, K., Wang, Y., Guo, J., Tang, Y., Wu, E.: Vision GNN: an image is worth graph of nodes (2022)
3. Sarkar, R., Abi-Karam, S., He, Y., Sathidevi, L., Hao, C.: FlowGNN: a dataflow architecture for real-time workload-agnostic graph neural network inference. In: 2023 IEEE International Symposium on High-Performance Computer Architecture (HPCA), Los Alamitos, CA, USA, pp. 1099–1112. IEEE Computer Society (2023)
4. Garg, R., et al.: Understanding the design-space of sparse/dense multiphase GNN dataflows on spatial accelerators (2021)
5. Peltekis, C., Filippas, D., Nicopoulos, C., Dimitrakopoulos, G.: FusedGCN: a systolic three-matrix multiplication architecture for graph convolutional networks. In: 2022 IEEE 33rd International Conference on Application-Specific Systems, Architectures and Processors (ASAP), pp. 93–97 (2022)
6. Li, J., Louri, A., Karanth, A., Bunescu, R.: GCNAX: a flexible and energy-efficient accelerator for graph convolutional neural networks. In: 2021 IEEE International Symposium on High-Performance Computer Architecture (HPCA), pp. 775–788 (2021)
7. Zeng, H., Prasanna, V.: GraphACT: accelerating GCN training on CPU-FPGA heterogeneous platforms. In: Proceedings of the 2020 ACM/SIGDA International Symposium on Field-Programmable Gate Arrays, FPGA 2020, pp. 255–265. Association for Computing Machinery, New York (2020)
8. Zhang, B., Zeng, H., Prasanna, V.: Hardware acceleration of large scale GCN inference. In: 2020 IEEE 31st International Conference on Application-Specific Systems, Architectures and Processors (ASAP), pp. 61–68 (2020)
9. Yuan, W., Tian, T., Wu, Q., Jin, X.: QEGCN: an FPGA-based accelerator for quantized GCNs with edge-level parallelism. J. Syst. Architect. **129**, 102596 (2022)
10. Kipf, T.N., Welling, M.: Semi-supervised classification with graph convolutional networks (2016)
11. Geng, T., et al.: AWB-GCN: a graph convolutional network accelerator with runtime workload rebalancing, pp. 922–936 (2020)
12. Zhang, C., et al.: H-GCN: a graph convolutional network accelerator on versal acap architecture. In: 2022 32nd International Conference on Field-Programmable Logic and Applications (FPL), Los Alamitos, CA, USA, pp. 200–208. IEEE Computer Society (2022)
13. Geng, T., et al.: I-GCN: a graph convolutional network accelerator with runtime locality enhancement through islandization. In: MICRO-54: 54th Annual IEEE/ACM International Symposium on Microarchitecture, MICRO 2021, New York, NY, USA, pp. 1051–1063. Association for Computing Machinery (2021)
14. Nunez-Yanez, J.: Fused architecture for dense and sparse matrix processing in tensorflow lite. IEEE Micro **42**(6), 55–66 (2022)

DNN Model Theft Through Trojan Side-Channel on Edge FPGA Accelerator

Srivatsan Chandrasekar[(✉)] [ID], Siew-Kei Lam[ID], and Srikanthan Thambipillai[ID]

Nanyang Technological University, Singapore, Singapore
{chan1000,assklam,astsrikan}@ntu.edu.sg

Abstract. In this paper, we present a novel hardware trojan assisted side-channel attack to reverse engineer DNN architectures on edge FPGA accelerators. In particular, our attack targets the widely-used Versatile Tensor Accelerator (VTA). A hardware trojan is employed to track the memory transactions by monitoring the AXI interface signals of VTA's submodules. The memory side-channel information is leaked through a UART port, which reveals the DNN architecture information. Our experiments demonstrate the effectiveness of the proposed attack and highlight the need for robust security measures to protect DNN intellectual property (IP) models that are deployed on edge FPGA platforms.

Keywords: Side-channel attacks · Deep learning accelerators · FPGA security · Machine learning security · Hardware trojans

1 Introduction

Deep neural networks (DNNs) have achieved state-of-the-art results in complex tasks across a multitude of applications including computer vision, natural language processing, speech recognition, autonomous vehicles, etc. [1–3]. DNNs have become prevalent in edge applications as well. In particular, FPGA-based accelerators have emerged as a viable solution that provides high performance and energy efficiency for DNN inference on the edge. However, the sensitive and confidential nature of DNN IP models coupled with the wide accessibility of edge devices, make them appealing targets for adversaries. If an attacker gains remote or physical access to a FPGA DNN accelerator, they may be able to reverse engineer the DNN model by exploiting side-channel leakages. These leakages include information from execution latency and memory access patterns [7,8], power consumption [9,10], electromagnetic emanation [11], etc. These side-channel attacks (SCAs) not only jeopardize the confidentiality of proprietary DNN models but can also pave the way for more potent adversarial attacks, such as adversarial examples [4] and membership inference attacks [5].

SCAs on FPGA-based DNN accelerators is still a nascent field of research. The work in [8] reverse engineered the structure of a convolutional neural network (CNN) model running on an FPGA-based accelerator by observing off-chip memory access patterns. They identified the number of layers, layer boundaries,

F. Palumbo et al. (Eds.): ARC 2023, LNCS 14251, pp. 146–158, 2023.
https://doi.org/10.1007/978-3-031-42921-7_10

connections between CNN layers, layer hyperparameters, and type of activation functions by distinguishing patterns of memory accesses to filters, input/output feature maps, etc. The work in [10] proposed a remote power SCA on a cloud-based FPGA accelerator, under the assumption that multi-tenancy (FPGA virtualization [12]) is enabled by the cloud ML provider. They deployed a hardware trojan circuit consisting of ring oscillators (RO) on the same FPGA board as the victim model. The frequency of the ROs fluctuate based on the operating state of the victim circuit, which is reflected by the victim's power trace. Power traces are collected as time series data, which is then used to train an inference model to predict the victim DNN architecture. The work in [13] presented a remote power SCA targeting the Versatile Tensor Accelerator (VTA) [6]. Time-to-digital converters (TDCs) are used to record voltage drops in the circuit during VTA's execution. Using the traces obtained from TDCs, they obtained the approximate configuration of GEMM instructions (input batch size, input and output channels) being executed on VTA. The work in [9] reverse engineered the weights of the DNN model running on a systolic-array based DNN accelerator. The attacker has physical access to the device and can measure the power consumption using physical probes. Using correlation power analysis (CPA) on the Hamming Distance of the accumulator register, they predicted the DNN model's weights.

To the best of our knowledge, none of the works in the literature explored the practicality of hardware trojan-induced SCAs on FPGA-based DNN accelerators on the edge. In this paper, we present a novel SCA that uses memory side-channel information to predict the structure of the victim DNN model being executed on an edge FPGA device. Our approach targets the widely-used VTA and employs a hardware trojan to monitor the AXI signals of VTA's submodules. The memory side channel information is leaked through a Universal Asynchronous Receiver-Transmitter (UART) port, which can be intercepted by an attacker with physical access to the device. We demonstrate that our hardware trojan can extract memory side channel information from the AXI signals, and the DNN's architecture can be predicted using this information. The main contributions of our paper are as follows:

1. We show that the AXI signals from the submodules of VTA provide insights into the DNN model's architecture, which can be exploited for model theft.
2. We present a hardware trojan with a stealthy triggering mechanism to extract memory side channel information from the AXI signals and leak this data through a UART port. The proposed hardware trojan has low overheads in terms of resource utilization, power consumption and execution time.
3. We demonstrate that the memory side channel information leaked by the hardware trojan can be used to predict DNN architecture characteristics such as model depth, layer types and layer hyperparameters, for widely-used DNNs such as ResNet18 and randomly constructed DNN models.

The rest of the paper is organized as follows. Section 2 gives a background on DNN architecture and VTA. In Sect. 3, we present our threat model, and describe our proposed attack and experiment setup used to evaluate its effectiveness. In Sect. 4, we present and discuss results of our experiments. We discuss directions for future research and conclude the paper in Sects. 5 and 6.

2 Background

2.1 Versatile Tensor Accelerator

The Versatile Tensor Accelerator (VTA) [6] is a customizable deep learning accelerator framework that is built upon the Apache TVM compiler stack. TVM is used to deploy deep learning models that are defined in popular frameworks such as PyTorch, TensorFlow, and MXNet, onto a variety of hardware, including CPUs, GPUs, and FPGAs. VTA serves as a FPGA accelerator backend for TVM that provides the benefits of specialized accelerators without compromising on flexibility. The VTA architecture, shown in Fig. 1, is designed as a Fetch ← Load ← Compute ← Store task pipeline, with its hardware organized based on the size of the GEMM core, the number of units in the tensor ALU, BRAM buffer sizes, and other parameters that can be customized to meet the demands of different deep learning (DL) workloads. VTA has gained interest due to its flexibility, which enables the deployment of evolving deep learning workloads on a variety of FPGAs. Its compatibility with off-the-shelf deep learning frameworks facilitates easy integration of DL software with specialized hardware, making it an attractive choice for several applications. Hence, we have chosen VTA as the target for our attack.

The TVM software stack transforms a DNN model defined in a high-level framework (e.g. PyTorch) into a computational graph. It schedules the workloads by tiling the computations and inserting virtual threading. The subcomputations of each layer of the DNN model are translated into a set of VTA instructions.

VTA's instruction set consists of 4 different types of instructions:

- LOAD - loads either a 2D tensor from the DRAM to the input/weight buffer, or a micro-op kernel to the micro-op cache.
- GEMM - executes a sequence of multiply and accumulate operations over input and weight tensors and stores the result in a register-file tensor.
- ALU - executes a sequence of arithmetic operations over tensor data stored in the register-file.
- STORE - transfers 2D tensor data in the output buffer to the DRAM.

Users also have the flexibility to execute some layers of the model on the CPU, while offloading the remaining layers to VTA.

For Xilinx FPGAs, VTA's pipeline tasks are implemented by four AXI memory-mapped peripherals (or IPs) - Fetch, Load, Compute and Store. These IPs communicate with each other via FIFO queues and local memory blocks implemented by Block RAMs (BRAM). They are connected to the processing system (PS) through AXI interfaces.

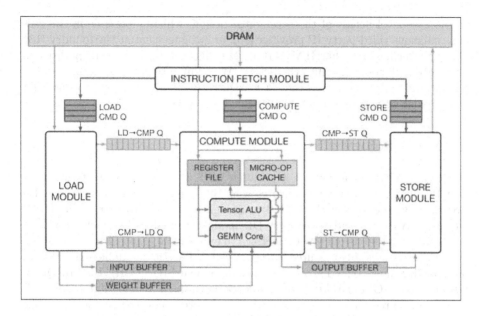

Fig. 1. VTA architecture, figure taken from [6].

2.2 Reverse Engineering DNN Architecture

To fully reverse engineer a DNN, the adversary would require information of the model's architecture and its parameters. The model's architecture encompasses the model depth (number of layers), type of each layer (convolution, fully connected, pooling, etc.), types of interconnections between the layers, and each layer's hyperparameters (input/output feature map dimensions, convolution kernel dimensions, number of neurons, pooling window dimensions, stride, padding, etc.). The model's parameters include layers' weight and bias matrices/vectors.

Previous research has shown that a substitute model from a reverse-engineered architecture is sufficient to create effective adversarial attacks ([7,14,15]). Obtaining the model's weights is only necessary if the attacker wants to create a substitute model that is functionally equivalent to the victim model ([21]). Predicting DNN model weights can be achieved using side channel analysis, such as correlation or differential power analysis (CPA/DPA) ([9,11]), which is tedious as a typical DNN model contains millions of parameters. Our paper focuses on predicting the victim model's architecture, rather than the weights, as the former is more practical and has high security impact (e.g., adversarial attacks on edge devices in autonomous vehicles).

2.3 Threat Model

In this work, we assume that the FPGA accelerator is deployed on the edge, making it physically accessible to potential adversaries. The attacker has access to the gate-level netlist of the accelerator design, which is possible in the case of a malicious third-party IP provider [16], or a rogue agent at the foundry [18]. The attacker has tools like HAL [17] at their disposal to modify the netlist and introduce malicious logic into the design. We assume that the attacker also has a high-level understanding of the VTA architecture, which is reasonable as VTA is a popular open-source DNN accelerator framework.

3   Methodology

We deploy VTA on a Zynq UltraScale+ MPSoC ZCU104 evaluation kit. A host PC running TVM communicates with the Linux OS running on the ARM Cortex-A53 processor of the ZCU104 through a remote procedure call (RPC) interface. We use TVM to convert DL models defined in PyTorch into VTA graph libraries and use the RPC interface to execute the graph libraries on VTA. We use Intel Labs' open source fork of TVM/VTA [19] to enable execution of max pooling layers on VTA. ZCU104 has an onboard FT4232HL USB-to-Quad-UART for JTAG and UART communications through a single micro-AB USB connector. Three out of the four UART ports are connected to the PS, while one is connected to the programmable logic (PL). We leverage the unused PL-side UART channel to leak side channel information to the adversary via the micro-AB USB connector.

3.1   Hardware Trojan Design

To detect patterns during the execution of a DNN model, our attack monitors the AXI interface signals of VTA's IPs, specifically the master AXI ports of the fetch, load, compute, and store modules. The compute module has two master AXI ports, one for micro-op kernels and the other for register file data. Our focus is on the AXI signals related to read operations for fetch, load, and compute modules, and on write operations for the store module. In our proposed attack, the *ARVALID* and *RVALID* signals for read operations and *AWVALID* and *WVALID* signals for write operations, are of importance. These signals indicate whether a channel is signaling valid read and write addresses, and transmitting valid read and write data, respectively.

   A significant number of clock cycles between two consecutive occurrences of the *ARVALID* signal in the fetch module implies the start of a new DNN layer, i.e., the fetch module is fetching instructions for a new DNN layer. During this interval, all the read and write transactions that occur in the load, compute, and store modules are associated with the operations performed in a single layer of the DNN model. The signals *RVALID* and *WVALID* denote the presence of valid data being read or written by the modules. By counting the number of occurrences of these signals and multiplying it with the size of each transferred data element, it is possible to determine the overall data volume that is being transferred during the execution of a DNN layer. This enables the identification of number of layers in the DNN model and the read/write volumes corresponding to each DNN layer. Figure 2 shows the timing diagram of AXI signals of VTA's sub-modules during the execution of two convolutional layers on VTA.

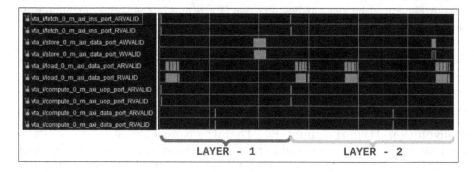

Fig. 2. AXI signals during execution of a DNN model with 2 convolutional layers. The large interval between two consecutive fetch_0_m_axi_ins_port_ARVALID signals indicates 2 different DNN layers.

Our hardware trojan is designed to monitor the intervals between successive ARVALID signals in the fetch module and track the data transmission volumes. These data volume counts, obtained from VTA's individual modules, are stored in FIFOs and subsequently transmitted through the UART port using a UART Tx module. To make the trojan more stealthy, we incorporate a triggering mechanism that activates the trojan only upon the receipt of a particular sequence of characters through the UART Rx port. Figure 3 shows the high-level design of the hardware trojan and an overview of the attack methodology.

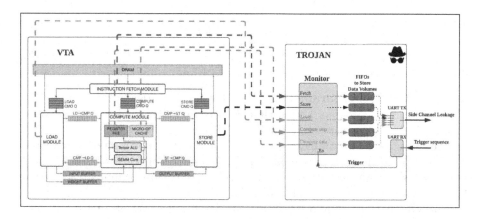

Fig. 3. Hardware trojan design and attack methodology.

3.2   Predicting the Layer Hyperparameters

Information regarding the number of layers in the DNN architecture and the read/write volumes associated with each layer is obtained through the serial output generated by the hardware trojan. Each line in the serial output represents a distinct layer. The transaction volumes are used to predict each layer's hyperparameters. The first convolutional layer and the final fully connected layer for classification are executed on the ARM CPU. These layers typically involve lower arithmetic intensity and perform well on CPUs [6]. The remaining layers are executed on VTA. We will describe our attack on models containing convolutions and max pooling layers in the following sub-sections.

Convolution Hyperparameters. The hyperparameters of a convolutional layer are input feature map height and width (I_h) and I_w), output feature map height and width (O_h, O_w), kernel height and width (K_h, K_w), input channels (IC), output channels (OC), stride (S) and padding (P). Most popular deep learning models use square matrices as inputs, output and kernels. Hence, we assume $I_h = I_w = I$, $O_h = O_w = O$ and $K_h = K_w = K$. These quantities are mathematically constrained as follows.

$$O = \lfloor (I + 2P - K)/S \rfloor + 1 \tag{1}$$

Also, the output feature map of a convolutional layer is the input feature map of the following layer i.e., $I^n = O^{n-1}$. The dimensions of the input feature map for the first convolutional layer can be estimated based on frequently used input image sizes for deep neural networks, such as 224x224 pixels. The write data volume (W_v) obtained from the VTA's store module is mathematically related to O and OC as below.

$$W_v = O * O * OC \tag{2}$$

$$\Downarrow$$

$$OC = W_v/(O * O) \tag{3}$$

Therefore, the prediction of K, P and S for any convolutional layer, enables the calculation of O from Eq. (1) and OC from Eq. (3).

Max-Pooling Hyperparameters. The same mathematical relationship in Eq. (1) applies to max-pooling layers. Here K is the pooling window size. OC of a max-pool layer is the same as the OC of the preceding layer.

We collected the hardware trojan side channel data for over 200 different convolution workloads used in popular DL models in PyTorch's torchvision model library (ResNet, AlexNet, VGG, Inception, etc.). The most common convolution kernel sizes used in these models are (1x1), (3x3), (5x5) and (7x7), with padding dimensions (0x0), (1x1) and (2x2), and strides 1 and 2. We also gathered data for commonly used max pooling workloads with window sizes (2x2) and (3x3), padding sizes (0x0) and (1x1), and strides 1 and 2. The side channel data is used to train XGBoost classifiers [20] for layer type identification (convolution or maxpool), and to predict K, P and S.

4 Experiment Results

In this section, we discuss the effectiveness of our attack in determining model depth, layer types and layer hyperparameters. In our experiments, we use a threshold interval of 50000 clock cycles (chosen empirically) between two successive DNN model layers.

4.1 Demonstration of Our Attack on ResNet18

To determine the number of layers being executed on VTA, we rely on number of lines in the serial output of the hardware trojan. Each line of the output contains 20 bytes of data, with 4 bytes coming from each of the fetch, load, compute_uop, compute_data, and store modules. The data from the fetch, load and compute modules represent read volumes in bytes, while that from the store module represents write volume in bytes. The hardware trojan outputs a line for each convolution and pooling operation being executed on VTA.

However, for other DNN computations such as batch normalization and activation functions (e.g., ReLU), TVM's graph optimizer combines these operations with the preceding convolution into a single fused VTA operation, resulting in no new instructions being fetched by the fetch module. As a result, the hardware trojan does not identify these computations as separate DNN layers.

Table 1. Demonstration of our attack on ResNet18.

S.No	Fetch	Store	Load	Compute_uop	Compute_data	Predicted layer type	Predicted (K, S, P)	Ground truth (K, S, P)
1	4848	200704	745472	464	1792	C	3, 1, 1	3, 1, 1
2	4624	200704	745472	464	1792	C	3, 1, 1	3, 1, 1
3	4848	200704	745472	464	1792	C	3, 1, 1	3, 1, 1
4	4624	200704	745472	464	1792	C	3, 1, 1	3, 1, 1
5	2832	100352	717824	744	2048	C	3, 1, 1	3, 2, 1
6	4240	100352	724992	800	1024	C	3, 1, 1	3, 1, 1
7	2704	100352	398848	128	2048	C	1, 2, 0	1, 2, 0
8	4368	100352	724992	800	1024	C	3, 1, 1	3, 1, 1
9	4240	100352	724992	800	1024	C	3, 1, 1	3, 1, 1
10	2256	50176	696320	1472	1024	C	3, 2, 1	3, 2, 1
11	3728	50176	790528	1472	1024	C	3, 1, 1	3, 1, 1
12	2192	50176	245248	128	2048	C	1, 2, 0	1, 2, 0
13	3792	50176	790528	1472	1024	C	3, 1, 1	3, 1, 1
14	3728	50176	790528	1472	1024	C	3, 1, 1	3, 1, 1
15	1888	25088	1280000	2760	2048	C	3, 1, 1	3, 2, 1
16	3392	25088	2409472	2760	2048	C	3, 1, 1	3, 1, 1
17	1856	25088	217600	128	2048	C	1, 2, 0	1, 2, 0
18	3424	25088	2409472	2760	2048	C	3, 1, 1	3, 1, 1
19	3392	25088	2409472	2760	2048	C	3, 1, 1	3, 1, 1

(a) Hardware trojan output - read/write volumes in bytes   (b) Predicted layer types and hyperparameters

Table 1 shows the side-channel information from the hardware trojan, and the predicted model depth, layer type, and layer hyperparameters for ResNet18. ResNet18 contains a total of 17 convolutional layers and one fully connected layer [22]. We assume that the first convolutional layer and the final fully connected layer are offloaded to the ARM CPU, while the remaining 16 convolutions are executed on VTA. These 16 convolutions are arranged into 8 residual blocks, with each block containing two 3x3 convolutions with the same number of output channels. To implement the skip connection between every alternate residual block's input and output, 3 additional 1x1 convolutions are used to ensure that the number of channels of the feature maps matches. Hence, a total of sixteen 3x3 convolutions and three 1x1 convolutions are executed on VTA. Table 1a shows that our hardware trojan's output accurately reflects the number of convolutions executed on VTA. From Table 1b, we see that the layer type classifier correctly identifies each layer as a convolution. The convolution hyperparmeters (K, S and P), are also predicted accurately for all layers except two.

4.2 Evaluation of Our Attack on Randomly-chained DNNs

We collected side channel data for 150 DNN models with chained convolutions randomly selected from a pool of over 200 convolution workloads. We also inserted maxpool operations into these networks, while ensuring that the selected convolutions and maxpool operations were dimensionally compatible. Our hardware trojan was able to accurately determine the number of layers in 130 out of the 150 models. The results from a sample 8-layer random network are presented in Table 2a and Table 2b. Additionally, Table 3 provides a summary of our classifiers' performance in predicting layer type and hyper-parameters for the 130 random networks.

Table 2. Demonstration of our attack on a 8-layer randomly-chained DNN.

S.No	Fetch	Store	Load	Comput_uop	Compute_data
1	25312	401408	11641888	10992	14336
2	5744	100352	8830976	36	1605632
3	1072	100352	724992	960	4096
4	592	50176	362496	484	2048
5	816	100352	362496	960	4096
6	400	25088	165888	512	512
7	1120	50176	618496	1380	2048
8	1648	12544	618496	16	200704

(a) Hardware trojan output - read/write volumes in bytes.

IFM dimensions	OFM dimensions	Predicted layer type	Ground truth layer type	Predicted (K, S, P)	Ground truth (K, S, P)
(28, 28, 256)	(28, 28, 512)	C	C	3, 1, 1	3, 1, 1
(28, 28, 512)	(14, 14, 512)	M	M	3, 2, 0	3, 2, 1
(14, 14, 512)	(14, 14, 512)	C	C	1, 1, 0	1, 1, 0
(14, 14, 512)	(14, 14, 256)	C	C	1, 1, 0	1, 1, 0
(14, 14, 256)	(14, 14, 512)	C	C	1, 1, 0	1, 1, 0
(14, 14, 512)	(14, 14, 128)	C	C	1, 1, 0	1, 1, 0
(14, 14, 128)	(14, 14, 256)	C	C	3, 1, 1	3, 1, 1
(14, 14, 256)	(7, 7, 256)	M	M	2, 2, 0	2, 2, 0

(b) Predicted layer types and hyperparameters.

Table 3. Layer type and hyperparameter prediction results for 130 random chained DNNs.

		Average F1 Score
Layer type		1.0
Convolution hyperparameters	K	0.9332
	S	0.9092
	P	0.929
Max-pool hyperparameters	K	1.0
	S	0.9619
	P	0.9619

From the results, it is evident that our attack is effective in identifying model depth, as well as convolution and max pooling hyperparameters. It also effectively distinguishes convolutions and max pooling operations from each other.

4.3   Hardware Trojan Overheads

We implemented the hardware trojan in Verilog and used Xilinx's Vivado tool suite to synthesize, place, and route the design. To measure the resource utilization and power consumption overheads, we referred to the post-implementation utilization and power analysis reports. Additionally, we measured the power and execution time overheads during VTA execution. To measure power during execution, we utilized the power sensors onboard ZCU104, with ResNet18 serving as the reference DNN workload for these measurements. The resource utilization overheads are presented in Table 4a as a percentage of the total available LUTs, FFs, and CARRY8s. From the power analysis report, we estimated the total on-chip power overhead as **0.45%**. Table 4b shows the power overheads during VTA execution and Table 4c shows the execution time overheads.

The results indicate that there is only a small resource utilization overhead. The impact on power consumption and execution times is negligible, as the measured values are within a margin of error. The implemented trigger enhances the trojan's stealthiness, as it cannot be detected if the end user attempts to probe the UART port when the trigger is off.

It is important to note that onboard power sensors often lack accuracy when measuring run time power consumption. Moreover, using PYNQ's PMBUS python library for power measurements allows low sampling rates and limited granularity. For more precise measurements of power consumption overheads, alternative tools such as current probes, power analyzers, or ring oscillator - based sensors are recommended.

5   Limitations and Future Work

Our trojan is limited in its ability to recognize certain aspects of the DNN architecture. For example, as mentioned in Subsect. 4.1, it cannot identify batch

Table 4. Trojan overheads

Utilization	VTA	VTA + Trojan	Overhead
LUT Utilization %	11.53	11.7	**0.17**
FF Utilization %	6.16	6.42	**0.26**
CARRY8 Utilization %	3.27	3.4	**0.13**

(a) Resource utilization overhead.

Power	VTA	VTA + Trojan (trigger off)	VTA + Trojan (trigger on)
Average (W)	11.84592	11.845869	11.842509
Peak (W)	12.554	12.566375	12.558125

(b) Average power consumption during execution of ResNet18, measured through the 12V power rail.

Execution time	VTA	VTA + Trojan (trigger off)	VTA + Trojan (trigger on)
Average (ms)	55.588072	55.531023	55.483124

(c) Average execution times of ResNet18, with and without the trojan present.

normalization and activation functions, nor can it interpret complex interconnections such as skip connections. Our attack can identify the 1x1 convolutions in the skip connections of ResNet18, but it is unable to determine their input feature map dimensions. The reason for this is that the inputs to the 1x1 convolutions are not the outputs of the convolution that immediately precedes them. Understanding these layer interconnections requires monitoring read-after-write (RAW) and write-after-read (WAR) memory dependencies. Additionally, our hardware trojan can infer DNN layers executed on the VTA, but not those executed on the ARM CPU. This is not a major drawback as typically the layers are executed on the VTA to take advantage of hardware acceleration.

Our future work will focus on enhancing the capabilities of the hardware trojan to overcome its current limitations. Specifically, we plan to equip the trojan with the ability to interpret RAW and WAR dependencies and to identify unique micro-op kernel signatures for various activation functions and batch normalization workloads.

6   Conclusion

This paper highlights the security concerns associated with the wide accessibility of FPGA DNN accelerators and presents a novel hardware trojan assisted side-channel attack to reverse engineer DNN models deployed on edge FPGA accelerators. By monitoring the AXI interface signals of VTA's submodules, our hardware trojan extracts memory side-channel information and leaks it through a UART port. Our experiments demonstrate that our trojan can effectively uncover key architectural details of DNN models with minimal overhead. This emphasizes the need for robust security techniques to be integrated into the design of FPGA DNN accelerators to mitigate potential security threats and maintain the confidentiality of the DNN model.

Acknowledgement. This work was supported in part by NTU-DESAY SV Research Program 2018–0980; and in part by the Ministry of Education, Singapore, under its Academic Research Fund Tier 2, under Grant MOE-T2EP20121-0008.

References

1. Simonyan, K., Zisserman, A.: Very deep convolutional networks for large-scale image recognition. arXiv preprint arXiv:1409.1556 (2014)
2. Vaswani, A., et al.: Attention is all you need. Adv. Neural Inf. Process. Syst. **30**, 5998–6008 (2017)
3. Luo, W., Sun, P., Zhong, F., Liu, W., Zhang, T., Wang, Y.: End-to-end active object tracking and its real-world deployment via reinforcement learning. IEEE Trans. Pattern Anal. Mach. Intell. **42**(6), 1317–1332 (2019)
4. Szegedy, C., et al.: Intriguing properties of neural networks. In: Proceedings of the 2014 Conference on Computer Vision and Pattern Recognition, IEEE (2014)
5. Shokri, R., et al.: Membership inference attacks against machine learning models. In: IEEE Symposium on Security and Privacy, IEEE (2017)
6. Moreau, T., et al.: A hardware-software blueprint for flexible deep learning specialization. IEEE Micro **39**(5), 8–16 (2019)
7. Hu, X., et al.: DeepSniffer: a DNN model extraction framework based on learning architectural hints. In: International Conference on Architectural Support for Programming Languages and Operating Systems - ASPLOS, pp. 385–399 (2020)
8. Hua, W., Zhang, Z., Suh, G.E.: Reverse engineering convolutional neural networks through side-channel information leaks. In: Proceedings of the 55th Annual Design Automation Conference, pp. 1–6, June 2018
9. Yoshida, K., Okura, S., Shiozaki, M., Kubota, T., Fujino, T.: Model reverse-engineering attack using correlation power analysis against systolic array based neural network accelerator. In: Proceedings - IEEE International Symposium on Circuits and Systems, pp. 42–46, October 2020
10. Zhang, Y., Yasaei, R., Chen, H., Li, Z., Faruque, M.A., et al.: Stealing neural network structure through remote FPGA Side-channel analysis. IEEE Trans. Inf. Forensics Secur. **16**, 4377–4388 (2021)
11. Batina, L., Bhasin, S., Jap, D., Picek, S.: CSI neural network: Using side-channels to recover your artificial neural network information. arXiv preprint arXiv:1810.09076 (2018)
12. Vaishnav, A., Pham, K.D., Koch, D.: A survey on FPGA virtualization. In: 2018 28th International Conference on Field Programmable Logic and Applications (FPL), pp. 131–1317. IEEE, August 2018
13. Tian, S., Moini, S., Wolnikowski, A., Holcomb, D., Tessier, R., Szefer, J.: Remote power attacks on the versatile tensor accelerator in multi-tenant FPGAs. In: 2021 IEEE 29th Annual International Symposium on Field-Programmable Custom Computing Machines (FCCM), pp. 242–246, May 2021
14. Wei, L., Luo, B., Li, Y., Liu, Y., Xu, Q.: I know what you see: power side-channel attack on convolutional neural network accelerators. In: Proceedings of the 34th Annual Computer Security Applications Conference (ACSAC 2018). Association for Computing Machinery, New York, NY, USA, pp. 393–406 (2018)
15. Liu, Y., Chen, X., Liu, C., Song, D.: Delving into transferable adversarial examples and black-box attacks. arXiv preprint arXiv:1611.02770 (2016)

16. Duncan, A., Rahman, F., Lukefahr, A., Farahmandi, F., Tehranipoor, M.: FPGA bitstream security: a day in the life. In: 2019 IEEE International Test Conference (ITC), pp. 1–10. IEEE, November 2019
17. Fyrbiak, M., et al.: Hal-the missing piece of the puzzle for hardware reverse engineering, trojan detection and insertion. IEEE Trans. Dependable Secure Comput. **16**(3), 498–510 (2018)
18. Perez, T., Imran, M., Vaz, P., Pagliarini, S.: Side-channel trojan insertion-a practical foundry-side attack via ECO. In: 2021 IEEE International Symposium on Circuits and Systems (ISCAS), pp. 1–5. IEEE, May 2021
19. Banerjee, S., et al.: A highly configurable hardware/Software stack for DNN inference acceleration. arXiv preprint arXiv:2111.15024 (2021)
20. Chen, T., Guestrin, C.: Xgboost: a scalable tree boosting system. In: Proceedings of the 22nd ACM sigkdd International Conference on Knowledge Discovery and Data Mining, pp. 785–794, August 2016
21. Jagielski, M., Carlini, N., Berthelot, D., Kurakin, A., Papernot, N.: High accuracy and high fidelity extraction of neural networks. In: Proceedings of the 29th USENIX Conference on Security Symposium, pp. 1345–1362, August 2020
22. He, K., Zhang, X., Ren, S., Sun, J.: Deep residual learning for image recognition. In: Proceedings of the IEEE Conference on Computer Vision and Pattern Recognition, pp. 770–778 (2016)

Towards Secure and Efficient Multi-generation Cellular Communications: Multi-mode SNOW-3G/V ASIC and FPGA Implementations

Evangelia Konstantopoulou[1,2]([envelope]) [ID], George S. Athanasiou[1] [ID], and Nicolas Sklavos[2] [ID]

[1] IC Services (ICS) Group, u-blox Athens S.A, Athens, Greece
{eva.konstantopoulou,george.athanasiou}@u-blox.com
[2] Computer Engineering & Informatics Department, SCYTALE Group, University of Patras, Patras, Greece
nsklavos@upatras.gr

Abstract. There is a definite upward trend in the number of cellular communication nodes that, together with high rate of digital content transactions, led to continuous progress on generational technologies (3G, 4G, 5G, and more recently 6G). To facilitate smooth deployments on multi-generation environments, communication systems have to be flexible, i.e., being able to support more than one security mechanisms. In this article, two multimode architectures are introduced, realizing both SNOW 3G and SNOW-V stream ciphers. The first SNOW-3G/V multimode architecture targets area efficiency. Thus, extensive and sophisticated resource sharing is performed, without degrading the overall performance. The second one, going one step further, aims at increasing the performance of underlying SNOW 3G mechanism through parallelism, without compromising the overall area efficiency. The introduced architectures are captured in SystemVerilog and implemented in FPGA (AMD Xilinx Virtex 7 - xc7v585tffg1761–3) and ASIC (22nm FD-SOI) technologies. Frequency, Area, and Throughput metrics are concerned and comparisons with existing implementations of individual SNOW 3G and SNOW-V mechanisms are made. Regarding the area, comparisons with the sum of the area of individual designs are also made. Experimental results showed that: (a) there is limited degradation of achieved performance of multimode architectures, (b) remarkable resource sharing is achieved in both multimode architectures, and (c) the overall performance of the proposed multimode architectures is great, comparable with almost all existing individual cipher designs. Finally, it has to be stressed that it is the first time that multimode designs are proposed that include SNOW 3G and SNOW-V mechanisms.

Keywords: 5G · cellular · SNOW 3G · SNOW-V · security · cryptography · ASIC · FPGA · multimode

F. Palumbo et al. (Eds.): ARC 2023, LNCS 14251, pp. 159–172, 2023.
https://doi.org/10.1007/978-3-031-42921-7_11

1 Introduction

Over the years, there is a significant increase in the number of cellular communication nodes as well as the amount and volume of data transmitted. This led to rapid progress of communication technologies, with more than one technology generations co-exist in cellular communication environments. The technological improvements from generation to generation, such as 3G, 4G, 5G, and the forthcoming 6G, are significant aiming at fast and responsive networks.

The latest 5G ecosystem provides very high data rates and higher coverage, with significantly improved Quality of Service (QoS) and extremely low latency. 5G began worldwide deployment in 2019 and will connect nearly all aspects of the human life to communication networks. Modern devices that will be connected with each other via 5G, spanning from traditional personal ones (e.g., smartphones, tablets and PCs) to smart appliances and vehicles, gather and analyze a high volume of data from different sources. Moving forward, 6G that is expected to be implemented around 2030 will further increase this volume and at the same time enable more devices in the network.

To facilitate compatibility and smooth deployments on multi-generation 3G/4G/5G/6G communication environments, flexible systems need to be able to support more than one communication protocols. Although this feature can be achieved by just implementing separate designs, a more efficient solution is the realization of multi-mode topologies that will be able to support more than one algorithm with one design. Such architectures significantly increase the flexibility of the whole communication module.

These high-demanding communication ecosystems form a challenging field regarding security and privacy, with increased threats and potential vulnerabilities. Cyberattacks may include Denial-of-Service (DoS), Eavesdropping, Tampering, and Spoofing. Thus, it is evident that there is a significant need for sufficient security-ensuring solutions based on cryptographic mechanisms. In cellular communications, confidentiality and integrity preserving algorithms based on SNOW, AES, and ZUC are used towards this direction.

Systems communicating within a multi-generation cellular environment are often resource-constrained, thus they need to be employed flexible security solutions. At the same time, it is important to meet specific performance requirements i.e., keeping throughput high-enough, to meet the applications' needs. To construct high performance systems in limited area resources, hardware solutions are essential. Figure 1 depicts the security threats of 3G through 5G, as well as the expected ones for 6G.

SNOW ciphers are word-based synchronous stream ciphers created by Patrik Ekdahl et. al. [1]. SNOW 1.0, introduced in 2000, was the first version of the mechanism [1]. An improved version, SNOW 2.0 was proposed later on, being stronger in terms of security [2]. After further modifications to increase the resistance against algebraic attacks, a new mechanism named SNOW 3G was introduced [3]. The latter is chosen from the third-generation partnership project (3GPP) to be included in the security mechanisms NEA and NIA, providing confidentiality and integrity, respectively, for 5G communications [4].

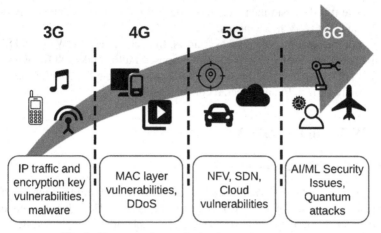

Fig. 1. The network security landscape from 3G to 6G.

In 2018, industry and university researchers developed a promising new cipher called SNOW-V, which is a thoroughly revised version of SNOW 3G showing increased 256-bit security level [5]. The main motivation for this algorithm was to move towards more speed-efficient realizations for 5G mobile communication systems.

Currently, there are several hardware designs of SNOW 3G algorithm, targeting performance or area efficiency. Most of these designs are implemented in FPGAs [6–12] and not in ASIC technologies [13]. Contrary, regarding SNOW-V, there fewer works regarding hardware designs [14–16]. What is more, it is apparent that both SNOW 3G and SNOW-V can play an important role in 5G security. SNOW 3G can offer backwards compatibility with 3G and 4G, whereas SNOW-V can be useful in encryption scenarios where high-throughput and a strong security level are needed. Therefore, there is a clear benefit in incorporating both ciphers in a single system that handles messages for multi-generation communications. In the literature, there are really few published works regarding multimode hardware implementations that consist of either SNOW-3G or SNOW V. SNOW-3G/ZUC-128 multi-mode hardware implementations are presented in [10, 17, 18], whereas a SNOW-V/ZUC-256 implementation was proposed in [19].

In this paper, two multimode architectures are introduced, realizing both SNOW 3G and SNOW-V stream ciphers. The first SNOW-3G/V multimode architecture targets area efficiency. Thus, extensive, and sophisticated resource sharing is performed, without degrading the overall performance. The second one, going one step further, aims at increasing the performance of underlying SNOW 3G mechanism through parallelism, without compromising the overall area efficiency. Two independent SNOW 3G operations are incorporated together with SNOW-V, achieving even higher throughput for SNOW 3G and at the same time not degrading SNOW-V performance. Experimental results showed that: (a) there is limited degradation of achieved performance of multimode architectures, (b) remarkable resource sharing is achieved in both multimode architectures, and (c) the overall performance of the proposed multimode architectures is great, comparable with almost all existing individual cipher designs. Finally, it has to be stressed that it is the first time that multimode designs are proposed that include both SNOW 3G and SNOW-V mechanisms.

The rest of the paper is organized as follows: In Sect. 2, the SNOW 3G and SNOW-V stream ciphers are briefly described. The proposed multi-mode SNOW-3G/V architectures are presented in detail in Sect. 3. In Sect. 4, the implementation results and comparisons are shown. Finally, Sect. 5 concludes the paper.

2 SNOW 3G and SNOW-V

2.1 The SNOW 3G Algorithm

SNOW 3G stream cipher receives a 128-bit key and a 128-bit initialization vector (IV) and generates a sequence of 32-bit words, i.e. the keystream. These keystream words as XORed with the 32-bit input data words producing ciphertext/plaintext words.

Algorithmic topology of SNOW 3G is shown in Fig. 2. Core parts of SNOW 3G are the following: functions MUL_a, DIV_a, and $MULxPOW$, the Linear Feedback Shift Register (LFSR) having 16 internal stages, each holding a 32-bit word, and a Finite State Machine (FSM) with two S-boxes S_1 and S_2. $MULxPOW$ maps 16 bits and a positive integer i to 8 bits. Let V and c be 8-bit input values, then if i equals 0, then $MULxPOW(V, i, c) = V$, else $MULxPOW(V, i, c) = MULx(MULxPOW(V, i-1, c), c)$. $MULx$ a function that maps 16 bits to 8 bits. Letting V and c be 8-bit input values: $MULx(V, c) = (V \ll_8 1) \oplus c$ if the MSB of V equals 1 or $MULx(V, c) = (V \ll_8 1)$ if not, where $\oplus$ is a bitwise XOR.

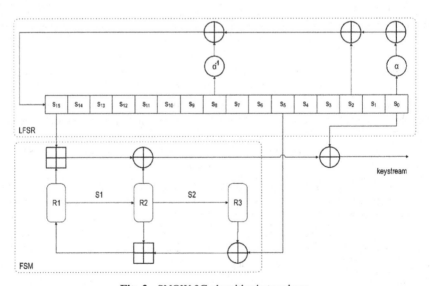

Fig. 2. SNOW 3G algorithmic topology.

Function MUL_a maps 8 bits to 32 bits. Letting c be the 8-bit input: $MUL_a(c)$ = $MULxPOW(c, 23, 0xA9)\|MULxPOW(c, 245, 0xA9)\|MULxPOW(c, 48, 0xA9)\|$ $MULxPOW(c, 239, 0xA9)$, where$\|$ denotes concatenation of two bitstreams.

The operation of SNOW 3G comprises of two modes that are performed consecutively, i.e. the *Initialization* and the *Keystream Generation*, respectively. During *Initialization* the input key and *IV* are consumed, the LFSR receives the 32-bit output of the FSM and no keystream / output produced. Right after, during the *Keystream Generation* the keystream is produced. During *Keystream Generation* the LFSR does not receive any input. R_1, R_2, R_3 are 128-bit registers and $\boxplus$ is an integer modulo 2^{32} addition.

2.2 The SNOW-V Algorithm

SNOW-V is based on the algorithmic pattern of all previous SNOW versions, consisting mainly of an LFSR part and an FSM part. The overall topology is shown in Fig. 3. The algorithm receives a 256-bit key and a 128-bit IV and generates a sequence of 128-bit keys. The LFSR is a circular construction including two interoperating Shift Registers (SRs), each feeding the other. Also, the FSM has three 128-bit registers and two instances of a single Advanced Encryption Standard (AES) encryption round function.

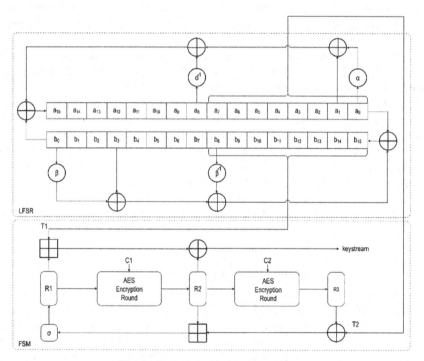

Fig. 3. SNOW-V algorithmic topology.

The two SRs of the LFSR structure are both of length 16 with a cell size of 16 bits. Each time the LFSR is updated, the two SRs are shifting 8 times, thus 256 bits will be updated in a single step, creating two new values of T_1 and T_2. FSM receives the T_1 and T_2 blocks and produces a 128-bit keystream as output. R_1, R_2, R_3 are the 128-bit registers and now $\boxplus$ denotes the parallel independent application of four modulo 2^{32} additions over 32-bit words, i.e., the carry does not propagate from a lower 32-bit word to the higher. Finally, zero round keys are considered for the two AES encryption rounds.

3 Proposed Multi-mode Architectures

This section describes the designed architectures. Firstly, a single area-efficient multi-mode architecture where the SNOW 3G and SNOW-V ciphers are combined is proposed. Then, an optimized version of this architecture in terms of performance is proposed. It supports the parallel operation of two SNOW 3G modules, thus offering double the throughput when encryption in this mode is selected.

3.1 SNOW-3G/V for Area Efficiency

The proposed design is an implementation of an architectural synthesis, consisting of ciphers SNOW-V and SNOW 3G, each of which are enabled on demand by the user (Fig. 4). A control signal allows data routing according to the choice of the encryption mode. Moreover, hardware components that are used for the functionality of both ciphers are shared for the highest area efficiency.

Firstly, the LFSR layer is shared, consisting of 16 register stages, each holding 32 bits. Out of these 32 bits, the SNOW-V cipher utilizes 16 bits in each cell for the design of the LFSR-A and 16 bits for the implementation of the LFSR-B.

In the Feedback layer, sub-block *mul_x* is re-designed to execute the GF(2^{16}) multiplication and division operations in SNOW-V, and to be used by functions $DIV\alpha$ and $MUL\alpha$ of SNOW 3G. The sub-block's inputs are the encryption mode signal, the operation mode signal, the two operands, and the coefficient number in the case of SNOW-V encryption. Following a parallel design for XORs, $DIV\alpha$ and $MUL\alpha$ computations, similarly to existing publications [15], the values of the 128-bit T_1 and T_2 are generated simultaneously in each clock cycle. The hardware section that refreshes the LFSR-A accepts the current values of the LFSR-A and the 128 least significant bits of the LFSR-B, and generates a 128-bit output, which is loaded into the most significant 128-bits of the LFSR-A. The 128 most significant bits of the LFSR-A are also loaded into the 128 least significant bits of LFSR-A in each clock cycle. LFSR-B is refreshed accordingly.

The 128-bit registers R_1, R_2, and R_3 of SNOW-V in the FSM layer are also used by SNOW 3G, but only the 32 least significant bits of each one. SNOW 3G also utilizes two of the eight parallel addition modulo 2^{32} adders that are implemented in SNOW-V, to execute two modulo 2^{32} additions. Based on the control selection of the desired cipher, the operands switch from the 32 least significant bits of $R_1 \boxplus_{32} T1$ and $R_2 \boxplus_{32} R_3 \oplus T_2$ to carry-out the additions in SNOW-V, to $s_{15} \boxplus_{32} R_1$, as well as $R_2 \boxplus_{32} s_5 \oplus R_3$ respectively to carry out the additions in SNOW 3G. What is more, another common element of the two ciphers is the usage of Rijandel's Sbox, which is manufactured using Look-Up Tables. Lastly, SNOW-V's 128-bit datapath is also shared by SNOW 3G, utilizing its 32 least significant bits.

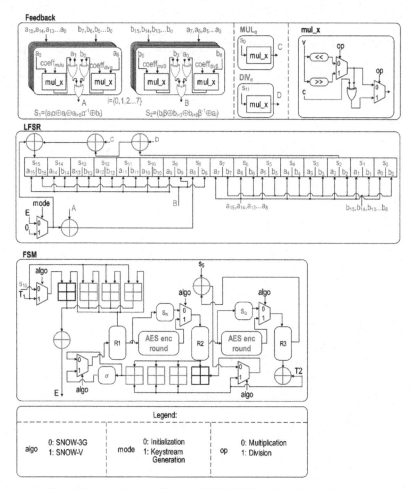

Fig. 4. Proposed area-efficient SNOW-3G/V multimode architecture.

3.2 SNOW-3G/V for High Performance

This design aims to achieving double the throughput when SNOW 3G encryption is selected. That is, two independent SNOW 3G realizations (denoted in this paper as SNOW-3G-1 and SNOW-3G-2), operate in parallel in a resource-sharing architecture combined also with SNOW-V encryption (Fig. 5). The architecture is described below.

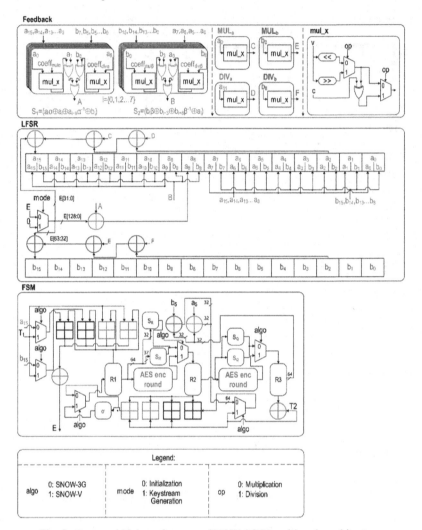

Fig. 5. Proposed high-performance SNOW-3G/V multimode architecture.

Firstly, the LFSR layer now consists of two LFSRs, one used by SNOW-3G-1 and the other by SNOW-3G-2. Both are of length 16 and with a cell size of 32 bits. SNOW-V uses SNOW-3G-1's LFSR to implement LFSR-A and LFSR-B. The shared hardware of the Feedback and FSM module is utilized by the second SNOW 3G in the same way the single SNOW 3G did, as described in the previous section. This time, four of the eight parallel modulo 2^{32} adders that are implemented in SNOW-V are used by the two SNOW 3Gs. When it comes to datapath sharing, one SNOW 3G will always occupy the 32 least significant bits of the 128-bit bus, with the second one occupying the 32 more important ones. The same principle applies to the storage of values in the three 128-bit registers of the FSM.

When two different 128-bit keys and 128-bit initialization vectors are inserted into the design, and SNOW 3G mode of operation is selected, a 64-bit keystream is produced every clock cycle, thus successfully executing two encryptions in parallel and doubling the achieved throughput.

4 Experimental Results and Comparisons

The introduced area-efficient (SNOW-3G/V-AE) and the high-performance (SNOW-3G/V-HP) were captured in SystemVerilog, verified over golden vectors provided by ETSI as well as using SW models for regression testing, and implemented in FPGA and ASIC technologies. Specifically, AMD Xilinx Virtex 7 (xc7v585tffg1761–3) and 22nm FD-SOI were used, respectively. The quality of the proposed architectures was measured in terms of Frequency, Area, and Throughput. Throughput is calculated taking into account that one word of the keystream is produced on every clock cycle, given the operational frequency. To offer a comparative analysis that will clearly showcase the value of the proposed designs and the trade-offs of using the multimode architectures, individual architectures of SNOW 3G and SNOW-V were used for comparisons. They were designed and implemented in the same technologies.

Table 1 presents the frequency of the individual and multimode architectures in FPGA and ASIC technologies. Regarding ASIC, 3ns period was set, thus 333 MHz operational frequency is achieved for all architectures. Concerning FPGA, as expected, individual architectures achieved better results due to the additional logic that is inserted in the multimode ones. However, this degradation was limited thanks to the careful addition of the extra logic.

Table 1. Frequency results and comparisons.

Architecture	Frequency (MHz)	
	FPGA	*ASIC*
SNOW 3G	448	333
SNOW-V	438	333
Proposed SNOW-3G/V-AE	380	333
Proposed SNOW 3G/V-HP	405	333

To further evaluate the proposed designs, area metrics are considered. Figures 6 and 7 presents the area of the individual and multimode architectures, as well as the sum of the area of the individual ones, for FPGA and ASIC implementations. Specifically, the first two bars correspond to the area of the individual architectures, the third bar correspond to the sum of the area of the individual architectures, whereas the last two bars correspond to the area of the proposed SNOW-3G/V-AE and SNOW-3G/V-HP ones.

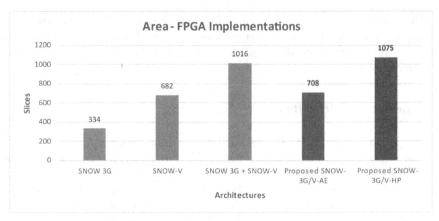

Fig. 6. Area comparisons of FPGA implementations.

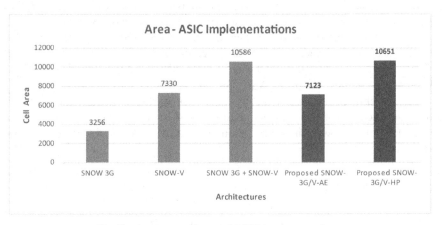

Fig. 7. Area comparisons of ASIC implementations.

Studying the FPGA implementations, it is derived that the area of the SNOW-3G/V-AE architecture (708 slices) is reduced by 30.3% compared the total area of the two individual designs (1016 slices). Concerning the SNOW-3G/V-HP architecture it is shown that the resulted area consumption is directly comparable to the one of the sum of two individual designs (negligible increase below 6%), even though it is able to support two parallel SNOW 3G computations. Similar conclusions are derived regarding ASIC implementations. Thus, the first outcome is that remarkable resource sharing is achieved in both multimode architectures.

Moving forward, Table 2 shows the resulted throughput in Gbps for the individual designs, as well as the proposed multimode, presented separately per cipher algorithm. Concerning ASIC implementations, there are not much to analyze except from the obvious doubling of the SNOW 3G HP throughput due to parallel execution of two independent SNOW 3G computations. Regarding FPGA implementations, beyond the double throughput of SNOW 3G HP it must be stressed that there is a degradation of throughput in the multimode architectures, ranging from 7.5% (SNOW-V) up to 15% (SNOW 3G). This small degradation is anticipated and is directly related with the small degradation of the maximum achieved operating frequency, analyzed in the beginning of this section, due to the additional logic that is inserted.

Table 2. Throughput results and comparisons.

Architecture	Throughput	
	FPGA	*ASIC*
SNOW 3G	14.34 Gbps	9.6 Gbps
SNOW-V	56.06 Gbps	38.4 Gbps
Proposed SNOW 3G AE	12.16 Gbps	9.6 Gbps
Proposed SNOW 3G HP	24.32 Gbps	19.2 Gbps
Proposed SNOW-V AE	48.64 Gbps	38.4 Gbps
Proposed SNOW-V HP	51.84 Gbps	38.4 Gbps

Finally, in Tables 3 and 4, a comparison of existing implementations of SNOW 3G and SNOW-V designs with the proposed multimode architectures is depicted. At this point it has to be stressed that comparing different implementation results based on different FPGA/ASIC structures and implementation options is almost impossible and sometimes unfair (e.g., in some cases the proposed architectures are not necessarily better, newer/better platforms are used, or different optimization techniques are employed). However, these comparisons are of value because they provide an overview of the status and state of the art regarding hardware implementations of SNOW 3G and SNOW-V ciphers and the relation of the proposed multimode ones with the corresponding research landscape. Another takeaway is that there are few published works regarding hardware implementations of SNOW-V.

Table 3. Performance and area comparisons with existing SNOW 3G architectures.

Reference	Platform (Family/Technology)	Metrics		
		Freq. (MHz)	*Area*	*Throughput (Gbps)*
[6]	FPGA (Xilinx Virtex-5)	322	188 Slices	10.3
[6]	FPGA (Xilinx Virtex-5)	376	356 Slices	12.04
[7]	FPGA (Xilinx Spartan-3A)	104	3559 Slices	3.33
[8]	FPGA (Xilinx Virtex-5)	28.84	-	0.92
[8]	FPGA (Xilinx Virtex-5)	287.81	-	8.3
[9]	FPGA (Xilinx Virtex-5)	28.84	-	0.92
[10]	FPGA (Xilinx Virtex-5)	309	-	6.29
[11]	FPGA (Altera Stratix V D8)	327.8	482 ALMs	10.49
[12]	FPGA (Xilinx Virtex-5)	226.6	-	7.22
Pr. SNOW 3G AE	FPGA (Xilinx Virtex-7)	380	708 Slices	12.16
Pr. SNOW 3G HP	FPGA (Xilinx Virtex-7)	405	1075 Slices	24.32
[11]	ASIC (SMIC 65 nm)	1000	11Kgates	32
[13]	ASIC (130 nm)	249	25K GEs	7.97
Pr. SNOW 3G AE	ASIC (FD-SOI 22 nm)	333	7123 Cell Area	9.6
Pr. SNOW 3G HP	ASIC (FD-SOI 22 nm)	333	10651 Cell Area	19.2

Table 4. Performance and area comparisons with existing SNOW-V architectures.

Reference	Platform (Family/Technology)	Metrics		
		Freq (MHz)	*Area*	*Throughput (Gbps)*
[14]	FPGA (Xilinx ARTIX 7)	224	530 Slices	2.6
[15]	FPGA (Xilinx Zynq UltraScale +)	637	384 CLBs	81.54
[15]	FPGA (Xilinx Zynq UltraScale +)	345	1367 CLBs	88.32
Pr. SNOW-V AE	FPGA (Xilinx Virtex-7)	380	708 Slices	48.64
Pr. SNOW-V HP	FPGA (Xilinx Virtex-7)	405	1075 Slices	51.84
[16]	ASIC (STM 90 nm)	134	4776 GEs	1.07
[16]	ASIC (TSMC 90 nm)	150	6210 GEs	1.19
[16]	ASIC (NanGate 15 nm)	5500	8227 GEs	44.7
Pr. SNOW-V AE	ASIC (FD-SOI 22 nm)	300	7123 Cell Area	38.4
Pr. SNOW-V HP	ASIC (FD-SOI 22 nm)	300	10651 Cell Area	38.4

5 Conclusions

In this paper, two SNOW-3G/V multimode architectures are introduced. They achieve high area efficiency, occupying same or less area compared to the sum of area resources of the corresponding individual architectures, with limited to no throughput degradation. Also, compared to existing individual implementations, their performance is not degraded. To the best of our knowledge, it is the first time that multimode designs are proposed that include both SNOW 3G and SNOW-V algorithms. Future research on SNOW-3G/V multimode architectures should propose further design optimizations in an algorithmic and circuit level, to lessen the trade-off between throughput and cost of resources. Also, depending on the frequency of switches between the two ciphers, dynamic partial reconfiguration could also be explored.

References

1. Ekdahl, P., Johansson, T.: SNOW – a new stream cipher. In: The NESSIE Submission Paper (2000)
2. Ekdahl, P., Johansson, T.: A new version of the stream cipher SNOW. In: Nyberg, K., Heys, H. (eds.) SAC 2002. LNCS, vol. 2595, pp. 47–61. Springer, Heidelberg (2003). https://doi.org/10.1007/3-540-36492-7_5
3. ETSI/SAGE. Specification of the 3GPP Confidentiality and Integrity Algorithms UEA2 & UIA2. Document 5: Design and Evaluation Report, Technical report (2006). https://www.gsma.com/aboutus/wp-content/uploads/2014/12/uea2designevaluation.pdf. Accessed 18 Feb 2022
4. ETSI/3GPP TS 33.501. Security Architecture and Procedures for 5G System, Version 15.4.0, Release 15, 3GPP (2019). https://www.etsi.org/deliver/etsi_ts/133500_133599/133501/15.04.00_60/ts_133501v150400p.pdf. Accessed 14 Feb 2022
5. Ekdahl, P., Johansson, T., Maximov, A., Yang, J.: A new SNOW stream cipher called SNOW-V. In: IACR Transactions on Symmetric Cryptology, vol. 2019(3), pp. 1–42 (2019). https://doi.org/10.13154/tosc.v2019.i3.1-42
6. Zhang, L., Xia, L., Liu, Z., Jing, J., Ma, Y.: Evaluating the optimized implementations of SNOW3G and ZUC on FPGA. In: IEEE 11th International Conference on Trust, Security and Privacy in Computing and Communications, Liverpool, UK, pp. 436–442 (2012). https://doi.org/10.1109/TrustCom.2012.150
7. Kitsos, P., Sklavos, N., Provelengios, G., Skodras, A.N.: FPGA-based performance analysis of stream ciphers ZUC, SNOW 3G, Grain V1, Mickey V2, Trivium and E0. Microprocess. Microsyst. 37(2), 235–245 (2013)
8. Madani, M., Benkhaddra, I., Tanougast, C., Chitroub, S., Sieler, L.: Digital implementation of an improved LTE stream cipher SNOW 3G based on hyperchaotic PRNG. Sec. Commun. Netw. 2017, 5746976 (2017). https://doi.org/10.1155/2017/5746976
9. Madani, M., Benkhaddra, I., Tanougast, C., Chitroub, S., Sieler, L.: FPGA implementation of an enhanced SNOW-3G stream cipher based on a hyperchaotic system. In: 4th International Conference on Control, Decision and Information Technologies (CoDIT), Barcelona, Spain, pp. 1168–1173 (2017). https://doi.org/10.1109/CoDIT.2017.8102758
10. Madani, M., Tanougast, C.: Combined and robust SNOW-ZUC algorithm based on chaotic system. In: 2018 International Conference on Cyber Security and Protection of Digital Services (Cyber Security), Glasgow, UK, pp. 1–7 (2018). https://doi.org/10.1109/CyberSecPODS.2018.8560677

11. Shen, C., et al.: An FPGA design and implementation of 4G network security algorithm based on SNOW3G. In: IEEE 19th International Conference on Software Quality, Reliability and Security Companion (QRS-C), Sofia, Bulgaria, pp. 387–392 (2019). https://doi.org/10.1109/QRS-C.2019.00078

12. Hulle, N.B., Prathiba, B., Khope, S.R., Anuradha, K., Borole, Y., Kotambkar, D.: Optimized architecture for SNOW 3G. Int. J. Electr. Comput. Eng. (IJECE) **11**(1), 545–557 (2021). https://doi.org/10.11591/ijece.v11i1.pp545-557

13. Kitsos, P., Selimis, G., Koufopavlou, O.: High performance ASIC implementation of the snow 3G stream cipher. In: Proceedings of the IFIP/IEEE VLSI-SOC, pp. 13–15 (2008)

14. Pyrgas, L., Kitsos, P.: 5G security: FPGA implementation of SNOW-V stream cipher. In: 2021 24th Euromicro Conference on Digital System Design (DSD), Palermo, Italy, pp. 381–384 (2021). https://doi.org/10.1109/DSD53832.2021.00064

15. Bahadori, M., Järvinen, K., Niemi, V.: FPGA implementations of 256-Bit SNOW stream ciphers for postquantum mobile security. In: IEEE Transactions on Very Large-Scale Integration (VLSI) Systems, vol. 29(11), pp. 1943–1954 (2021). https://doi.org/10.1109/TVLSI.2021.3108430

16. Caforio, A., Balli, F., Banik, S.: Melting SNOW-V: improved lightweight architectures. J. Cryptogr. Eng. **12**, 53–73 (2022). https://doi.org/10.1007/s13389-020-00251-6

17. Sen Gupta, S., Chattopadhyay, A., Khalid, A.: Designing integrated accelerator for stream ciphers with structural similarities. Crypt. Commun. **5**, 19–47 (2013). https://doi.org/10.1007/s12095-012-0074-6

18. Cavo, L., Fuhrmann, S., Liu, L.: Implementation of an area efficient crypto processor for a NB-IoT SoC platform. In: 2018 IEEE Nordic Circuits and Systems Conference (NORCAS): NORCHIP and International Symposium of System-on-Chip (SoC), Tallinn, Estonia (2018). https://doi.org/10.1109/NORCHIP.2018.8573517

19. Konstantopoulou, E., Athanasiou, G.S., Sklavos, N.: Securing 5G/6G communications in SmartCities: novel SNOW-V/ZUC-256 multimode architectures. In: The 2023 International Conference on Security and Management (SAM 2023), Las Vegas, USA (2023)

A Convolution Neural Network Based Displaced Vertex Trigger for the Belle II Experiment

Kai Unger[1]([✉]) [iD], Jürgen Becker[1] [iD], Christian Kiesling[2] [iD], Yichuan Ma[1],
Felix Meggendorfer[2], Marc Neu[1] [iD], Elia Schmidt[2], and Ulrike Zweigart[1]

[1] Institut für Technik der Informationsverarbeitung,
Engesserstraße 5, 76131 Karlsruhe, Germany
kai.unger@kit.edu
[2] Max-Planck-Institut für Physik, Föhringer Ring 6, 80805 München, Germany
https://www.itiv.kit.edu/ , https://www.mpp.mpg.de/

Abstract. The Belle II experiment in Tsukuba, Japan, searches for physics beyond the Standard Model. Electrons and positrons are accelerated in the SuperKEKB collider to collide at the interaction point in the Belle II detector. Since the resulting data volume is too large, a multi-stage trigger system is installed to sort out physically irrelevant events. In order to find decays with displaced vertex, which are candidates for the indirect detection of dark matter, the FPGA-based level 1 trigger has to be upgraded. A convolution neural network (CNN) with parallel convolution presented in this work enables the finding of displaced vertex tracks. To do this, the CNN must process 32,000,000 frames per second in parallel and provide an estimate of the origin of these tracks for each frame. The complete system has been successfully implemented on the FPGA platform (XCVU160) used in the experiment and meets the specified requirements of the trigger system.

Keywords: FPGA · CNN · Belle II

1 Introduction

The Belle II experiment, located in Tsukuba, Japan, aims to discover new physics by accelerating electrons and positrons in the SuperKEKB accelerator and colliding them in the Belle II detector, resulting in a luminosity record of $L = 4.7 \cdot 10^{34}$ cm^{-2}s^{-1} on June 2022 [1]. The resulting decay products are measured to identify deviations from the Standard Model of particle physics, providing insight into new theories. The experiment comprises various detectors, including the pixel detector (PXD) and the strip vertex detector (SVD), both situated closest to the interaction point (IP) or collision point. The Central Drift Chamber (CDC), which is crucial for track reconstruction, surrounds these detectors. The CDC contains 14,336 sense wires and 42,240 field wires, and each sense wire is surrounded by eight field wires. These sense wires are organized into 56 layers and combined in 9 so-called super layers (SL). The chamber is filled with gas that gets ionized by particles flying through. This ionization resulting in

F. Palumbo et al. (Eds.): ARC 2023, LNCS 14251, pp. 173–184, 2023.
https://doi.org/10.1007/978-3-031-42921-7_12

a current flow from the field wires to the sense wires, is measured to reconstruct the track. The present work focuses on the tracks from the CDC. The CDC is further encompassed by the Electromagnetic Calorimeter (ECL), which gives us the energy information from a particle, and the KL Muon Detector (KLM), which detect Muones [2].

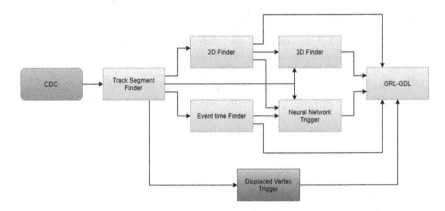

Fig. 1. Belle II CDC level 1 trigger chain. In red the new CNN based displaced vertex trigger system presented in this work. (Color figure online)

Figure 1 illustrates the CDC trigger chain. The data from the 14,336 sensing wires are continuously read out at a rate of 32 MHz and sent to the Level 1 Trigger System in a reduced data format. These data contain various timing information as well as a one-bit hit information [3]. The trigger system has 5 μs for the entire processing from the readout from the detector to the final decision. The transmission of data between the individual systems takes place via latency-optimized fiber optics. The entire detector data is pre-filtered by the Track Segment Finder (TSF) [4] with a geometric filter and then forwarded to the following systems. The Event Time Finder [5] primarily receives timing information to determine the collision time. The 2D Finder, on the other hand, receives hit information with, which it performs a 2D Hough transformation to determine a track. This 2D track serves as the basis for the 3D Finder [6], which performs a 3D Hough transformation, and the Neural Network Trigger [7], which estimates the origin of the collision on the z-axis and the polar scattering angle with the help of the 2D track. The Displaced Vertex Trigger presented in this work operates on the hit information provided by the TSF and runs parallel to the existing trigger system. Finally, all the information collected in the trigger systems is delivered to the Global Reconstruction Logic, which matches the information from different detectors, and the Global Decision Logic, which decides whether to record an event or not based on the information from all trigger systems bevor [8].

2   State of the Art

High-energy physics experiments, particularly their trigger systems, have unique hardware requirements, making it challenging to compare them with one another. The application of neural network-based triggers is even more limited. One of the early instances of a neural network trigger system [9,10] was employed in the level 2 trigger of the H1 experiment at DESY in Hamburg. In this case, pattern recognition was performed on specialized CNAPS chips. By utilizing physics information from the level 1 trigger, a neural network was employed to improve decision-making.

Another example of a currently utilized neural network trigger system [11–14] can be found in the Belle II level 1 trigger. This system comprises a multilayer perceptron (MLP) with 27 inputs, 81 hidden layer neurons, and two outputs. The MLP calculates the origin of a particle on the beam axis and the polar scattering angle of the particle. This information is used to implement a z-cut to identify the collision origin. The found origin serves as a noise filter and an unbiased singular track trigger. The system has been operational in the experiments since 2019.

Neural network triggers on FPGA Hardware are also being developed for experiments at CERN, specifically for the phase 2 update in 2024. The CMS detector will receive an auto-encoder-based anomaly detector [15], and there is a prototype for a CNN-based calorimeter trigger [16] for the CMS experiment.

To simplify the implementation of neural networks, CERN has developed the hls4ml framework [17–20], which is also used in this work. The aim of this framework is to enable the automated implementation of neural networks on FPGA for level 1 trigger systems. It emphasizes crucial properties in physics experiments, such as low latency and high data throughput.

Another overview is given in the white paper [21] resulting from the Fast Machine Learning workshop.

3   Concept of a Displaced Vertex Trigger

The expansion of the L1 trigger system aims to detect displaced vertex tracks and determine their specific displaced vertex. These decays hold potential as candidates for dark matter research. It is crucial to identify cases where two electrons emerge from the displaced vertex to exclude triggering events caused by known effects like electron scattering.

Figure 2 illustrates selected instances of displaced vertex decay events within the Central Drift Chamber (CDC) as a cross-section. The interaction point (IP) where the beams intersect, and new decay products are formed is situated at the center of the figure. In a typical particle decay, the particle track emanates from the IP and extends outward. The current L1 trigger system is optimized for decays originating from the IP. Particles originating from outside the IP are currently classified as background and discarded at the L1 stage. The cross symbol represents the origin of the displaced vertex, while the dots indicate the resulting particle tracks.

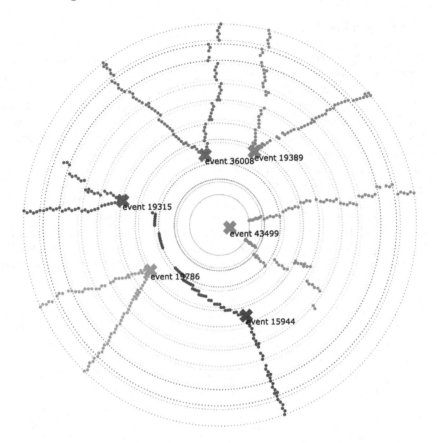

Fig. 2. 6 example events vertices in the displaced vertices dataset

In this study, we focus on determining the offset origin of these two tracks using a Convolutional Neural Network (CNN). By employing the CNN, we aim to identify the precise location of the displaced vertex in these specific cases.

To interpret each wire as a pixel in a black-and-white image (with values of 1 or 0), the system needs to satisfy the experiment's latency requirements of processing time below 1 microsecond (μs). Additionally, it must handle the high data rate of 32,000,000 frames per second (fps). Furthermore, the system needs to be compatible with the low latency Universal Trigger Boards 4 (UT4), which are specifically designed for the experiment and feature a Xilinx Ultrascale 160 (XCVU160) FPGA.

Unlike a typical camera, it is crucial that all data arrives at the system in parallel and is processed in parallel. This parallel processing capability is essential to handle high-speed data and meet the real-time processing requirements of the experiment.

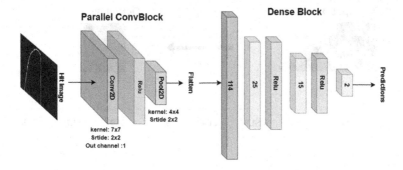

Fig. 3. Basic structure for the CNN Architecture of the displaced vertex trigger

Figure 3 illustrates the structure of the basic CNN. It begins with a convolutional layer, which performs feature extraction, followed by a pooling layer. Subsequently, the classification process takes place, utilizing a flattening layer and several fully connected layers. For all layers, the Rectified Linear Unit (ReLU) function is employed as the activation function. The output of the CNN represents the coordinates of the track's origin in the x and y dimensions.

3.1   Hit Image Converter

Before utilizing the CNN, preprocessing of the incoming data is necessary. The incoming data consists of hit information, indicating whether a sensor wire has been triggered or not. The CDC detector is constructed in a circular shape around the interaction point (IP) to provide complete 360-degree coverage. The circular data is split at a specific point to generate a 2-dimensional image.

To maintain uniform resolution as the radius increases, the inner sensor layer consists of 160 wires, while the outer sensor layer consists of 384 wires. However, this results in non-uniformity in the image. The 56 sensor layers are organized into 9 super layers (SL) according to a predetermined combination, where each layer is a multiple of 32 Table 1.

To achieve better results, a mapping rule is applied to obtain a uniform image. The detector is mapped onto a 160 × 56 image. This mapping results in merging several sensor wires into one pixel in the outer layers, as depicted in Fig. 4. Consequently, an 8,960-pixel image is obtained from the 14,336 sensor wire inputs, leading to a reduction in input data by 37.5%. This reduction causes lower resolution in the outer SL, but it is deemed acceptable since determining the vertex in that region is challenging due to the short tracks resulting from those layers.

Table 1. Sens wire per SL

SL0	SL1	SL2	SL3	SL4	SL5	SL6	SL7	SL8
160	160	192	224	256	288	320	352	384
5	5	6	7	8	9	10	11	12

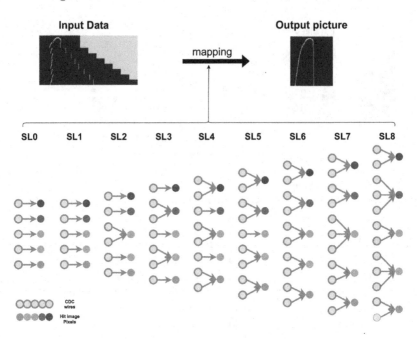

Fig. 4. Mapping rules for the input data for each SL

3.2   Parallel Convolution Layer

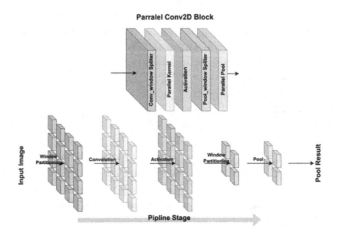

Fig. 5. Structure of the CNN's parallel convolution unit

In our case, where all input data is available in parallel and low latency is essential, it is crucial to ensure parallel processing in the convolution layer. The initial approach was to utilize standard tools like hls4ml for network synthesis on

FPGA. However, a limitation arises due to the for-loop unrolling in Vivado High-Level Synthesis (HLS), as hls4ml currently supports only Vivado HLS 2020.1, while the newer versions of Vitis HLS are only supported experimentally. This limitation is not significant for most applications, such as camera image processing, where the image is processed pixel by pixel. However, in our scenario, an alternative solution is needed (Fig. 5).

One possible approach is to divide the image into smaller sections and process them in parallel using multiple CNNs. However, this approach has the disadvantage of reduced recognition accuracy for longer tracks. Hence, in this work, the Convolution operation itself was implemented to overcome this limitation. The convolution kernel is fixed to a predefined 2D matrix. It should be noted that this choice may have a slight impact on the accuracy of the model. However, the primary objective is to significantly enhance processing speed, which is crucial for practical applications of the model.

The convolution layer, including the convolution kernel, consists of a multiplier with weights and a pipeline-add pipeline tree. A hardware generator can automatically generate the entire convolution layer, facilitating adjustments and customization as needed.

3.3   Training

During the training process, a baseline model is initially created using Keras. This baseline model is then trained using a dataset consisting of created hit images. The data set contains 11 million simulated decays with a displaced vertex. For each hit image, the known origin from the simulation is utilized as the target or objective function for training. Since the output represents a 2D coordinate, the Mean Squared Error (MSE) is employed as the loss function to measure the dissimilarity between the predicted and target coordinates.

Following the training of the baseline model, the best configuration is selected and rebuilt using QKeras. In this step, the standard Keras layers are replaced with QLayers, which are designed specifically for quantization-aware training. A fixpoint value of <16.8> bit is employed for quantization during this process.

Subsequently, the QKeras model undergoes another round of training to further refine its performance. This training process takes into account the quantization aspects, ensuring that the model is trained to produce accurate results even with reduced precision due to quantization.

3.4 Hardware Generator

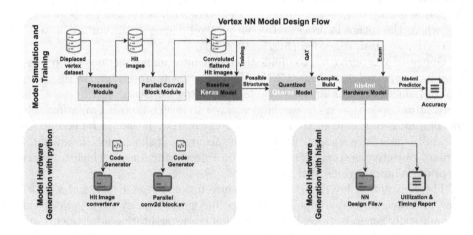

Fig. 6. The toolfolow from a dataset to the generated hardware

A Python-based tool flow has been developed to facilitate the generation of hardware, as depicted in Fig. 6. This tool flow leverages a collection of Dark Matter events as input. Initially, events from the Belle II simulation are utilized, which can later be substituted with real experimental data. The data is processed within the processing module, which encompasses the mapping and conversion of the hit image. In this module, the data is resized to achieve a uniform image size. Subsequently, a Verilog module is automatically generated from the Python code to execute this mapping process.

The processed data is then fed into the parallel Conv2d block module, where the convolution operation is performed, and the results are stored as new training data. Additionally, the corresponding convolutional hardware code is generated to ensure consistency between the training data and the hardware implementation. The automated hardware generation process guarantees that the training data aligns with the hardware specifications, and any necessary modifications to the mapping or convolution can be quickly implemented.

The newly generated training data is employed to train a Multi-Layer Perceptron (MLP). Various configurations of the MLP are trained on the software side using QKeras. The best design is then selected and synthesized using hls4ml, a tool that enables the synthesis of neural networks onto FPGAs. By utilizing the generated hardware modules and the trained MLP, a CNN trigger with pipelines is constructed. This iterative process can be repeated at each step to further enhance the performance and effectiveness of the trigger system. Furthermore, a comprehensive software simulation of the trigger is available for analysis by physicists involved in the experiment. This tool flow ensures the consistency between the software and hardware code, eliminating the need for time-consuming adaptation and maintenance of trigger software simulation and actual hardware code.

4 Result

Using the designfolow described earlier, a range of Vertex MLP Qkeras models are investigated for potential improvements. The Table 2 shows the training outcomes using the same flattened dataset with different MLP configurations. These models are then subjected to quantization-aware training, although the optimization of the training was not the aim of this paper. From experience with previous neural network triggers, we know that resolution improves as soon as training is switched from simulated data to real data.

The Qkeras MLP model with a hidden layer configuration of 20, 15 achieves the highest accuracy and is subsequently used for further FPGA firmware generation with Hls4ml and with our approach.

When combining the Hls4ml MLP Model with the developed Parallel ConvBlock in Table 3, there is a slight decrease in accuracy due to the fixed convolution kernel parameters. However, the hls4ml-generated MLP model shows significant disadvantages in terms of stage latency and total latency. Or short of saying it doesn't meet the latency requirement from the Belle II L1 Trigger System with $<1\,\mu s$.

Table 4 provides a comparison of resource usage, specifically Block RAM (BRAM), DSP, and Lookup Tables (LUT), for the implemented design.

When the MLP model is integrated with additional components, such as the hit image converter, the configured parallel ConvBlock, and a Gigabit Transceiver module, a fully functional operational setup is established. The

Table 2. Accuracy and timing report of the implemented NN module

Hidden layer 0	Hidden layer 1	Parameter	Train Error	Val. Error
25	25	3525	11.60 cm	11.94 cm
25	20	3390	11.79 cm	12.04 cm
25	15	3255	11.23 cm	11.58 cm
25	10	3120	12.46 cm	12.84 cm
25	5	2850	12.84 cm	13.14 cm
20	20	2720	11.77 cm	12.02 cm
20	15	2610	10.97 cm	11.14 cm
20	10	2500	11.84 cm	12.44 cm
20	5	2390	13.23 cm	13.54 cm
15	15	1965	13.19 cm	13.28 cm
15	10	1880	13.02 cm	13.14 cm
15	5	1795	13.45 cm	13.64 cm

Table 3. Model performance and timing report

	precision	latency clk	latency
hls4ml CNN	7.25 cm	8978	71,82 μs
parallel CNN (our)	10.83 cm	24	192 ns

Table 4. Resources used on a Xilinx XCVU160 FPGA

Model	DSP	BRAM_18K	LUT
Hit Image converter	0%	0%	1%
Parallel ConvBlock	0%	0%	5%
Vertex MLP	75%	0%	19%
Full System	76%	8%	22%

results reveal that the complete system utilizes only a portion of its available resources, suggesting significant room for further optimization. This surplus of resources presents opportunities to enhance the model's capabilities, improve system performance, or incorporate additional features to create a more robust and efficient solution.

5   Summary

The design of the displaced vertex trigger is implemented and tested using a dataset of simulated events from the Belle II experiment. The dataset contained examples of displaced vertex decay events within the Central Drift Chamber (CDC) detector. The goal is to determine the origin of the two electron tracks originating from the displaced vertex.

Before feeding the data into the CNN, a preprocessing step is performed to convert the hit information from the CDC detector into a 2D image format. This involved mapping the sensor wires onto a 160×56 image grid, where each pixel represented the presence or absence of a hit on a wire. The mapping process ensured uniform resolution across the detector.

A Convolutional Neural Network (CNN) architecture is employed for this work. The CNN consisted of multiple layers, including convolutional layers for feature extraction, pooling layers for downsampling, and fully connected layers for classification.

To handle the high data rate and low latency requirements of the Belle II experiment, a parallel convolution layer was developed. This layer performed the convolution operation in parallel, allowing for efficient processing of the incoming data. The convolution kernel was fixed to a predefined 2D matrix, which simplified the hardware implementation.

The CNN model was trained using the simulated dataset, with the known origins of the electron tracks serving as the target values. The model was initially trained using Keras and then refined using QKeras, which enabled quantization-aware training to handle reduced precision due to quantization.

A hardware generator tool flow was developed to automate the generation of hardware code from the trained CNN model. The tool flow processed the dataset, performed the mapping and conversion of the hit information, and generated Verilog modules for the hardware implementation. The training data was used to train a Multi-Layer Perceptron (MLP) on the software side using QKeras. The best MLP design was synthesized using hls4ml, enabling the synthesis of the neural network onto FPGAs.

The results of the study demonstrated the feasibility of implementing a displaced vertex trigger using a CNN architecture. The trained CNN model achieved an accurate determination of the origin of the electron tracks from the displaced vertex. The hardware implementation of the trigger system showed promising performance, meeting the high-speed data processing requirements of the Belle II experiment.

The automated hardware generation process ensured consistency between the software and hardware code, allowing for quick iterations and enhancements of the trigger system. A software simulation of the trigger system was also available for further analysis by physicists involved in the experiment.

Overall, the results of the study showed the potential of using neural network-based triggers, specifically CNNs, in high-energy physics experiments. The displaced vertex trigger presented in this work provided a new capability for identifying and studying decays originating from displaced vertices, which are of particular interest in dark matter research.

Acknowledgments. Funded by the German Federal Ministry of Education and Research under "Verbundprojekt 05H2021 (ErUM-FSP T09) - Belle II: Pixeldetektor, Software und erste Datenanalysen"

References

1. Belle II Collaboration. Accessed 03 May 2023. https://www.belle2.org/
2. Abe, T.: Belle II Collaboration 2010 "Belle II Technical Design Report". arXiv arXiv:1011.0352
3. Lai, Y.T., et al.: Development of the Level-1 track trigger with Central Drift Chamber detector in Belle II experiment and its performance in SuperKEKB 2019 Phase 3 operation. J. Instrument. **15**(06), C06063 (2020)
4. Unger, K.L., Bähr, S., Becker, J., Iwasaki, Y., Kim, K., Lai, Y.T.: Realization of a state machine based detection for Track Segments in the trigger system of the Belle II experiment. In: Proceedings of Topical Workshop on Electronics for Particle Physics Proceedings of Science, vol. 370 (2020). https://doi.org/10.22323/1.370.0145
5. Won, E., Moon, H.: Development of an event time finding algorithm for multi-wire drift chamber-based Level-1 trigger system in the Belle II experiment. J. Korean Phys. Soc. **80**, 1–6 (2022)
6. Won, E., Kim, J.B., Ko, B.R.: Three-dimensional fast tracker for the central drift chamber based level-1 trigger system in the Belle II experiment. J. Korean Phys. Soc. **72**(1), 33–37 (2018). https://doi.org/10.3938/jkps.72.33

7. Baehr, S., et al.: Low latency neural networks using heterogenous resources on FPGA for the Belle II trigger. In: Connecting the Dots and Workshop on Intelligent Trackers (2019)

8. Iwasaki, Y., Cheon, B., Won, E., Varner, G.: Level 1 trigger system for the Belle II experiment. In: 2010 17th IEEE-NPSS Real Time Conference, pp. 1–9. IEEE (2010)

9. Köhne, J.K., et al.: "Realization of a second level neural network trigger for the H1 experiment at HERA" nuclear instruments and methods in physics research section A: accelerators. Spectromet. Detect. Assoc. Equip. **389**, 128–133 (1997). https://doi.org/10.1016/S0168-9002(97)00062-4

10. Kiesling, C.M., et al.: The H1 neural network trigger project. In: AIP Conference Proceedings, vol. 583, pp.36–44 (2002). https://doi.org/10.1063/1.1405259

11. Baehr, S., et al.: A neural network on FPGAs for the z-vertex track trigger in Belle II. J. Instrument. (2017). https://doi.org/10.1088/1748-0221/12/03/C03065

12. Baehr, S., et al.: Data reduction and readout triggering in particle physics experiments using neural networks on fpgas. In: 2018 IEEE 18th International Conference on Nanotechnology (IEEE-NANO), pp. 1–4 (2018). https://doi.org/10.1109/NANO.2018.8626239

13. Baehr, S., et al.: Low latency neural networks using heterogenous resources on fpga for the Belle II trigger. arXiv https://doi.org/10.48550/arXiv.1910.13679 (2019)

14. Unger, K.L., et al.: Operation of the neural z-vertex track trigger for Belle II in 2021-a hardware perspective. In: Journal of Physics: Conference Series (2023). https://doi.org/10.1088/1742-6596/2438/1/012056

15. Hartmann, F., et al.: The phase-2 upgrade of the CMS level-1 trigger. CERN-LHCC-2020-004, CMS-TDR-021 (2020)

16. Alimena, J., et al.: Fast convolutional neural networks for identifying long-lived particles in a high-granularity calorimeter. J. Instrument. **15**, P12006 (2020). https://doi.org/10.1088/1748-0221/15/12/P12006

17. Duarte, J., et al.: FPGA-accelerated machine learning inference as a service for particle physics computing. Comput. Softw. Big Sci. **3**(1), 1–15 (2019). https://doi.org/10.1007/s41781-019-0027-2

18. Coelho, C.N., Kuusela, A., Zhuang, H., Aarrestad, T., Loncar, V., Ngadiuba, J., et al.: Automatic deep heterogeneous quantization of deep neural networks for ultra low-area, low-latency inference on the edge at particle colliders. Nat. Mach. Intell. (2020). https://doi.org/10.1038/s42256-021-00356-5

19. Loncar, V., Pierini, M., Summers, S., Di Guglielmo, G., Duarte, J., Harris, P., et al.: Compressing deep neural networks on FPGAs to binary and ternary precision with hls4ml. Mach. Learn. 2, 015001 (2020). https://doi.org/10.1088/2632-2153/

20. Aarrestad, T., Loncar, V., Ghielmetti, N., Pierini, M., Summers, S., Ngadiuba, J., et al.: Fast convolutional neural networks on FPGAs with hls4ml'. Mach. Learn. Sci. Tech. **2**, 045015 (2021). https://doi.org/10.1088/2632-2153/ac0ea1

21. Deiana, A., et al.: Applications and techniques for fast machine learning in science. Front Big Data Sec. Big Data AI High Energy Phys. **5**, 787421 (2022). https://doi.org/10.3389/fdata.2022.787421

On-FPGA Spiking Neural Networks for Multi-variable End-to-End Neural Decoding

Gianluca Leone[(✉)], Luca Martis, Luigi Raffo, and Paolo Meloni

Università degli studi di Cagliari, Cagliari, Italy
{gianluca.leone94,raffo,paolo.meloni}@unica.it,
l.martis2@studenti.unica.it

Abstract. In the field of brain-machine interface (BMI), deep learning algorithms have been steadily advancing as the go-to instrument for the key task of neural decoding. However, to function in real-time on portable devices, these algorithms must adhere to stringent limitations on computational power and memory. In this work, we exploit spiking neural networks (SNNs) within a real-time neural decoding system deployed on a low-end Artix-7 FPGA. The system is capable of decoding the spike activity in intracortical neural signals, recorded by a 96-channels microelectrode array, to continuously and concurrently track five target variables in a reach-to-grasp experiment. We have assessed our approach on a widely used reference dataset, achieving a decoding accuracy comparable with alternatives in literature, which exploit more complex deep learning models on the same dataset to decode a single target variables. Our system uses around 20 times less parameters than other non-SNN approaches and consumes 56.4 mW.

Keywords: Neural decoding · SNN · FPGA · Low power

1 Introduction

Brain-machine interface (BMI) is a constantly evolving area of scientific study and technological development, with the ultimate goal of establishing a direct communication pathway between the human brain and external devices. This objective is achieved through the utilization of neural interfaces that acquires and interprets neural signals, which are then transformed into commands for external devices. BMIs have a broad range of practical applications that have been demonstrated to enhance the quality of life of disabled patients, including controlling hand prostheses with sensory restoration for patients with transradial amputations [1], and speech decoding for patients with motor speech disorders

The authors acknowledge funding from Sardegna Ricerche, Bando "PROOF of CONCEPT - Valorizzazione dei risultati della ricerca in biomedicina" - PO FESR 2014–2020 - Deep-ECGEE project.

F. Palumbo et al. (Eds.): ARC 2023, LNCS 14251, pp. 185–199, 2023.
https://doi.org/10.1007/978-3-031-42921-7_13

[2]. To be utilized and have an impact on a long-term basis on the life of people, BMIs must operate in real-time while undergoing strict power limitations. In the case of implantable chip developments, the electronic systems must guarantee to limit any temperature increase of the tissue to below 0.5°C [3]. Even in the case of non-implantable BCIs, power constraints still hold if the device is intended to be portable or wearable [4].

Among several solutions for decoding the neural signal, Spiking Neural Networks (SNNs) are prospectively promising instruments for developing real-time solutions under strict computational, power, and memory limitations. Although the non-differentiability of the spiking output is incompatible with the back-propagation gradient descent algorithm utilized for the supervised learning of neural networks [5] and held back from using these event-based models in the past, thanks to the efforts of the scientific community, nowadays several open-source platforms dedicated to SNNs training are available [6,7]. SNN models are event-based processing systems that in response to input spike trains generate output spike trains. The sparsity of the events is the reason why these algorithms are so efficient compared to other deep-learning models [8,9]. However, in the majority of the cases, the problem is not specified in terms of events, but rather by continuous time series of values, and it is necessary to translate the format of the data to make the SNN compatible with the problem. Nevertheless, in the case of intracortical recordings, the most common approach for processing the neural data consists in detecting the cortical spikes along the multi-channel recording, therefore, the data format is already in the proper shape to be elaborated by SNN models.

Field Programmable Gate Arrays (FPGAs) are well suited target platform for hosting portable low-power electronic systems embedding SNN models and multi-channel digital signal processing algorithms that need to be executed in real-time and with low latency. In particular: 1) Hardwired Digital Signal Processor (DSP) slices are specifically designed for the most computationally demanding part of the signal processing, which involves multiplications and multiply-and-accumulate operations, mainly for filtering applications; 2) A fabric of programmable logic (PL) is included and is flexible enough to accelerate even the most specific aspects of SNN inference algorithms; 3) Configurable dual-port block RAM (BRAMs) with customizable port widths are essential for hosting a wide choice of SNN models, accelerated with a selectable throughput chosen depending on the requirements of the application. In fact, a beneficial aspect of using FPGAs is promoting hardware adaptability over a wide range of possible experiments.

In this work, we present a multi-variable real-time neural decoder hosted by a low-end Artix-7 FPGA. The decoding system embeds a 128-channel neural signal processing chain and an SNN model for decoding kinetic and kinematic variables of a handle moved during a delayed reach-to-grasp task, i.e. velocity displacement of the handle and fingers pressure. The main findings of this study can be summarized as follows:

- A hardware SNN is utilized to continuously decode kinetic and kinematic quantities in real-time, which, to the best of our knowledge, is a first in the field of neural signal decoding;
- The accuracy of the system is evaluated on a benchmark dataset achieving results comparable to state-of-the-art methods. Remarkably, it utilized 19.27 times fewer parameters compared to the smallest non-SNN neural decoder tested on the same dataset, focusing on decoding one of the five variables only;
- The study demonstrates the computational efficiency of SNN-based decoders in neural applications, with an average energy consumption of 56.4 μJ per inference.

2   Related Works

During the last few decades, several studies have been presented for interfacing neural tissue and analyzing neural information. BMIs have a wide scope of applications: collecting information for upcoming offline elaboration [10], enabling closed-loop low-latency analysis for studying neural cell's level interactions [11], etc. In this study, we focus on extracting kinetic and kinematic information from neural intracortical data in real-time, while guaranteeing low power consumption and low latency responses. Table 1 contains a list of works related to this study, either because of the similarity of the decoding task, the computing platform, or the deep learning model. Kinetic information, such as the fingers' force, can be extracted from the motor cortex. For example, in [12] a Linear Ridge Regression (LRR) model was used for continuously tracking the finger's pressure, decoding the information from the Local Field Potential (LFP). Moreover, in [13] a multilayer perceptron (MLP) and a Support Vector Machine (SVM) models have

Table 1. Related works

Work	Year	Sbj	Signal	Task	Type	Model	Platform
[12]	2015	M	LFP	Fingers forces	Regr	LRR	PC
[13]	2015	M	SUA	Finger forces	Class	MLP	PC
[14]	2016	R	LFP	Paw force	Regr	PLS	PC
[15]	2021	M	MUA	Hand velocity	Regr	QRNN	PC
[16]	2021	M	SUA	Hand velocity	Regr	LSTM	PC
[17]	2023	M	MUA	Hand velocity	Regr	SNN	FPGA
[18]	2019	H	EEG	Motor imagery	Class	CNN	FPGA
[19]	2016	H	ECoG	Finger movements	Class	MLP	FPGA
[20]	2017	H	EEG	Hand gestures	Class	BC	uC
[21]	2022	H	sEMG	Elbow angle	Regr	SNN	PC
[22]	2022	M	SBP	Finger velocity	Regr	SNN	PC

Sbj = Subject, M = Macaque monkey, R = Rat, H = Human

been compared on a force classification problem using intracortical data. Furthermore, in [14] Partial Least Square (PLS) regression algorithm was used for decoding the pressure applied to a button by freely moving rats (R). These three studies among others are preliminary works that gave proof of the feasibility of extracting kinetic information from intracortical neural signals.

As regards kinematic data decoding from the neural signal, in [15] and [16] several deep learning models such as Quasi-Recurrent Neural Networks (QRNNs) and Recurrent Neural Networks (RNNs) were tested for decoding the handle velocity during a delayed reach-to-grasp task. Although both the studies presented offline analysis, and are presumably not optimal solutions for at-the-edge processing because of the memory requirements (reported only in [16]), they achieved state-of-the-art accuracy in decoding the velocity on the same dataset utilized in this work, and are therefore reported.

Examples of real-time neural decoders are given in [18] and [19], where two FPGA-based systems were tested on motor imagery and finger movements decoding, respectively. Moreover, in [18] the Electroencephalographic (EEG) signal was used for classifying which movement the human subject (H) is imagining of doing relying on the accelerated inference of a Convolutional Neural Network (CNN), whereas in [19] the Electrocorticographic (ECoG) signal were used for classifying if the fingers are moving or not individually by using an MLP in conjunction with Principal Component Analysis (PCA) to reduce the data dimensionality from 62 to 3.

SNNs hold great potential as tools for creating real-time solutions that can operate within strict constraints on computational power and memory usage. In the domain of neuroscience numerous SNN accelerators have been presented in the literature, some of which are focused on understanding brain functionality through the use of FPGA-based prototypes [23], others aim at executing larger networks of spiking neurons targeting higher-end emulators, like SpiNNaker [24]. The main objective of this research is to create an end-to-end accelerator capable of processing and decoding neural information in real-time while ensuring low power consumption using SNNs, taking advantage of spike sparsity to reduce memory read/write operations and computations. This work extends a previously published work [17] that only decoded the kinematics information from intracortical recorded spikes. We extended our previous design by decoding four additional variables in real-time, representing the kinetic data of the behavioral task, and by re-designing our system to work without the support of an ARM processor, but with a softcore mapped in the PL to reduce the power consumption.

3   Methods

3.1   Neural Recording and Decoding Problem

The system has been tested relying on electrophysiological data recorded in the motor cortex of a macaque monkey during a delayed reach-to-grasp task [25]. The dataset consists of multiple trials where the subject pulls a cuboid handle with two grip types and two force levels. The neural activity was obtained using a chronically implanted 10×10 microelectrode Utah array in the motor cortex sampled at 30 kHz, downsampled by a factor of 3 in this study. In addition to neural data, the dataset included behavioral data, such as handle displacement and the forces applied to the cuboid handle, that was recorded using force-sensitive sensors sampled at 1 kHz. Before the neural network training phase, the handle position and the forces have been smoothed using a moving average filter of order 64. Moreover, the handle velocity was calculated by computing the first derivative of the smoothed handle position, which was determined by subtracting adjacent samples and further smoothed using a mean average filter of order 16.

3.2   Signal Processing: Spike Detection

In this study, we rely on a previously presented spike detection pipeline, therefore we only provide a brief overview of this part and refer the reader to the original paper for more details about the hardware implementation [17].

The spike detection modules operate on signals sampled at a frequency of 10 kHz, which is ten times higher than the frequency of signals processed by the SNN at 1 kHz. Therefore, we aimed to minimize the computational load of the spike detection pipeline, proposing a configuration that only requires five additions per channel and zero multiplications. The spike detection processing chain can be summarized as follows:

- Filter: a second-order moving average difference (MAD) filter is applied to remove low-frequency components, simplifying the process of finding a threshold to verify the spike condition.
- Spike emphasis: the absolute value is used to emphasize the spike shape and improve detection reliability;
- Threshold: the mean value of the rectified signal multiplied by four is used as the threshold above which a spike event is detected;
- Threshold update time: the spike threshold is updated every 0.82 ms;
- Refractory period: a 1 ms period of insensitivity follows a spike detection event (per channel) in order not to detect twice or more the same spike;
- Spike bins: spike trains are downsampled accumulating the spikes during non-overlapped windows of 1 ms; the procedure supplies another series of 0 s and 1 s because of the insensitivity period of 1 ms imposed during detection.

3.3   Neural Decoding

The SNN model has been trained with the LAVA Deep Learning framework[1] and the Spike LAYer Error Reassignment (SLAYER) packet[2], a library for backpropagation-based SNNs learning. We used Loihi CUrrent BAsed Leaky Integrate and Fire (CUBA) Neurons as base units [26], represented by Eq. (1).

---

[1] https://lava-nc.org/index.html.
[2] https://lava-nc.org/lava-lib-dl/slayer/slayer.html.

$$S(t) = \sum ws(t-1)$$

$$i(t) = \alpha i(t-1) + S(t)$$

$$v(t) = \beta v(t-1) + i(t)$$

$$s(t) = v(t) > \theta$$

$$v(t) = v(t)(1 - s(t)) \tag{1}$$

Where, w represents the synaptic weights, s is the input spike vector, and $S(t)$ is the convolution of the spikes and weights. The result of this convolution, $S(t)$, serves as the input for the neuron. The current state variable, $i(t)$, is calculated by decaying its previous value using a factor α and adding the convolved spiking activity, $S(t)$, to it. The voltage state variable, $v(t)$, follows a similar process to $i(t)$, with its previous value decayed by a factor β and added to the current $i(t)$. The neuron produces a spike when the value of $v(t)$ reaches the threshold θ. When this occurs, the value of $v(t)$ is reset to zero.

A network of four dense layers of CUBA neurons is used to decode the target variables. The binned spiking activity is already in the right format to be processed by the SNN model, however, the target variables are sequences of numbers rather than series of events, therefore, it is necessary to convert the spikes into numbers. To carry out the conversion we placed five spiking neurons on the last layer of the model, one for each target variable. The thresholds, θ, of the neurons are set at infinite so that it would be impossible for the neurons to generate a spike [21]. The potentials of the neurons, $v(t)$, are directly the decoded variables.

3.4   Training Scheme

The dataset used consists of 157 trials, which were divided into 94 for training, 15 for validation, and 48 for testing. During training, the loss function was defined as the mean squared error (MSE) between the output neuron potentials and the ground truth. In addition, a penalty term was introduced to increase the loss for networks that generated more spikes as in the library's example[3]. After training, the network with the lowest loss on the velocity variable measured on the validation set was selected as the best model. The decision to monitor the velocity output more accurately during the training process was motivated by the fact that this variable initially produced the worst results in terms of correlation. The learning rate used was 0.001 and was divided by 3.33 every 50 epochs. The number of epochs was set to 400, while an early exit criterion based on the MSE of the velocity was used to interrupt the training process if no improvements were observed for 50 consecutive epochs.

4   Hardware Architecture

The system is composed of three primary modules: 1) a MicroBlaze softcore used for handling input/output data flow; 2) a spike detector that processes raw samples obtained from the array of sensors, detecting the spikes along the

---

[3] https://github.com/lava-nc/lava-dl/blob/main/tutorials/lava/lib/dl/slayer/pilotnet/train.ipynb.

neural recording and computing 1-ms bins, 3) an SNN that directly processes the spike bins to infer the handle velocity and the four forces applied to the handle (Fig. 1). These modules are implemented on a low-end Artix-7 FPGA (XC7A100T-CSG324). The FPGA's programmability allows for adjusting the deployment of the parametric design to suit the needs of various experimental setups. These setups may include different datasets, adjustments of the spike detection hyper-parameters, or changes in the chosen neural network topology.

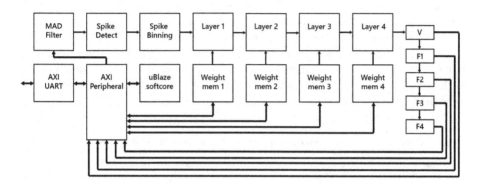

Fig. 1. System architecture

4.1 PC-FPGA Communication

The communication between the FPGA and the PC occurs through an AXI UartLite module. On the PC side, a Python script controls the communication, whereas the FPGA softcore firmware is written in C. At the beginning of the program, the weights are sent to the FPGA and loaded into the BRAMs. Once the weights are set, the system is ready to receive data streams. Each sample is sent at regular time intervals of 0.1 ms determined by an AXI Timer. When the interrupt is generated, the softcore sends a handshake to the PC to require a stream of data. The first 8,192 samples are used to set the thresholds of the spike detection module, then the inference generation begins. Inferences are generated cyclically every 10 data samples at a frequency of 1 kHz and sent to the PC.

4.2 Spiking Neural Network Architecture

The SNN is composed of four dense layers which process the binned spiking activity and infer concurrently the handle velocity and the forces applied to the handle. Each SNN's layer is mapped on a dedicated hardware layer core that hosts the spike and the weight memories, a DSP-based accumulator for computing the synaptic current, and two identical cascade-connected integrator modules used to evaluate the Loihi CUBA neuron model described by Eq. 1.

The weight and spike memories are dynamically addressed by using a stack storing pointers to the active input synapses. The stack permits taking advantage of the spike sparsity of the neural signal only considering the active inputs that effectively contribute to the output values, saving memory accesses, and computation cycles. The layer module updates the neurons' states by performing several steps in a pipelined fashion: 1) the addresses stored in the stack are used to access spikes and weights of the active set of synapses; 2) the synaptic weights are accumulated according to the spike condition of the associated synapses; 3) the integrator modules update the neuron's states, the updated states are stored in two FIFOs connected between the integrator's input and output; 4) the spikes, before being streamed to the next layer of the network, are re-organized in groups of four bits, and appended with the active set signal, which is the or-reduced value of the set of spikes which is used as a write enable to add new entries to the stack pointer of the following layer. Figure 2 provides an overview of the layer module architecture.

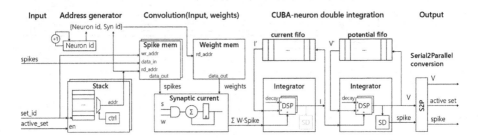

Fig. 2. Layer module architecture

5   Discussion

5.1   Accuracy

We selected a four-layer topology following the example given in [21]. The hyperparameters are shown in Table 2.

Table 2. SNN hyperparameters

Layer	Inputs	Neurons	Parameters
1	96	64	6,144
2	64	128	8,192
3	128	64	8,192
4	64	5	320

The box plot in Fig. 3 shows the distribution accuracy in terms of the Pearson correlation coefficient of the five target variables in the training and test sets. The decoding accuracy of the forces was measured by only considering the trials where the subject was effectively touching the force sensors, and a measure of the force was available. Figure 4 shows the superimposition between the model output and the target variables. The system is capable of tracking the target variables' trajectory without deviating from it.

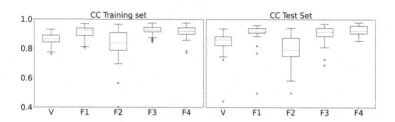

Fig. 3. Neural decoding accuracy distribution in the training set, on the left, and in the test set, on the right.

5.2   Resource Utilization

The presented system can handle up to 128 input channels, however, the design is parametric, and the number of channels can be extended for supporting bigger MEA or multiple MEAs, requiring only the memory to grow linearly with it, neither the look-up table (LUTs), nor the registers (REGs), nor the DSPs utilization would increase. The hardware modules are deployed on an Artix-7 FPGA mounted on a Nexys-4 prototype board, the clock frequency is set at 8 MHz and the chip provides a real-time response with a typical latency of 0.45 ms that varies depending on the spiking activity level up to 1.0 ms in the worst-case scenario, where a spike is detected concurrently on each channel.

Table 3 shows the hardware resources required by the current setup: 15,168 LUTs and 15,893 REGs, distributed between the AXI peripheral module (48% and 58%), the spike decoder (15% and 15%), the MicroBlaze softcore (8% and 6%), and other modules such as the BRAM controllers, the timer, etc. Moreover, 28 DSPs are used to speed up the neuron integration during the SNN inference, and 18 BRAMs are used for storing the SNN's weights, whereas the remaining 5 BRAMs are utilized for storing the softcore firmware.

Finally, it is shown the design under test (DUT) resource requirements, where the capacity of the softcore memory has been augmented for hosting a test signal and measure the on-chip power consumption excluding the I/O component.

5.3   Power Consumption

We determined the power consumption of the FPGA chip by measuring the voltage drop across a shunt resistor of 1.0±0.05 Ω connected between the 1.0 V power

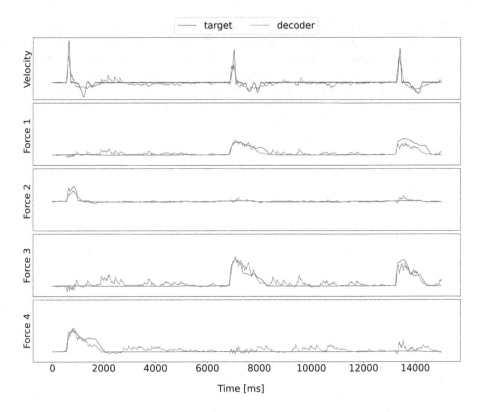

Fig. 4. Spike decoder output behavior.

supply and the chip itself. We used a Digilent Analog Discovery 2 oscilloscope for measuring the voltage difference between the resistor's pins and the ground. Moreover, in order not to account for the I/O power, which would be the same independently by the system considered, the softcore memory has been extended for storing about 13 ms of data samples. We measured a voltage drop of 60 mV across the resistor, which corresponds to a current of 60 mA absorbed from the chip and overall power consumption on the 1.0 V power supply of 56.4 mW.

The voltage absorbed from the 1.8 V supply voltage is not easily accessible since there are no test points available. However, by relying on the post-implementation power report of Vivado 2019.2, the power does not change by modifying the switching activity of the implemented netlist, therefore we consider it to be constant, and equal to 138.6 mW. As regards the 3.8 V power supply, the estimation available in the power report of Vivado 2019.2 is 132 mW.

Table 3. Hardware resource utilization

	System	Decoder	Detection	SNN	DUT	Available	Utilization
LUT	15,168	2,253	460	1,783	15,568	63,400	23.92%
REG	15,893	2,415	499	1,907	15,893	126,800	12.53%
DSP	28	28	0	28	28	240	11.67%
BRAM	23	18	1	17	83	135	17.04%

5.4 Adaptability to Different Experiments

The intrinsic characteristics of FPGA align well with the general requirements for executing SNNs for neural decoding, as dedicated hardware allows for:

- Exploiting sparsity, activating the computation of neuron dynamics only when input events are detected;
- Utilizing custom arithmetic operations, for instance using arbitrary fixed point formats to represent weights and neuron/synapse internal variables;
- Adapting to various experimental setups, featuring, for example, different number of input channels or sampling frequencies, diverse spike detection techniques, different binning approaches, or distinct output decoding methods.

To demonstrate the architecture's versatility, we present as an example synthesis results for several decoder configurations that facilitate diverse experiments with varying numbers of MEA channels. The following tables showcase the system's adaptability. Table 4 exhibits the system's ability to accommodate an increasing number (up to 4096) of input channels under latency constraints (e.g., to be used in closed-loop feedback scenarios). Table 5 demonstrates a similar exploration where the increasing workload is obtained through the instantiation of additional processing elements on a fixed clock frequency. As the number of input channels increases, the workload of the spike detection and binning front-end modules, as well as the computational load of the first SNN layer, also rise.

This involves instantiating multiple spike detection and binning modules (a pair for every 128 input channels) and deploying the first layer of the SNN across multiple hardware layer modules (one for every 128 input channels).

These configurations exemplify the flexibility of the FPGA architecture to be adapted to different setups by modifying its structural parameters. The main limit is posed by the number of synaptic weights that can be stored in the BRAMs available in the target device.

6 Comparison with State of Art

The BMI presented in this work is the first to employ intracortical recorded spikes extracted from raw neural recordings in conjunction with an SNN for real-time

Table 4. Frequency scaling

Channels	128	1024	2048	4096
CLK [MHz]	8	28	50	100
LUT [10^3]	15.2	18.4	22.1	29.4
REG [10^3]	15.9	20.6	25.9	36.7
DSP	28	28	28	28
BRAM	23	48	76	133
Latency [ms]	0.45	0.42	0.42	0.41

Table 5. Resource scaling

Channels	128	1024	2048	4096
CLK [MHz]	8	8	8	8
LUT [10^3]	15.2	21.3	28.3	42.3
REG [10^3]	15.9	21.9	28.8	42.5
DSP	28	77	133	240
BRAM	23	48	76	133
Latency [ms]	0.45	0.45	0.45	0.45

decoding of kinetic and kinematic data. Table 6 reports offline decoders tested on the same or similar datasets of this study and a former work of ours where we decoded in real-time kinematic data only. Table 6 reports the type of neural signal, the kind of decoder, the platform hosting the algorithm, and the number of parameters used. Moreover, since different studies decoded either the force or the velocity using several accuracy metrics, we provided four accuracy columns to make the comparison possible. From left to right the Pearson correlation coefficient measured between the decoded velocity and the ground truth v_{cc}, the Pearson correlation coefficient measured between the decoded force and the ground truth f_{CC}, the coefficient of determination of the force f_{R^2} and the fraction of accounted variance of the force f_{FAV}.

Table 6. Related works

Works	Year	Signal	Model	Platform	Parameters	v_{CC}	f_{cc}	f_{R^2}	f_{FAV}
This work	2023	MUA	SNN	FPGA	22.3 k	0.84	0.87	0.60	0.68
[17]	2023	MUA	SNN	FPGA	56.0 k	0.83	–	–	–
[15]	2021	MUA	QRNN	PC	–	0.84	–	–	–
[16]	2021	SUA	RNN	PC	430 k	0.91	–	–	–
[22]	2022	SBP	SNN	PC	152.5 k	0.75	–	–	–
[12]	2015	LFP	LRR	PC	–	–	–	–	<0.6
[14]	2016	LFP	PLS	PC	–	–	0.68	0.45	–

In [17] we presented a real-time system for decoding the velocity using the same dataset utilized in this work. However, in this study, we changed the SNN topology and training paradigm, obtaining a model that requires only the 40% of the parameters used in [17], while maintaining the same decoding accuracy for the velocity, and providing support for decoding four additional kinetic quantities. Moreover, we changed the target device and deployed the system on a low-end Artix-7 FPGA which does not embed a power-draining ARM processor as in [17].

In [15] and [16] two deep learning recurrent algorithms were tested for decoding the handle velocity of the same dataset utilized in this study. The correlation we obtained is similar to [15], and slightly lower than [16]. However, the number of parameters required by the presented decoding algorithm is only 5.2% of [16], making our solution better suited for at-the-edge processing applications.

In [22] an SNN-based algorithm was used for decoding the velocity of a finger from intracortical recordings using the spiking band power (SBP) signal. A direct accuracy comparison is not possible since the dataset is different. Nevertheless, in [22], the accuracy was found to be slightly lower than the one we obtained in this work. However, considering that similar decoding algorithms were tested on similar tasks, the results are reasonably close. The networks used in [22] utilized 6.84 times more parameters than in this study to decode only the velocity.

In [12] and [14] LRR and PLS regression algorithms were used for decoding the forces generated from the fingers of a monkey and from the forelimb of a rat respectively, using intracortical recorded data. The force decoding accuracy found in [12], measured using the FAV coefficient, is smaller than 0.6, whereas our FAV accuracy, averaged across the four forces, is 0.68. In [14] the force decoding accuracy is given both in terms of CC and R^2, and reached 0.68 and 0.45, whereas we got higher values of 0.87 and 0.60.

7 Conclusion

In this study, we presented a resource and power-efficient intracortical BMI for concurrent and continuous neural decoding of kinetic and kinematic quantities in real-time. The decoding system is deployed on an Artix-4 FPGA and hosts a multiplier-less spike detection pipeline for the extraction of intracortical spikes and an SNN model for directly processing the neural spikes and inferring the values of the target variables.

The system reached accuracy comparable with other works in the literature in decoding the velocity of a handle during a delayed reach-to-grasp task and state-of-the-art accuracy in decoding the finger forces applied to a handle. The number of parameters required by the algorithm is 19.3 times lower than state-of-the-art approaches tested on the same dataset and the power consumption of the chip during inference is 56.4 mW.

References

1. Petrini, F.M., et al.: Six-month assessment of a hand prosthesis with intraneural tactile feedback. Ann. Neurol. **85**(1), 137–154 (2019)
2. Moses, D.A., et al.: Neuroprosthesis for decoding speech in a paralyzed person with anarthria. N. Engl. J. Med. **385**(3), 217–227 (2021)
3. Nurmikko, A.: Challenges for large-scale cortical interfaces. Neuron **108**(2), 259–269 (2020)
4. Busia, P., et al.: EEGformer: transformer-based epilepsy detection on raw EEG traces for low-channel-count wearable continuous monitoring devices. In: 2022 IEEE Biomedical Circuits and Systems Conference (BioCAS), pp. 640–644 (2022). https://doi.org/10.1109/BioCAS54905.2022.9948637

5. Wang, X., Lin, X., Dang, X.: Supervised learning in spiking neural networks: A review of algorithms and evaluations. Neural Netw. **125**, 258–280 (2020)
6. Shrestha, S.B., Orchard, G.: Slayer: Spike layer error reassignment in time. In: Advances in Neural Information Processing Systems, vol. 31 (2018)
7. Lee, C., Sarwar, S.S., Panda, P., Srinivasan, G., Roy, K.: Enabling spike-based backpropagation for training deep neural network architectures. Front. Neurosci., 119 (2020)
8. Yan, Z., Zhou, J., Wong, W.-F.: Energy efficient ECG classification with spiking neural network. Biomed. Signal Process. Control **63**, 102170 (2021)
9. Xiping, J., Fang, B., Yan, R., Xiaoliang, X., Tang, H.: An FPGA implementation of deep spiking neural networks for low-power and fast classification. Neural Comput. **32**(1), 182–204 (2020)
10. Sun, B., Feng, H., Chen, K., Zhu, X.: A deep learning framework of quantized compressed sensing for wireless neural recording. IEEE Access **4**, 5169–5178 (2016). https://doi.org/10.1109/ACCESS.2016.2604397
11. Leone, G., Raffo, L., Meloni, P.: ZyON: enabling spike sorting on APSoC-based signal processors for high-density microelectrode arrays. IEEE Access **8**, 218145–218160 (2020). https://doi.org/10.1109/ACCESS.2020.3042034
12. Milekovic, T., Truccolo, W., Grün, S., Riehle, A., Brochier, T.: Local field potentials in primate motor cortex encode grasp kinetic parameters. Neuroimage **114**, 338–355 (2015)
13. Tagliabue, M., et al.: Estimation of two-digit grip type and grip force level by frequency decoding of motor cortex activity for a BMI application. In: 2015 International Conference on Advanced Robotics (ICAR), pp. 308–315. IEEE (2015)
14. Khorasani, A., Heydari Beni, N., Shalchyan, V., Daliri, M.R.: Continuous force decoding from local field potentials of the primary motor cortex in freely moving rats. Sci. Rep. **6**(1), 1–10 (2016)
15. Ahmadi, N., Constandinou, T.G., Bouganis, C.S.: Robust and accurate decoding of hand kinematics from entire spiking activity using deep learning. J. Neural Eng. **18**(2), 026011 (2021)
16. Yang, S.-H., Huang, J.-W., Huang, C.-J., Chiu, P.-H., Lai, H.-Y., Chen, Y.-Y.: Selection of essential neural activity timesteps for intracortical brain-computer interface based on recurrent neural network. Sensors **21**(19), 6372 (2021)
17. Leone, G., Raffo, L., Meloni, P.: On-FPGA spiking neural networks for end-to-end neural decoding. IEEE Access **11**, 41387–41399 (2023). https://doi.org/10.1109/ACCESS.2023.3269598
18. Ma, X., Zheng, W., Peng, Z., Yang, J.: FPGA-based rapid electroencephalography signal classification system. In: 2019 IEEE 11th International Conference on Advanced Infocomm Technology (ICAIT), pp. 223–227. IEEE (2019)
19. Agrawal, M., Vidyashankar, S., Huang, K.: On-chip implementation of ECoG signal data decoding in brain-computer interface. In: 2016 IEEE 21st International Mixed-Signal Testing Workshop (IMSTW), pp. 1–6. IEEE (2016)
20. McCrimmon, C.M., et al.: Performance assessment of a custom, portable, and low-cost brain-computer interface platform. IEEE Trans. Biomed. Eng. **64**(10), 2313–2320 (2017)
21. Du, Y., Jin, J., Wang, Q., Fan, J.: EMG-based continuous motion decoding of upper limb with spiking neural network. In: 2022 IEEE International Instrumentation and Measurement Technology Conference (I2MTC), pp. 1–5. IEEE (2022)

22. Liao, J., et al.: An energy-efficient spiking neural network for finger velocity decoding for implantable brain-machine interface. In: 2022 IEEE 4th International Conference on Artificial Intelligence Circuits and Systems (AICAS), pp. 134–137. IEEE (2022)

23. Leone, G., Raffo, L., Meloni, P.: A bandwidth-efficient emulator of biologically-relevant spiking neural networks on FPGA. IEEE Access **10**, 76780–76793 (2022). https://doi.org/10.1109/ACCESS.2022.3192826

24. Furber, S.B., Galluppi, F., Temple, S., Plana, L.A.: The spinnaker project. Proc. IEEE **102**(5), 652–665 (2014)

25. Brochier, T., et al.: Massively parallel recordings in macaque motor cortex during an instructed delayed reach-to-grasp task. Sci. Data **5**(1), 1–23 (2018)

26. Davies, M., et al.: Loihi: a neuromorphic manycore processor with on-chip learning. IEEE Micro **38**(1), 82–99 (2018)

Implementation of a Perception System for Autonomous Vehicles Using a Detection-Segmentation Network in SoC FPGA

Maciej Baczmanski, Mateusz Wasala⬤, and Tomasz Kryjak$^{(\boxtimes)}$⬤

Embedded Vision Systems Group, Computer Vision Laboratory,
Department of Automatic Control and Robotics, AGH University of Krakow,
Al. Mickiewicza 30, 30-059 Krakow, Poland
mbaczmanski@student.agh.edu.pl, {mateusz.wasala,tomasz.kryjak}@agh.edu.pl

Abstract. Perception and control systems for autonomous vehicles are an active area of scientific and industrial research. These solutions should be characterised by both high efficiency in recognising obstacles and other environmental elements in different road conditions, real-time capability, and energy efficiency. Achieving such functionality requires an appropriate algorithm and a suitable computing platform. In this paper, we have used the MultiTaskV3 detection-segmentation network as the basis for a perception system that can perform both functionalities within a single architecture. It was appropriately trained, quantised, and implemented on the AMD Xilinx Kria KV260 Vision AI embedded platform. By using this device, it was possible to parallelise and accelerate the computations. Furthermore, the whole system consumes relatively little power compared to a CPU-based implementation (an average of 5 W, compared to the minimum of 55 W for weaker CPUs, and the small size (119mm × 140 mm × 36 mm) of the platform allows it to be used in devices where the amount of space available is limited. It also achieves an accuracy higher than 97% of the mAP (mean average precision) for object detection and above 90% of the mIoU (mean intersection over union) score for image segmentation. The article also details the design of the Mecanum wheel vehicle, which was used to test the proposed solution in a mock-up city.

Keywords: detection-segmentation neural network · perception · embedded AI · SoC FPGA · eGPU · Vitis AI · Mecanum wheel vehicle

1 Introduction

Today, we are witnessing the rapid development of advanced mobile robotics, including autonomous cars and drones (unmanned aerial vehicles, UAV). This would not be possible without advances in the implementation of perception and control systems, including the use of deep neural networks (DNN). DNNs make

F. Palumbo et al. (Eds.): ARC 2023, LNCS 14251, pp. 200–211, 2023.
https://doi.org/10.1007/978-3-031-42921-7_14

it possible to achieve high accuracy, but memory and computational complexity remain significant challenges. In order to meet the requirements of mobile platforms, i.e. low latency and low energy consumption, it becomes necessary to use specialised hardware platforms such as SoC FPGAs (System on Chip Field Programmable Gate Arrays) or eGPUs (embedded Graphic Processing Units). These solutions also have the advantage of relatively small size and weight. It is also worth noting that a major challenge is the reliability analysis of network-based solutions, including their explainability [1]. This is of particular importance when traffic safety, for example, depends on DNNs detections or control.

In perception systems, two basic tasks can be roughly distinguished: object detection and segmentation (semantic and instance). Object detection is the marking of objects belonging to the considered classes (e.g. cars, pedestrians, cyclists, traffic signs, etc.) in the image with bounding boxes or sometimes binary masks. Semantic segmentation involves assigning to each pixel a label that tells what object it belongs to (e.g. drivable area, horizontal road sign, vegetation, buildings, persistent, or sky). Instance segmentation, on the other hand, allows different labels to be given to pixels belonging to two separate objects of the same class (e.g. two pedestrians). It should be noted that object detection is a simpler and thus computationally less complex task. A typical solution /changeusingthat uses DNNs is the YOLO (You Only Look Once) family of algorithms [2]. In contrast, segmentation, especially of instances to obtain similar information, is much more complex – requiring both longer learning and inference. U-Nets [3] are typically used for semantic segmentation and Mask R-CNN-based [4] solutions for instances.

For autonomous vehicle perception systems, the tasks of detection and segmentation appear together. For objects such as pedestrians, vehicles, bicycles, vertical road signs, or traffic lights, the use of detection is sufficient. However, for the detection of drivable area or horizontal road signs (including pedestrian crossings), it is better to use segmentation. Hence, detection-segmentation networks have been proposed in the literature, which combine the advantages of both approaches and, at the same time, thanks to a common backbone (encoder), are characterised by lower computational complexity and an easier learning process than instance segmentation approaches. A detection-segmentation network, in addition to the aforementioned backbone, consists of a segmentation head and several detection heads. Examples of such networks are YOLOP [5], HybridNets [6] and MultiTask V3 [7] discussed in Sect. 2.

Taking into account the properties of the detection segmentation networks discussed above, we decided to use this solution as the basis for the perception system of our autonomous vehicle model. We used the MultiTask V3 network, which we implemented and deployed on two embedded platforms: SoC FPGA Kria KV260 and an eGPU (NVIDIA Jetson Nano and Xavier NX). The experiments performed showed that detection-segmentation networks represent a good compromise between accuracy, performance, and power consumption. We also discussed the design of the Mecanum wheeled vehicle used. To the best of our knowledge, this is the first paper that discusses the hardware implementation of a perception system based on a detection-segmentation network implemented in an SoC FPGA, the results of which were applied to the control of an autonomous vehicle model.

The remainder of this paper is structured as follows. In Sect. 2 we discuss the relevant prior works on detection-segmentation networks and DNNs acceleration on SoC FPGA. Section 3 discusses the methods used, including the hardware implementation of the considered DNNs, and the design of the autonomous vehicle model. The results obtained are summarised in Sect. 4. The paper ends with conclusions and a discussion of possible future research.

2   Previous Work

Three types of deep neural networks can be distinguished in current vision systems: detection, segmentation, and detection-segmentation. As mentioned in the introduction, detection-segmentation networks represent a compromise between the accuracy of instance segmentation and the speed of simple detection and are therefore an interesting solution for autonomous vehicle perception systems. Several architectures of detection-segmentation networks have been proposed in the literature.

The first is YOLOP [5]. It allows object detection and segmentation of drivable area and horizontal road markings. It consists of a common encoder and 3 separate decoders (one for detection and two for segmentation). It has been trained and evaluated on the popular *BDD100k* dataset [8]. The second is HybridNets [6], which is very similar to YOLOP in terms of functionality. It consists of 4 components: encoder (EfficientNet V2 architecture), neck, detection head (inspired by YOLOv4), and segmentation head. The *BDD100k* dataset was also used for training and evaluation. The third architecture, used in this work, is the MultiTask V3 [7] proposed by AMD Xilinx. It is worth noting that it is included in the Vitis AI library as a demonstrator of its capabilities, but to our knowledge, it has not been described in a scientific publication. Details of its construction are presented in Sect. 3.1. Unlike YOLOP and HybridNets, it also includes a depth estimation module. However, it has not been evaluated on a publicly available dataset.

The topic of hardware acceleration of deep neural networks, especially for embedded computing, is the subject of intense academic and industrial research due to its very high practical importance. A whole spectrum of solutions is encountered, from dedicated chips for AI acceleration (e.g. Intel Neural Compute Stick, Google Coral, Tesla FSD Chip), through programmable SoC FPGAs to eGPU platforms. A detailed overview of the solutions is beyond the scope of this article, and we refer interested readers, for example, to the review [9] or the work [10].

In this work, we have chosen to use an SoC FPGA platform and also run the selected network on an eGPU platform for comparison. Reprogrammable devices have been a proven platform for implementing vision algorithms for years, which was the main reason for our choice. In addition, they tend to have lower power

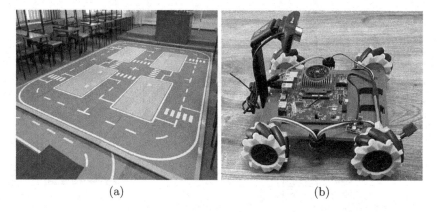

(a)   (b)

Fig. 1. The mock-up of a city made by us (a) and the model of an autonomous vehicle (b) with Mecanum wheels and all equipment.

consumption than eGPUs. Of the available detection-segmentation networks, we chose MultiTask V3 for two reasons. First, from our previous experiments, it had the highest efficiency and relatively low computational complexity for our scenario. Second, it was well-prepared by AMD Xilinx for acceleration in SoC FPGAs, which facilitated its use in the target perception and control system.

3   Implementation of the Perception and Control System

The starting point for our research was the FPT'22 [11] competition, the aim of which is to create a model of an autonomous vehicle capable of driving according to the road traffic rules in a mock-up city. Figure 1a shows the used mock-up city. It is equipped with horizontal markings (traffic lanes, pedestrian crossings), traffic lights, figures imitating pedestrians, and various objects (obstacles) to be avoided on the road. Thanks to this test environment, it is possible to evaluate the perception and control system of an autonomous vehicle. The research presented can be divided into four phases: the design and construction of an autonomous vehicle equipped with Mecanum wheels, the design of electronics and assembly equipment, the implementation of the perception and control algorithm on the AMD Xilinx Kria KV260 platform, and the programming of a low-level algorithm to control the motors for the Mecanum wheels. The most important part of the work is the implementation of the perception and control system. It uses a detection-segmentation deep convolutional neural network architecture that is parallelised, quantised, and accelerated on an embedded SoC FPGA platform. On the other hand, the Mecanum wheels allow for precise manoeuvring, and the detection-segmentation network provides the necessary information about obstacles and other elements of the environment. In addition, the PID controller implemented in the motor controllers ensures stable driving, which is essential for the safety of the vehicle.

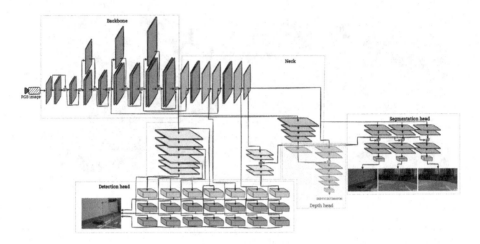

Fig. 2. Scheme of the MultiTask V3 deep neural network, showing layers of neurons grouped into sections. An input image is processed within successive layers to extract features. The features are used to generate output data: detections, segmentation, and also a depth map.

3.1   Detection-Segmentation Network in SoC FPGA

MultiTask V3 is a deep convolutional neural network, designed by the developers of Vitis AI (AMD Xilinx) as part of an open source library made available for the development process [7][1]. Its architecture is shown in Fig. 2 and allows the simultaneous execution of five tasks: detection, three types of segmentation, and depth estimation (not used in this work).

The segmentation part of the architecture is divided into three branches. Each branch can focus on a different task, such as segmenting detected objects, lanes (drivable area), or road markings. This approach makes it easier to prepare training sets, as these can be separated from each other, allowing a pixel to be classified in more than one class (e.g. a road marking should still be detected as a lane). The additional use of detection means that an in-depth analysis of detected objects (e.g. in terms of shape or occupied area in the image) is optional and performed only in special cases. The MultiTask V3 network architecture consists of several elements. First, the input image is transferred to the *Backbone* segment, which is used for feature extraction. This is based on the ResNet-18 convolutional neural network. Then, thanks to the use of encoders and convolutional layers, the *Neck* segment allows further feature extraction and the combination of low-level and high-level features. The features obtained are transferred to the appropriate branches: *Detection*, *Depth*, and *Segmentation* heads. In them, again, thanks to the use of convolution, activation operations, and normalisation, the corresponding result tensors are generated.

---

[1] MultiTask V3 has not been described in a published scientific paper.

Due to the specificity of the project and the high complexity of the training set for depth estimation, the *Depth* head training was not considered. For the remaining branches, three training sets were prepared, one common for object detection and segmentation and two for drivable area segmentation and road markings. The data for the training sets were obtained from recordings made on a city mock-up, which made it possible to prepare them strictly for the assumed task. 250 photos were obtained for the set containing the detected objects and 500 photos for the set showing the drivable area. The images were then manually labelled using the LabelMe software. To speed up the process of labelling lanes, a preprocessing script was created, which used binarisation with a given threshold to create initial masks of lane markings, which then could be corrected manually in the software. This method could be useful to speed up the process of labelling for bigger datasets for real-life deployment. The generated datasets were converted into a format compatible with the framework used to train the network. The framework is open source, based on Python, uses the PyTorch libraries, and is published in the Vitis AI libraries. As the software was written for older versions of the libraries and Python, corrections had to be made in order for the code to run properly. Once the modifications had been made, the software was launched using the prepared datasets. The model was trained using the GTX 1060 M GPU on sets split 80/20 between training and validation. The training was stopped after 450 epochs if there was no improvement in network performance.

The next step was to quantise the network model so that it could be run on an embedded SoC FPGA platform. This was done using the software described above. The quantisation is based on the vai_p_pytorch API provided by AMD Xilinx. Finally, the model was compiled into an architecture-compatible format using the vai_c_xir program, also provided by AMD Xilinx.

The final detection-segmentation model has been launched on the Kria KV260 SoC FPGA platform [12]. Kria is designed for the development of advanced image processing applications, allowing the acceleration of neural networks thanks to the use of DPU(Deep Processing Unit). The platform's operating system is Ubuntu, with PYNQ software installed, which allows a program to be created in Python on notebooks using the DPU overlay. In addition, by using the WiFi USB adapter and modifying the operating system's network settings, it is possible to communicate with the platform via SSH (Secure Shell) and through the Jupyter Notebook server created, allowing the algorithm to be executed and its operation to be analysed in real-time. This communication also makes it possible to continuously monitor the consumption of resources and the performance of the algorithm. Thanks to the libraries used, it is possible to collect image frames from a connected USB camera with a resolution of 512×320 pixels, convert them into the network input tensor, and then analyse the output tensors using methods from the OpenCV library. DPU overlay's API accepts and returns only tensors of shape compatible with the model's input and output layers. Preprocessing of input images, consisting of rescaling and changing colour models, and postprocessing, focused on gathering output data from raw tensors, were implemented in Python language. The implemented algorithm imports the necessary libraries and defines data pre-processing and processing functions.

3.2 Vehicle Control Algorithm

The algorithm captures the last frame from the USB camera, pre-processes it (size, colour space), and converts it into tensors, which are then fed into the MultiTaskv3 neural network. The network returns tensors which are then converted into masks: segmentation of detected objects, segmentation of drivable area, segmentation of road markings, and bounding boxes of detected objects. The received data is then analysed: first, it is checked that the pedestrian or obstacle is not in the ROI(Region of Interest), which is defined as a short distance in front of the vehicle. In the case of a pedestrian, the vehicle should stop, and in the case of an obstacle, the overtaking manoeuvre should be initiated. The lines are then checked. The detection of a continuous cross-line marking triggers a vehicle stop. Based on the sideline, it is possible to determine the trajectory of movement. If the sideline is not in the ROI – on the left side of the image, the segmentation of the drivable area allows checking if the vehicle is at an intersection or in a curve, which means it needs to turn. Based on the results of the analysis, a trajectory is determined and transmitted to the Arduino microcontroller, which controls the motors. The loop then returns to the initial step and continues indefinitely.

3.3 Hardware Setup

The electronics project consisted of placing the Arduino Nano Every microcontroller, based on the ATMega4809, on the breadboard, allowing the use of hardware interrupts on any pin. The microcontroller is directly connected to the motor encoders and four Pololu DRV8838 motor controllers, which allow control using the PWM (Pulse-width Modulation) signal. The power section consists of a LiPo package and step-down converters: 12V for the FPGA platform and 6V for the motors. The microcontroller communicates and is powered via a USB connection to the FPGA platform. The motor control was programmed on the microcontroller in the language provided by Arduino, based on C++. The program receives the set values from the FPGA platform through the UART protocol in the format V_x, V_y, ω, where V_x is the longitudinal velocity vector, V_y is the transverse velocity vector, and ω is the given angular velocity of rotation relative to the geometric centre of the vehicle. From the above values, the angular velocities set values for each of the motors are determined. The rotation of each wheel changes the signals on the encoder connected to it. Using hardware interrupts, it is possible to determine the angle that each of the motors has turned, which is counted in the counter assigned to it, and stored in the cache. The interrupt timer has been implemented in the program, which calls the function exactly every 0.1 s. This function retrieves the current counter reading and compares it with the previous one. This is used to determine the angular velocity, the previous values of which are also stored and differentiated for the purposes of the PID (Proportional Integral Derivative) controller. Then, for each motor, the control set for the given speed, the control error and its differential are determined, which makes it possible to determine the P and D terms of the PID controller. The values obtained are used to determine the filling of the PWM signal sent to the motor controllers. The program runs in an infinite loop, and in asynchronous mode, the microcontroller is constantly waiting for a new reference to be sent.

In order to better adapt the vehicle to the dimensions of the city mock-up, all its elements were made using 3D printing technology, such as adapters for the motors to mount the wheels, USB camera holder, base platform adapted to mount the motors, cameras, electronics, power supply, and the main computing platform. Four Pololu HP micromotors with 150:1 gears and encoders were attached to the base platform, on which the shaft was mounted using Mecanum 80mm diameter wheels with adapters. On the underside of the platform is a breadboard with electronics to control the motors and a 14.8V nominal LiPo pack. At the top of the chassis there is a computer platform and a USB camera mount. Figure 1b shows the model of the autonomous vehicle described above.

4   Evaluation of the Detection-Segmentation Network

The first experiment was to compare the quality (efficiency, accuracy) of network model inference before and after quantisation. The tests were performed using the libraries provided by AMD Xilinx, discussed earlier. Each branch was evaluated on the test set and the results are summarised in Tabels 1, 2, 3 and 4. As can be seen, quantisation resulted in a slight quality decrease (of the order of less than one per cent). This means, therefore, that the model used by the SoC FPGA platform will behave almost identically to the one run on a PC equipped with a graphics card in the environment provided by AMD Xilinx. The conducted experiment also shows that a prepared dataset of 750 pictures in total was enough to train the model for the given task. It is worth noting that it was created for a small mock-up with repetitive scenery, so shooting more pictures could result in overfitting of the model. The dataset seems to be a good base which could be extended for models that could be run on similar, but larger mock-ups. For real-life deployment of the model, it would be worth considering using bigger datasets, which take into consideration environmental variability (different times of day, weather, etc.). There are some datasets available, such as BDD100K, or a custom dataset could be created, similarly as described in Sect. 3.1.

To test the efficiency and cost-effectiveness of the proposed solution, a series of performance tests were carried out on the Kria KV260 platform. The input to the algorithm was a pre-prepared dataset derived from footage recorded on a mock-up of the city. During operation, the use of the quad-core Cortex-A53 processor clocked at 1.3 GHz used in the platform, the use of RAM (Random Access Memory) and CMA (Contiguous Memory Allocator), and the power consumption of the SOM (System on Module) platform were checked. The results are shown in Table 5. It is worth noting that the platform makes full use of one CPU core. According to the manufacturer's documentation, it is possible to run the algorithm using multithreading, but this would involve higher power consumption. The results show that the platform consumes only around 5W of power when running, which allows it to be considered energy efficient.

In order to compare the performance of the platform used, the inference time of the MultiTask V3 network and the execution time of one iteration of the algorithm was examined. The same algorithm was then run on the NVIDIA Jetson Nano and NVIDIA Jetson Xavier NX eGPU platforms, using the pre-quantisation model and the PyTorch library to run the network. The results of the algorithm's efficiency on the platforms are shown in Table 6.

Experiments show that the Kria KV260 platform has demonstrated the best performance in its power consumption class. In terms of processing speed, it clearly outperforms the NVIDIA Jetson Nano platform, with the same power consumption. It also runs faster than the NVIDIA Jetson Xavier NX platform in 10W consumption mode. Only when using the 20W consumption mode does the NX platform achieve approximately 0.5 fps (frames per second) more, but at the cost of four times higher power consumption.

The achieved processing speed of almost 5 FPS is sufficient for the algorithm to make a decision in a satisfactory time. However, the results show that the application of deep neural networks on energy-efficient embedded platforms is still a significant challenge.

To sum up. The best results were obtained on the Kria KV260 SoC FPGA platform. The SoC FPGA platform allows us to obtain satisfactory results in terms of accuracy, efficiency, and power consumption. It should be noted that the currently implemented algorithm is still under development, and the results show that it would be beneficial to focus more on code optimisation and system reconfiguration to utilise all CPU cores. This could slightly increase power consumption, but even 10W of consumption can be considered low for a platform that would be the most important element of an autonomous car. The code used in the experiments described is available at https://github.com/vision-agh/mt_kria.

Table 1. Comparison of results for object detection (mAP – mean Average Precision).

Quantisation state	mAP$_{50}$ [%]	mAP$_{70}$ [%]	mAP$_{75}$ [%]
Before	99.4	99.4	97.2
After	99.3	99.3	97.0

Table 2. Comparison of results for drivable area segmentation (MIoU – Mean IoU, IoU – Intersection over Union).

Quantisation state	MIoU [%]	IoU [%]	
		Background	Drivable area
Before	97.31	97.88	96.75
After	97.29	97.86	96.72

Table 3. Comparison of results for lane segmentation (MIoU – Mean IoU, IoU – Intersection over Union).

Quantisation state	MIoU [%]	IoU [%]	
		Background	Lanes
Before	90.72	99.04	82.40
After	90.69	99.04	82.33

Table 4. Comparison of results for object segmentation (MIoU – Mean IoU, IoU – Intersection over Union).

Quantisation state	MIoU [%]	IoU [%]					
		Background	Pedestrian	Amber Light	Red Light	Green Light	Obstacle
Before	96.52	99.85	88.69	93.90	95.13	94.66	94.88
After	92.08	99.81	88.69	92.56	90.49	89.45	91.46

Table 5. Comparison of resource consumption on the Kria KV260 platform.

Resource usage	CPU cores				RAM	CMA	Power
	CPU_0	CPU_1	CPU_2	CPU_3			
Used	85 %	22 %	3 %	3 %	38 %	6 %	4.95 W

Table 6. Comparison of algorithm's performance on different computing platforms.

Embedded platform	Power [W]	Speed [fps]	Execution time [s]	Model Inference time [s]
Kria KV260	5	4.85	0.206	0.073
Nvidia Jetson Nano	5	2.07	0.483	0.223
Nvidia Jetson Xavier NX	10	4.35	0.230	0.093
	20	5.48	0.182	0.068

5   Conclusion

In this paper, we have discussed the implementation of a perception system for autonomous vehicles using a detection-segmentation network deployed in an SoC FPGA. We have presented the process of preparing a custom dataset according to the requirements of the FPT'22 competition and the training of a neural network model. We have also given a detailed description of the construction of a Mecanum wheel-based autonomous vehicle model, focusing on mechanical and electrical aspects. A fully autonomous control algorithm has been implemented and run on the discussed platform, as well as on two eGPUs. Several experiments have been performed, showing the efficiency and low power consumption of the proposed solution, which supports our thesis that the FPGA Kria KV260 using the MultiTask V3 neural network is a suitable solution for autonomous cars and robots with limited space and resources.

In future work, we will first refactor the code to further improve its efficiency. We also plan to test the vehicle model on the mock-up. Secondly, we will try to use the *weakly supervised learning* and *self-supervised learning* methods, which, in the case of an atypical, custom dataset, would allow a significant reduction in the labelling process of the learning data. We would also like to consider adding modules for depth estimation and optical flow, as these are often used in autonomous vehicle perception systems. The next step would be to use the depth estimation branch in the MultiTask V3 model. This could be beneficial to further improve the vehicle's perception. Using the branch will require creating an additional dataset, based on the mock-up, as the pre-trained model did not give satisfactory results during testing. The dataset can be obtained by recording the environment using a depth sensor, such as the Intel RealSense L515, a device equipped with an RGB camera and a LiDAR sensor. We would also like to consider adding optical flow modules, as these are often used in autonomous vehicle perception systems.

Acknowledgements. The work presented in this paper was supported by the programme "Excellence initiative - research university" for the AGH University of Krakow.

References

1. Minh, D., Wang, H.X., Li, Y.F., et al.: Explainable artificial intelligence: a comprehensive review. Artif. Intell. Rev. **55**, 3503–3568 (2022). https://doi.org/10.1007/s10462-021-10088-y
2. Terven, J., Cordova-Esparza, D.: A comprehensive review of YOLO: from YOLOv1 to YOLOv8 and beyond (2023). https://doi.org/10.48550/arXiv.2304.00501
3. Ronneberger, O., Fischer, P., Brox, T.: U-Net: convolutional networks for biomedical image segmentation. In: Navab, N., Hornegger, J., Wells, W.M., Frangi, A.F. (eds.) MICCAI 2015. LNCS, vol. 9351, pp. 234–241. Springer, Cham (2015). https://doi.org/10.1007/978-3-319-24574-4_28
4. He, K., Gkioxari, G., Dollár, P., Girshick, R.: Mask R-CNN. In: 2017 IEEE International Conference on Computer Vision (ICCV), Venice, Italy, pp. 2980–2988 (2017). https://doi.org/10.1109/ICCV.2017.322

5. Wu, D., et al.: YOLOP: you only look once for panoptic driving perception. Mach. Intell. Res. **19**, 1–13 (2022)
6. Vu, D., Ngo, B., Phan, H.: HybridNets: end-to-end perception network. arXiv preprint: arXiv:2203.09035 (2022)
7. Vitis AI library user guide (UG1354). https://docs.xilinx.com/r/en-US/ug1354-xilinx-ai-sdk/MultiTask-V3. Accessed 18 May 2023
8. Yu, F., et al.: BDD100K: a diverse driving dataset for heterogeneous multitask learning. In: 2020 IEEE/CVF Conference on Computer Vision and Pattern Recognition (CVPR), pp. 2633–2642 (2018)
9. Seng, K.P., Ang, L.-M.: Embedded intelligence: state-of-the-art and research challenges. IEEE Access **10**, 59236–59258 (2022). https://doi.org/10.1109/ACCESS.2022.3175574
10. Wu, R., Guo, X., Du, J., Li, J.: Accelerating neural network inference on FPGA-based platforms-a survey. Electronics **10**, 1025 (2021). https://doi.org/10.3390/electronics10091025
11. The international conference on field-programmable technology (FPT'21) FPGA design competition. https://wp.rs.cs.okayama-u.ac.jp/design-contest-fpt2022/. Accessed 16 May 2023
12. Kria KV260 Vision AI starter kit product brief. https://www.xilinx.com/content/dam/xilinx/publications/product-briefs/xilinx-kv260-product-brief.pdf. Accessed 18 May 2023

Architectures

Increasing the Fault Tolerance of COTS FPGAs in Space: SEU Mitigation Techniques on MPSoC

George Pagonis[1], Vasileios Leon[1], Dimitrios Soudris[1],
and George Lentaris[1,2(✉)]

[1] National Technical University of Athens
School of Electrical and Computer Engineering, Zografou 15780, Greece
{gpagonis,vleon,dsoudris,glentaris}@microlab.ntua.gr
[2] University of West Attica, Department of Informatics and Computer Engineering,
Egaleo 12243, Greece
glentaris@uniwa.gr

Abstract. The increasing need for more powerful onboard computing in space applications contributes in a shift towards the use of Commercial-Off-The-Shelf (COTS) accelerators for payload processing, which offer superior performance compared to traditional radiation-hardened devices. To address the reliability concerns associated with the use of COTS accelerators, this paper investigates and evaluates fault-tolerance techniques for the UltraScale+ MPSoC FPGA, which is being considered into multiple research and industrial space avionics. For testing purposes, as a representative DSP circuit, we develop in parametric VHDL and modify a custom Fast Fourier Transform (FFT) kernel. On the accelerator side, the proposed techniques include temporal, spatial, and hybrid redundancy, as well as application-specific triple modular redundancy. On the system side, partial and full reconfiguration methods are used to correct faulty components. The paper also explores the fault resilience of different computational FPGA blocks (i.e., LUTs and DSPs) when implementing the key processing elements. The results show that the use of DSPs is beneficial for decreasing downtime compared to the respective LUT implementation. Our best approach results in a reduction of downtime by 95% and 65% for the 8-point and 32-point FFT, respectively, when compared to the baseline implementation without fault tolerance.

Keywords: Fault Tolerant · COTS · Space Applications · UltraScale+ · FPGA · Xilinx · Redundancy · SEM · Reconfiguration

1 Introduction

The "New Space" era is heavily reliant on innovative technological approaches for space applications. The advent of small-form-factor satellites, such as SmallSats and CubeSats, has significantly broadened the scope of Earth Observation (EO) and communication-oriented missions, while it is also attracting new research

F. Palumbo et al. (Eds.): ARC 2023, LNCS 14251, pp. 215–229, 2023.
https://doi.org/10.1007/978-3-031-42921-7_15

opportunities for payload processing in space. More than 80% of communication and 79% of technology and development satellites belong to the small-form-factor category [9]. The proliferation of small satellites and sensor instruments has resulted in a vast amount of data that must be processed efficiently onboard. At the same time, modern Digital Signal Processing (DSP) and Artificial Intelligence (AI) algorithms with increased computational demands pose significant challenges for onboard computing, especially when considering the power budget and dependability constraints of space missions. Thus, the space industry is compelled to re-evaluate the computing architectures for space avionics.

Classical space-qualified general-purpose processors, such as the radiation-hardened Power-PC and LEON CPUs [16], are stressed to keep up with the constantly evolving trends in space avionics mentioned above. Consequently, the space industry is shifting towards mixed-criticality architectures that combine radiation-hardened components with Commercial-Off-The-Shelf (COTS) accelerators, such as GPUs, TPUs, VPUs, and FPGAs [8,13,14]. The primary purpose of COTS accelerators is to improve the payload processing performance compared to their radiation-hardened variants or classical general-purpose processors. Specialized COTS System-on-Chips (SoCs) offer an attractive trade-off between Size, Weight, Power, and Cost (SWaP-C), processing performance, and development flexibility [12]. Despite their advantages, however, these COTS devices are not radiation-hardened-by-design, and thus, they are vulnerable to ionizing radiation, increasing the risk of failure. To address this risk, Fault-Tolerance (FT) architectures and fault-mitigation techniques are applied. These techniques commonly include radiation-hardened components supervising the COTS devices, Error Correction Coding (ECC), Error Detection and Correction (EDAC) in memories, and redundant processing (spatial and temporal).

In this context, the current work investigates and evaluates fault-mitigation techniques for Xilinx's UltraScale+ MPSoC FPGA, which is a device integrated in industrial computing boards for space avionics [10,19]. The main contributions of this paper are summarized as follows: (i) we apply our FT techniques in the UltraScale+ MPSoC architecture, which has received less attention by the space community than other FPGAs like Zynq-7000, (ii) on the hardware accelerator front, we propose both coarse-grained and fine-grained FT architectures, which incorporate spatial and temporal redundancy, as well as a combination of both approaches, (iii) on the system side, we apply correction of the FPGA configuration memory using full reconfiguration or dynamic partial reconfiguration as complementary FT technique, (iv) we design a custom software fault injection and evaluation campaign to evaluate the proposed FT techniques in terms of reliability and resource utilization, (v) we explore the fault resilience of the computational FPGA blocks (DSPs and LUTs) and the impact of the kernel size on the accelerator's reliability.

We utilize a ZCU106 commercial board featuring the UltraScale+ MPSoC architecture (Quad Arm Cortex-A53 and 16nm FinFET+ programmable logic). As a representative test case for DSP application, we develop a custom Fast Fourier Transform (FFT) kernel with parametric VHDL. Our implementation facilitates full control on the memory size and logic resources towards examining various test cases for our FT techniques. To evaluate our FT techniques, we develop a fault-injection campaign that gathers addresses of the FPGA's configuration memory to apply bit-flips via Xilinx's SEM IP, similarly to [3,4]. Our best-performing architecture is based on a combination of Triple Modular Redundancy (TMR) and reconfiguration, which achieves a downtime reduction of 89%–95% at the 8-point FFT and 66%–58% at the 32-point FFT (depending on the use of DSPs or LUTs for the computations), with only a slight increase in resource utilization of $1.63 \times$ –$1.89 \times$ and $2.59 \times$ –$2.74 \times$, respectively.

The remainder of this paper is organized as follows. In Sect. 2, we present a review of relevant literature works, including a comparison with our approach. Section 3 outlines our proposed architectures and fault-tolerant techniques, detailing how they are incorporated into our design. In Sect. 4, we evaluate the effectiveness of our approach by describing our campaign to extract results, presenting the obtained outcomes, and highlighting significant experimental results. Finally, Sect. 5 concludes our work.

2   Related Work

As COTS FPGAs for space applications are increasingly utilized in orbit, FT techniques have attracted significant attention. Numerous studies have investigated the impact of failures and ways to improve reliability in COTS FPGAs.

In [2], the authors correct errors in MPSoC at system level. Their approach is to divide the device into secure and non-secure sides, and protect the data exchanges between the two sides. In addition, an external supervisor acts as a watchdog timer. While this study focuses primarily on improving the reliability via system-level mitigation techniques, in our paper we explore FT architectures for the FPGA programmable logic. The work in [11] introduces system-level hardening techniques by employing multiple processing nodes for redundancy and triple modular redundant memories for Zynq's bootloaders and operating system. However, also in this case, the FPGA is not under any FT technique, thus the calculations on the programmable logic are susceptible to ionizing radiation. The authors of [15] develop fault-tolerant architectures based on Zynq's features (e.g., redundancy, dynamic partial reconfiguration, configuration memory scrubbing). In this paper, the techniques are deployed in an older architecture, i.e., Zynq-7000, whereas our work focuses on a newer one, i.e., UltraScale+ MPSoC, which is also gaining traction in space avionics.

The literature includes other relevant works for MPSoC, such as the study of [6], which presents non-blocking partial reconfiguration options. In the same context, the work of [17] integrates Fault Detection, Isolation, & Recovery (FDIR) features, among other functionalities, into the MPSoC-based on-board processor. However, the novelty of our approach lies in the cooperation of accelerator-based mitigation techniques and reconfiguration on cutting-edge architecture. More specifically, our fault-mitigation techniques for the accelerator include spatial, temporal, and hybrid redundancy, while our correction approaches for the faulty components rely on partial and full reconfiguration. The extensive analysis of both the size of the hardware kernel (application) and the use of different FPGA computational blocks also sets our study apart from existing works in literature.

3   Development of Fault-Tolerance Techniques

3.1   HW/SW Fault-Tolerant Architecture

We propose the FT architecture depicted in Fig. 1. This architecture comprises two primary modules: the SEM sub-system and the Application sub-system. The SEM sub-system is responsible for the emulation of ionizing radiation faults (i.e., Single-Event Upsets – SEUs), by injecting bit-flips into the configuration memory. The Application sub-system includes the example hardware accelerator (FFT) and the communication components between MPSoC's processing system and programmable logic. The SEM sub-system includes the SEM IP provided by Xilinx, along with the monitor interface and UART communication between this sub-system and the ARM processor. The SEM IP has access to the configuration memory through the Internal Configuration Access Port (ICAP).

The proposed FT techniques, implemented in the programmable logic of MPSoC, include various redundancy techniques such as Dual Modular Redundancy (DMR), Triple Modular Redundancy (TMR), Temporal N-Modular Redundancy (NMR), Hybrid DMR & NMR, and Fine-Grained Spatial Redundancy (at the level of FFT stages and butterfly processing units). To correct faulty components, we utilize either Full Reconfiguration (FR) or Dynamic Partial Reconfiguration (DPR). To emulate the use of an external fault-tolerant flash memory, the bitstreams required for reconfiguration are initially stored on an SD card and transferred to the Double Data Rate (DDR) memory during the application initialization. Furthermore, we employ Xilinx's Xilfpga library, which acts as a bridge between MPSoC's Processing System (PS) and Programmable Logic (PL), enabling us to perform either FR or DPR via the Processor Configuration Access Port (PCAP).

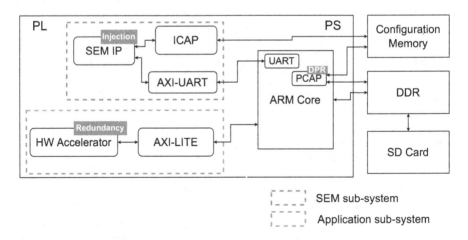

Fig. 1. The proposed FT architecture on Xilinx's UltraScale+ MPSoC FPGA.

3.2   Coarse-Grained Application-Independent Redundancy

Spatial DMR. By duplicating the FFT kernel, we detect mismatches between the outputs of the two FFT modules. However, this approach cannot determine which FFT module provides the correct output. Consequently, when an error is detected, both modules require correction to guarantee the correct functionality of the accelerator. The key advantage over the TMR is the smaller area occupied on the FPGA fabric.

Spatial TMR. The triplication of the FFT kernel offers both error detection & correction capabilities, as the voter can determine which FFT module produces the correct output. In case of a single faulty FFT module, the voter forwards the correct result to the final output (correction), while raising the appropriate flag to signal the detection of an error. This approach enables the reconfiguration of the single faulty module, while allowing the other 2 FFT modules to remain operational and continue to accept inputs and produce outputs.

Temporal NMR. The proposed temporal NMR architecture is illustrated in Fig. 2. This technique reuses a single FFT module to perform the exact same computation multiple times during a period, contrary to spatial redundancy performing the same FFT with different HW modules. The goal of this architecture is to exploit the internal parallelism/pipelining offered by the accelerator, e.g., by our FFT kernel. Assuming applications with imbalanced data-compute rate, e.g., serial input, we utilize the idle/wait time for data queuing to apply temporal redundancy. In particular, our hardware accelerator includes a repeater component feeding N times the previously received input to the FFT kernel to redo the same computation N times (where N is the number of the FFT points). Besides the repeater, this architecture also includes an error detection component to compare the outputs of redundant FFT executions. Moreover, we implement an FSM to handle the error flags upon detection and protect the system from forwarding new data to the faulty FFT. This architecture has the ability for both error detection & correction. However, we have a probability of $1/N$ to miss the upset, because it might occur in-between distinct FFT inputs when there is no reference data for valid comparison. Furthermore, during the correction phase, the accelerator is not operational as there is no redundant HW to continue operation (single FFT module).

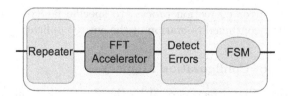

Fig. 2. The proposed Temporal NMR FT architecture.

Hybrid DMR and NMR. Hybrid redundancy combines both the spatial and temporal redundancy techniques, by employing two FFT modules for the computation, while also repeating the FFT execution N times (as in temporal NMR). This approach allows for both error detection & correction. The benefit compared to temporal NMR is that it eliminates its limitation to detect an error that occurs during the redundant iterations. This issue is resolved due to the duality of the kernel, which allows for error detection in case the two outputs differ. Moreover, compared to temporal NMR, the FSM for ensuring the detected errors is more complex, as now there are two FFT modules instead of one. Finally, regarding error correction, it is performed if the error is detected during the repetition of the FFT execution for the same input, and not if the output of the two modules differs from the start of the repeating operation.

3.3 Fine-Grained Application-Specific Redundancy

Our custom FFT kernel comprises butterfly blocks arranged in stages. To enhance its resilience, we incorporate an application-specific mitigation architecture that ensures the protection of the FFT kernel at every level of abstraction. In contrast to the coarse-grained approach, which focuses on protecting the entire FFT kernel, this architecture seeks to correct smaller components, i.e., the stage and the butterfly blocks. This architecture leverages the benefits of spatial redundancy by triplicating smaller components of the kernel, and hence, presumably, enabling faster fine-grained reconfiguration/correction of smaller HW areas.

TMR at FFT-Stage Level. In the developed architecture (Fig. 3a), we apply triplication at each stage of the FFT computation. We replicate the entire FFT stage and a voter compares the outputs of the three identical stages. This approach extends the voting scheme used in the coarse-grained TMR implementation, where the outputs of three identical FFT's are compared, however, here, we detect and correct errors at each one of the $\log N$ FFT stages, individually. Upon error, only the corresponding component is reconfigured/corrected, while the application continues to function and output correct values.

TMR at Butterfly Processing Unit Level. The butterfly-level TMR architecture, illustrated in Fig. 3b, implements triplication at every butterfly component, similar to the stage-level TMR architecture. This approach enables the localization of the error correction process to specific faulty butterflies, while accommodating the continued operation of the entire application.

3.4 Correction of Configuration Memory

Reconfiguration. The correction of SEUs (bit-flips in the configuration memory) is performed at the configuration layer by applying either FR or PR of the programmable logic. FR involves reloading the entire bitstream, which corrects

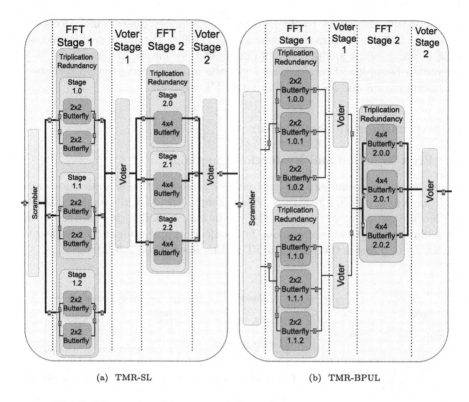

(a) TMR-SL   (b) TMR-BPUL

Fig. 3. The proposed fine-grained FT architecture in the FFT kernel.

any malfunction or error that may have occurred and altered the accelerator's functionality. On the other hand, DPR employs smaller blocks within the FPGA fabric, which are created by dividing the design into partitions using PBlocks. This method is dynamic, as it can be performed while the application continues to operate and produce results. We select to implement this correction method only for the computational blocks i.e., the entire FFT kernel, as well as FFT's stage and butterfly components.

We exclude the components required for the redundancy techniques (e.g., voters, FSMs) and the communication protocol.

Configuration Memory Scrubbing. The SEM IP offers an internal memory scrubber that utilizes CRC and ECC algorithms to detect and correct faults in the configuration memory via ICAP. However, the internal scrubbers suffer from certain integrity problems [5]: (i) fault accumulation when multiple errors occur in a single configuration frame, as the ECC algorithm of SEM can correct up to 4-bit errors per frame [1], (ii) faults in the internal scrubber circuit may result in erroneous operation, inserting errors in the configuration memory and thus altering the functionality of the rest components, (iii) faults in the ICAP interface may constitute the access to the configuration memory unavailable. Moreover, the study of [20] demonstrates that in specific designs, the above problems could occur in a significant amount, depending on the percentage of the critical SEM sub-system being hit. Therefore, we avoid the internal configuration scrubbing in our exploration and focus on alternative FT methods.

4   Experimental Evaluation

4.1   Fault Injection and Evaluation Campaign

To assess our FT techniques, we customize a fault-injection & evaluation campaign for Xilinx's ZCU106 MPSoC board (with Vivado Vitis version 2020.2). The block diagram of our testing and validation methodology is illustrated in Fig. 4. Subsequently, we present our fault-injection and evaluation campaigns, which target to assess the proposed FT techniques for 200,000 faults.

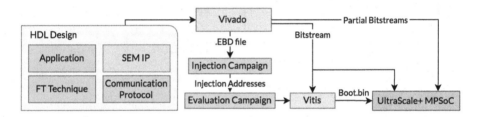

Fig. 4. Our testing and validation methodology for Xilinx's UltraScale+ MPSoC.

Fault-Injection Campaign. We induce errors in 200,000 configuration memory addresses, and specifically, apply one bit-flip (SEU) per address. Put into perspective, this test corresponds to approximately 17 years of an LEO mission [18], considering the possibility of SEUs per day equal to 2.4E-7 and the 132M bits of MPSoC's configuration memory, which results in 31 SEUs per day. We focus on single-bit errors, which have a much higher occurrence possibility compared to multiple-bit errors (the occurrence ratio is 20:1) [7].

Initially, we identify the FPGA clock regions in the .EBD file (mask of the configuration memory) to determine where our design is placed in the configuration memory. The analysis of the .EBD file is performed from top to bottom, which is equivalent to examining the FPGA in upward raster-scan order (from bottom-left to top-right). Next, we translate the position of the injecting bits into Linear Frame Addresses (LFAs). The bits' addresses are predetermined and constant in all the evaluations performed. The LFA transformation is accomplished by considering that the UltraScale+ configuration memory is partitioned into frames, each of which contains 93 32-bit words. From the address selection, we exclude the SEM sub-system (see Fig. 1), as it is necessary for the fault injection process. The 200K LFA 1-bit addresses are inserted into an array to be serially fed in the SEM's monitor interface for fault injection. The injection command performs a bit-flip in the selected configuration memory address.

Evaluation Campaign. Algorithm 1 presents our evaluation campaign, which is based on the PS–PL cooperation. The initialization phase involves loading the bitstreams in the DDR memory, initializing the SEM IP, and establishing the communication between PS and PL. Subsequently, in an iterative manner, we inject faults in the addresses of the Configuration Memory (CRAM), execute our application, and perform error detection and correction (reconfiguration). More specifically, we feed one CRAM address per iteration into the monitor interface of SEM to inject fault in it, and then we transmit the input data to the accelerator via AXI-Lite and execute the HW kernel. Simultaneously, we execute the kernel on ARM to obtain the expected HW results. The results of the HW execution and the error flags of the FT architecture are received by PS. The error detection is performed on ARM, which compares the SW and HW results and analyzes the raised error flags. If an error is detected, error correction is commanded through the use of reconfiguration (PR or FR), as indicated by the error flags (e.g., some faulty components may require only PR to be reconfigured). Finally, in the report phase, we calculate the number of SEU errors and the downtime of the architecture. All the clocks of the design are operating at a frequency of 100MHz (PS–PL communication interface, SEM IP, UART port, hardware kernel). Moreover, with this frequency, the SEM's monitor interface allows us to inject 1 error every 4 ms.

Algorithm 1. Evaluation Campaign

Initialization Phase: FPGA configuration, SEM/ICAP init., PS–PL commun.
Fault-Injection Phase:
for $i \leftarrow 1$ to 200K **do**
    Inject i-th fault in CRAM
    Execute HW & SW
    Receive HW Results
    Check HW flags and Data Correctness
    if Error Detected **then**
        if Error in accelerator IP **then**
            Partial Reconfiguration
        else
            Full Reconfiguration
        end if
    end if
end for
Report Phase: calculation of downtime and number of apparent SEU impacts

---

4.2   Experimental Results

Resource Utilization and Memory Size. Table 1 reports the resource utilization of our designs (FFT kernel & FT technique) on ZCU106 MPSoC. We note that the RAMB utilization is constant (1.2%), while the BUFG usage is in the range 0.3%–1.2%. Moreover, we report that some fine-grained TMR designs do not fit in the FPGA, i.e., the butterfly-level TMR for the 16-point FFT as well as both the stage-level and butterfly-level TMR for the 32-point FFT. Besides the FT technique, each design applies either FR or PR for error correction.

As shown in Table 1, the LUT-based implementations utilize on average 1.48× more essential bits of configuration memory than the respective DSP-based implementations. Another observation is that the spatial redundancy technique increases the resources only by 0.44% and 0.5% in the DSP- and LUT-based implementation, respectively. Furthermore, as expected, the temporal redundancy requires less resources than the spatial redundancy, i.e., only 0.1% and 0.16% more resources compared to the FFT kernel. Finally, as we divide the design into partitions to support PR in the fine-grained FT techniques (TMR SL, TMR BPUL), the floor-planning optimizations of the placement tool are disabled, and thus, the resources are increased. For example, in the 8-point FFT, the partial bitstream size of the stage component is on average 1/2 of the FFT's bitstream size (rather than 1/3, as expected, given that the FFT has 3 stages).

Table 1. Resource utilization of FFT & FT techniques on ZCU106 MPSoC (230K LUTs, 1.7K DSPs, 459K FFs, 132M ess. bits). The ranges refer to 8/16/32-pt FFT (32-pt TMR SL and 16/32-pt TMR BPUL are missing due to resource over-utilization).

FT Techn.	DSP Implementation				LUT Implementation		
	DSPs	LUTs	FFs	Ess. Bits	LUTs	FFs	Ess. Bits
only FFT	2.7–29%	2.7–6%	1.2–1.4%	2.1–6.1%	4.0–19%	1.3–2%	2.7–11%
Temp NMR	2.7–29%	3.4–6.8%	1.5–2.5%	2.3–7.1%	4.7–20%	1.5–3.1%	3–12%
DMR	5.3–58%	3.4–10%	1.4–2.1%	2.7–11%	5.9–37%	1.5–3.4%	3.9–21%
DMR &NMR	5.3–58%	4.3–13%	1.6–3.2%	3.1–12%	6.9–39%	1.8–4.5%	4.2–22%
TMR	8–87%	4.2–15%	1.5–2.6%	3.4–16%	8–55%	1.6–4.5%	5.1–30%
TMR SL	9–21%	4.7–9%	1.7–2.6%	4.3–8%	8.5–20%	1.8–2.9%	6–13%
TMR BPUL	9%	5.4%	1.9%	4.3%	9.3%	2%	6.3%

Correction Latency. Next, we evaluate the time needed to restore the functionality of the device, either by reconfiguring the entire FPGA (FR) or specific blocks of faulty components (PR). All the relevant experimental results are presented in Table 2, where we also report results for memory scrubbing via SEM (CMS).

Firstly, we observe that FR is is 28.3×, 7.8× and 2.5× more time-consuming than the PR of the 8-point, 16-point, and 32-point FFT, respectively. It is important to note that the bitstream size is fixed and independent of the design size,

Table 2. Experimental results for the PR, FR, & CMS techniques on ZCU106 MPSoC.

Partial Reconfiguration		Module Size	Config. Time
Kernel Size	Partial Module		
8	FFT kernel	661 KB	1 ms
	Average Stage component	330 KB	0.6 ms
	Average Butterfly component	174 KB	0.363 ms
16	FFT kernel	2354 KB	3.59 ms
	Average Stage component	338 KB	0.9 ms
32	FFT kernel	7492 KB	11.46 ms
Full Reconfiguration		19.3 MB	28.3 ms
Configuration Memory Scrubbing via SEM (default solution)	Detection Time		26ms
	Repair Time (Correctable)		44 μs
	Repair Time (Uncorrectable)		22 μs
	Any CRC-Only Time (Uncorrectable)		9 μs

thus, the FR time is always constant. In contrast, the PR time is increased linearly to the size of the components to be re-configured. However, when PR targets small FPGA regions, the initialization time takes up a significant part of the whole PR time. In addition, the PR of specific components, i.e., stage and butterfly, is only 1.6× and 2.75× faster, respectively, than the PR of the entire FFT kernel. The small difference in the PR times is justified by the fact that the cross-PBlock optimization is disabled when creating small PBlocks, as calculations from different regions cannot be merged, and thus, the sizes of the partial bitstreams are not very small. Finally, when compared with the vendor's internal memory scrubber, FR is only 1.08 × slower than the CMS approach. Nevertheless, as shown in Table 2, the most time-consuming task of CMS is the error detection (26 ms), while the error correction requires only a few μs.

SEU and Downtime. Figure 5 evaluates the reliability of our FT techniques by examining the number of SEU errors and the downtime for different kernel sizes (i.e., 8, 16, 32) and FPGA computational blocks (i.e., DSPs, LUTs). On average for all the FT techniques, the number of SEU errors in the LUT implementation is 2.7× , 3.6× and 2.9× larger than the DSP one for the different kernel sizes. The downtime follows a similar trend, being 2.2× , 3.6× and 2.7× larger when using LUTs. These results are justified by the fact that the DSP implementations utilize less resources than the respective LUT ones, whose larger utilized area increases the fault possibility. Regarding the impact of different kernel sizes, we observe that the smaller designs (e.g., 8-point FFT) suffer from less errors, and thus, their downtime is reduced. More specifically, the 8-point FFT has on average 1.2× |3.4× and 2× |4.2× (DSP|LUT) smaller downtime than the 16-point and 32-point FFTs, respectively.

The plots of Fig. 5 demonstrate that the **Temporal NMR** and **TMR** techniques are the most effective in terms of downtime. The superiority of Temporal NMR can be attributed to its capability to detect errors with only a small resource overhead compared to the other approaches. On the other hand, besides error detection, TMR also provides error correction compared to the other approaches, increasing the reliability. In contrast, the fine-grained approaches (TMR SL, TMR BPUL) improve the downtime of the accelerator without FT, however, they fail to match the downtime of Temporal NMR and TMR. As already explained, this outcome is highly associated with the increased resource utilization that increases the fault possibility and derives from: (i) not optimizing the placement due to the partition into FPGA regions (PBlocks) and (ii) using extra logic to apply fine-grained redundancy (i.e., more voters). Moreover, as the voters of TMR SL and TMR BPUL are not included into PBlocks, their reconfiguration cannot be performed with PR but only with FR, increasing even more the downtime. In particular, we apply 134|183 and 438|638 (DSP|LUT) FRs in TMR SL and TMR BPUL, respectively, while the respective numbers in TMR are 17|19.

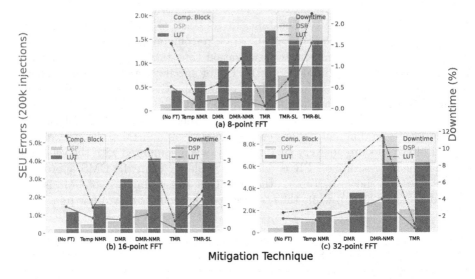

Fig. 5. Evaluation of FT techniques on MPSoC with respect to: (i) the number of injections that affect the functionality (bars & left vertical axes) and (ii) the percentage of downtime (lines & right vertical axes). Every technique employs PR or FR for correction.

Summary of FT Results. Table 3 summarizes the most important results from our experiments, reporting the downtime reduction and the memory overhead versus the kernel without FT. It is evident that the TMR approach provides the most significant improvements in downtime, in exchange, however, for increased utilization of the configuration memory. In particular, the downtime is reduced up to 95.4% (LUT-based 8-point FFT), while the largest memory overhead is 2.74× (LUT-based 32-point FFT). On the other hand, the gains of Temporal NMR in downtime are up to 84.5%, while the memory overhead is 1.2×.

In the proposed design, we rely on the PR/FR methods to correct errors, rather than utilizing the configuration memory scrubbing via SEM. By adopting this approach, we are able to avoid the integrity issues associated with SEM, which were discussed in detail in Sect. 3.4. In addition, as illustrated in Table 2, the time required for the PR of FFTs is 3%–44% of the time in the worst-case scenario of CMS (26 ms for detection and some μs for correction). It is also worth noting that the detection time of our FT techniques is in the order of tens of nanoseconds, including the time needed for reading the error flags and comparing the HW output with the SW results. Overall, instead of the continuous reading of the configuration memory to detect a fault and correct a single configuration memory frame, our reconfiguration process is carried out by PS based on the error flags and the SW–HW comparison.

Another significant outcome is that the fine-grained techniques (TMR SL, TMR BPUL) are more susceptible to faults that alter the functionality than the coarse-grained techniques (e.g., TMR). This susceptibility can be attributed to two main factors: (i) the increase in resource utilization due to the extra redundancy logic and the limited floor-planning optimization (segmentation into PBlocks), and (ii) the use of additional voters (not included in the PBlocks), which leads to an increased need for FR. Regarding the first explanation, the fine-grained approaches utilize significantly more essential bits, and hence, the fault possibility is increased. As a result, the average increase of 1.2× in the number of essential bits results in ∼1.3× more SEU errors that alter the functionality. Finally, the second factor has a bigger impact on downtime, and thus, it is required to apply 9.78× and 25.7× more FRs in TMR SL, TMR BPUL, respectively, than in TMR.

Table 3. Evaluation of FT techniques in terms of downtime and configuration memory utilization (essential bits). The downtime reduction and memory overhead are versus the respective implementation without the FT technique.

Kernel Size	FPGA Impl	FT Technique	Downtime	Downtime Reduction	Memory	Memory Overhead
8	DSP	only FFT	4.1 s	–	2.1%	–
		Temp NMR	1.14 s	72.7%	2.4%	1.2×
		TMR	0.46 s	89.5%	3.5%	1.63×
	LUT	only FFT	12.4 s	–	2.7%	–
		Temp NMR	1.93 s	84.5%	3.0%	1.09×
		TMR	0.57 s	95.4%	5.2%	1.89×
32	DSP	only FFT	13.9 s	–	6.1%	–
		TMR	4.6 s	66.7%	15.8%	2.59×
	LUT	only FFT	19.9 s	–	11.1%	–
		TMR	8.32 s	58.1%	30.4%	2.74×

5   Conclusion

In this work, we proposed and developed various FT techniques for the UltraScale+ MPSoC FPGA, which is a COTS chip already being considered extensively in space avionics. We explored both application-independent and application-specific and FT architectures by using the FFT as our example. Furthermore, we examined the impact on reliability when utilizing diverse FPGA computational blocks to implement our circuits, i.e., DSPs vs LUTs. To evaluate our proposed FT techniques, we employed a custom injection and evaluation campaign. Based on the experimental results, our key conclusions are: (i) the DSP-based FT designs feature less downtime than the corresponding LUT-based FT designs, (ii) the fine-grained FT designs are more susceptible to faults and feature larger downtime than the coarse-grained ones, as they utilize more resources (increasing the possibility of fault in essential bits) and require additional full reconfigurations in our scheme, (iii) the best-performing FT architecture relies on the DSP-based TMR technique and PR/FR, achieving only 0.05% downtime (0.46 s in a total execution of 13.3 min), as well as a downtime reduction of 89.5% versus the baseline design without TMR.

Acknowledgment. The current work is partially supported by the EU H2020 project EVOLVE with grant agreement ID 825061.

References

1. AMD Xilinx: UltraScale Architecture Soft Error Mitigation Controller Logi-CORE IP Product Guide (PG187) (2022). https://docs.xilinx.com/r/en-US/pg187-ultrascale-sem
2. Amorim, R.C., Martins, R., Harikrishnan, P., Ghiglione, M., Helfers, T.: Dependable MPSoC framework for mixed criticality applications. In: European Workshop on On-Board Data Processing (OBDP) (2021). https://doi.org/10.5281/zenodo.5521521
3. Aranda, L.A., Ruano, O., Garcia-Herrero, F., Maestro, J.A.: ACME-2: improving the extraction of essential bits in Xilinx SRAM-based FPGAs. IEEE Trans. Circuits Syst. II Express Briefs **69**(3), 1577–1581 (2022). https://doi.org/10.1109/TCSII.2021.3105558
4. Aranda, L.A., Sánchez-Macián, A., Maestro, J.A.: ACME: A tool to improve configuration memory fault injection in SRAM-based FPGAs. IEEE Access **7**, 128153–128161 (2019). https://doi.org/10.1109/ACCESS.2019.2939858
5. Berg, M., et al.: Effectiveness of internal vs. external SEU scrubbing mitigation strategies in a Xilinx FPGA: Design, test, and analysis. In: European Conference on Radiation and Its Effects on Components and Systems (RADECS), pp. 1–8 (2007). https://doi.org/10.1109/RADECS.2007.5205603
6. Bucknall, A., Shanker, S., Fahmy, S.: Build automation and runtime abstraction for partial reconfiguration on Xilinx Zynq UltraScale+, pp. 215–220 (2020). https://doi.org/10.1109/ICFPT51103.2020.00037
7. Chapman, K.: Seu strategies for Virtex-5 devices (2010)

8. Furano, G., et al.: Towards the use of Artificial Intelligence on the edge in space systems: Challenges and opportunities. IEEE Aerospace Electron. Syst. Mag. **35** (2020). https://doi.org/10.1109/MAES.2020.3008468

9. Kongsberg NanoAvionics: How many satellites are in space?. https://nanoavionics. com/blog/how-many-satellites-are-in-space/

10. KP Labs: Leopard DPU: A new chapter in on-board data processing. https:// kplabs.space/wp-content/uploads/Leopard-technical-sheet.pdf

11. Kuligowski, P., Gajoch, G., Nowak, M., Sładek, W.: System-level hardening techniques used in the COTS-based data processing unit. In: European Workshop on On-Board Data Processing (OBDP) (2021). https://doi.org/10.5281/zenodo. 5521575

12. Lentaris, G., Stratakos, I., Stamoulias, I., Soudris, D., Lourakis, M., Zabulis, X.: High-performance vision-based navigation on SoC FPGA for spacecraft proximity operations. IEEE Trans. Circuits Syst. Video Technol. **30**(4), 1–14 (2020). https:// doi.org/10.1109/TCSVT.2019.2900802

13. Leon, V., et al.: FPGA & VPU co-processing in space applications: Development and testing with DSP/AI benchmarks. In: IEEE International Conference on Electronics, Circuits, and Systems (ICECS), pp. 1–5 (2021). https://doi.org/10.1109/ ICECS53924.2021.9665462

14. Leon, V., Lentaris, G., Soudris, D., Vellas, S., Bernou, M.: Towards employing FPGA and ASIP acceleration to enable onboard AI/ML in space applications. In: IFIP/IEEE International Conference on Very Large Scale Integration (VLSI-SoC), pp. 1–4 (2022). https://doi.org/10.1109/VLSI-SoC54400.2022.9939566

15. Leon, V., et al.: Combining fault tolerance techniques and COTS SoC accelerators for payload processing in space. In: IFIP/IEEE International Conference on Very Large Scale Integration (VLSI-SoC), pp. 1–6 (2022). https://doi.org/10.1109/ VLSI-SoC54400.2022.9939621

16. Leon, V., et al.: Development and testing on the European space-grade BRAVE FPGAs: evaluation of NG-Large using high-performance DSP benchmarks. IEEE Access **9**, 131877–131892 (2021). https://doi.org/10.1109/ACCESS.2021.3114502

17. Pérez, A., et al.: Run-time reconfigurable MPSoC-based on-board processor for vision-based space navigation. IEEE Access **8**, 59891–59905 (2020). https://doi. org/10.1109/ACCESS.2020.2983308

18. Xilinx: RT Kintex UltraScale FPGAs for ultra high throughput and high bandwidth applications (2020)

19. Xiphos Technology: Q8s specifications. https://xiphos.com/wp-content/uploads/ 2020/06/XTI-2001-2025-f-Q8S-Rev-B-Spec-Sheet-1.pdf

20. Yang, W., Du, B., He, C., Sterpone, L.: Reliability assessment on 16nm UltraScale+ MPSoC using fault injection and fault tree analysis. Microelectron. Reliab. **120**, 114–122 (2021). https://doi.org/10.1016/j.microrel.2021.114122

Scalable and Energy-Efficient NN Acceleration with GPU-ReRAM Architecture

Rafael Fão de Moura$^{(\boxtimes)}$ and Luigi Carro

Informatics Institute, Federal University of Rio Grande do Sul, Porto Alegre, Brazil
`{rfmoura,carro}@inf.ufrgs.br`

Abstract. As AI techniques are increasingly adopted in various industry sectors, reducing energy consumption in Neural Network applications has become a priority for researchers. One potential solution is analog ReRAM processing, which outperforms GPU-based approaches in terms of both performance and energy consumption. However, the scalability of ReRAM-based architectures for large-scale NN applications with billions of parameters remains a major challenge. To address this issue, this paper proposes a novel GPU-ReRAM architecture that uses a heuristic approach to identify the best NN layers for ReRAM acceleration, thus enabling ReRAM to be scalable for complex NNs while significantly reducing energy consumption. The effectiveness of this approach was tested on real-world models, resulting in a meaningful 6x reduction in energy consumption without sacrificing inference accuracy.

Keywords: Neural Networks · In-memory computing · Scalability

1 Introduction

Neural Networks (NNs) are widely used for various applications, but their growing popularity has raised concerns about power consumption on embedded computing platforms. Graphics Processing Units (GPUs) offer fast and parallel processing for NNs, allowing for larger and more complex NN models. However, the energy requirements of computing NN models in von Neumann architectures make the long-term sustainability of Artificial Intelligence (AI) solutions questionable [15]. As NN model sizes increase, embedded platforms face limitations in processing, memory, and battery capacities, making deployment challenging. Alternatively, utilizing powerful GPUs for computation becomes costlier due to energy-intensive arithmetic circuits, memory systems, and communication systems [31].

In-memory Resistive RAM (ReRAM) computing addresses the energy constraints of GPUs and the memory bottleneck in von Neumann architectures. ReRAMs excel in performing Matrix-Vector Multiplication (MVM) operations in parallel with a time complexity of $O(1)$, enabling the deployment of advanced AI algorithms with reduced energy consumption. Combining the analog computing capabilities of ReRAMs with a GPU can create a GPU-ReRAM device

F. Palumbo et al. (Eds.): ARC 2023, LNCS 14251, pp. 230–244, 2023.
https://doi.org/10.1007/978-3-031-42921-7_16

to enhance NN inference on edge and embedded platforms. However, the current state of ReRAM fabrication technology poses scalability issues, preventing analog ReRAM accelerators from handling deeper NN models. Figure 1 highlights the scalability issue that ReRAM-based NN accelerators are facing. The storage capacity of ReRAM chips falls short of the increasing model sizes of NNs, and recent designs face challenges due to evolving manufacturing processes, random noises, and parasitic voltage drop [8,13]. Consequently, ReRAM chips currently have limited capacity, ranging from a few kilobytes to megabytes.

Despite attempts to reduce NN model size, such as pruning and transforming techniques [17], huge NN models can still reach hundreds of megabytes, creating a gap of five orders of magnitude (10^5) compared to current ReRAMs. Hence, the adoption of state-of-the-art NNs such as Generative Pre-trained Transformer (GPT) requires supporting a plethora of parameters, ranging from 20 millions to 175 billions. This observation presents an opportunity for an optimal solution that can tackle ReRAM scalability by reducing the gap between NN model size and ReRAM capacity, enabling ReRAM devices to support the increasingly complex NN models that are being developed, with the potential to reduce energy consumption and improve NN processing speed.

To fully leverage the potential of ReRAM devices in modern neural networks, we present a solution that bridges the gap between ReRAM storage capacity and the growing demand for deeper and more complex models. Our approach introduces a GPU-ReRAM architecture that incorporates a heuristic for selecting the most beneficial ReRAM-accelerated layers in neural networks. This novel solution combines the scalability of GPUs with the energy efficiency of analog computing, delivering unparalleled performance gains and significant energy savings. Our main contributions are:

- Our work presents a solution to overcome the scalability issue of ReRAM-based NN accelerators and highlights the enormous potential of our GPU-ReRAM architecture in tackling the challenges associated with deploying advanced AI algorithms on energy-constrained devices.
- Our offloading heuristic selects the NN layers that most benefit from ReRAM acceleration, achieving the best trade-off between performance and scalability for a ReRAM constrained device.

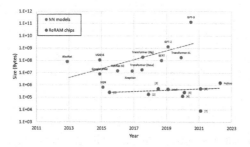

Fig. 1. Size growth comparison of state-of-the art NNs and fabricated ReRAM chips over the years.

– We present the results of our experiments on real-world human activity recognition and image classification tasks, which demonstrate that our heuristic significantly reduces energy consumption by 6x when compared to a powerful RTX 3080 GPU.

2   Background: ReRAM for In-Memory NN Computing

Figure 2a) shows the structure of a ReRAM cell, which is made up of a resistive layer sandwiched between two electrodes. To store data, a voltage is applied between the electrodes, creating an electric field across the oxide layer, causing a filament to form or break between them [27]. The state of the ReRAM cell is determined by the presence or absence of the filament, which can be detected by applying a voltage and measuring the resulting current [11].

The ReRAM arrangement that performs synaptic computations in a NN is called the *synaptic array*, depicted in Fig. 2c). The synaptic array comprises an $N \times M$ crossbar of ReRAM cells, where the WordLine (WL) electrodes connect to the input neurons, and the BitLine (BL) electrodes connect to the output neurons. The conductance of each ReRAM cell represents the weight of the corresponding synapse between input and output neurons. To perform a dot-product operation using the synaptic array, an input voltage signal is applied to the WL, and the ReRAM cell conductances modulate the signal, resulting in a weighted sum at the output BL.

Due to the limited precision of ReRAM devices, it is necessary first to normalize the floating-point weights to decimal integers, and then map them to conductance levels into the synaptic array [27]. As shown in Fig. 2b), one way to achieve this is to define a fixed precision for the synaptic weights, such as 3 bits, and represent them as decimal integers ranging from 0 to 7.

In current implementations of ReRAM, it is not feasible to have the minimum conductance representing the 0 value if the G_{max}/G_{min} ratio is not infinite [11]. Thus, small on/off ratios will introduce non-ideal zeros and distort the inference accuracy. To eliminate these non-ideal zeros, a dummy column filled with $g_{mid} =$

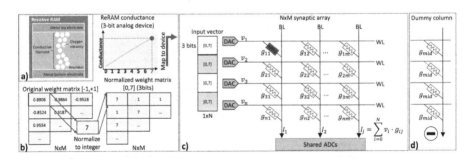

Fig. 2. a) Physical model of conductive filament-based ReRAM cell, b) Mapping weight to synaptic device conductance, c) Parallel dot-product implemented in a ReRAM crossbar, and d) Introducing a dummy column to cancel out the off-state current effects.

$(G_{min} + G_{max})/2$ values is added to multiply-accumulate with the input, as illustrated in Fig. 2d). By subtracting the real outputs with the dummy outputs, the truncated conductance range becomes $[-(G_{max} - G_{min})/2, +(G_{max} - G_{min})/2]$, which is zero-centered as $[-1, +1]$ and perfectly removes the off-state current effects.

3   Related Work

ReRAM-based architectures have gained significant popularity for accelerating both inference [6,34] and training of neural networks [5,35]. To facilitate NN training, the REGENT architecture [21] performs the backward phase of the training algorithm (which necessitates high precision) on GPUs, as does a similar strategy employed in [26]. However, both of these approaches ([21,26]) sacrifice performance since a significant proportion of NN execution is conducted by the relatively slower GPUs rather than ReRAMs. It is well established that ReRAMs can more efficiently implement vector dot-product, the core computation during NN processing, than GPUs [19]. To address this problem and enable the execution of precision-critical layers, the GRAMARCH architecture has been proposed in [20]. However, none of these works considers the scalability challenges of ReRAM in their designs, and most assume ideal operating conditions and infinite ReRAM chip capacity.

Prior works try to mitigate the scalability issue of ReRAMs by reducing the impact of the fabrication limitations caused by physical issues, and hence increasing the capacity of chips. A major concern of performing MVM on ReRAMs is the relatively large current, due to the parallel activation of several devices at the same time. The large current results in a relatively large parasitic voltage drop across the array rows and columns, referred to as IR drop [13]. IR drop was previously taken into account by on-line training in hardware [33] or by including the effects of IR drop in off-line software training via circuit simulations [4,9]. More general compensation schemes have been proposed via calibration of scaling factors [14,16] calibration of the synaptic weights [1,25], or mapping and partitioning algorithms [37]. Other mitigation techniques involve device optimization by conductance limitation [7,10]. However, none of these techniques can enable the increasing of the ReRAM by more than two times.

Other works try to mitigate the scalability issue of ReRAMs by reducing the NN model size, such as reducing the number of bits in the weights, or even employing binary and ternary operations. ReMaGN [2] proposes a ReRAM-based 3D many-core processing-in-memory architecture tailored for on-chip training of Graph Neural Networks. ReMaGN implements Graph Neural Networks training using reduced-precision representation to make the computation faster and reduce the load on the communication backbone. Kim et al. [22] minimize redundant operations in Binary Neural Networks and reduce the number of ReRAM arrays with ADCs approximately by half. Laborieux et al. [24] implement synapses in a differential fashion to reduce bit errors, and read synaptic weights using precharge sense amplifiers, showing that the same memory array architecture can be used to implement ternary weights instead of binary weights. However, such related works do not properly solve the scalability issue of ReRAMs. Despite being capable of reducing the NN model by a factor of 8, thei fall far from mitigating the current gap of ReRAM chips and NN model sizes (currently, a gap of five orders of magnitude).

Our Contributions: Our work differs from the previous by providing an orthogonal heuristic to select the best fit layers to execute in the ReRAM accelerator. As the main result, we achieve significant energy reduction on the fraction of the NN running in the accelerator and considerable energy reduction for the overall system, while maintaining accuracy.

4   Proposed Architecture

4.1   Overall Architecture

Figure 3 illustrates the proposed GPU-ReRAM architecture, which aims to exceed the performance of solitary GPU-based models in neural network applications. The configuration comprises two flat layers of ReRAMs and GPUs, respectively, linked through a 3D arrangement. It is a recognized fact that 3D configurations offer superior throughput, energy efficiency, and area footprint compared to their planar equivalents. As ReRAM tiles are smaller than their GPU counterparts, four ReRAM tiles are grouped with one GPU tile to form a 3D structure called Vault. The GPU tiles and ReRAM clusters are interconnected through a 3D mesh NoC, where the vertical connection within each Vault is established using through silicon vias (TSVs). To ensure extracting the maximum performance and minimal energy consumption of the proposed architecture, Sect. 4.4 describes how to create the best NN layer scheduling with ReRAMs and GPUs to minimize energy consumption or execution time.

4.2   GPU Layer

ReRAMs are relatively more cost-effective in conducting MVM operations compared to GPUs. However, GPUs provide a computing platform with full-precision

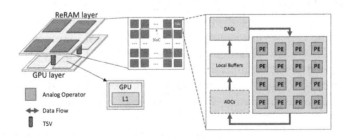

Fig. 3. Overview of the proposed architecture for the energy-efficient versatile acceleration of NN applications.

and are scalable to track deeper NN models. Therefore, GPUs are utilized to implement the remaining layers not chosen for ReRAM acceleration. Each GPU tile consists of a GPU core (SM in NVIDIA terms) with its private L1 cache and a segment of Last-Level Cache (LLC).

4.3 ReRAM Layer

The ReRAM layer provides a low-power computational platform that is capable of efficiently executing MVM operations, utilized for computing convolution and fully-connected layers, along with the necessary activation functions. The ReRAM configuration comprises interconnected tiles, each containing several components, including a Local Buffer, Processing Elements (PEs), DACs, and ADCs. The 3D NoC interconnects the tiles that compose the same Vault, enabling efficient communication and data transfer between them. Inside each tile, the PEs conduct coarse-grained computations. Each PE houses either an instance of the MVM Unit, or a Programmable Non-linear ReRAM Unit (PNRU). The MVM Unit performs a ubiquitous operation used in several neural network models: multiplying a weight matrix with an input vector. In contrast, the PNRU is programmable to execute a wide spectrum of activation functions, such as rectified linear units (ReLU), tanh, sigmoid, etc.

Data Flow and Pipeline. Figure 3 illustrates the data flow within each tile using dark red dashes. The Local Buffers provide input data, which is converted to the analog domain by DACs and sent to the MVM Unit PEs. These PEs perform dot-product operations in parallel, and the results are then processed by PNRU PEs. The PNRU PEs handle non-linearities, such as activation functions and pooling layers, in the analog domain. The resulting outputs are converted back to the digital domain by ADCs and stored in the Local Buffer. To simplify control circuits, each layer of the neural network (NN) is treated as a pipeline stage. The clock cycle of the entire pipeline is determined by the longest latency among all the layers. Consequently, smaller-latency layers may experience idle periods, leading to wasted energy, as they are constrained by the slowest layer.

To mitigate this issue, when the ReRAM layer has available capacity, weights of smaller-latency layers are duplicated, enabling the processing of multiple Input Feature Maps (IFMs) concurrently. This approach reduces idle time and energy leakage by allowing smaller-latency layers to handle more data in parallel. However, duplicating weights and processing multiple IFMs simultaneously may increase hardware complexity and energy consumption. Thus, it is crucial to strike a balance between performance improvement and energy efficiency to optimize the overall system performance. The duplication of a layer is limited to a maximum of 2x, resulting in a maximum of four instances of the same layer on the accelerator.

Local Buffers. Our architecture has two types of memory in the Local Buffers: a memory buffer and a cache memory. The memory buffer is made of Dynamic

RAM (DRAM), while the cache memory uses Static RAM (SRAM). This two-level memory hierarchy is a common practice in architectures based on ReRAM [34]. We assume that the on-chip memory is enough to store the synaptic weights of the entire NN layers mapped to the ReRAM accelerator, so we only need to access off-chip memory to fetch input data and store output data from each tile. We set the cache size to hold all the necessary input/output data for PEs that are mapped to one tile. This way, the cache can reduce the time required for memory access, which improves the overall system performance. We also map the layers of the NN that share the same input onto one tile, allowing buffer sharing to reduce the hardware overhead of local buffers. This technique effectively reduces the hardware complexity and energy consumption of the architecture while maintaining the system's performance.

MVM Unit. The MVM Unit is shown in detail in Fig. 4. Each MVM Unit has a square ReRAM array that stores the synaptic weights and performs dot products in parallel for the NN layers. The MVM results are then sent to the PNRU in the analog domain to perform non-linear computations, as required by each layer. A voltage follower op-amp circuit grounds the BLs and isolates neighbor layers to prevent voltage division from affecting the signal between the MVM Unit and PNRU. By using parallel processing and analog domain processing, the system's performance can be significantly improved, while careful circuit design can ensure accurate signal propagation and minimize interference between layers.

ReRAM technology currently only provides cells with a limited range of conductance, which are typically 2-bit or 3-bit cells. Therefore, some implementations use multiple ReRAM crossbars to combine the weight bits and perform shift-and-add operations to combine the results. However, such an approach can introduce unwanted AD-DA steps in the digital domain or noise sources to the analog signal if linear scaling is used. To address this issue, we use the add method proposed by [18] to represent the entire weight bits. This method involves adding several memory cells with smaller levels to represent a weight with a higher number of levels. For instance, eight 2-bit ReRAM cells are required to compose a 5-bit weight cell (32 levels). Generally, if the ReRAM crossbar cells have L_c levels and the NN weights are represented with L_w levels, where $L_c < L_w$, then $L_w \div L_c$ ReRAM cells are necessary to represent the target weight.

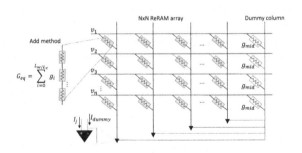

Fig. 4. MVM Unit in detail.

Programmable Non-linear ReRAM Unit (PNRU). The image in Fig. 5 displays the PNRU, which consists of two parts: the ReRAM crossbars compute linear MVM operations, while the op-amp arrangement implements the non-linearity programmed in the PNRU. The ReRAM crossbars have the same structure as the MVM Unit. To enable the calculus of activation functions in the ReRAM crossbar, we approximate the target function with Piece-Wise Linear (PWL) interpolation. PWL interpolates any given function $f(x)$ within N linear segments, as described in Eq. 1.

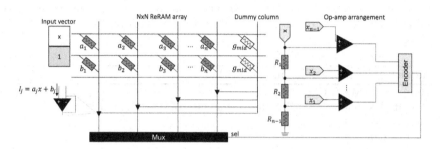

Fig. 5. The Programmable Non-linear ReRAM Unit (PNRU) for the calculus of activation functions: all programmable elements are shown in the orange color. (Color figure online)

$$f(x) \approx \begin{cases} f_1(x) = a_1 x + b1 & x_0 \leq x < x_1 \\ f_2(x) = a_2 x + b2 & x_1 \leq x < x_2 \\ f_n(x) = a_n x + bn & x_{n-1} \leq x < x_n \end{cases} \tag{1}$$

Also, in Fig. 5, the PNRU programming for the PWL computation is shown. The input to the ReRAM crossbar is represented by the column-vector $[\mathbf{x}, 1]^T$, which is multiplied with the $[a_i, b_i]$ coefficients to produce N linear functions, denoted as $f_i(x)$. The outputs of all $f_i(x)$ line segments are computed in parallel through the sum of currents on each BL. The op-amp arrangement works as an analog mux that bypasses only the $f_i(x)$ output corresponding to the current input x value, represented by the voltage level V_x. The op-amps operate as a series of parallel analog comparators, where each op-amp has its negative feedback switched off and compares the input signal (V_x) to an individual reference voltage level ($x_{n-1}, x_n \ldots x_1$). The highest-order active input generates a signal control for the mux, ignoring all other active inputs.

4.4 Offloading: Selecting the Best Layers for ReRAM Acceleration

This section outlines a heuristic for determining which neural network (NN) layers should be offloaded to ReRAMs in order to improve performance. We approach this problem by modeling layer offloading as a variant of the Knapsack problem, which involves selecting a set of items with different weights and values in order to maximize the total profit, while staying within a certain weight limit.

Similarly, the layer offloading problem seeks to select a subset of NN layers to run on ReRAM accelerators, maximizing performance while staying within the capacity of the accelerators.

Hence, we use a dynamic programming solution for the knapsack problem. Our algorithm takes as the input the number of layers (L) in the NN, the total number of ReRAM tiles (W), an array indicating the number of tiles needed for each NN layer (Wt), and an array indicating the corresponding costs (energy consumption or execution time) to run each layer in the ReRAMs (C). The algorithm iterates through the layers and W in bottom-up order, calculating the best offloading solution for each layer (i) based on the remaining number of tiles in the ReRAM accelerator (w), as described in the algorithm below.

Algorithm 1: Layer offloading algorithm

Data: L, W, Wt[.], C[.]
Result: NN mapping to GPU-ReRAM architecture with minimal cost
1 Initialize(Wt, C)
2 **for** $i \leftarrow 1$ *to* L **do**
3   **for** $w \leftarrow 1$ *to* W **do**
4   **if** *Wt[i]* $> w$ **then**
5 | Sol[i][w] = Sol[i-1][w]
6   **else**
7   Sol[i][w] = min(Sol[i-1][w] , Sol[i-1][w - Wt[i]] + C[i])

If the weight of the current layer ($Wt[i]$) exceeds the remaining capacity of the ReRAM accelerator, we skip the layer and keep the solution from the previous step. Otherwise, we add the cost of the current layer to the solution set and reduce the problem size by the weight of that layer. This dynamic programming approach has a time and space complexity of $O(W*L)$, which is much faster than the brute force approach of examining all subsets to find the optimal solution, which would require a time complexity of $O(2^L)$ and is unacceptable for larger L values.

5   Evaluation Methodology

To evaluate the proposed work, we used a simulation framework based on the GPGPU-Sim simulator [3] and DNN+NeuroSim [32]. GPGPU-SIM is used to simulate the GPUs along with the memory layers to obtain execution time and power information of the GPU layer. The GPU cores are based on the NVIDIA Pascal architecture. Also, GPGPU-SIM provides a compatible version of the Pytorch, which helps to model the NNs and works as the wrapper for the DNN+NeuroSim. DNN+NeuroSim simulates the behavior of in-situ analog computing for the ReRAM layer, such as the variability of the ReRAM, and error of ADC and DAC converters within a PyTorch wrapper, to obtain the inference accuracy. Then, the framework employs an analytical model of the ReRAM crossbar computation, including converters, memristor non-idealities, and weight splitting/mapping to compute the design's energy, area, and timing statistics. Initially, DNN+NeuroSim did not support LSTM and GPT cells or weights composed of several RRAM cells, so we added these features and the simulation of the PNRU for the Pytorch wrapper. All activation functions were interpolated by a PWL function composed of 3 line segments.

We use the power, area, and timing model of ReRAM crossbar arrays and the Op-Amp from [27] to design the MVM Unit and the PNRU. The ReRAM accelerator capacity is set to 8MB, following state-of-the-art reports of ReRAM fabricated chips. To compose a design with all components under the same technology, we scale some parameters of the circuits (i.e., transistor sizes) accordingly to work with the 32 nm model. The ReRAM devices have a resistance range of $50k\Omega$ - $800k\Omega$, and the read voltage is 0.15 V. Each ReRAM cell has four bits (16 available conductance levels). Hence, 16 cells are used to represent an 8-bit weight value with the add method. We set the sub-array size to 128×128 for the MVM Unit and 32 × 3 for the PNRU. The ADC and DAC models are from a fabricated chip [23]. CACTI 6.5 [30] is used to model the overhead of buffers and memories. We limit the frequency of tiles to 10 MHz to hold the critical path of our design. The size of the local buffers and the number of DACs/ADCs are determined accordingly to match the throughput of the MVM Unit and the PNRU. The NN weights are quantized to 8-bit under the WAGE8 format before being mapped to the device conductance values.

The device variation of ReRAM, ADC, DAC, and op-amp can significantly deteriorate the accuracy of the system. Variations can be caused by read or write operation, properties of resistive materials, and various fabrication factors. In this work, we use the Gaussian noise to represent the device variation for the MVM Unit and the PNRU. We use Eq. 2 to represent the Gaussian noise of device conductance. Where $output_{ideal}$ is the expected output value from the MVM Unit or PNRU circuits; $N(0, \sigma^2)$ is the normal distribution of the device error with a mean equal to zero and standard deviation σ. It has been measured that the variation is normally 0.2% for the ReRAM cells, 0.3% for the op-amps, and half LSB for the AD-DA converters.

$$ouput = output_{ideal} \times (1 + N(0, \sigma^2)) \tag{2}$$

Two CNN-LSTM models are used to evaluate this works on two Human Activity Recognition datasets: Kinetics-700 and UCF-101. The NN models consist of CNNs AlexNet and ResNet18 backbones, followed by an LSTM layer. Also, a GPT-3-XL model is employed for the task of reading comprehension over the CoQA dataset. The choice for these NNs is explained by the fact they are modern networks, and their applications can be easily found in the current market.

6   Results

6.1   Synthesis Results

Table 1. Tile power and area breakdown of a ReRAM tile

Component	Power (uW)	Area (um^2)	Quantity
eDRAM;8kB	2098.0	4357.0	1
I/O Buffer;640B	652.0	1856.0	1
Local Buffers	**2750.0**	**6213.0**	**1**
ADC;8 bits;1.3GSps	**3100.0**	**1500.0**	**2**
DAC;8bits;1.3GSps	**200.0**	**500.0**	**128**
ReRAM XBAR 128 × 128	10.0	148.0	16
Op-AMP	15.0	0.4	128
MVM Unit	**2080.0**	**2419.2**	**4**
ReRAM XBAR 32 × 3	0.1	0.9	1
Op-AMP	15.0	0.4	5
PNRU	**75.1**	**2.9**	**32**
Router	**4498.0**	**11227.0**	**1**
TOTAL TILE	**49771.2**	**94208.6**	**N/A**

Table 1 presents the power and area breakdown of a tile of the ReRAM layer. Each tile has four instances of the MVM Unit, 32 instances of the PNRU, 128 DAC, and two ADC. Each ReRAM tile has roughly 64kBytes of capacity. Therefore, the ReRAM layer can support 128 ReRAM tiles, and hence we can have 32 vaults (the grouping of four ReRAM tiles + a GPU core) with the capacity to compute both on GPU and ReRAM. Also, we set the GPU layer to have 256 GPU cores. This means that 32 of the 256 GPU cores compose vaults with the 128 ReRAM tiles. The remaining GPU cores do not have a connection with the ReRAM tiles. We experimentally found such a tile dimensioning as the one that best fits power efficiency and throughput together.

6.2   Computing Efficiency

Table 2. Computing efficiency comparison.

Accelerator name	Approach/ Device	Computing Efficiency (GOPs/s/W)
ISAAC [34]	ReRAM + digital IC	380
DaDianNao [28]	Digital IC	286
ReRAM-PIM [27]	ReRAM + digital IC	116
ERA [12]	ReRAM + analog IC	714
FPAA [29]	ReRAM + AN221E04-FPAA	250
FPGA [36]	Virtex7-VX690t	66
GPU	Nvidia Geforce RTX 3080	372
This work	**GPU-ReRAM**	**1177**

Table 2 compiles the computing efficiency of our design with state-of-the-art accelerators, including several ReRAM and Digital accelerators, as FPAA-based and FPGA-based implementations. Compared with the Digital design, our approach achieves 10.14x its efficiency. ERA is 1.64x less efficient than our design. Compared to the Field Programmable approaches (FPAA and FPGA), our approach achieves 4.7x and 17.8x more efficiency. Such a result can be achieved due to its simple logic inside the PNRU, which has considerably smaller costs of reprogrammability for non-linearities than a conventional programmable circuit.

6.3 Inference Accuracy

Table 3 presents the inference accuracy comparison. In the *Retrained NN* column, we present the accuracy of our technique after retraining the NN models with the simulation of PNRU, where our design is able to reach near-optimal accuracy levels.

Table 3. Top-one int8 inference accuracy comparison

NN backbone	Dataset	Inference accuracy(%)		
		Original(software)	This work	Retrained NN
AlexNet	UCF101	61.97	**58.80**	**61.72**
	Kinetics-700	57.35	**55.14**	**57.21**
ResNet18	Kinetics-700	70.81	**69.91**	**70.44**
	UCF101	76.97	**74.18**	**76.31**
GPT-3	CoQA	64.83	**61.86**	**64.37**

6.4 Energy Consumption

Fig. 6 presents the normalized energy consumption comparison for the experimented scenarios. We compare our results to a GPU-only execution on an RTX 3080 GPU, and two GPU-ReRAM related works: AccuRed [19] and REGENT [21]. By using the proposed architecture and mapping heuristics presented in this work, one can achieve energy reduction levels of 6.32x, 4.21x, and 3.26x for the AlexNet, ResNET-18, and GPT-3 NN compared to the RTX 3080 GPU, respectively.

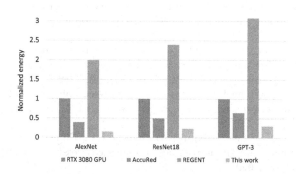

Fig. 6. Energy consumption comparison.

7 Conclusion and Future Work

This work presented a methodology to tackle the scalability issue of ReRAM accelerators and enable the execution of NNs on GPU-ReRAM devices. By employing the proposed offloading heuristic, one can select the best offloading layer schedule for the NN layers that most benefits from ReRAM acceleration. Also, this paper presented PNRU, a programmable ReRAM-based unit that exploits the inherent energy-efficient capacity of ReRAMs in performing MVM to reduce the energy consumption of the calculus of non-linearities in ReRAM accelerators. Our results show that our approach reduces energy consumption by up to 6.32x compared to an Nvidia RTX 3080 GPU. In future work, we intend to expand our PNRU to deal with other non-linearities, explore the acceleration of communication devices, for example, and combine our heuristics with a NN model reduction approach.

References

1. Aguirre, F.L., Gomez, N.M., Pazos, S.M., Palumbo, F., Suñé, J., Miranda, E.: Minimization of the line resistance impact on memdiode-based simulations of multilayer perceptron arrays applied to pattern recognition. J. Low Power Electron. Appl. **11**(1), 9 (2021)
2. Arka, A.I., Joardar, B.K., Doppa, J.R., Pande, P.P., Chakrabarty, K.: Performance and accuracy tradeoffs for training graph neural networks on reram-based architectures. IEEE Trans. Very Large Scale Integr. (VLSI) Syst. **29**(10), 1743–1756 (2021)
3. Bakhoda, A., Yuan, G.L., Fung, W.W., Wong, H., Aamodt, T.M.: Analyzing cuda workloads using a detailed GPU simulator. In: 2009 IEEE International Symposium on Performance Analysis of Systems and Software, pp. 163–174. IEEE (2009)
4. Chakraborty, I., Roy, D., Roy, K.: Technology aware training in memristive neuromorphic systems for nonideal synaptic crossbars. IEEE Trans. Emerg. Topics Comput. Intell. **2**(5), 335–344 (2018)
5. Cheng, M., et al.: Time: a training-in-memory architecture for RRAM-based deep neural networks. IEEE Trans. Comput. Aided Des. Integr. Circuits Syst. **38**(5), 834–847 (2018)
6. Chi, P., Li, S., Xu, C., Zhang, T., Zhao, J., Liu, Y., Wang, Y., Xie, Y.: Prime: a novel processing-in-memory architecture for neural network computation in ReRAM-based main memory. ACM SIGARCH Comput. Architect. News **44**(3), 27–39 (2016)
7. Cosemans, S., et al.:Towards 10000tops/w dnn inference with analog in-memory computing-a circuit blueprint, device options and requirements. In: 2019 IEEE International Electron Devices Meeting (IEDM), pp. 22–2. IEEE (2019)
8. Du, Y., et al.: Exploring the impact of random telegraph noise-induced accuracy loss on resistive ram-based deep neural network. IEEE Trans. Electron Devices **67**(8), 3335–3340 (2020)
9. Fouda, M.E., Lee, S., Lee, J., Kim, G.H., Kurdahi, F., Eltawi, A.M.: Ir-qnn framework: an Ir drop-aware offline training of quantized crossbar arrays. IEEE Access **8**, 228392–228408 (2020)

10. Gokmen, T., Vlasov, Y.: Acceleration of deep neural network training with resistive cross-point devices: design considerations. Front. Neurosci. **10**, 333 (2016)

11. Grossi, A., et al.: Experimental investigation of 4-kb rram arrays programming conditions suitable for tcam. IEEE Trans. Very Large Scale Integr. (VLSI) Syst. **26**(12), 2599–2607 (2018)

12. Han, J., Liu, H., Wang, M., Li, Z., Zhang, Y.: Era-LSTM: an efficient ReRam-based architecture for long short-term memory. IEEE Trans. Parallel Distrib. Syst. **31**(6), 1328–1342 (2019)

13. Ielmini, D., Pedretti, G.: Device and circuit architectures for in-memory computing. Adv. Intell. Syst. **2**(7), 2000040 (2020)

14. Jain, S., Raghunathan, A.: CxDNN: hardware-software compensation methods for deep neural networks on resistive crossbar systems. ACM Trans. Embedded Comput. Syst. (TECS) **18**(6), 1–23 (2019)

15. Jeong, D.S., Kim, K.M., Kim, S., Choi, B.J., Hwang, C.S.: Memristors for energy-efficient new computing paradigms. Adv. Electron. Mater. **2**(9), 1600090 (2016)

16. Jeong, Y., Zidan, M.A., Lu, W.D.: Parasitic effect analysis in memristor-array-based neuromorphic systems. IEEE Trans. Nanotechnol. **17**(1), 184–193 (2017)

17. Ji, Y., Liang, L., Deng, L., Zhang, Y., Zhang, Y., Xie, Y.: Tetris: Tile-matching the tremendous irregular sparsity. In: Advances in Neural Information Processing Systems, vol. 31 (2018)

18. Ji, Y., et al.: Fpsa: A full system stack solution for reconfigurable reram-based nn accelerator architecture. In: Proceedings of the Twenty-Fourth International Conference on Architectural Support for Programming Languages and Operating Systems, pp. 733–747 (2019)

19. Joardar, B.K., Doppa, J.R., Pande, P.P., Li, H., Chakrabarty, K.: Accured: high accuracy training of CNNs on ReRAM/GPU heterogeneous 3-D architecture. IEEE Trans. Comput. Aided Des. Integr. Circuits Syst. **40**(5), 971–984 (2020)

20. Joardar, B.K., Jayakodi, N.K., Doppa, J.R., Li, H., Pande, P.P., Chakrabarty, K.: GRAMARCH: A GPU-ReRAM based heterogeneous architecture for neural image segmentation. In: 2020 Design, Automation and Test in Europe Conference and Exhibition (DATE), pp. 228–233. IEEE (2020)

21. Joardar, B.K., Li, B., Doppa, J.R., Li, H., Pande, P.P., Chakrabarty, K.: Regent: A heterogeneous ReRAM/GPU-based architecture enabled by NoC for training CNNs. In: 2019 Design, Automation and Test in Europe Conference & Exhibition (DATE), pp. 522–527. IEEE (2019)

22. Kim, H., Jung, Y., Kim, L.S.: ADC-free ReRAM-based in-situ accelerator for energy-efficient binary neural networks. IEEE Trans. Comput. (2022)

23. Kull, L., et al.: A 3.1 mw 8b 1.2 GS/s single-channel asynchronous SAR ADC with alternate comparators for enhanced speed in 32 nm digital soi cmos. IEEE J. Solid-State Circ. **48**(12), 3049–3058 (2013)

24. Laborieux, A. et al.: Low power in-memory implementation of ternary neural networks with resistive ram-based synapse. In: 2020 2nd IEEE International Conference on Artificial Intelligence Circuits and Systems (AICAS), pp. 136–140. IEEE (2020)

25. Lee, Y.K., et al.: Matrix mapping on crossbar memory arrays with resistive interconnects and its use in in-memory compression of biosignals. Micromachines **10**(5), 306 (2019)

26. Li, B., Doppa, J.R., Pande, P.P., Chakrabarty, K., Qiu, J.X., Li, H.: 3D-ReG: A 3D ReRAM-based heterogeneous architecture for training deep neural networks. ACM J. Emerg. Technol. Comput. Syst. (JETC) **16**(2), 1–24 (2020)

27. Long, Y., Na, T., Mukhopadhyay, S.: ReRAM-based processing-in-memory archi-tecture for recurrent neural network acceleration. IEEE Trans. Very Large Scale Integr. (VLSI) Syst. **26**(12), 2781–2794 (2018)

28. Luo, T., et al.: Dadiannao: a neural network supercomputer. IEEE Trans. Comput. **66**(1), 73–88 (2016)

29. Moreno, D.G., Del Barrio, A.A., Botella, G., Hasler, J.: A cluster of FPAAs to recognize images using neural networks. IEEE Trans. Circ. Syst. II Express Briefs **68**(11), 3391–3395 (2021)

30. Muralimanohar, N., Balasubramonian, R., Jouppi, N.: Optimizing NUCA organi-zations and wiring alternatives for large caches with cacti 6.0. In: 40th Annual IEEE/ACM International Symposium on Microarchitecture (MICRO 2007), pp. 3–14. IEEE (2007)

31. Murshed, M.S., Murphy, C., Hou, D., Khan, N., Ananthanarayanan, G., Hussain, F.: Machine learning at the network edge: a survey. ACM Comput. Surv. (CSUR) **54**(8), 1–37 (2021)

32. Peng, X., Huang, S., Jiang, H., Lu, A., Yu, S.: Dnn+ neurosim v2. 0: An end-to-end benchmarking framework for compute-in-memory accelerators for on-chip training. IEEE Trans. Comput.-Aided Design of Integr. Circ. Syst. **40**(11), 2306–2319 (2020)

33. Rao, M., et al.: Learning with resistive switching neural networks. In: 2019 IEEE International Electron Devices Meeting (IEDM), pp. 35–4. IEEE (2019)

34. Shafiee, A., et al.: Isaac: a convolutional neural network accelerator with in-situ analog arithmetic in crossbars. ACM SIGARCH Comput. Architect. News **44**(3), 14–26 (2016)

35. Song, L., Qian, X., Li, H., Chen, Y.: Pipelayer: A pipelined reram-based accelerator for deep learning. In: 2017 IEEE International Symposium on High Performance Computer Architecture (HPCA), pp. 541–552. IEEE (2017)

36. Zhang, C., Wu, D., Sun, J., Sun, G., Luo, G., Cong, J.: Energy-efficient cnn imple-mentation on a deeply pipelined FGPA cluster. In: Proceedings of the 2016 Inter-national Symposium on Low Power Electronics and Design, pp. 326–331 (2016)

37. Zhang, F., Hu, M.: Mitigate parasitic resistance in resistive crossbar-based convo-lutional neural networks. ACM J. Emerg. Technol. Comput. Syst. (JETC) **16**(3), 1–20 (2020)

On Guaranteeing Schedulability of Periodic Real-Time Hardware Tasks Under ReconOS⁶⁴

Lennart Clausing[1]([✉]), Zakarya Guettatfi[1,3], Paul Kaufmann[2],
Christian Lienen[1], and Marco Platzner[1]

[1] Computer Science Department, Paderborn University, Paderborn, Germany
{clausl,zakarya,clienen,platzner}@mail.uni-paderborn.de
[2] Westfälische Hochschule, Gelsenkirchen, Germany
paul.kaufmann@w-hs.de
[3] Center for Development of Advanced Technology, Algiers, Algeria
zguettatfi@cdta.dz

Abstract. Many papers proposed the execution of real-time tasks on FPGA hardware. Most of these works do not demonstrate fully working systems and suffer from either unrealistic assumptions about the placement, reconfigurability, and connectivity of hardware tasks to memory and peripherals, or do not come with an efficient schedulability test that guarantees that real-time constraints are met.

In this paper, we present a practical way of executing a set of periodic real-time tasks under static priority assignment on a platform FPGA, comprising a processing system and programmable logic. The platform FPGA is operated under the ReconOS⁶⁴ architecture and operating system layer which enables practical realization. The hardware tasks follow a 3-phase task model with memory-in, execution, and memory-out phases. All memory phases compete for shared memory, which forms a resource that must be accessed mutually exclusive. While our task and system models are relatively simple as they map each hardware task to a separate region in the programmable logic, they lead to an efficient schedulability test covering memory accesses. We present our task and ReconOS⁶⁴ system models, describe the runtime scheduler, and derive a corresponding schedulability test.

1   Introduction

Over the years, the logic capacities of field-programmable gate arrays (FPGAs) have grown substantially, allowing the mapping of several accelerators or hardware tasks, respectively, to one FPGA. There is substantial earlier work that deals with the problem of placing and executing hardware tasks to reconfigurable fabrics. These works differ in the characteristics of the task sets, the area model used for the reconfigurable fabric, the optimization goals, and whether they deal with off-line or on-line problems.

FPGAs are also employed in embedded system scenarios with real-time constraints, where design time guarantees for meeting deadlines are required. Many

F. Palumbo et al. (Eds.): ARC 2023, LNCS 14251, pp. 245–259, 2023.
https://doi.org/10.1007/978-3-031-42921-7_17

works targeting FPGA-based real-time systems relied on area models that could and still can not be realized with commercial FPGAs, or propose preemptive hardware task execution which is possible but bears huge overheads in execution time and memory. Further, the complexity of the intertwined placement and scheduling problems pose a formidable challenge for schedulability analysis and often prevented the development of schedulability tests.

In this paper, we present a practical implementation of a real-time system on FPGA. We leverage ReconOS[64] [4], an existing operating system approach for FPGAs that organizes the reconfigurable resources into predefined areas, so-called reconfigurable slots, and maps hardware tasks to these reconfigurable slots. We define a three-phase task model for periodic real-time tasks, where each task requires a memory-in phase, followed by an execution phase and, finally, a memory-out phase. The phases are executed non-preemptively. A runtime system including a runtime scheduler controls the execution of the tasks and ensures that accesses to the shared memory are done in a mutually exclusive manner. For the given task model and runtime system, we are able to provide a schedulability analysis and a schedulability test to decide whether all deadlines will be met. The novelty of the paper is thus that it combines a practical FPGA implementation of a real-time system with the ability to provide design-time guarantees for schedulability.

The remainder of this paper is structured as follows: In Sect. 2, we review selected related work and in Sect. 3, we summarize features of the ReconOS[64] operating system. Section 4 presents our task model and details the runtime system. We elaborate on the schedulability analysis in Sect. 5, and apply the resulting schedulability test to an exemplary task set in Sect. 6. Finally, Sect. 7 concludes the paper with a discussion of current limitations and an outlook to future work.

2   Related Work

In this section, we discuss a selection of related work in real-time scheduling on FPGAs considering shared resources, FPGA operating systems, and one relevant previous multi-processor schedulability result.

2.1   Real-Time Scheduling and Shared Resources on FPGAs

Many authors studied the situation where an FPGA cannot accommodate all hardware tasks at once and, thus, (partial) runtime reconfiguration is needed to load and execute hardware tasks whenever needed. In such scenarios the configuration port forms a shared resource that must be used in exclusive mode. Early work on real-time systems on FPGAs, e.g., [21,22] or [5] did not consider the configuration port but simply assumed the reconfiguration time to be negligible.

Later works considered the reconfiguration time to be constant, and added it to the hardware task execution time, e.g., [6] or [11]. Following the same model, the authors of [18] proposed a novel resource allocation scheme and an online admission control test. Real-time guarantees were given for applications supporting mode changes, i.e., tasks can either be executed in software on a CPU or in hardware on the FPGA. In [20], the authors presented an admission control strategy and a preemptive scheduling methodology for combined execution of periodic and aperiodic real-time tasks to minimize the aperiodic task rejections.

The first paper considering the configuration port as a shared resource which has to be be accessed exclusively is [7]. The authors addressed the analysis of reconfiguration requests through considering the configuration port as a single core scheduling problem. As has been noted later in [3], it is not clear how response-time bounds follow from that since no proofs have been provided. In [15], 1D reuse and partial reuse techniques that reuse already configured tasks to minimize reconfiguration time are discussed, again without giving a schedulability test.

To the best of our knowledge, [3] was the first work to view the configuration port as a shared resource *and* to derive worst-case response times bounds for task executions. In [19], the configuration port is considered to be a preemptive shared resource, where configuration processes can be interrupted and later on resumed to increase the schedulability of tasks. Another line of papers started with [8] and focused on so-called scalability of dynamic partial reconfiguration (DPR). In [9], the authors provided a theoretical analysis and a practical evaluation of multiple DPR offloadings in the context of hard real-time systems. They derived a new worst-case bound to evaluate the DPR time in case of offloading. Recently, [23] dealt with DPR profitability, which determines whether DPR to accelerate a task is useful or not in the context of a real-time system. The authors provided an approach to calculate the DPR time and derive its worst-case bound.

In contrast to related work, we focus on a scenario where all hardware tasks can be accommodated on the reconfigurable fabric. The hardware tasks can be pre-loaded and no runtime reconfiguration is required. Consequently, during runtime the configuration port idles. Although from the point of view of runtime configuration our scenario is simpler than that considered in many of the above mentioned related works, we do model and analyze the *memory accesses* of the hardware tasks, which is often neglected in related work. In architectures where all hardware tasks access the same memory subsystem, the shared memory also forms a resource that must be used mutually exclusive.

2.2   Operating Systems for FPGAs

A number of approaches attempt to extend known operating system functionality across the software/hardware boundary and offer fundamental synchronization, communication and scheduling services to hardware tasks. Examples for such FPGA operating systems include ReconOS [1, 16], BORPH [14], Hthreads [2], FUSE [12], SPREAD [24], R3TOS [13], or LEAP [10]. These operating system approaches provide practical and proven FPGA execution and area models and ready-to-use interfaces for hardware tasks. However, with the exception of Hthreads their focus is on improving the average system performance and not on real-time scheduling.

For the work presented here, we leverage ReconOS[64], the 64 bit version of ReconOS. ReconOS is open source and extends Linux as guest operating system to feature multi-threaded programming in software and hardware based on a shared memory architecture. Compared to related approaches, ReconOS has proven to be highly flexible and portable, and has been made available for several guest operating systems and FPGA technologies over time.

2.3 Fixed-Priority Multi-processor Scheduling

The scheduling scenario discussed in this paper shares some similarity with the work in [17], and our schedulability analysis in Sect. 5 partly adopts the analysis approach used there. In [17], the authors considered the execution of a set of real-time tasks on a multi-core processor with a memory bus as shared resource. Each task comprises three distinct phases, (data) acquisition, execution, and (data) restitution. Acquisition and restitution phases compete for the shared memory bus. The tasks' code and data are assumed to fit into the cores' private caches. Hence, during the execution phase shared memory is not accessed. The three phases are executed non-preemptively, and the tasks are scheduled under a global static priority scheme. Importantly, the schedulability analysis in [17] defines a so-called problem window for each task τ_k that starts at the latest time instant earlier than the release of an instance of τ_k at which at least one core is idle, and ends when the instance of τ_k misses its deadline. The system was shown to be schedulable if the maximum interference each task can suffer is less than the minimum supply in its problem window. The authors then develop upper bounds for the interference time and a schedulability test.

3 System Architecture

We leverage ReconOS[64] for our work, the 64 bit version of the ReconOS reconfigurable hardware operating system and architecture [1,16]. ReconOS provides a practical platform for realizing the real-time scheduling system described in this paper. ReconOS[64] has been described in more detail in [4], hence, in the following we summarize its main features relevant for this paper.

Figure 1 shows an example ReconOS[64] architecture on the platform FPGA Xilinx UltraScale+ MPSoC comprising the processing system, the programmable logic, as well as shared memory and peripherals. The processing system includes a 64 bit quad-core CPU running the 64 bit Xilinx PetaLinux as guest operating system. ReconOS[64] adds several libraries to the user space for thread management, thread communication, bitstream loading, etc., and the ReconOS[64] driver to the kernel. The programmable logic of the platform FPGA comprises so-called reconfigurable slots that constitute rectangular areas of the programmable logic resources. Reconfigurable slots accommodate hardware threads, that in addition to the software threads running on the CPU comprise an application. Hardware threads can make use of the operating system via their operating system interface (OSIF) and access shared memory via their memory interface (MEMIF) exactly in the same way as software threads.

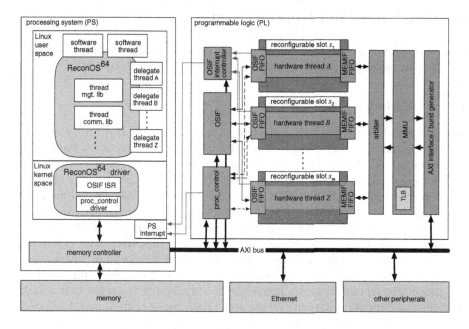

Fig. 1. Simplified ReconOS^{64} architecture (adopted from [4])

As detailed in green color in Fig. 1, the operating system interface comprises an OSIF FIFO for each reconfigurable slot to queue requests and return values of operating system calls, an OSIF component to collect these data from all reconfigurable slots, and the OSIF interrupt controller. When a hardware thread wants to execute an operating system call, an interrupt to the processing system is raised and a corresponding interrupt service route (OSIF ISR) is executed in kernel space. The OSIF ISR wakes up a so-called delegate thread, which then executes the operating system call on behalf of the hardware thread. Hardware thread management functions such as starting, stopping and resetting threads, or setting clock frequencies for individual reconfigurable slots, require the proc_control component in hardware and a corresponding driver in kernel space.

The ReconOS^{64} components that implement the memory interface for hardware threads are shown in orange color in Fig. 1. Each reconfigurable slot includes a MEMIF FIFO to queue the read and write requests of the corresponding hardware thread. Competing memory accesses among the hardware threads are resolved by an arbiter module. A memory management unit (MMU) with an integrated translation look-aside buffer (TLB) supports virtual addressing. Finally, an AXI interface connects to the memory controller.

4   Task Model and Runtime System

This section describes the task model we use for our real-time scheduling scenario and the corresponding runtime system implemented under ReconOS[64].

4.1   Task Model

We consider a set of n periodic, independent hardware tasks $\Gamma = \{\tau_1, \tau_2, ..., \tau_n\}$, where each task τ_i has a period T_i, a relative deadline $D_i \leq T_i$, and a worst-case execution time C_i. Each task is assigned a static priority P_i.

Further, each task comprises the three distinct phases shown in Fig. 2: In the memory-in phase, the hardware task reads input data from shared memory and stores it in task-internal RAM. In the execution phase, the hardware task operates solely on internal RAM. In the memory-out phase, the hardware task writes its results back to shared memory. We require that worst-case execution times are known for the memory-in, execution, and memory-out phases and denote them with A_i, E_i and R_i, respectively. Each of the three phases runs non-preemptively, and there are precedence constraints in the sense that a task must first read input data, then execute and, finally, write output data. Executed in isolation, the worst-case execution time of τ_i is thus given by $C_i = A_i + E_i + R_i$. The shared memory constitutes a resource shared between the hardware tasks (and software tasks) that must be used mutually exclusive.

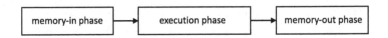

Fig. 2. Task model with 3-phases

4.2   Runtime System

Figure 3 outlines the ReconOS[64]-based runtime system. The programmable logic includes m reconfigurable slots $S = \{s_1, s_2, \ldots, s_m\}$. On the software side, the runtime system comprises a timer, a runtime scheduler, and two queues Q_A and Q_R that also maintain empty flags. Algorithm 1 outlines the functionality of the runtime scheduler, including the dispatch() routine as core function.

To control access to shared memory, the runtime system uses the global flag mem_in_use, initialized to FALSE, to indicate whether the ReconOS[64] memory subsystem is in use or free. The dispatch() routine is called on three events: First, when the timer, programmed to trigger whenever a new job for some task τ_i, expires (event ①). Released jobs are enqueued in the priority queue Q_A based on their priorities to await start of their memory-in phases. Second, the dispatch() routine is called when a hardware task's A or R phase has completed (event ②). Then, the flag mem_in_use is set to FALSE again to indicate that the

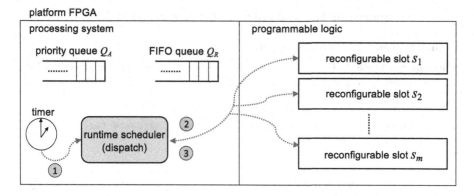

Fig. 3. Components of the runtime system implemented in the processing system

memory subsystem is idling. Third, the `dispatch()` routine is called when a hardware task's E phase has completed (event ③). Then, the job is enqueued in the FIFO queue Q_R to await start of its memory-out phase.

When the `dispatch()` routine is invoked, it first checks whether there are tasks enqueued in Q_A awaiting their A phase. If so, and the memory subsystem is free, the task with highest priority, which is at the head of Q_A, is removed from Q_A, the memory subsystem is marked busy, and the task's A phase is started (lines 15–19 of Algorithm 1). Next, it is checked whether there are tasks enqueued in Q_R awaiting their R phase. If so, and the memory subsystem is free, the task that was enqueued in Q_R the earliest, which is at the head of Q_R, is removed from Q_R, the memory subsystem is marked busy, and the task's R phase is started (lines 21–25 of Algorithm 1). Following the approach of [17], our runtime system exhibits two characteristics: First, the choice of the FIFO policy for Q_R ensures that also lower priority tasks will eventually write back their results and cannot starve. Second, serving memory-in phases has priority over serving memory-out phases.

5   Schedulability Analysis

In this section we present a schedulability analysis for the task model and runtime system of Sect. 4. Our analysis is partly adopted from [17], where the authors study schedulability of a set of periodic, non-preemptible real-time tasks under a static priority policy. They consider a multi-core processor with shared memory, where tasks also have three phases, but can be executed on any of the cores.

From the analyzability point of view our scenario is of lesser complexity, as we map each task to a separate reconfigurable slot, i.e., $m = n$. Since all jobs of a task run in the same reconfigurable slot, we can—without loss of generality— sort task indices such that τ_1 is the task with highest priority P_1 and assigned to reconfigurable slot s_1, and τ_m has the lowest priority P_m and is assigned to s_m. The following analysis assumes that the software threads implementing the

Algorithm 1: Pseudo code for the runtime scheduler

```
1  initialization: mem_sin_use = FALSE;
2  job of τ_i released {                          // timer event ①
3      enqueue τ_i into Q_A;
4      dispatch();
5  }
6  A phase or R phase of τ_i completed {          // hardware task event ②
7      mem_in_use = FALSE;
8      dispatch();
9  }
10 E phase of τ_i completed {                     // hardware task event ③
11     enqueue τ_i into Q_R;
12     dispatch();
13 }
14 dispatch() {                 // core function of the runtime scheduler
15     if (Q_A.not_empty ∧ (mem_in_use = FALSE )) then
16         τ_i = Q_A.head;
17         dequeue τ_i from Q_A;
18         mem_in_use = TRUE;
19         start A/E phases of τ_i;
20     end
21     if (Q_R.not_empty ∧ (mem_in_use = FALSE )) then
22         τ_i = Q_R.head;
23         dequeue τ_i from Q_R;
24         mem_in_use = TRUE;
25         start R phase of τ_i;
26     end
27 }
```

runtime system do not compete with the hardware tasks' memory accesses. This assumption is justified since the runtime system is light-weight and can run out of the processing system's cache. Moreover, aligned with [17] it is important to note that a task's job is not released before its previous job has completed. Hence, at any time there is at most only one job of each task in the system, i.e., either in the priority queue Q_A, the memory-in phase, in execution, in the FIFO queue Q_R, or in the memory-out phase.

Figure 4 sketches a set of four tasks τ_1, τ_2, τ_i and τ_m assigned to reconfigurable slots. At time r_i, a job of task τ_i assigned to s_i with relative deadline D_i is released. Obviously, for the task to be schedulable, its worst-case execution time must not be higher than its relative deadline, i.e., $C_i = A_i + E_i + R_i \leq D_i$. Additionally, the task's memory-in and memory-out phases might be delayed due to other tasks using the memory subsystem. We denote these delays as blocking times for A_i and R_i, respectively, and aim at determining upper bounds for these blocking times, denoted as I_i^A and I_i^R.

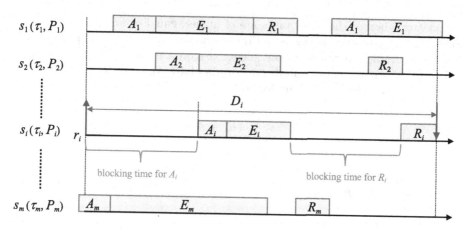

Fig. 4. Blocking time analysis

An upper bound I_i^A for the interference τ_i can experience by other tasks through blocking its memory-in phase can be derived as follows: When the job of τ_i is released, we have to consider higher and equal priority tasks on one side and lower priority tasks on the other side. In the worst case, jobs of all higher and equal priority tasks $\tau_k, k = 1, \ldots, i-1$, have already been released and are enqueued in the priority queue Q_A to wait for their memory-in phases to start. In the example of Fig. 4, this applies to τ_1 and τ_2. In addition, one lower priority job could have just started its memory-in phase, as shown by τ_m in Fig. 4. We do not need to consider other lower priority jobs that have been released since they will be sorted in the priority queue behind the job of τ_i. To upper bound I_i^A it is thus sufficient to consider the low priority job with the longest memory-in phase. Whether we consider equal priority jobs together with higher or lower priority jobs depends on the detailed implementation of the queuing policy. We pessimistically assume for the analysis that equal priority jobs can indeed interfere with jobs of τ_i. An upper bound on I_i^A is thus given by:

$$I_i^A \le \sum_{k=1}^{i-1}(A_k) \quad + \max_{i+1 \le k \le m} \{A_k\}. \tag{1}$$

We derive an upper bound I_i^R for the interference τ_i can experience by other tasks through blocking its memory-out phase as follows: When the execution phase of τ_i is completed and its memory-out phase is ready to start, in the worst-case all other tasks have already enqueued their memory-out phases in the FIFO and will be served first. In the example of Fig. 4 this applies to τ_1, τ_m and τ_2 in exactly that order. Whenever such a task completes its memory-out phase it can have its next job released and the corresponding memory-in phase will have priority over τ_i's memory-out phase. In the worst case, every other task has its next job released before τ_i can start its memory-out phase. Importantly, it does not matter whether the other tasks are of higher, equal or lower priority, since for the memory-out phases we use a FIFO queue and the memory-in phases have generally priority over memory-out phases. Figure 4 exemplarily shows that τ_1 receives another job release and its memory-in phase A_1 blocks R_i. The response time I_i^R can thus be upper bounded by:

$$I_i^R \leq \sum_{\substack{k=1 \\ k \neq i}}^{m} (R_k + A_k). \tag{2}$$

Given I_i^A and I_i^R, the jobs of task τ_i will meet their deadlines if (see Fig. 4) $I_i^A + A_i + E_i + I_i^R + R_i \leq D_i$. The overall task set Γ is thus schedulable if $\forall \tau_i \in \Gamma$:

$$\left(\sum_{k=1}^{i-1} A_k + \max_{i+1 \leq k \leq m} \{A_k\} \right) + A_i + E_i + \left(\sum_{\substack{k=1 \\ k \neq i}}^{m} (R_k + A_k) \right) + R_i =$$

$$\left(\sum_{k=1}^{i-1} A_k + \max_{i+1 \leq k \leq m} \{A_k\} \right) + E_i + \sum_{k=1}^{m} (A_k + R_k) \leq D_i. \tag{3}$$

6   Practical Example

In this section, we explain how we have implemented the discussed real-time scheduling system on ReconOS^{64} and then demonstrate the computation of our schedulability test on an exemplary task set.

6.1   Implementation Based on ReconOS^{64}

ReconOS^{64} uses Linux with virtual memory support as guest operating system and is, thus, not per se suitable for implementing a real-time system. To realize the task model and runtime system presented in Sect. 4, we have essentially bypassed the memory-management unit (cf. Fig. 1), technically by making sure that all address translations for the hardware tasks' memory accesses are pre-stored in the TLB of the ReconOS^{64} MMU.

The runtime system presented in Sect. 4, including the runtime scheduler and the queues Q_A and Q_R, has been implemented in form of software threads and ReconOS^{64} objects in user space. Further, we have implemented mechanisms for hardware tasks to signal the completion of their A, E and R phases, and mechanisms for the runtime scheduler to start the A and R phases of hardware tasks. Technically, these mechanisms rely on message box communication and semaphore synchronization between the software threads of the runtime scheduler and the hardware tasks.

6.2   Exemplary Task Set

To characterize the required times for the different task phases, we have implemented a task set comprising the five following hardware tasks:

- *InvKin* is an inverse kinematics task that computes control signals for driving a servo motor that sets a joint angle based on a desired position and orientation of a robotic manipulation platform. The computation involves coordinate transformations and an iterative implementation of the arctan() function. The input are two fixed-point numbers that represent the desired rotation angles of the platform around the x-axis and the y-axis. The output sets the pulse width coded control signal for the motor.
- *Sobel, RGB2Gray* are image processing functions processing images of dimension 640 × 480 with three channels (24 bit). The Sobel image filter applies two filter kernels on each channel, and calculates the arithmetic mean as an approximation for the geometric mean. RGB2Gray converts an RGB image into a gray-scale representation by weighting the color values by Luma factors according to the ITU 709 standard.
- *SHA256* determines the SHA256 hash value for an input of 1 MiB size.
- *Sort* takes an array of 2048 elements of 64 bit unsigned integers and sorts it with a Bubble sort like algorithm.

All tasks match well our task model, as they read a constant-sized block of data from shared memory, operate on that data, and write a constant-sized block of data back to shared memory. We have synthesized and mapped all hardware tasks to a Zynq UltraScale+ XCZU7EV device using Xilinx Vivado and Vitis HLS, Version 2020.2. The *Sort* tasks has been synthesized from a VHDL specification, all other tasks with high-level synthesis from C/C++ specifications.

We have augmented the ReconOS[64] system with cycle-accurate hardware timers to measure the number of cycles spent for the three task phases. Table 1 presents the characterization of the memory-in and memory-out phases. The table lists the amount of data read and written and the measured number of required cycles. The MEMIF of the used ReconOS[64] is clocked with 100 MHz. The resulting times for the memory-in and memory-out phases, A_i and R_i, are also given in the table.

We have repeated the measurements for five times and noted that the required cycles for the memory-in phases show slight variations which are due to the memory controller's behavior when reading. Table 1 reports the maximal values measured. For *Sobel* and *RGB2Gray*, the deviations are 508 and 423 cycles, respectively, which amounts to 0.19% and 0.16% of the maximal values. For *SHA256* the deviation was 6'333 cycles, or 0.69%, and for *Sort* 11 cycles, or 0.47%. The largest deviation was for *InvKin*, which has a very small input data size of only 8 bytes. There, the deviation was 8 cycles, which amounts to 22.22%. For the memory out phases, there we no variations in the measured number of cycles, presumably due to buffering in the memory controller.

Table 2 displays the number of cycles required for each hardware task, the maximum clock frequency at which the task can run, and the corresponding

Table 1. Characterization of memory-in and memory-out phases

τ_i	task name	input data size	output data size	A_i [cycles]	R_i [cycles]	$f_{A,R}$ [MHz]	A_i [ms]	R_i [ms]
τ_1	InvKin	8 B	8 B	44	7	100	0.0004	0.0001
τ_2	Sobel	900 kiB	900 kiB	266'283	462'601	100	2.6628	4.6260
τ_3	RGB2Gray	900 kiB	900 kiB	266'207	462'601	100	2.6621	4.6260
τ_4	Sort	16 kiB	16 kiB	2'325	2'090	100	0.0233	0.0209
τ_5	SHA256	1 MiB	32 B	915'796	13	100	9.1580	0.0002

execution time E_i in seconds. Additionally, the table lists the total task execution times C_i that is required if the tasks run in isolation, i.e., no other hardware tasks are active and there is no interaction with the operating system or software tasks.

Table 2. Characterization of execution phase and hardware task parameters

τ_i	task name	E_i [cycles]	f_{max} [MHz]	E_i [ms]	C_i [ms]	$T_i = D_i$ [ms]
τ_1	InvKin	11'095	122.16	0.0908	0.0913	40
τ_2	Sobel	21'282'222	294.72	72.2117	79.5005	110
τ_3	RGB2Gray	3'193'393	151.19	21.1217	28.4098	120
τ_4	Sort	10'487'746	390.63	26.8483	26.8925	150
τ_5	SHA256	9'413'071	236.91	39.7327	48.8909	150

6.3   Applying the Schedulability Test

In the last column of Table 2, we give assumed relative deadlines for the hardware tasks. Without loss of generality, we set $D_i = T_i$ and assign priorities P_i according to increasing periods, i.e., analogously to the rate monotonic scheme. The tasks in the tables are listed in priority order. Based on the characterization given in Tables 1 and 2, we can apply the schedulability test of Eq. 3.

The last term of the left-hand side of Eq. 3, $\sum_{k=1}^{m}(A_k + R_k)$, amounts to $(0.0004 + 0.0001) + (2.6628 + 4.6260) + (2.6621 + 4.6260) + (9.1580 + 0.0002) + (0.0233 + 0.0209) = 23.7798$ ms. The maximum memory-in phase of any lower priority task, $\max_{i+1 \leq k \leq m}\{A_k\}$ is always $A_5 = 9.1580$ ms, since τ_5 has the longest memory-in phase overall and is also the lowest priority task.

Computing the schedulability test for all tasks according to Eq. 3, we get the following result that shows that all jobs of the five tasks will easily meet their deadlines:

$$\tau_1 : 0 + 9.1580 + 0.0908 + 23.7798 = 33.0286 \text{ ms} \leq 40 \text{ ms} \quad \checkmark$$
$$\tau_2 : 0.0004 + 9.1580 + 72.2117 + 23.7798 = 105.1499 \text{ ms} \leq 120 \text{ ms} \quad \checkmark$$
$$\tau_3 : 2.6632 + 9.1580 + 21.1217 + 23.7798 = 56.7227 \text{ ms} \leq 140 \text{ ms} \quad \checkmark$$
$$\tau_4 : 5.3253 + 9.1580 + 26.8483 + 23.7798 = 65.1114 \text{ ms} \leq 150 \text{ ms} \quad \checkmark$$
$$\tau_5 : 5.3486 + 48.8909 + 23.7798 = 78.0193 \text{ ms} \leq 150 \text{ ms} \quad \checkmark$$

7 Conclusion and Future Work

In this paper, we have shown the realization of a real-time scheduling system on FPGA that is both practical and comes with a schedulability test giving a design-time guarantee that all deadlines will be met. Practicability is established by leveraging an operating system layer, in our case the ReconOS[64] architecture, and the schedulability test holds for the presented task model and runtime system.

Currently, our schedulability analysis and the corresponding test do not consider times required for the operating system and the runtime scheduler. In real-time literature, such overhead times are often treated as negligible or assumed to be known and lumped into the worst-case task execution time. Since we signal the completion of the task phases to the runtime system, and the runtime system starts the A/E and R phases, there will be non-negligible overhead times. The use of Linux as guest operating system further means that we cannot reasonably bound these overhead times. To improve predictability, we had to replace Linux with a real-time operating system (RTOS) that allows us to analyze and time-bound operating system calls. Alternatively, the operating system implementation itself could be mapped to hardware as has been done, for example, in the Hthreads [2] project.

Besides switching to a ReconOS version with an RTOS as guest operating system, future work also includes studying how pessimistic our schedulability test actually is. Relying on upper bounds for blocking times, our test is sufficient but not necessary, and there might be task sets where the test fails but actually all deadlines are being met. Also of interest is conducting a schedulability analysis for scheduling with dynamic priority assignments. Finally, extending our work to a scenario where we have more hardware tasks than reconfigurable slots and, thus, need (partial) runtime reconfiguration to load hardware tasks on demand, is a challenging goal. In addition to the memory subsystem, the configuration port is then another shared resource and we can apply the same analysis technique as in this paper. However, determining upper bounds for blocking times will be quite involved in such a case.

Acknowledgments. This work was partially supported by the German Research Foundation (DFG) within the Collaborative Research Centre On-The-Fly Computing (GZ: SFB 901/3) under the project number 160364472.

References

1. Agne, A., et al.: ReconOS - an operating system approach for reconfigurable computing. IEEE Micro **34**(1), 60–71 (2014). https://doi.org/10.1109/MM.2013.110
2. Andrews, D., et al.: Achieving Programming Model Abstractions for Reconfigurable Computing. IEEE Trans. Very Large Scale Integr. (VLSI) Syst. **16**(1), 34–44 (2008)
3. Biondi, A., Balsini, A., Pagani, M., Rossi, E., Marinoni, M., Buttazzo, G.: A framework for supporting real-time applications on dynamic reconfigurable FPGAs. In: 2016 IEEE Real-Time Systems Symposium (RTSS), pp. 1–12 (2016). https://doi.org/10.1109/RTSS.2016.010
4. Clausing, L., Platzner, M.: ReconOS[64]: A hardware operating system for modern platform FPGAs with 64-Bit support. In: 2022 IEEE International Parallel and Distributed Processing Symposium Workshops (IPDPSW), pp. 120–127. IEEE (2022). https://doi.org/10.1109/ipdpsw55747.2022.00029
5. Danne, K., Platzner, M.: Periodic real-time scheduling for FPGA computers. In: Third International Workshop on Intelligent Solutions in Embedded Systems, 2005, pp. 117–127 (2005). https://doi.org/10.1109/WISES.2005.1438720
6. Danne, K., Platzner, M.: An edf schedulability test for periodic tasks on reconfigurable hardware devices. SIGPLAN Not. **41**(7), 93–102 (2006). https://doi.org/10.1145/1159974.1134665
7. Dittmann, F., Frank, S.: Hard real-time reconfiguration port scheduling. In: 2007 Design, Automation & Test in Europe Conference & Exhibition, pp. 1–6 (2007). https://doi.org/10.1109/DATE.2007.364578
8. D'Andrea, G., Valente, G.: Work-in-progress: Cyber-physical systems and dynamic partial reconfiguration scalability: opportunities and challenges. In: 2020 IEEE Real-Time Systems Symposium (RTSS), pp. 399–402 (2020). https://doi.org/10.1109/RTSS49844.2020.00048
9. D'Andrea, G., Valente, G., Pomante, L., Di Mascio, T.: An investigation of dynamic partial reconfiguration offloading in hard real-time systems. In: 2021 24th Euromicro Conference on Digital System Design (DSD), pp. 192–198 (2021). https://doi.org/10.1109/DSD53832.2021.00039
10. Fleming, K., Yang, H.J., Adler, M., Emer, J.: The LEAP FPGA operating system. In: International Conference on Field Programmable Logic and Applications (FPL), pp. 1–8. IEEE (2014)
11. Guan, N., Deng, Q., Gu, Z., Xu, W., Yu, G.: Schedulability analysis of preemptive and nonpreemptive edf on partial runtime-reconfigurable FPGAs. ACM Trans. Des. Autom. Electron. Syst. 13(4) (2008). https://doi.org/10.1145/1391962.1391964
12. Ismail, A., Shannon, L.: FUSE: front-end user framework for o/s abstraction of hardware accelerators. In: International Symposium on Field-Programmable Custom Computing Machines (FCCM). IEEE (2011)
13. Iturbe, X., et al.: R3tos: a novel reliable reconfigurable real-time operating system for highly adaptive, efficient, and dependable computing on fpgas. IEEE Trans. Comput. **62**(8), 1542–1556 (2013). https://doi.org/10.1109/TC.2013.79

14. Kwok-Hay So, H., Brodersen, R.: Runtime Filesystem Support for Reconfigurable FPGA Hardware Processes in BORPH. In: International Symposium on Field-Programmable Custom Computing Machines (FCCM) (2008)
15. Lu, Y., Marconi, T., Bertels, K., Gaydadjiev, G.: Online task scheduling for the FPGA-based partially reconfigurable systems. In: Becker, J., Woods, R., Athanas, P., Morgan, F. (eds.) Reconfigurable Computing: Architectures, Tools and Applications, pp. 216–230. Springer, Berlin Heidelberg, Berlin, Heidelberg (2009)
16. Lübbers, E., Platzner, M.: ReconOS: Multithreaded programming for reconfigurable computers. ACM Trans. Embedded Comput. Syst. 9(1), 8:1–8:33 (2009). https://doi.org/10.1145/1596532.1596540
17. Maia, C., Nelissen, G., Nogueira, L., Pinho, L.M., Pérez, D.G.: Schedulability analysis for global fixed-priority scheduling of the 3-phase task model. In: 2017 IEEE 23rd International Conference on Embedded and Real-Time Computing Systems and Applications (RTCSA), pp. 1–10 (2017). https://doi.org/10.1109/RTCSA.2017.8046313
18. Pellizzoni, R., Caccamo, M.: Real-time management of hardware and software tasks for FPGA-based embedded systems. IEEE Trans. Comput. 56(12), 1666–1680 (2007). https://doi.org/10.1109/TC.2007.70763
19. Rossi, E., Damschen, M., Bauer, L., Buttazzo, G., Henkel, J.: Preemption of the partial reconfiguration process to enable real-time computing with FPGAs. ACM Trans. Reconfigurable Technol. Syst. 11(2), 10:1–10:24 (2018). https://doi.org/10.1145/3182183
20. Saha, S., Sarkar, A., Chakrabarti, A., Ghosh, R.: Co-scheduling persistent periodic and dynamic aperiodic real-time tasks on reconfigurable platforms. IEEE Trans. Multi-Scale Comput. Syst. 4(1), 41–54 (2018). https://doi.org/10.1109/TMSCS.2017.2691701
21. Steiger, C., Walder, H., Platzner, M.: Operating systems for reconfigurable embedded platforms: online scheduling of real-time tasks. IEEE Trans. Comput. 53(11), 1393–1407 (2004). https://doi.org/10.1109/TC.2004.99
22. Steiger, C., Walder, H., Platzner, M., Thiele, L.: Online scheduling and placement of real-time tasks to partially reconfigurable devices. In: RTSS 2003. 24th IEEE Real-Time Systems Symposium, 2003, pp. 224–225 (2003). https://doi.org/10.1109/REAL.2003.1253269
23. Valente, G., Mascio, T.D., Pomante, L., D'Andrea, G.: Dynamic partial reconfiguration profitability for real-time systems. IEEE Embed. Syst. Lett. 13(3), 102–105 (2021). https://doi.org/10.1109/LES.2020.3004302
24. Wang, Y., et al.: SPREAD: A Streaming-Based Partially Reconfigurable Architecture and Programming Model. IEEE Trans. Very Large Scale Integr. (VLSI) Syst. 21, 2179–2192 (2013)

Evolutionary FPGA-Based Spiking Neural Networks for Continual Learning

Andrés Otero[1]($\boxtimes$), Guillermo Sanllorente[1], Eduardo de la Torre[1], and Jose Nunez-Yanez[2]

[1] Centro de Electrónica Industrial, Universidad Politécnica de Madrid, Madrid, Spain
{joseandres.otero,g.sanllorente,eduardo.delatorre}@upm.es
[2] Department of Electrical Engineering, Linköping University, Linköping, Sweden
jose.nunez-yanez@liu.se

Abstract. Spiking Neural Networks (SNNs) constitute a representative example of neuromorphic computing in which event-driven computation is mapped to neuron spikes reducing power consumption. A challenge that limits the general adoption of SNNs is the need for mature training algorithms compared with other artificial neural networks, such as multi-layer perceptrons or convolutional neural networks. This paper explores the use of evolutionary algorithms as a black-box solution for training SNNs. The selected SNN model relies on the Izhikevich neuron model implemented in hardware. Differently from state-of-the-art, the approach followed in this paper integrates within the same System-on-a-chip (SoC) both the training algorithm and the SNN fabric, enabling continuous network adaptation in-field and, thus, eliminating the barrier between offline (training) and online (inference). A novel encoding approach for the inputs based on receptive fields is also provided to improve network accuracy. Experimental results demonstrate that these techniques perform similarly to other algorithms in the literature without dynamic adaptability for classification and control problems.

Keywords: Spiking Neural Networks · Evolutionary Algorithms · FPGAs

1 Introduction

Neuromorphic computing is gaining momentum in a new scenario emerging from the end of Moore's law. As an alternative to Von Neumann processors, neuromorphic computers substitute CPUs and memories with neurons and synapses and traditional binary encoding with spikes. The change in the computing architecture mitigates the CPU/memory bottleneck, moving to an inherently parallel strategy. At the same time, the use of spikes makes computation event-driven, obtaining low-power operation. As a complete revolution in the computing paradigm, neuromorphic computing requires novel physical realizations,

This project has been funded by the European Commission under the project A-IQ Ready (GA. 101096658) and by the Knut and Alice Wallenberg Foundation under the Wallenberg AI autonomous systems and software (WASP) program.

F. Palumbo et al. (Eds.): ARC 2023, LNCS 14251, pp. 260–274, 2023.
https://doi.org/10.1007/978-3-031-42921-7_18

which have recently become available to the research community. Among them are solutions provided by academia (such as ODIN [1]) and industry (such as Intel Loihi [2] or ARM spinnaker [3]). Also, analog solutions based on memristors or in-memory computing paradigms are available in the state-of-the-art [4].

Although using neuromorphic computing principles for general-purpose computing is still in the future, it is already a reality for artificial intelligence workloads in which biological brains inspire architectures, such as SNNs. SNNs are envisaged as a high-potential technology but still with many challenges to reach the computational capabilities of other Artificial Neural Network (ANN) models, such as deep neural networks. Open research questions are related to the network (and neuron's) structure, the learning paradigms, and how to preserve the biological plausibility, temporal encoding, and low-power and low-rate features inherent to SNNs.

Mathematical models for biological neural behaviors have been known since the mid-20th century. The Hodgkin-Huxley model [5] describes the physiological mechanisms of neurons and prioritizes natural precision over mathematical simplicity. Alternatively, spiking-based models, such as the Izhikevich [6] or the Integrate and Fire [7], were proposed to reduce the mathematical complexity by describing the temporal behavior of cortical spike trains.

Along with the mathematical representation of the neuron behavior, it is also required to implement a learning model for the neural network. In this regard, this paper investigates the use of an evolutionary strategy for training biologically accurate spiking neural networks based on the Izikevich model. The SNN and the learning algorithm are integrated into the same SoC FPGA device, enabling continuous learning throughout the system's lifetime. This system has been adapted to solve various benchmarks and problems using supervised and reinforcement learning to demonstrate the usage of the network in complex real-time tasks. A novel receptive field strategy is proposed to encode the temporal information into spikes. Experimental results demonstrate the suitability of using evolution strategies for SNNs with hardware acceleration.

The rest of this paper is structured as follows. Section 2 reviews state-of-the-art learning techniques for SNNs. In Sect. 3, the architecture proposed in this paper is described, while the learning algorithm is described in Sect. 4. Section 5 describes the data encoding strategy, and the evaluation setup is described in Sect. 6. Experimental results are described in Sect. 7, while conclusions and future work are shown in Sect. 8.

2   Learning Techniques for SNNs

This section describes the main approaches available in the state-of-the-art for learning in SNNs, including unsupervised, supervised, and reinforcement learning strategies.

The most popular unsupervised learning method targeting SNNs is Spike Timing-Dependent Plasticity (STDP). It is based on Hebb's rule introduced in 1949. In STDP, synaptic connections are reinforced based on interconnected neurons' pre-synaptic and post-synaptic spike timings. Modifying the synaptic strengths leads to a new organization of the links in the neural network that may result in a learning phenomenon [8]. This learning technique is considered unsupervised since any explicit goal does not guide the learning process.

SpikeProp was one of the first attempts to use a supervised learning algorithm in multilayer SNNs [9]. It is an adaptation of the backpropagation algorithm used in ANNs, by introducing simplifications to cope with the discontinuous nature of spiking neurons. It is, therefore, one of the best-known, most extended learning methods based on Gradient Evaluation for SNNs. SpikeProp has been shown to deal effectively with complex problems. The algorithm was tested on various UCI datasets, such as the Iris dataset, the Wisconsin breast cancer dataset, and the Statlog Landsat dataset, using a feedforward network topology. One of the main drawbacks of SpikeProp is that it can only train a single spike for each neuron, which limits the diversity and information transmission in the SNN. Dealing with multiple spikes would be more biologically accurate than single-spike training [10].

Remote Supervised Method (ReSuMe) is another solution for single-spike training. As a supervised learning model, ReSuMe is based on error minimization between the recorded output spikes and the expected ones, which are calculated a priori based on the problem to solve. It is a temporally local algorithm, meaning that at every time step, the algorithm updates synaptic weights only for the nearest target firing times [11]. One of its main advantages is that the algorithm has been proven independent of the used neuron models. However, ReSuMe is also unsuitable for multilayer SNNs, and different algorithm adaptations have been proposed to overcome this issue [12].

In contrast to the previous learning strategies, evolution strategies are optimization techniques inspired by nature, using concepts such as mutation and selection as critical elements for exploring the design space and finding solutions in a neural network. This technique uses generations to represent the number of loops tested on a particular problem, creating new individuals through mutation for each generation. A. Belatreche et al. [13] proposed an evolutionary strategy for SNNs and tested its functionality through a Spike Response Model network. However, to the best of the author's knowledge, these evolutionary methods have not yet been tested in more biologically accurate models, such as the Izhikevich model, using hardware implementations to accelerate its computation times.

3   The Proposed SNN-Based SoC Architecture

Taking inspiration from biological neural models makes SNNs computing demanding architectures. However, the simultaneous operation of all the neurons in the network makes them suitable for parallel implementations using hardware accelerators such as FPGAs or GPUs. In this work, the Izhikevich SNN model is implemented in an FPGA, which enables fast and parallel computation. In particular, the provided solution targets an FPGA SoC device (the Zynq MPSoC) to perform both training and inference at run-time, enabling the continuous evolution of the network. MPSoCs combine different computing fabrics in a single device: CPUs, referred to as the Processing System (PS), and an FPGA, known as the programmable logic (PL). This combination generally results in higher computing performance, lower power consumption, and higher flexibility than homogeneous multi-core solutions. The spiking neural network is implemented as an accelerator in the PL, and the embedded dual-core ARM Cortex-A9 processor handles the learning tasks and the input spike generation. The spiking neural network is integrated as an Intellectual Property (IP) module, which is integrated with the PS using a Direct Memory Access (DMA) mechanism. In addition to using the same IP for training and inference, this structure has other advantages, such as the ability to embed more than one SNN accelerator inside the PL. In this work, solutions based on one and two IPs will be shown.

The SNN accelerator integrated as an IP is based on the work proposed at [14], consisting of an Izhikevich-based SNN architecture with up to 250K neurons initially implemented in a single Zynq 7020 device. Note that this implementation has not been tested on complex datasets before, so this work validates both the proposed evolution strategies and the SNN implementation. The SNN uses a fully connected feed-forward network, as shown in Fig. 1.

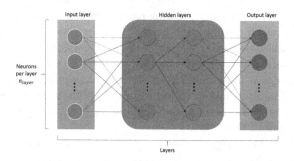

Fig. 1. Fully connected feed-forward topology.

It contains an input layer that serves as an interface with the processor in the PS. The hidden layers are internally allocated inside the IP and transparent to the user. Finally, the output layer is a delivery point for the network's results. The processor can adjust each neuron's internal weights at each time step, allowing the network parameters to be changed and trained even during runtime. This accessibility is crucial during the learning process guided by the evolutionary strategy. The same IP will be used with many candidate solutions with different weights as evolution parameters.

The IP can be customized using the network and the neuron model parameters. The network parameters constitute the main configuration points for the SNN, and they include the neurons per layer (n_layer), the number of inputs, the number of outputs, and the number of hidden layers (L). The number of inputs cannot exceed the neurons per layer parameter. Suppose a different number of neurons is required in each network layer. In that case, the IP must be synthesized using the maximum number of neurons in a single layer as the neurons per layer n_{layer} parameter. The network architecture can be adjusted during runtime by setting the unused weights to zero, turning the synapses or even complete neurons into inactive ones. On the other hand, internal neuron parameters include the minimum time step, simulation time step, excitatory and inhibitory neuron probability, weight data precision, and internal Izhikevich neuronal model parameters. In this project, floating-point weights have been selected. The design provided initially in [14] is described in C++, targeting a High-level synthesis design methodology.

4   Proposed Learning Strategy

The learning strategy proposed in this work requires selecting a population size defined as a parameter (P) which can be modified depending on the complexity of the target application. An initializing function $(\lambda())$ fills all the genomes with random weights, creating a diverse spectrum of possible individuals at the beginning of the program. The total number of generations (G) is also a parameter that will be adapted depending on the complexity of the problem. The error or fitness function (E) represents a comparison between the actual and the target value. It is used to evaluate the achieved performance of a candidate SNN. This function will be defined, together with the algorithm parameters, for each problem to be solved. Finally, the mutation function, used as the bioinspired operator to create new individuals from the current population, uses a Gaussian distribution to generate random values from the previous ones. The overall goal of the algorithm is to obtain an optimal individual that, after some generations, can solve the required task.

More in detail, the proposed algorithm is based on an evolution strategy that uses mutation and elitism as bioinspired operators (Algorithm 1). The SNN weights (θ_i) are the parameters that the evolutionary procedure uses to explore the design space of candidate solutions, maintained as a population of individuals, each with a randomly initialized set of weights (*lines 2–4*). After initializing the original weights, each individual is evaluated by executing the evolved SNN against the target problem (*lines 7–8*). In each generation, the error achieved with the candidate under evaluation (E_i) is compared with the error previously stored for this member of the population (E_i^{Prev}) (*line 11*). When the performance of the new individual surpasses its predecessor, the parent is substituted in the population by the descendant, which is therefore preserved for future generations $(\theta_i^{Prev} = \theta_i)$. This way of maintaining better predecessors is called elitism. In every iteration, an offspring is generated based on the parent's weight through mutation (*lines 13 and 15*).

The processors in the PS store the weight information for every individual during training. In each iteration, the weights are transferred to the SNN IP in the PL to evaluate the performance of the current individual for a given problem. Since the population comprises multiple independent individuals, several can be evaluated simultaneously. This can be easily achieved when multiple SNN IPs are

---

Algorithm 1. Evolutionary Strategy for Learning in SNN

1: **Require:** population size P, error function E, number of generations G.
2: **for** $i = 0, 1, \ldots, P-1$ **do**
3:     Initialize population with random sets of weights: $\theta_i = \lambda()$
4: **end for**
5: **for** $g = 1, 2, \ldots, G$ **do**
6:     **for** $i = 0, 1, \ldots, P-1$ **do**
7:         Initialize SNN IP with weights θ_i
8:         Compute error: E_i
9:         **if** g=1 **then**
10:             Store individual: $\theta_i^{Prev} = \theta_i$, $E_i^{Prev} = E_i$
11:         **else if** $E_i < E_i^{Prev}$ **then**
12:             Store and substitute individual: $\theta_i^{Prev} = \theta_i$, $E_i^{Prev} = E_i$
13:             Create new individual from mutation: θ_i=mutate(θ_i^{Prev})
14:         **else**
15:             Create new individual from mutation: θ_i=mutate(θ_i^{Prev})
16:         **end if**
17:     **end for**
18: **end for**
19: return θ_P, E_P, A_P

---

included in the SoC. This inherent parallelism is another benefit of the proposed strategy.

5 Data Encoding Strategy

One of the more relevant decisions needed when implementing SNN-based systems is how to encode the input data to be processed by the network. Different approaches exist in the literature, ranging from the most straightforward rate coding (i.e., information is provided by the number of spikes in a time window) to temporal encoding (i.e., information is provided by the exact time of spikes, for instance, the first one). In this work, a more complex approach is followed, exploiting the model of receptive fields proposed by S. M. Bohte et al. [21]. This approach utilizes a population of neurons with Gaussian activation functions, and each input variable is encoded using a variable number of neurons. The accuracy can be improved by sharpening the receptive fields and increasing the neurons affected by each input variable.

The data range for each input variable is filled with Gaussian fields that cover the entire data spectrum with an adjustable number of inputs per variable. For a variable n with range $[I_{max}^n, \ldots, I_{min}^n]$, m neurons are used. The width for all the neurons is set to $\sigma = \frac{1}{\beta} \cdot \frac{(I_{max}^n - I_{min}^n)}{(m-2)}$ and for every neuron i, its center is set to $I_{min}^n + \frac{(2i-3)}{2} \cdot \frac{(I_{max}^n - I_{min}^n)}{(m-2)}$. A value of 1.5 was experimentally decided to be used for β in the proposed implementation. Figure 2 shows a graphical representation of this technique. For a given input (shown as the blue line in the top figure), the crossing points with each Gaussian field are calculated (green triangles). These crossing points can be obtained using the probability density function for the input data. Higher values at these intersection points indicate stronger excitation for that variable, and these are transformed into lower delay times, rounded to the nearest discrete time step. For example, a value of 1 would be the maximum possible value obtained by the probability density function formula and would be then transformed into an input spike at time t=0. With the example of an input window of ten steps, values for each spike delay can go up to t = 10. In this project, spike delays higher than t = 9 are coded not to fire, as considered to be insufficiently excited.

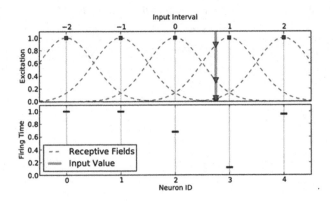

Fig. 2. Input Data encoding based on Gaussian receptive fields.

The encoding of the output produced by the SNN is also highly relevant. In supervised learning problems, the dataset's total number of instances is split into a training and a validation subset. The network is then evaluated using the training set as a reference, taking the exact timings of the output neuron spikes as the classification value assigned to a given label in the dataset. The classification error for novel samples in the dataset is computed as the distance between the target and actual spikes, as shown in Fig. 3.

The processors in the PS running the evolutionary algorithm must be aware of the SNN evaluation time to provide the inputs at the right time stamps and to understand the output in its context.

6   Evaluation Setup

The system proposed in this work has been implemented on the PYNQ-Z1 development board with a ZYNQ XC7Z020-1CLG400C MPSoC device. Two different sets of problems are used to demonstrate the adaptation capabilities of the system: classic classification problems from the UCI datasets, and control problems, from the Gymnasium API (formerly, OpenAI's Gym library [15]). The selected problems are described next.

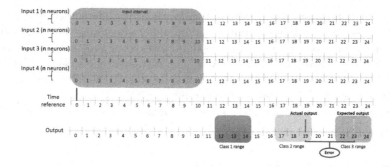

Fig. 3. Computing error in the network.

6.1 Iris Problem

The first of the UCI datasets selected is the Iris dataset [16]. It is one of the most well-known databases in the pattern recognition field. It contains three classes of 50 instances each, two of which are not linearly separable. The Iris dataset uses four attributes representing specific characteristics of different types of plants. The objective is to classify each instance into one of the three types of iris plants. Four Gaussian receptive fields have been selected for each variable to convert the original dataset into input spikes for the SNN. This results in 16 inputs, with an extra input used as a time reference. A single output neuron is included, with three different time windows used for classification. A complete scheme of the network's input and output encodings, including the time windows, is presented in Fig. 4. The size of the input time window is set to 9 execution time steps (light blue).

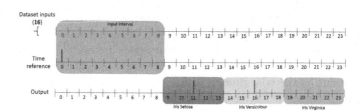

Fig. 4. Network configuration for the Iris dataset. (Color figure online)

The dataset is divided into a training (70% of the instances) and a testing set (30%). Both groups are randomly selected, with the same proportion of classes as in the original dataset. The error function is calculated using the accumulated time-step distances between the actual and expected spikes as its main parameter. However, during the experimental tests, it has been observed that including penalties for non-desired behaviors helps the network to converge faster. The proposed penalty system favors if the spikes for the different classes are correctly ordered, even if they are out of the bounds reserved for the classification. For example, an Iris Virginica instance that spikes after time step 23 (following Fig. 4) is less penalized than an Iris Virginica instance that spikes at time step 16. However, if the output neuron does not spike during the trial time (100 ms), a maximum penalty is applied to the candidate SNN.

The complete list of parameters used to adapt the system for each of the datasets is included in Table 1.

Table 1. Parameters of the Evolutionary Strategy for the different datasets.

Parameter	Iris	Brest Cancer	Pima Diabetes	Wine	Montain Car
Training trials	105 (70%)	350 (50.07%)	385 (50.13%)	125 (70.22%)	—
Testing trials	45 (30%)	349 (49.93%)	383 (49.87%)	53 (29.78%)	—
Hidden layers	1	1	1	1	1
Neurons per layer	17	37	33	53	17
Hidden neurons	17	37	33	14	17
Input neurons	17	37	33	53	17
Output neurons	1	1	1	1	1
Total neurons	35	75	67	68	35
Population	20	20	20	20	5
Trial time (ms)	100	100	100	100	100

6.2   Breast Cancer Wisconsin Dataset

This dataset uses nine different attributes, resulting in 37 inputs for the network (with 4 Gaussian receptive fields for each feature). A single neuron classifies the data, dividing the output spectrum into two windows. The error function implemented for this dataset also penalizes the case in which the output neuron does not fire during the trial time. If it does fire, the error is computed using the distance to the correct time window for the output spike.

6.3   Pima Indian Diabetes Dataset

The following dataset considered was the Pima Indian Diabetes dataset, whose purpose is to predict whether a patient has diabetes based on diagnostic measurements included as attributes of the dataset. In this dataset, eight features are used to classify the instances into two classes, corresponding to either a positive or a negative prediction. For this purpose, 33 input neurons are used, with just one output neuron. The output window is split into two parts, representing the two classes. The error function is the same as seen in the Breast Cancer dataset.

6.4   Wine Dataset

The last dataset selected from the UCI repository is the Wine dataset. It includes data about the chemical analysis of wines derived from three different cultivars, which comprise the three possible output classes. The network configuration is derived from the one used for the Iris dataset. An error function favoring the correct order of spikes for the three different classes is applied, as already seen in the case of the Iris dataset. The list of parameters corresponding to this implementation is listed in Table 1, with an initial proposal of 53 neurons inside of the hidden layer. Because of the limited number of instances of the dataset and the large number of neurons and synapses included, the network had difficulty converging within a reasonable time. To solve this problem, some neurons' weights were set to zero to implement only 14 neurons in the hidden layer, which proved more effective, as shown in the experimental results.

6.5   The Mountain Car Environment

The mountain car environment is a deterministic Markov Decision Process in which the goal is to accelerate a car placed at the bottom of a valley to reach the top of the right hill. The rendered environment can be observed in Fig. 5. It belongs to Gymnasium, a standard API for RL, created as a maintained version of the original OpenAI's Gym library [15]. The observation space of the mountain car environment consists of two attributes: the position of the car along the x-axis and the car's velocity. Three discrete actions form the action space: accelerating the car in both directions and not accelerating.

Fig. 5. Mountain car environment.

Eight Gaussian receptive fields are used to encode each one of the attributes of the environment. A multiplying factor is also applied for both attributes (after centering the x-axis position attribute at zero) to improve accuracy for the initial values when the car is at the bottom of the valley with little changes in position. The spike timings of the output neuron dictate the action to be taken. The goal of the mountain car is to reach the flag placed on the right hill as quickly as possible. The agent is then penalized with a reward of -1 for each timestep. After 200 timesteps, the episode ends. This variable number of trials constitutes one of the main differences between this environment and the UCI datasets described before. To help the system converge, the evolution strategy running inside the

Zynq device will use this reward information about the time duration of the episode and the maximum x-axis position achieved during it. This allows that, at the first evolution steps, individuals that get closer to the flag are selected. A population of just five individuals is used to accelerate the simulations, as shown in Table 1.

7   Experimental Results

7.1   Resource Utilization

The resource utilization presented in Table 2 covers the implementations for each of the four UCI datasets used for the single IP solution. It can be observed that having only one SNN in the system, the resource occupation is relatively small, with up to 43% of the LUTs used in the worst-case scenario, corresponding to the Wine dataset. This value decreases when implementing smaller networks, such as the one used for the Iris dataset, containing only 17 neurons per layer. In this case, it utilizes 25% of the available LUTs.

Table 2. Resource Utilization with a single SNN (ZYNQ XC7Z020 MPSoC)

Dataset	LUTs	FFs	BRAMs	DSPs
Iris	25%	18%	19%	15%
Breast Cancer Dat	35%	26%	23%	22%
Pima Indian Diabetes	33%	25%	23%	20%
Wine	43%	29%	24%	30%

Table 3. Resource Utilization with two SNNs (ZYNQ XC7Z020 MPSoC)

Dataset	LUTs	FFs	BRAMs	DSPs
Iris	51%	37%	37%	31%
Breast Cancer Dat	70%	53%	46%	45%
Pima Indian Diabetes	67%	49%	46%	40%
Wine	98%	59%	47%	59%

When scaling the implementation to two SNN IPs, the resource utilization increases almost by the same factor, as seen in Table 3. All the resource utilization values are approximately doubled, going from a 51% LUT occupation in the Iris implementation to almost a complete occupation in the case of the Wine dataset.

7.2   Accuracy Results

Figure 6 shows the maximum, minimum, and average accuracy results achieved for the different datasets during training. The maximum classification accuracy rate of the best individual achieved during training for the Iris dataset is 98.1%. Similar behavior is obtained for the rest of the datasets. The X-axis represents the generation number.

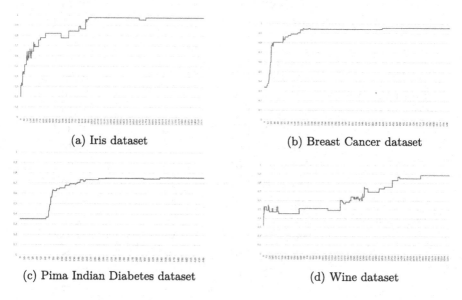

(a) Iris dataset   (b) Breast Cancer dataset

(c) Pima Indian Diabetes dataset   (d) Wine dataset

Fig. 6. Accuracy results for the different training sets.

After training, the goal is to see if the trained networks can extrapolate the knowledge acquired for a given dataset and achieve good results for new input data (during inference with the test dataset). A comparison of the performance in testing achieved over the different datasets against other state-of-the-art solutions that have previously addressed the same problems is provided in Table 4. The comparison table includes results from other machine-learning solutions DoB-SNN [17], SWAT [18], SpikeProp [19], SRESN [20], DANNA and NIDA [21], differential evolution (DE) [22] and Cuckoo Search (CS) [23]. The table presents the accuracy achieved for the testing dataset and neuron type for the solutions considered.

Note that the solution presented in this work is the only one found to use the Izhikevich neuron model in a hardware-accelerated implementation for these datasets. Other solutions use neuron models like LIF or other Integrate-and-Fire derived models. Additionally, most solutions are tested using software implementations rather than leveraging the parallel capabilities of hardware-accelerated platforms. From the information in the table, it can be seen that the accuracy results for this work are comparable to those obtained by other solutions.

Table 4. Results comparison

Dataset	Algorithm	Neuron type	Hardware impl.	Accuracy
Iris	DANNA	I&F	Yes	99.30%
	NIDA	I&F	No	99.30%
	DE	Izhikevich	No	98.33%
	This work	Izhikevich	Yes	97.78%
	DoB-SNN	LIF	No	97.75%
	SRESN	LIF	No	97.01%
	SpikeProp	LIF	No	96.13%
	CS	Izhikevich	No	94.67%
	SWAT	LIF	No	93.88%
Breast Cancer Wisc.	NIDA	I&F	No	98.60%
	DANNA	I&F	Yes	98.10%
	DoB-SNN	LIF	No	97.35%
	SRESN	LIF	No	97.10%
	SpikeProp	LIF	No	97.04%
	This work	Izhikevich	Yes	95.70%
	SWAT	LIF	No	95.66%
Pima Indian Diab.	NIDA	I&F	No	81.00%
	DANNA	I&F	Yes	78.00%
	SpikeProp	LIF	No	77.38%
	DoB-SNN	LIF	No	76.57%
	CS	Izhikevich	No	74.77%
	DE	Izhikevich	No	73.71%
	SWAT	LIF	No	72.11%
	This work	Izhikevich	Yes	72.06%
	SRESN	LIF	No	70.06%
Wine	NIDA	I&F	No	99,4%
	DANNA	I&F	Yes	97.2%
	CS	Izhikevich	No	90.78%
	This work	Izhikevich	Yes	88.679%
	DE	Izhikevich	No	87.44%

Regarding the mountain car problem, L. Custode and G. Iacca [24] propose evolutionary solutions based on orthogonal and oblique Decision Trees (DT) to solve different reinforcement learning problems. By also computing ten episodes per individual and calculating their mean score, they obtain a maximum score value of 101.72 timesteps for the orthogonal DT method and 106.02 timesteps for the oblique DT method. For the same problem, Z. Xiao [25] obtains a maximum average score of 102.61 timesteps using a closed-form policy method.

The solution presented in this work solved the mountain car problem with an average episode duration time of 97.3 timesteps, outperforming previous solutions. Three of the five individuals in the original randomly generated population were able to converge and solve this problem in less than 100 timesteps (on average), taking less than 500 generations to do it. This also validates the design for real-time reinforcement learning problems and demonstrates the ability to reliably obtain optimal individuals within a few generations.

8   Conclusions and Future Work

The SNN-based SoC presented in this work has been successfully tested on both supervised learning and reinforced learning problems, achieving positive results for accuracy rates and performance in each case. The results are comparable to other state-of-the-art solutions for the four UCI datasets. For the reinforcement learning test conducted, the results show slightly better performance than other ANN solutions. The tests demonstrate the proposed system's adaptability, flexibility, and real-time capabilities, providing a solid foundation for future development and research. This opens up a wide range of possibilities to improve the system and extend its applications, including the integration of fault models in the neurons to show the fault-tolerance of the proposed integrated SoC, expanding the evolution strategy capabilities by incorporating crossover or more complex selection and mutation algorithms or developing a concurrent solution using several Zynq devices to enable faster computing targeting more complex tasks.

References

1. Frenkel, C., Lefebvre, M., Legat, J.-D., Bol, D.: A 0.086-mm2 12.7-pj/sop 64k-synapse 256-neuron online-learning digital spiking neuromorphic processor in 28-nm cmos. IEEE Trans. Biomed. Circuits Syst. **13**(1), 145–158 (2018)
2. Lines, A., et al.: Loihi asynchronous neuromorphic research chip. In: 2018 24th IEEE International Symposium on Asynchronous Circuits and Systems (ASYNC), pp. 32–33. IEEE (2018)
3. Furber, S.B., Galluppi, F., Temple, S., Plana, L.A.: The spinnaker project. Proc. IEEE **102**(5), 652–665 (2014)
4. Li, C., et al.: Efficient and self-adaptive in-situ learning in multilayer memristor neural networks. Nat. Commun. **9**(1), 2385 (2018)
5. Hodgkin, A.L., Huxley, A.F.: A quantitative description of membrane current and its application to conduction and excitation in nerve. J. Physiol. **117**(4), 500 (1952)
6. Izhikevich, E.M.: Simple model of spiking neurons. IEEE Trans. Neural Networks **14**(6), 1569–1572 (2003)
7. Brette, R., Gerstner, W.: Adaptive exponential integrate-and-fire model as an effective description of neuronal activity. J. Neurophysiol. **94**(5), 3637–3642 (2005)
8. Ponulak, F., Kasinski, A.: Introduction to spiking neural networks: information processing, learning and applications. Acta Neurobiol. Exp. **71**(4), 409–433 (2011)
9. Bohte, S.M., Kok, J.N., La Poutre, H.: Error-backpropagation in temporally encoded networks of spiking neurons. Neurocomputing **1–4**, 17–37 (2002)

10. Xu, Y., Zeng, X., Han, L., Yang, J.: A supervised multi-spike learning algorithm based on gradient descent for spiking neural networks. Neural Netw. **43**, 99–113 (2013)
11. Ponulak, F., Kasiński, A.: Supervised learning in spiking neural networks with resume: sequence learning, classification, and spike shifting. Neural Comput. **22**(2), 467–510 (2010)
12. Sporea, I., Grüning, A.: Supervised learning in multilayer spiking neural networks. Neural Comput. **25**(2), 473–509 (2013)
13. Belatreche, A., Maguire, L.P., McGinnity, M., Wu, Q.X.: An evolutionary strategy for supervised training of biologically plausible neural networks. In: The Sixth International Conference on Computational Intelligence and Natural Computing, pp. 1524–1527 (2003)
14. Sanchez, F.G., Nunez-Yanez, J.: Energy proportional streaming spiking neural network in a reconfigurable system. Microprocess. Microsyst. **53**, 57–67 (2017)
15. Brockman, G., et al.: Openai gym. arXiv preprint arXiv:1606.01540 (2016)
16. Asuncion, A., Newman, D.: UCI machine learning repository (2007)
17. Saranirad, V., McGinnity, T.M., Dora, S., Coyle, D.: DOB-SNN: a new neuron assembly-inspired spiking neural network for pattern classification. In: 2021 International Joint Conference on Neural Networks, pp. 1–6 (2021)
18. Wade, J.J., McDaid, L.J., Santos, J.A., Sayers, H.M.: Swat: a spiking neural network training algorithm for classification problems. IEEE Trans. Neural Networks **21**(11), 1817–1830 (2010)
19. Bohte, S.M., Kok, J.N., La Poutré, J.A.: Spikeprop: backpropagation for networks of spiking neurons. In: ESANN, vol. 48, pp. 419–424 (2000)
20. Dora, S., Subramanian, K., Suresh, S., Sundararajan, N.: Development of a self-regulating evolving spiking neural network for classification problem. Neurocomputing **171**, 1216–1229 (2016)
21. Schuman, C.D., Plank, J.S., Disney, A., Reynolds, J.: An evolutionary optimization framework for neural networks and neuromorphic architectures. In: 2016 International Joint Conference on Neural Networks (IJCNN), pp. 145–154. IEEE (2016)
22. Vazquez, R.: Izhikevich neuron model and its application in pattern recognition. Aust. J. Intell. Inf. Process. Syst. **11**(1), 35–40 (2010)
23. Vazquez, R.A.: Training spiking neural models using cuckoo search algorithm. In: 2011 IEEE Congress of Evolutionary Computation (CEC), pp. 679–686 (2011)
24. Custode, L.L., Iacca, G.: Evolutionary learning of interpretable decision trees. IEEE Access (2023)
25. Xiao, Z.: Reinforcement Learning: Theory and Python Implementation. Springer, Singapor (2022)

More Efficient CMMs on FPGAs: Instantiated Ternary Adders for Computation Coding

Alexander Lehnert[1,2](✉) [ID], Hans Rosenberger[3] [ID], Ralf Müller[3] [ID],
and Marc Reichenbach[2] [ID]

[1] Chair of Computer Engineering, Brandenburg University of Technology, Cottbus,
Germany
`alexander.lehnert@b-tu.de`
[2] Institute of Applied Microelectronics and Computer Engineering, University of
Rostock, Rostock, Germany
`{alexander.lehnert,marc.reichenbach}@uni-rostock.de`
[3] Institute for Digital Communications, Friedrich-Alexander University
Erlangen-Nürnberg, Erlangen, Germany
`{hans.rosenberger,ralf.r.mueller}@fau.de`

Abstract. With the ever increasing complexity of modern algorithms, especially Artificial Neural Networks, the acceleration of linear operations becomes highly beneficial. Computation Coding (CC) matrix decomposition methods promise great reductions in operational cost of Constant Matrix Multiplication. Implementations of such decompositions rely on shifts followed by additions only. Recent FPGAs enable efficient addition of three operands by using multiple-output Lookup-Tables (LUTs) and CC decompositions naturally enable fine control over operand counts in each addition. However, synthesis does not always infer these efficient adder structures.

To better utilize the resources present on FPGAs, we use primitive instantiation via a Python-based hardware generation framework allowing for fine control over implemented logic. We show, that designs based on instantiated primitive ternary-input adders reduce hardware cost in LUTs by up to 1.8× compared to inferred designs and decompositions based on binary input adders only, but also perform well with regards to pipelining and timing restrictions.

1 Introduction

Linear Operations, i.e. matrix multiplications are fundamental operations used in many algorithms. One prominent example is inference in Artificial Neural Networks (ANNs) and many digital signal processing algorithms [6]. Inference in

---

This work was partially founded by the German Research Foundation (DFG - Deutsche Forschungsgemeinschaft) under the project Berechnungskodierung (RE 4182/4-1 and MU 3735/8-1).

trained ANNs relies on Constant Matrix Multiplication (CMM), i.e. the matrices underlying are fixed. Therefore, the computation of CMMs benefits from the utilization of prior knowledge. Methods using this prior knowledge of constant matrices are Canonically Signed Digit (CSD) based computation paradigms and matrix decomposition methods such as Computation Coding (CC).

CC approximate matrix decomposition methods enable highly efficient implementations of CMMs on Field Programmable Gate Arrays (FPGAs). Implementations of CC decompositions are multiplierless designs which rely on adders bit shifting implemented by wiring alone [12]. The decomposition takes advantage of prior knowledge of matrices, which is given as matrices in CMMs are fixed. FPGAs enable implementations of different CMMs as they offer reconfigurability. Therefore, combining CC designs with FPGA implementations combined the benefits from both worlds, maximal use of prior knowledge and flexibility of implementation.

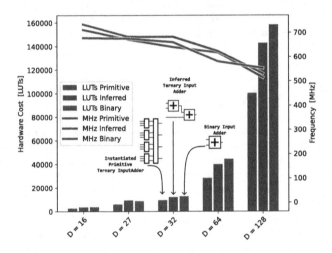

Fig. 1. Comparison of Hardware Cost (LUTs) and Frequency (MHz) of designs based TIAs using Primitive Instantiation, inferred TIAs and inferred BIAs for matrices of dimension D.

Recent FPGAs offer the unique opportunity of Ternary-Input Adders (TIAs) with similar resource utilization as traditional Binary-Input Adders (BIAs) thanks to two-output Lookup-Tables (LUTs) [20]. As the binary system stands at the core of traditional hardware designs, we often do not see the potential reduction in hardware resource utilization realized, e.g. CSD based approaches do only achieve a 11% reduction in hardware cost [6]. Our designs directly benefit from more input adders by subsequently requiring less sequential additions and thus decreasing the overall number of additions and also the hardware cost required to implement them drastically.

CC decomposition algorithms naturally enable control over operand counts to additions, i.e. we can setup the algorithm to produce TIAs only. Designs with inferred adders in synthesis still does not achieve the desired 2× reduction in hardware cost. To improve the efficiency of implementations of CC designs, i.e. hardware designs implementing CC decompositions, we directly map to FPGA primitives within CLBs and come close to the desired improvement. Such a mapping to primitives is enabled by i) the properties of CC decompositions and ii) means of hardware description generation using a HLI tool. The graphical abstract, Fig. 1, summarizes our exploration. As shown, the three CCs implementations compared are traditional BIAs (green), inferred TIAs (red) during synthesis, as well as primitive mapped TIAs (blue).

Summarizing our findings, this paper provides the following two contributions.

- We analyze mappings of TIA designs on FPGAs and show that implementations CC naturally enable TIAs based designs and thus efficient CMM implementations.
- By means of hardware description generation, we demonstrate how an efficient implementation technique for adder design based on primitive instantiation is derived.

Our designs based on primitive mapped adders enable a reduction in required LUTs by 1.41× compared to inferred adder designs and 1.85× compared to BIA based designs with negligible impact on maximal achievable frequencies. Compared to designs from HLS, we perform 1.87× better on average for scaled integer representations and on average 8.09× for the fixed-point implementation at a bit-width of 8 bit. Similarly, for the comparison to the CSD method presented by Kumm et al. [11] with improvements ranging from 1.85× to 2.43×.

The paper is structured as follows. First of all, related work regarding algorithms for efficient CMM execution and corresponding hardware architectures is presented in Sect. 2. Afterwards, Sect. 3 explains the CC decomposition algorithm and the corresponding hardware designs first presented in [12]. The hardware generation workflow and the incorporation of primitive-mapped adder structures are covered in Sect. 4. Section 5 provides an experimental evaluation of our methods. This evaluation includes i) an overview over both hardware cost and timing properties of our designs for a selected range of matrix dimensions, ii) a comparison to current State-of-the-Art (SoA) FPGA approaches to CMM implementation, i.e. HLS and CSD based methods [10,11] and iii) a performance comparison to SoA processing architectures, meaning Graphics Processing Unit (GPU) and Central Processing Unit (CPU) implementations of CMMs. Lastly, the work is concluded by Sect. 6.

2 Related Work

Along with the increasing complexity of recent ANNs, methods for efficient accelerators have become immensely important. Current literature can be divided into two approaches to lowering the computational complexity of CMMs, quantization and arithmetical optimization.

Quantization of matrices in combination with pruning is by far the most popular approach to efficient CMMs. For a fixed bit-width B, matrix entries are mapped to the fixed-point number of bit-width B that is closest. Matrix-elements with low impact on the results of computation are pruned for further reductions in computation cost. The quantization approach reduces the representation space of numbers, e.g. to 4 bit or 8 bit, and thereby enables cheaper computation [3,5].

Further optimization comes from CSD based approaches. The CSD number representation yields the lowest number of 1-bits and thus the lowest number of additions (or subtractions) required to implement a multiplication. Several works propose optimizations of these representations over larger sums of products enabling resource sharing and reducing the required hardware for implementing the overall operation even further [1,6,10,11]. This problem is NP-hard [1] and finding an optimal solution for large operations often is expensive or practically infeasible. CSD based approaches promise multiplierless implementations of multiplications, though this is only true when splitting up multiplications into their corresponding additions and subtractions.

For FPGAs, there is wide range of frameworks aimed at finding efficient quantization and pruning parameters and infer corresponding hardware designs, e.g. FINN [2] and ZigZag [15]. As for CSD based approaches, there are frameworks aiming at finding approximative solutions to the optimization problem [1], as well as an elaborate framework by Kumm et al. [10,11] for finding optimal solutions. The work by Kumm et al. is well recognized and extended to also support TIAs [6].

Our work focuses on the second category of CMM optimization, i.e. new algorithmic optimization approaches. Recent advances in matrix decomposition methods make implementations based on the same viable. CC decomposition methods do not require quantization or pruning. They enable matrix approximations which only rely on shifting and addition, thus enabling actual multiplierless implementations [16–19]. These CC methods promise the lowest number of additions required for computation yet.

CC algorithms used in this work are presented in detail in Sect. 3.1. In short, the decomposition yields matrices which consist of signed powers of two only, i.e. the multiplication with such a operand does actually only require shifting. By fixing the number of operands in each matrix row, the datapaths in the computation are all of equal length, resulting in hardware designs with minimal clock slips [12]. Further, we propose a hardware generation framework to implement CC designs. Tools such as PagSuite [9] rely on FloPoCo [4] for the generation of hardware descriptions of operators [11]. With the prior knowledge of CC matrices, we can provide very efficient hardware designs without such operators from FloPoCo. As a further benefit, we have full control over the implemented operations, i.e. we can instantiate primitive-based adders and achieve very efficient TIAs.

Several hardware architectures are viable for implementation of some or most of the presented algorithmic approaches to efficient CMMs. We want to focus mainly on FPGA mapped hardware architectures. These include CC and CSD based methods along with Digital Signal Processor (DSP) and other LUT based solutions. Application-Specific Integrated Circuit (ASIC) architectures can achieve power efficient computation while enabling high performance.

In general, processing close to memory is desirable, as memory access becomes the bottle-neck of modern applications. Recent GPUs provide efficient acceleration for 4×4 matrix multiplication [14]. Google's Tensor Processing Units (TPUs) provides means for acceleration of larger operations, being based on systolic array-like structures [7,8]. For these fixed processing units, especially for GPUs and CPUs, quantized CMMs yield good performance. The implementation of CC decomposed matrices on these processing structures is not beneficial over naive implementations, as the required control overhead makes up for the cheaper computations. Therefore, our work focuses on FPGAs, presenting a method to map additions efficiently to LUT based TIAs and shows how to benefit from modifications to the CC algorithm accordingly.

3   Computation Coding on FPGAs

3.1   Decomposition Algorithm

The goal of this variant of CC algorithms is to find a decomposition for a constant, but arbitrary matrix $\boldsymbol{W} \in \mathbb{R}^{M \times N}$, such that the matrix vector product $\boldsymbol{W}\boldsymbol{v}$ can be efficiently computed on an FPGA.

We accomplish this by first cutting the target matrix into multiple tall submatrices [12]

$$\boldsymbol{W} = [\boldsymbol{W}_1 | \boldsymbol{W}_2 | \ldots | \boldsymbol{W}_S]. \tag{1}$$

The slicing of matrices is beneficial as the subsequent decomposition algorithm works much better for tall matrices than for approximately square matrices.

Each matrix slice $\boldsymbol{W}_s$ is then decomposed into a product of several nontrivial matrix factors

$$\boldsymbol{W} \approx \sum_{s=1}^{S} \prod_{p=1}^{P} \boldsymbol{F}_{s,p} \quad \text{with} \quad \boldsymbol{F}_{s,0} = [\boldsymbol{I}|\boldsymbol{0}]. \tag{2}$$

as suggested by the framework of CC [18]. A more efficient implementation on reconfigurable hardware is achieved by placing the following two restrictions on the matrix factors $\boldsymbol{F}_{s,p}$:

1. The matrix factors are sparse. At most E entries are allowed to be nonzero in each row of a matrix factor. This means when multiplying with a row of a matrix factor exactly $E - 1$ additions are required.

2. The entries of the matrix factors are restricted to the set of zero and (sums of) signed powers of two.

Formally, these restrictions correspond to recursively solving the following optimization problem with $p > 0$, and some parameter E controlling the computational cost,

$$f_{s,p,m} = \underset{\varphi \in \mathcal{A}}{\operatorname{argmin}} \| w_{s,}, - \varphi F_{s,p-1} \cdots F_{s,0} \|_2 \quad \forall m \tag{3}$$

$$\mathcal{A} = \left\{ \varphi \mid \varphi = \sum_{e=1}^{E} i_e 1_{j_e,M}, \ i_e \in \{0, \pm 2^Z\}, \ j_e \in \{1, \dots, M\} \ \forall e \right\}. \tag{4}$$

Further, $w_{s,m}$ corresponds to the m-th row in W_s and $f_{s,p,m}$ is the m-th row of a matrix factor $F_{s,p}$. In general, this problem is NP-hard and thus infeasible to solve optimally. We therefore consider in the following two suboptimal algorithms:

1. **Discrete Matching Pursuit (DMP)** [18]: The vector φ is updated successively in one component at a time until E updates are performed. Similar to the matching pursuit in each iteration the component of φ is updated that yields the largest reduction in distance to the target vector $w_{s,m}$.
2. **Reduced State Algorithm (RSA)** [19]: This algorithm operates on the principle of DMP. However, instead of updating φ directly, we keep a list of the L best vectors in each iteration and find in the subsequent iteration again the L distinct vectors for each vector obtained in the previous iteration. We then only use the L best vectors out of the set of L^2 vectors obtained for the following iteration. On termination, we choose the vector that yields minimum error. This approach offers a performance close to the optimal solution and is significantly improved over DMP for $E > 2$ and therefore well suited for an implementation with three input adders. For details see [19].

The decomposition algorithm does not place any restriction on the signs of the entries of the matrix factors. However, for an adder with two negative inputs an additional inverter is required. For an adder with three inputs the additional inverter is required as well if all inputs are negative. The additional hardware cost by the extra inverter is to be avoided as far as possible. This can be either achieved by placing an additional side constraint on the number of negative elements per row of a matrix factor on the optimization problem, leading to a degraded performance in terms of the distortion-cost trade-off. An alternative is to multiply each row with -1 if more than one entry is negative and then compensate for the sign change by multiplying the corresponding column in the subsequent matrix factor with -1 as well. This procedure is applied recursively throughout all matrix factors and the subsequent adder trees. Upon reaching the output, some elements may be inverted and require additional complementing. Note, that this procedure does not put restrictions on the optimization algorithm.

3.2 Hardware Designs

Implementations of CC designs save hardware resources based on the utilization of prior knowledge of CC matrices. These CC matrices or factors F of the decomposition satisfy the three following conditions

1. Factors F consist of E entries per row.
2. Each non-zero element of F is a sum of signed powers of two.
3. Rows of F feature at most $E - 1$ negative entries.

The constant number of signed power-of-two operands E in each row of a CC matrix is implemented using one E-input adder per row preceded by a set of E shifters. On FPGAs, shifts are mapped to wiring and thus are do not contribute to hardware cost.

We differentiate between BIAs ($E = 2$) and TIAs ($E = 3$). CC designs based on BIAs are explored in [12]. TIAs can be implemented very efficiently on FPGAs.

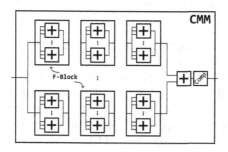

Fig. 2. CC design with TIAs ($E = 3$).

F-Blocks$_E$ implement one CC matrix each. Complying to (2), multiple F-Blocks are combined for the implementation of a full CMM. The corresponding hardware design for $E = 3$ operands per row of CC matrix is shown in Fig. 2. The important improvement over existing CC designs [12] is the omission of inverters. We guarantee at most $E - 1$ negative operands, i.e. one operand is either positive or zero, thus no operation requires additional complements of the input vector.

4 Hardware Generation Using Primitive Instantiation

4.1 Python Hardware Interface

We want our hardware designs to be compatible with a wide range of workflows [12]. Further, we need to bridge the semantic gap between CC decomposition algorithms and hardware descriptions while maintaining fine control over implemented adders. Therefore, we use a Python-based hardware generation workflow to generate all hardware designs which are shown in Sect. 3.2. Doing so joins two desirable properties, i) the ease of use with the decomposition algorithm and interfaces of e.g. ANN-frameworks such as TensorFlow or PyTorch and ii) VHDL-description of hardware designs consisting of low-level assertion only and thus being widely compatible.

One aspect of interest to design generation is pipelining. As explained in Sect. 3.2, CC designs achieve minimal slack. All computation paths traverse the same number of additions. Thus, the length of any path is very close to the critical path length resulting in a proper data-flow design without the need for any buffering of signals.

Our hardware generation workflow allows for end-to-end solutions from network-topology to training to hardware synthesis. It consists of two to three stages.

1. Operation Transformation (Optional): Transform linear operations to CMMs.
2. Matrix Decomposition: Decomposition using a CC algorithm with a chosen set of parameters.
3. Hardware Generation: HLI enables generation of VHDL-description of architectures from the matrix decomposition.

The first, optional step is the transformation to CMMs. In our applications, we focus on acceleration of inference in ANNs. Thus, this step provides the connection to Neural Network Frameworks such as PyTorch and extracts the weight matrices from e.g. fully connected layers. Secondly, matrices resulting from the previous stage are decomposed. This requires the choice of decomposition parameters, such as slice width W, operand count E and target accuracy. As a result, we get an approximations, i.e. sequences of CC matrices, for each slice. Hardware generation, as previously explained, leverages the HLI tool to generate low-level VHDL descriptions for the CC matrices, as well as for the composed design. For this last stage, design parameters are chosen, e.g. the pipelining configuration. After hardware generation, the hardware designs are ready for synthesis and implementation for FPGAs using e.g. Vivado 2022.2.

Adder designs and the mapping of the same to FPGAs are well explored [13]. Typically, hardware architectures designed for are built around BIAs. Many-Input Adder implementations based on compression trees in ASIC designs are well known. Recent FPGAs, such as Xilinx 7-Series [21], feature CLBs which enable efficient implementation of TIAs designs. This section shows methods of implementing TIAs and explains the mapping to FPGA resources in detail.

4.2   TIAs on FPGAs

There are two relevant adder designs for the analysis of TIAs in CC on FPGAs, Carry Look-Ahead Adders (CLAs) and Ripple-Carry-Adders (RCAs). RCAs feature a dedicated carry chain, which can be mapped to CARRY8 instances for fast computation. Such Carry structures reduce the delay of adders by means of fast carry forwarding [22]. CLAs feature low overall delay but come with high implementation costs [13]. Resource sharing for the carry calculation logic allows for reduction of CLB cost.

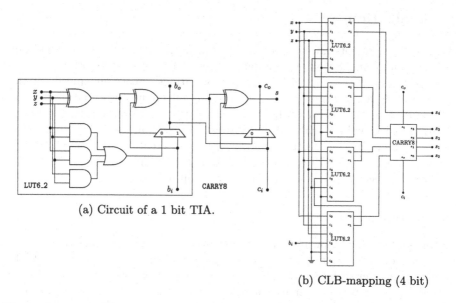

(a) Circuit of a 1 bit TIA.

(b) CLB-mapping (4 bit)

Fig. 3. Circuit of TIA and mapping to CLBs to a Xilinx 7-Series FPGA, first presented in [20].

Methods of implementing adders can be grouped into two categories: Inference and Primitive Instantiation. In recent versions of Vivado, e.g. Vivado 2022.2, inference of high level additions results in efficient adders designs. Still, we can also define the corresponding primitives directly. Xilinx proposed a TIA design, which requires the same hardware resources as a BIA [20]. The logic circuit, which is implemented for 1 bit of such an adder is shown in Fig. 3. Depending on the interpretation of the TIA design by Xilinx, there is either a 3:2 compressor followed by a BIA [20] or two separate carry paths, as depicted in Fig. 3a. A full 8 bit TIA with this design requires eight LUT6_2 and one CARRY8 instance, i.e. it utilizes one CLB.

4.3 Primitive Generation

The benefit of mapping TIAs as they are presented in Sect. 4.2 compared to inferred adder designs during synthesis depend heavily on the bit-width of the adders. Mainly, the limiting factor is the CARRY8. In Xilinx FPGAs, CARRY8s can be instantiated as one 8 bit carry or as two separate 4 bit carrys. Also, the multiplexing of CLB outputs is handled globally within one CLB. If a carry block is used only partially, the remaining LUTs connected to its other half cannot be used independent of the second carry block. The hardware generation tool makes use of primitives directly by instantiating them for different addition operations.

5   Evaluation

This section presents an evaluation of the primitive instantiation method and compares implementations to SoA hardware architectures. First of all, we will analyze the hardware cost of CC designs for various dimensions and decomposition and design parameters to determine a collection of optimal designs. In a second step, the desirable designs, i.e. the respective ones with the lowest hardware cost, will be analyzed under timing constraints to find the maximum or target frequency. From these numbers, we can create a comparison to SoA architectures such as GPUs. The exact details of the experiments conducted are explained in Sect. 5.1, followed by the evaluation in Sect. 5.2.

5.1   Setup

In this section, the following naming convention is used: Decomposition parameters include the dimension $D \times D$ of the original matrix, the slice width W, resulting number of factors P for each slice approximation and the number of operands E in rows of CC matrices. Further, we compare designs with registers after each factor and within each level of adder-trees, i.e. the critical path is determined by the individual maximal paths of implemented TIAs and BIAs.

A comparison between TIAs based on Primitive Instantiation (Pri), inferred TIAs (Inf) and BIAs (Bin) requires a sufficient search space. We achieve this by analyzing implementation costs for $D \in \{16, 27, 32, 64, 128\}$. Note, that all matrices are square but sliced vertically. Thus, rectangular matrices of dimension $M \times N$ require either less slices ($M < N$) or more slices ($M < N$) than their square counterparts of dimension $M \times M$.

All decompositions achieve at least 48 dB, i.e. they are at least as accurate as 8 bit fixed-point integer arithmetic. Decomposition for Pri and Inf, i.e. when $E = 3$, are determined using the RSA method, while we use DMP for the decomposition underlying Bin designs. These choices coincide with the best decompositions overall for both methods and the comparison is fair. Both methods are explained in Sect. 3.1. We use a Virtex UltraScale+ HBM (xcvu37p-fsvh2892-2L-e) board and Vivado 2022.2 for all experiments, which features the required LUT6_2s and CARRY8 blocks for the TIAs implemented using primitive instantiation.

First of all, we conduct a Design Space Exploration (DSE) to find the optimal slice widths for $E = 3$ and primitive instantiated TIAs. Slice widths should be powers of two (three) for optimal adder-trees in the resulting designs, i.e. in the CMM blocks in Fig. 2. We chose the optimal decomposition parameters based on minimal LUTs for each dimension. Table 1 presents the best results for each parameter set.

Note, that by implementing TIAs by instantiating primitives directly, we achieve the desired CARRY8 usage. Analysis of inferred adder designs shows, that inference during synthesis typically maps adders only to LUTs, rather than using CARRY8s. This observation can be related to routing strategies [22].

Table 1. Matrices of dimension $D \times D$ are decomposed with a slice width of D, $E = 3$ operands per row resulting in P factors. Resource costs shown include LUTs, CLBs, CARRY8 used as well as the number of registers (Regs). The maximum frequency is denoted as f in MHz.

Parameters			Resources				Pipelining	
D	W	P	LUTs	CLBs	CARRY8	$\frac{\text{CARRY8}}{\text{TIA}}$	f	Regs
16	4	5	3024	523	163	100.0%	711	2622
27	3	3	6942	1066	620	96.9%	672	6635
32	4	4	10576	1793	528	100.0%	640	7912
64	8	7	35163	5148	2653	116.9%	618	31689
128	8	6	124603	17803	9789	122.4%	514	107325

5.2 Comparison Between CMM Designs and SoA

This section presents comparisons between the proposed implementation based on CC and primitive instantiated TIAs with i) previous implementations of CC designs, ii) SoA FPGA based implementations and iii) GPU and CPU implementations for an architectural comparison.

CC Implementations. We compare our new TIA based method to the inferred TIAs, purely BIA based designs, as well as a quantized implementation of the CMM (STD) as the base-line. With the optimal designs from DSE, we can now focus on the comparison to designs based on inferred TIAs and ones only using BIAs and $E = 2$. Results of this comparison are presented in Table 2. The same Virtex UltraScale+ HBM board and target accuracy of 48 dB (SQNR of 8 bit fixed-point integer arithemtic) is used.

Table 2. Improvement $(\frac{\text{Method}}{(\text{Pri})})$ of designs with Primitive Instantiated TIAs (Pri) over Inferred TIAs (Inf) and BIAs (Bin). The underlying matrices are of dimension $D \times D$ and are decomposed using a slice width of W, and $E = 3$ using the RSA method for Pri, Inf and $E = 2$ using the DMP method for Bin.

Parameters				Resources					Pipelining			
D	W			LUTs		CLB		CARRY8	Registers		Frequency	
	Pri	Inf	Bin	Inf	Bin	Inf	Bin	Inf	Inf	Bin	Inf	Bin
16	4	4	2	1.19×	1.44×	1.40×	1.50×	4.53×	1.15×	1.47×	0.97×	1.05×
27	3	3	3	1.41×	1.85×	1.84×	1.74×	6.97×	0.99×	1.75×	0.98×	0.99×
32	4	4	4	1.19×	1.32×	1.33×	1.50×	2.49×	1.00×	1.76×	0.94×	0.97×
64	8	8	4	1.17×	1.28×	1.73×	1.80×	6.41×	1.00×	1.67×	0.99×	1.06×
128	8	8	8	1.16×	1.40×	1.53×	1.74×	5.23×	1.00×	1.57×	0.97×	0.93×

The factors in Table 2 denote the improvement from using primitive instantiation (Pri) for TIAs in the corresponding category over the denoted methods. This includes inferred adders (Inf) and BIAs designs (Bin).

First of all, we see that compared to Inf, Pri can achieve a reduction of up to 1.41× in LUTs required for implementation, while relying on the same number of factors in the decomposition. This reduction is the result of utilization of CARRY8s, which is also reflected in the reduction of required CLBs. Note, that for designs with binary adder trees, i.e. $D = 2^n, n \in \mathbb{N}$, the improvement is lower. Adder-trees in such cases consist of BIAs and no efficient TIAs are used. As the Pri and Inf designs rely on the same decomposition, the changes in number of implemented registers are very small. The same is true for the maximal frequency, which is higher for inferred designs, as our TIA design increases delay slightly [20].

A comparison to Bin shows, that a reduction in LUTs of up to 1.85× can be achieved. The comparison of frequencies between Bin and Pri is inconsistent. As already suggested, routing complexity may be one issue leading to these results, but also a larger variety in inferred BIAs implementations can contribute. Note, that with a larger number of factors required for the decomposition, also the number of registers increases drastically. Generally, we see that CC designs implemented using Primitive Instantiation lead to a notable reduction in resource utilization while impacts on timing constraints are negligible.

FPGA Implementations. Our implementation of CMMs based on TIAs and CC outperforms current SoA FPGA implementations. As alluded to in Sect. 2, there is a wide range of approaches of implementing CMMs on FPGAs. We choose the following subset as a basis for comparison.

HLS tools such as Vivado HLS by Xilinx are the most accessible method of implementing hardware accelerators. As input, the user is only required to provide a software kernel, e.g. using the C programming language in the case of Vivado HLS. The HLS tool then infers a hardware design implementing the kernel. For the application of CMMs, we generate the C-kernel of a CMM containing all constant matrix entries. All variables have an 8 bit bit-width, we present results for the actual fixed-point implementation, as well as a scaled Integer implementation, which guides the HLS tool towards the intended implementation not relying on floating-point representation. The latency of all HLS designs is set to a 10 ns delay.

CSD based approaches offer optimization potential based on the knowledge of constant matrix entries. Kumm et al. provide the PagSuite Framework [9] for implementing adder graphs with either BIAs [11] or TIAs [6,10]. The resulting graphs are passed to a hardware description generation framework, e.g. Kumm et all propose to use FloPoCo [4]. We compare two implementations of CSD based approaches, a BIA based one [11], as well as the optimized version relying on TIAs [6].

These two approaches cover current SoA methods of implementing CMMs, as HLS provides maximal accessibility and the CSD based optimization uses prior knowledge to lower hardware cost.

Table 3. Comparison ($\frac{\text{Method}}{\text{(CC-TIA-PRI)}}$) of FPGA-based CMM implementations. All implementations features the bit-width $B = 8$ and a frequency of $f = 100\,\text{MHz}$.

CC-TIA-PRI			HLS			CSD [10,11]	
D	W	LUT	FixPoint	Integer		BIA	TIA
16	4	3024	16.7×	1.69×		2.60×	1.85×
27	3	6942	8.23×	2.00×		3.22×	2.29×
32	4	10576	5.39×	1.84×		2.91×	2.07×
64	8	35163	2.10×	1.96×		3.42×	2.43×

We present a comparison of our approach to implementing CMMs using our hardware generation framework and CC to HLS and a CSD based approach in Table 3. It is clear, that the FixPoint HLS implementation struggles with unnecessary floating point representation. Here we are clearly better with an improvement of at least 2× in hardware resources. Compared to the scaled implementation relying on integers only, we still achieve an improvement of at least 1.69×. Note, that for comparison between the methods the frequency is set to 100 MHz, while the hardware cost increase of our approach at frequencies of up to 711 MHz is negligible. The comparison to CSD based optimizations shows a reduction in hardware cost ranging from 1.85× to 2.43×, when comparing TIAs. For smaller matrix sizes, we can expect CSD based approaches to perform better than CC ones, while its the opposite for large dimensions. Each matrix is split into 16 × 16 slices first, and each slice is optimized individually. The chosen dimension coincides with the maximal explored dimension in previous explorations [10,11]. We found, that the optimization problem for larger dimensions is not solvable in a similar time-frame to the CC decomposition.

Architecture Comparison. Finally, we compare our design on architecture level, including our FPGA implementation, and implementations for GPU and CPU at a bitwidth of $B = 8$. Using CUDA and the Numba Python framework, we execute the same CMMs presented before on a GPU and CPU. The computation-delay, i.e. execution time excluding memory transfers, is then compared to the estimated performance of our FPGA-based approach by considering the respective target frequency and memory bandwidth limitations of board (xcvu37p-fsvh2892-2L-e). For the GPU implementation, we parallelize the Sum of Products from one matrix row and use the high degree of parallelism for multiple rows of multiple CMMs without forcing the usage of Tensor cores. The benchmarked GPU is a NVIDIA A100 and the respective CPU a AMD EPYC Rome 7352. All numbers are rounded to four significant digits. Compared to the GPU, we achieve a speedup ranging from 31.63× ($D = 16$) to 1067× ($D = 128$). GPUs are generally optimized towards floating point processing, here we compare fixed point execution times. Further optimization potential can be assumed. Speedup over the CPU implementation ranges from 578.0× ($D = 27$) to 1688× ($D = 128$) The speedup generally increases with the dimension of the underlying matrix, as the FPGA implementation delay is determined by a single pipeline step, while the competing architectures are limited by parallelization.

6   Conclusion

Within this paper, we present a hardware cost and timing analysis of CC designs for FPGAs. By means of primitive instantiation, we achieve 1.8× reduced hardware cost at similar frequencies for our architecture.

There are several directions, that future research will explore. In this work, we do not analyze power results in detail. First results suggest a similar reduction in power to the reduction in hardware cost [12]. Also, we only analyze designs at a bit-width of 8 bit, but varying bit-widths and the impact on decomposition results are of interest as well. The aspect of parallelization in combination with CGRA designs or partial reconfiguration on FPGAs is a subject of future research.

References

1. Aksoy, L., Flores, P.M.: A novel method for the approximation of multiplierless constant matrix vector multiplication. Embedded Syst. 12 (2016). https://doi.org/10.1186/s13639-016-0033-y
2. Blott, M., et al.: FINN-R: an end-to-end deep-learning framework for fast exploration of quantized neural networks. ACM Trans. Reconfigurable Technol. Syst. **11**(3) (2018). https://doi.org/10.1145/3242897
3. Demidovskij, A., Smirnov, E.: Effective post-training quantization of neural networks for inference on low power neural accelerator. In: 2020 International Joint Conference on Neural Networks (IJCNN), pp. 1–7 (2020). https://doi.org/10.1109/IJCNN48605.2020.9207281
4. de Dinechin, F.: Reflections on 10 years of FloPoCo. In: 26th IEEE Symposium of Computer Arithmetic (ARITH-26) (2019)
5. Fan, A., et al.: Training with quantization noise for extreme model compression. arXiv preprint arXiv:2004.07320 (2020)
6. Hardieck, M., Kumm, M., Sittel, P., Zipf, P.: Constant matrix multiplication with ternary adders. In: 2018 25th IEEE International Conference on Electronics, Circuits and Systems (ICECS), pp. 85–88 (2018). https://doi.org/10.1109/ICECS.2018.8617860
7. Jia, L., Lu, L., Wei, X., Liang, Y.: Generating systolic array accelerators with reusable blocks. IEEE Micro **40**(4), 85–92 (2020). https://doi.org/10.1109/MM.2020.2997611
8. Jouppi, N.P., Young, C., Patil, N., et al.: In-datacenter performance analysis of a tensor processing unit. In: Proceedings of the 44th Annual International Symposium on Computer Architecture, pp. 1–12. ISCA 2017, New York, NY, USA. Association for Computing Machinery (2017). https://doi.org/10.1145/3079856.3080246, https://doi.org/10.1145/3079856.3080246
9. Kumm, M., Möller, K., Hardieck, M., Zipf, P.: Pagsuite project website (2018)
10. Kumm, M.: Optimal constant multiplication using integer linear programming. IEEE Trans. Circuits Syst. II Express Briefs **65**(5), 567–571 (2018). https://doi.org/10.1109/TCSII.2018.2823780

11. Kumm, M., Hardieck, M., Zipf, P.: Optimization of constant matrix multiplication with low power and high throughput. IEEE Trans. Comput. **66**(12), 2072–2080 (2017). https://doi.org/10.1109/TC.2017.2701365
12. Lehnert, A., Holzinger, P., Pfenning, S., Müller, R., Reichenbach, M.: Most resource efficient matrix vector multiplication on FPGAs. IEEE Access **11**, 3881–3898 (2023). https://doi.org/10.1109/ACCESS.2023.3234622
13. Luu, J., et al.: On hard adders and carry chains in FPGAs. In: 2014 IEEE 22nd Annual International Symposium on Field-Programmable Custom Computing Machines, May, pp. 52–59 (2014). https://doi.org/10.1109/FCCM.2014.25
14. Markidis, S., Chien, S.W.D., Laure, E., Peng, I.B., Vetter, J.S.: NVIDIA tensor core programmability, performance & precision. In: 2018 IEEE International Parallel and Distributed Processing Symposium Workshops (IPDPSW), pp. 522–531 (2018). https://doi.org/10.1109/IPDPSW.2018.00091
15. Mei, L., Houshmand, P., Jain, V., Giraldo, S., Verhelst, M.: Zigzag: Enlarging joint architecture-mapping design space exploration for DNN accelerators. IEEE Trans. Comput. **70**(8), 1160–1174 (2021). https://doi.org/10.1109/TC.2021.3059962
16. Müller, R.R., Gäde, B., Bereyhi, A.: Efficient matrix multiplication: the sparse power-of-2 factorization. In: 2020 Information Theory and Applications Workshop (ITA), pp. 1–6 (2020). https://doi.org/10.1109/ITA50056.2020.9244952
17. Müller, R.R., Gäde, B., Bereyhi, A.: Linear computation coding. In: ICASSP 2021–2021 IEEE International Conference on Acoustics, Speech and Signal Processing (ICASSP), pp. 5065–5069 (2021). https://doi.org/10.1109/ICASSP39728.2021.9414317
18. Müller, R., Gäde, B., Bereyhi, A.: Linear computation coding: a framework for joint quantization and computing. Algorithms **15**(7), 253 (2022)
19. Rosenberger, H., Fröhlich, J.S., Bereyhi, A., Müller, R.R.: Linear computation coding: Exponential search and reduced state algorithms. In: Data Compression Conference. Snowbird, UT (03 2023, accepted)
20. Simkins, J.M., Philofsky, B.D.: Structures and methods for implementing ternary adders/subtractors in programmable logic device; United States Patent US7274211B1 (2007)
21. Xilinx, I.: UltraScale Architecture Configurable Logic Block User Guide (UG574). Xilinx, Inc. (2017). https://docs.xilinx.com/v/u/en-US/ug574-ultrascale-clb
22. Xilinx, I.: Vivado Design Suite Properties Reference Guide. Xilinx, Inc. (2022). https://www.xilinx.com/support/documents/sw_manuals/xilinx2022_1/ug912-vivado-properties.pdf

Energy Efficient DNN Compaction for Edge Deployment

Bijin Elsa Baby[1]([✉]), Dipika Deb[2], Benuraj Sharma[3], Kirthika Vijayakumar[3], and Satyajit Das[1]

[1] Indian Institute of Technology Palakkad, Palakkad, Kerala, India
112114006@smail.iitpkd.ac.in, satyajitdas@iitpkd.ac.in
[2] Indian Institute of Technology Guwahati, Guwahati, Assam, India
d.dipika@iitg.ac.in
[3] MulticoreWare Inc., Chennai, Tamil Nadu, India
{benuraj,kirthika}@multicorewareinc.com

Abstract. Deep Neural Networks (DNNs) are popular deep learning models due to their numerous learnable parameters, which are required for both the training and inference phases. However, deploying these models on mobile and edge devices with limited hardware resources and power budgets is a significant challenge. To meet real-time requirements and energy efficiency, it is essential to compact DNN models. This paper proposes a fixed partition compaction technique exploiting consecutive zeros and non-zero weights/parameters in sparse DNN models. This approach reduces memory storage requirements, memory transactions and computations for DNNs. We implemented convolution and fully connected layers with the compact weights on Virtex-7 FPGA VC707. Our experiments demonstrate that compact layers have better performance and energy efficiency than layers without compaction. Results show that the compact convolution layers achieved an average performance improvement of 32.51% and 29.43% compared to state-of-the-art SMM and direct convolution respectively performed on several convolution configurations. Moreover, an energy consumption reduction of 34.14% over SMM and 29.58% over direct convolution. Experiments on the compact fully connected layers achieved an average performance improvement of 26.61% and energy consumption reduction of 30.85% over layers without compaction.

Keywords: Compact convolution · Pruning · DNN compaction · Energy efficiency

1 Introduction

Deep Neural Networks (DNNs) are widely used in edge vision applications such as surveillance, medical imaging, automatic driver assistance system, satellite imaging, military and industry applications. Among DNNs, Convolutional Neural Networks (CNNs) are the most popular for vision tasks [17]. However, CNNs

F. Palumbo et al. (Eds.): ARC 2023, LNCS 14251, pp. 290–303, 2023.
https://doi.org/10.1007/978-3-031-42921-7_20

are computationally intensive, with millions of learnable parameters necessary for training and inference. It is challenging to deploy large CNN models on mobile/edge devices that have restricted hardware resources and limited power budgets. Edge vision applications are highly intensive and energy-consuming since CNN models require costly off-chip DRAM access due to on-chip memory limitations. Studies indicate that a 32-bit DRAM access consumes 640 pJ of energy, which is 128 times greater than the energy required for on-chip memory access [7]. Such applications deployed on edge/mobile devices with limited resources lack performance and reliability guarantees [14].To satisfy the real-time demands and enhance energy efficiency on edge/mobile devices, compressing DNN models has become an unavoidable necessity [2].

In this paper, we proposed an energy efficient compaction technique for deep neural networks that can be applied to edge vision applications with limited resources. The overview of the proposed work is shown in Fig. 1. It involves two stages. To induce sparsity in the layers of DNN, initially we employed various pruning techniques provided by the PyTorch library namely random, L1, global random, global L1 unstructured pruning [12]. We have analyzed the classification accuracy and distribution of consecutive zero weights on various pruned models at different sparsity. Global L1 and L1 pruned models have better accuracy compared to other pruning techniques. It has chosen for the next stage compaction. The first major contribution of this work is a novel compaction technique called fixed partition compaction. This technique partitions the weights in a pruned DNN layer by two and compacts in such a way that it stores only one encoding value for consecutive two weights. The encoding overhead is fixed irrespective of sparsity. The existing compression techniques have encoding values for all non-zero weights and are sparsity dependent. As the sparsity decreases, the encoding overhead increases for such techniques, resulting in a higher computational burden and increased memory traffic. Consequently, this diminishes the potential benefits that can be obtained from the compression scheme. The second major contribution is that we have implemented different configurations of compact convolution and fully connected layers on Virtex-7 FPGA and assessed the performance and energy efficiency. A comparative analysis of performance improvement and energy consumption reduction was conducted to evaluate the effectiveness of the proposed compact layers in contrast to non-compact convolution and fully connected layers. For this purpose, Scalar Matrix Multiplication (SMM) convolution [10], direct convolution and General Matrix Multiplication (GEMM) were implemented on FPGA. The implemented design of compact convolution could achieve an average performance improvement of 32.51% and 29.43% against SMM and direct convolution respectively. It acquired an average of 34.14% and 29.58% energy efficiency higher than the state-of-the-art. Similarly, compact fully connected layers attained an average performance improvement of 26.61% and energy consumption reduction of 30.85% over layers without compaction.

The rest of the paper is structured as follows: Sect. 2 provides an overview of related works on different DNN model compression techniques. Section 3 describes the proposed approach in detail and presents the implementation

Fig. 1. Overview of the proposed approach.

methodology. In Sect. 4, the experimental results are discussed. Finally, Sect. 5 concludes the paper, summarizing the findings and contributions.

2   Related Works

DNN models often require expensive off-chip DRAM accesses because they are too large to fit in on-chip memory. Due to on-chip constraints, reducing the size of DNN models has become a widespread practice. To reduce the memory storage requirements, memory transactions, and computations of DNN models, several techniques have been developed for model compression. Various techniques such as pruning, sparsity encoding, low-rank factorization, quantization, and knowledge distillation have been developed to achieve this goal. Pruning eliminates redundant or unimportant weights/ parameters from the model, which results in the introduction of sparsity in the network [9]. This sparsity can then be compressed using various encoding techniques. In contrast, quantization aims to decrease the number of bits necessary to represent the weights and activations in DNN. By using a smaller number of bits, quantization reduces the memory storage and computational requirements of the model [3]. Knowledge distillation is a technique in which knowledge acquired by a large complex network called the teacher model, trained on a large dataset with strong generalization capabilities is imparted to a smaller network known as the student model [16]. It allows the student model to leverage the expertise of the teacher model. Low rank factorization involves decomposing tensors or matrices to estimate informative parameters. By representing the original parameters in a lower-dimensional space, low rank factorization reduces the complexity of the model, leading to improved computational efficiency and enhanced generalization capabilities [5].

The proposed work primarily emphasizes on pruning and sparsity encoding techniques. Pruning selectively removes insignificant parameters or weights within the network, leading to a more concise and streamlined model. It yields a sparse model as outcome where it contains zero and non-zero weights. Sparse DNN models can be represented in different encoding formats, including Coordinate (COO) [1], Run Length Encoding (RLC) [11], Compressed Sparse Row (CSR) [6], Compressed Sparse Column (CSC) [18], and Compressed Sparse Fibre (CSF) [15]. These encoding techniques store the indices or encoding values of all non-zero weights, along with the elements themselves. Many accelerators for sparse DNNs utilize these encoding techniques to enhance throughput and energy efficiency. The EIE (Efficient Inference Engine) accelerator utilized a variation of the CSC format that specifically supports matrix multiplication operations [8]. By leveraging the sparse nature of DNNs and the CSC encoding, EIE achieved improved throughput and energy efficiency in processing sparse DNNs. Chen et al. proposed a flexible accelerator called Eyeriss-v2, which also adopted the CSC encoding format to process the sparse data [4]. It extended the capabilities of the CSC format to support both convolution and matrix multiplication operations. This enhancement enabled the accelerator to efficiently handle both types of operations in sparse DNNs, further improving performance and energy efficiency. The work presented in [19], introduces Cambricon-X as a novel accelerator that leverages the Coordinate (COO) encoding format. This encoding format is utilized to represent sparse DNNs by storing the coordinates corresponding to non-zero weights, enabling efficient handling of sparse matrices within the accelerator. However, the existing encoding techniques are reliant on the amount of sparsity in the model. It requires additional index/encoding information for less sparse models, increasing storage overhead and limiting the accommodation of data into on-chip memory. Merely removing zero weights are not enough to obtain a compressed DNN model, as the indices or encoding values of every non-zero weight also need to be retained. Managing sparse representation with these encoding techniques during convolution and matrix multiplication operations can add significant complexity during the inference phase.

However, while selective pruning can aid in generalizing the models, compressing and decompressing them can result in additional software and hardware overhead. It will negatively impact the overall performance of the DNNs. To address this challenge, this paper proposes a novel compaction technique to facilitate the energy-efficient mapping of DNNs onto edge devices. Compact models are an optimal choice for resource-constrained edge environments due to their efficient memory utilization, faster processing time, reduced data transfer requirements, and improved energy conservation. In comparison to dense models, compact models provide superior performance in these aspects, making them well-suited for edge devices with limited resources. We compared the performance improvement and energy consumption reduction achieved by compact layers (convolution and fully connected layers) to that of non-compact dense layers. Besides evaluating compact convolution against direct convolution, we also conducted a comparison to SMM convolution. SMM convolution utilizes scalar matrix multiplication instead of matrix-matrix multiplication, and minimizes overhead to nearly one copy of the output tensor while reusing the same memory buffer.

3   Proposed Approach

In this section, we propose a novel compaction technique called fixed partition compaction which exploits the occurrences of consecutive zero weights. It occurs in two stages: pruning and compaction. In the pruning stage, various DNN models were subject to experiments involving four distinct unstructured weight pruning techniques in order to analyze the sparsity distribution across multiple levels. Four weight pruning techniques were employed, namely random unstructured, L1 unstructured, global random unstructured, and global L1 unstructured pruning. We used PyTorch library to implement the pruning techniques. The random

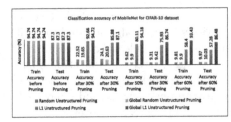

Fig. 2. Experimental observations of different pruning techniques on DNN models.

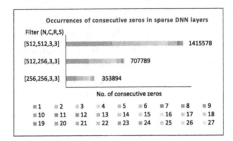

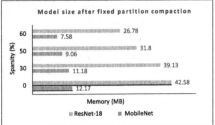

Fig. 3. Occurrences of consecutive zeros in 60% L1 pruned convolutional filters. Model size after fixed partition compaction on pruned models at various levels of sparsity (sparsity = 0%, original model without compaction).

unstructured method randomly eliminates a certain number of units from each layer, while the L1 Unstructured technique prunes weights with the lowest L1 norm. Global random/L1 unstructured pruning, on the other hand, removes weights globally from all layers by a specific amount of units using either random unstructured or L1 unstructured pruning. Global L1 pruning results in minimal accuracy degradation, while L1 pruning results in significant accuracy loss that requires fine-tuning. In contrast, random and global random pruning lead to substantial accuracy degradation as shown in Fig. 2. Consequently, L1 and global L1 pruned models are chosen for the next stage of compaction.

The observation resulting from the pruning experiments led us to investigate the potential utilization of consecutive zero and non-zero weights, inspiring us to introduce a compaction method named fixed partition compaction. This technique comprises three primary steps:

- Convert each filter of DNN layer into 1D vector and partition it with size 2.
- Encode partitions with at least one non-zero as **1** and partitions with all zeros as **0**.
- Eliminate the partitions with all zeros.

A partition size of 2 was chosen for fixed partition as it corresponds to the highest frequency of consecutive pairs of zeros found within each layer as depicted in Fig. 3. The size of MobileNet for CIFAR-10 dataset has been reduced from 12.17 MB to 7.58 MB, and ResNet-18 has been decreased from 42.58 MB to

---

Algorithm 1: Fixed Partition Compaction

Input: *wt* - weight tensor
Output: *comp_wt* - array of compact weights
  enc - array of encoding values of all filters
Data: *split_size* - no. of weights in a filter
Data: *no_of_filters* - no. of filters in a DNN layer

1 Convert *wt* into vector
2 *weights_per_filter* ← split *wt* into chunks of *split_size*
3 **for** $i \leftarrow 0$ **to** *no_of_filters* **do**
4   Initialize a list *enc_per_filter*
5   *partition* ← partition *weights_per_filter[i]* by 2
6   **for** $j \leftarrow 0$ **to** *len(partition)* **do**
7   **if** *len(partition[j])==2* **then**
8   **if** *count_non_zeros(partition[j])==0* **then**
9   *enc_per_filter* ← 0
10   **else**
11   *enc_per_filter* ← 1
12   *comp_wt* ← *partition[j][0], partition[j][1]*
13   **else**
14   **if** *count_non_zeros(partition[j])==0* **then**
15   *enc_per_filter* ← 0
16   **else**
17   *enc_per_filter* ← 1
18   *comp_wt* ← *partition[j][0]*
19   *enc* ← *enc_per_filter*

26.78 MB at sparsity 60%, which can be seen in Fig. 3. The procedure of fixed partition compaction of weights in convolution layer is presented in Algorithm 1. Given a 4D sparse weight tensor *wt* with dimensions $NCRS$ where N represents the number of filters, C denotes the input channels, R and S are the filter dimensions. The initial step involves converting *wt* into 1D vector and segregate the weights in each filter. Each filter is split into partitions of two weights and check whether each partition contains all zeros. If a partition has all zeros, it is denoted as 0. Otherwise, 1. The number of weights in each filter can be either even or odd. If it is odd, the final partition contains only one element, then the encoding is applied to the last single weight. Finally, elements in the non-zero partitions are included in the *compt_wt* array by excluding the partitions with all zeros. The same algorithm can be applied to compact fully connected layer as well. The number of bits required to encode the weights within a convolution and fully connected layer for even and odd filters can be represented as Eqn. 1 and Eqn. 2.

Table 1. Encoding overhead of different sparse representations

Technique	Encoding Overhead	Required Sparsity
COO	3*(R*S*C*N)*(1-SP)	SP≥0.667
CSR	(R*S*C*N)*(1-SP)+N*C	SP≥0.5(1/R*S)+1)
CSC	(R*S*C*N)*(1-SP)+R*S	SP≥0.5(1/C*N)+1)
Fixed Partition, filter =odd	R*S*C+1/2) * N	SP>0
Fixed Partition, filter =even	(R*S*C/2) * N	SP>0

Filter[N,C,R,S] – [2,3,3,3]

1	2	0		5	1	0		1	0	0		1	0	0		2	1	0		1	0	1
0	4	3		0	0	2		0	1	1		1	2	3		0	0	0		2	0	0
0	0	4		1	0	1		0	1	0		0	0	1		0	0	1		0	4	0

Filter[N,CRS] – [2,27]

1	2	0	0	4	3	0	0	4	5	1	0	0	0	2	1	0	1	1	0	0	0	1	1	0	1	0
1	0	0	1	2	3	0	0	1	2	1	0	0	0	0	0	0	1	1	0	1	2	0	0	0	4	0

Fixed Partition Compaction

Compact weights	1 2 4 3 4 5 1 0 2 1 0 1 1 0 1 1 0 1 1 0 0 1 2 3 1 2 1 0 0 1 1 0 1 2 0 4
Encoding values (1-bit)	1 0 1 0 1 1 0 1 1 1 0 1 1 0 1 1 1 0 1 1 0 0 1 1 1 0 1 0

Compressed Sparse Row (CSR)

Non-zero weights	1 2 4 3 4 5 1 2 1 1 1 1 1 1 1 2 3 1 2 1 1 1 2 4
Column indices	0 1 4 5 8 9 10 14 15 17 18 22 23 25 0 3 4 5 8 9 10 17 18 20 21 25
Row pointer	0 14 26

Compressed Sparse Column (CSC)

Non-zero weights	1 1 2 1 4 2 3 3 4 1 5 2 1 1 2 1 1 1 1 1 2 1 1 4
Row indices	0 1 0 1 0 1 0 1 0 1 0 1 0 1 0 0 0 1 0 1 1 1 0 0 0 1
Column pointer	0 2 3 3 4 6 8 8 8 10 12 14 14 14 14 15 16 16 18 20 20 21 22 23 24 24 26 26

Coordinate (COO)

Non-zero weights	1 2 4 3 4 5 1 2 1 1 1 1 1 1 1 2 3 1 2 1 1 1 1 2 4
Row indices	0 0 0 0 0 0 0 0 0 0 0 0 0 0 1 1 1 1 1 1 1 1 1 1 1
Column indices	0 1 4 5 8 9 10 14 15 17 18 22 23 25 0 3 4 5 8 9 10 17 18 20 21 25

Fig. 4. Different compression formats for DNN filters

$$Encoding\ overhead_{conv} = \begin{cases} (R * S * C/2) * N, \ filter = even \\ [(R * S * C + 1)/2] * N, \ filter = odd \end{cases} \quad (1)$$

$$Encoding\ overhead_{fc} = \begin{cases} (C/2) * N, \ filter = even \\ [(C + 1)/2] * N, \ filter = odd \end{cases} \quad (2)$$

Fixed partition compaction provides independent encoding regardless of the level of sparsity. Conversely, the state-of-the-art techniques like CSR, CSC, COO are sparsity-dependent encoding techniques. CSR compression processes each row of the matrix as a sparse vector; storing non-zero values with their corresponding column indices and uses a pointer to track the starting index of non-zero values in each row, indicating the total non-zero elements in that row. In contrast, CSC compression is the opposite of CSR as it compresses

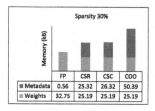 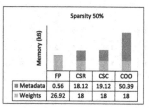 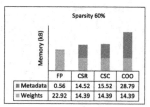

Fig. 5. Memory footprint of different compression techniques at various sparsity.

the matrix column-wise, storing non-zero values with their corresponding row indices, and the column pointer indicates the total number of non-zero elements in each column. COO format stores the absolute positions of non-zero values within the matrix. An example of proposed compaction and different compression techniques for 4D sparse tensor are illustrated in Fig. 4. The encoding overhead and the minimum sparsity (SP) required for different techniques are given in Table 1 [13]. The number of encoding values increases as the sparsity level decreases. Figure 5 shows the memory footprint of filter [32,32,3,3] with different compression formats at various sparsity. Fixed partition (FP) has constant metadata across various levels of sparsity. If the model is not highly sparse, the overall size of the compressed model is larger than the dense model for other existing compression techniques.

4 Experiments and Results

4.1 Experimental Setup

To assess the efficacy of our approach, we conducted a series of experiments with compact and non-compact DNN layers on Virtex-7 FPGA VC707 platform. Virtex 7 consists of soft 32bit RISC MicroBlaze with 1GB DDR3 SODIM memory up to 800 MHz / 1600 Mbps. It is equipped to manage both hardware acceleration tasks and general-purpose processing tasks through the MicroBlaze CPU. Vivado design suite (Vivado 2018.2) was used to implement compact and non-compact layers on FPGA. Each layer is implemented as a custom hardware IP, then integrated with the MicroBlaze soft processor and DDR3 memory through a memory-mapped interface. The layers have been implemented to operate at a frequency of 50 MHz. The purpose of these experiments was to evaluate the performance and energy consumption of 60% L1 pruned compact layers in comparison to the non-compact layers (dense layers). Compact convolution layers were compared with SMM and direct convolution layers. SMM convolution employs scalar matrix multiplication. It slides the filter over the input and multiplying the corresponding sub-matrices of the input with the kernel weights. The resulting products are then accumulated to generate the final convolution output. Direct convolution employs the MAC (Multiply-Accumulate) operation, which involves sliding a filter over the input data, performing element-wise multiplications between the filter and input elements, and then accumulating the products

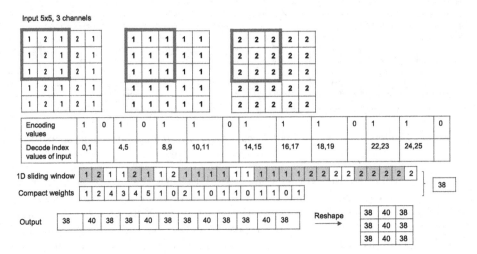

Fig. 6. Compact convolution.

to generate an output value at each location. Table 2 lists out the convolution configurations used for the experiments where I_h and I_w are the input dimensions. These configurations are taken from popular DNN models. The algorithm of hardware implementation of compact convolution is given in Algorithm 2. The first step involves capturing each sliding window of the input and then convert it into 1D vector. Then decode the matching indices of input that corresponds to the compact weight from the indices of the encoding values using energy-efficient shift and logical operators to perform the mac operation. It eliminates the ineffectual computations by selecting the inputs matching with the indices of weights in the array *comp_wt*. An example of compact convolution is also shown in Fig. 6. Similarly, compact fully connected layers were compared with non-compact layers. The hardware implementation of compact fully connected layers is shown in Algorithm 3. In addition to evaluating the performance of compact layers on FPGA, we also measured the performance on the CPU. 11th Gen Intel Core i7-1165G7 processor running at a base clock speed of 2.80GHz with 15.6GiB of RAM was the CPU configuration considered for the experiments.

4.2   Results and Discussion

This section presents performance improvement and energy consumption reduction of compact layers over non-compact layers on Virtex-7. Furthermore, we conducted a comparison of the results on the CPU platform. The layer's performance improvement on FPGA was evaluated based on the measured latency on Virtex-7. The energy consumption was determined by multiplying the power with the measured latency. Power can be measured in Vivado using the power analyzer tool. The power analyzer tool provides an estimation of the power consumption for a given design implemented on a specific FPGA device. pyRAPL

Algorithm 2: Compact Convolution

Input: *comp_wt* - compact weights
       enc - encoding values
       inp - input activation
Output: *out* - output activation

Data: H,W - height and width of output feature map
       enc_len - no. of encoding bits in a filter
       C - no of input channels
       N - no. of output channels
       R, S - filter dimensions
       inp_batch - input batch
       st - stride

1 Initialize SW, $m=0$, $m1=0$, $sum=0.0$, $sum1=0.0$, $sum2=0.0$
2 **for** $k \leftarrow 0$ **to** *inp_batch* **do**
3   **for** $i \leftarrow 0$ **to** H **do**
4   **for** $j \leftarrow 0$ **to** W **do**
5   **for** $l \leftarrow 0$ **to** C **do**
6   **for** $i1 \leftarrow 0$ **to** R **do**
7   **for** $j1 \leftarrow 0$ **to** S **do**
8                    $SW[m] = inp[k][l][i*st+i1][j*st+j1]$
9                    $m = m+1$

10           $m=0$, $m1=0$
11   **for** $p \leftarrow 0$ **to** N **do**
             // for odd filter, iterate upto q=enc_len -1
12   **for** $q \leftarrow 0$ **to** *enc_len* **do**
13                 $sum1 = enc[p][q]==1$? $SW[q<<1] * comp\_wt[m1]$: 0
14                 $sum2 = enc[p][q]==1$? $SW[q<<1|1] * comp\_wt[m1+1]$: 0
15                 $sum = enc[p][q]==1$? $sum + sum1 + sum2$: sum
16                 $m1 = enc[p][q]==1$? $m1+2$: $m1$

             /* for odd filter, include the following statements
                q = enc_len -1
                sum1 = enc[p][q]==1 ? SW[q<<1] *comp_wt[m1]: 0
                sum = enc[p][q]==1 ? sum + sum1: sum
                m1 = enc[p,q]==1 ? m1+1: m1   */
17              $out[k][p][i][j] = sum$
18              $sum = 0.0$

---

software toolkit was used to measure the CPU's energy consumption during the execution of compact and non-compact layers.

Figure 7 depicts the performance improvement and energy consumption reduction of compact convolution layers over SMM and direct convolution layers on Virtex-7 FPGA and Intel i7 CPU. Results show that the compact convolution attains an average performance improvement of 32.51% (with a minimum of

---

Algorithm 3: Compact Fully Connected Layer

Input: $comp\_wt$ - compact weights
      enc - encoding values
      inp - input activation
Output: out - output activation
Data: C - no of input channels
      enc_len - no. of encoding bits in a output channel
      N - no. of output channels

1 Initialize $m = 0$, $sum = 0.0$, $sum1 = 0.0$, $sum2 = 0.0$
    `// If C is odd, iterate upto j=enc_len -1`
2 **for** $i \leftarrow 0$ **to** C **do**
3   **for** $j \leftarrow 0$ **to** enc_len **do**
4         $sum1 = enc[i][j]{==}1 \,?\, inp[j{<}{<}1] * comp\_wt[m]: 0$
5         $sum2 = enc[i][j]{==}1 \,?\, inp[j{<}{<}1|1] * comp\_wt[m{+}1]: 0$
6         $sum = enc[i][j]{==}1 \,?\, sum + sum1 + sum2: sum$
7         $m = enc[i][j]{==}1 \,?\, m{+}2: m$

        `/* If C is odd, include the following statements`
        `j = enc_len -1`
        `sum1 = enc[i][j]==1 ? inp[j<<1] *comp_wt[m]: 0`
        `sum = enc[i][j]==1 ? sum + sum1: sum`
        `m = enc[i][j]==1 ? m+1: m`   `*/`
8     $out[i] = sum$
9     $sum = 0.0$

28.02% and a maximum of 34.24%) and 29.43% (with a minimum of 25.68% and a maximum of 32.12%) compared to the SMM and direct convolution on Virtex-7. It is observed that irrespective of the convolution configurations, the performance improvement is almost similar, thanks to the proposed compaction algorithm. The proposed approach achieves an average energy consumption reduction of 34.14% and 29.58% with a maximum of 37.61% and 32.61% as well as a minimum of 31.53% and 24.03% over SMM and direct convolution on Virtex-7.

The compact convolution demonstrates an average performance improvement of 65.72% compared to SMM convolution on CPU with a minimum improvement of 50.46% and a maximum improvement of 79.13%. In comparison to the direct convolution, compact layers exhibited a substantial average performance improvement of 54.78% with a range of improvement spanning from 45.47% as the minimum to 68% maximum. The proposed convolution yields an average reduction in energy consumption of 66.41% and 59.81% when compared to SMM and direct convolution. Moreover, it achieved a maximum reduction of 79.74% and 69.48% as well as minimum of 54.39% and 54.96%. CPU results are also depicted in Fig. 7.

The performance improvement and energy consumption reduction of fully connected layers are shown in Fig. 8. The compact fully connected layer has an average performance improvement of 26.61% with a maximum of 31.62% while a minimum of 12.14% and energy consumption reduction of 30.85% with

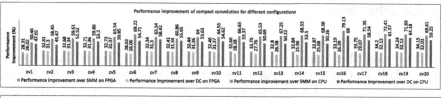

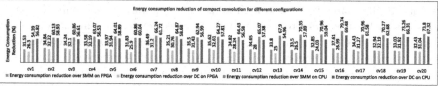

Fig. 7. Performance improvement and energy consumption reduction of compact convolution for different configurations.

a maximum of 40.10% and minimum of 16.21% over layers without compaction on Virtex-7 FPGA. Likewise, it achieved an average performance improvement of 12.39% (with minimum of 5.35% and maximum of 20.61%) and an average energy consumption reduction of 30.53% (with minimum of 2.58% and maximum of 96.97%) over non-compact layers on CPU.

Table 2. Different convolution configurations.

Name	Input (I_hxI_wxC)	Kernel (RxSxN)	stride	padding	Name	Input (I_hxI_wxC)	Kernel (RxSxN)	stride	padding
cv1	$32 \times 32 \times 1$	$3 \times 3 \times 32$	1	0	cv11	$64 \times 64 \times 32$	$5 \times 5 \times 32$	1	0
cv2	$32 \times 32 \times 16$	$3 \times 3 \times 32$	1	0	cv12	$64 \times 64 \times 32$	$7 \times 7 \times 32$	1	0
cv3	$32 \times 32 \times 32$	$3 \times 3 \times 32$	1	0	cv13	$64 \times 64 \times 32$	$9 \times 9 \times 32$	1	0
cv4	$32 \times 32 \times 64$	$3 \times 3 \times 32$	1	0	cv14	$64 \times 64 \times 32$	$11 \times 11 \times 32$	1	0
cv5	$32 \times 32 \times 128$	$3 \times 3 \times 32$	1	0	cv15	$64 \times 64 \times 32$	$13 \times 13 \times 32$	1	0
cv6	$64 \times 64 \times 1$	$3 \times 3 \times 32$	1	0	cv16	$227 \times 227 \times 3$	$11 \times 11 \times 96$	4	0
cv7	$64 \times 64 \times 16$	$3 \times 3 \times 32$	1	0	cv17	$27 \times 27 \times 96$	$5 \times 5 \times 256$	1	2
cv8	$64 \times 64 \times 32$	$3 \times 3 \times 32$	1	0	cv18	$13 \times 13 \times 256$	$3 \times 3 \times 384$	1	1
cv9	$64 \times 64 \times 64$	$3 \times 3 \times 32$	1	0	cv19	$13 \times 13 \times 384$	$3 \times 3 \times 384$	1	1
cv10	$64 \times 64 \times 128$	$3 \times 3 \times 32$	1	0	cv20	$13 \times 13 \times 384$	$3 \times 3 \times 256$	1	1

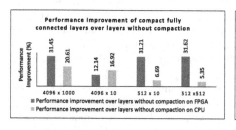

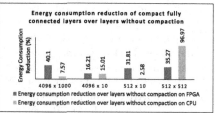

Fig. 8. Performance improvement and energy consumption reduction of fully connected layers over layers without compaction.

5   Conclusion

In this paper, we presented a novel compaction technique for deep neural networks to boost the performance and energy efficiency in resource limited edge nodes. The fixed partition compaction partitions the pruned model and compact in such a manner that it stores only 1-bit one encoding value for consecutive two weights. It eliminates partitions with all zero weights and retain only the partitions with atleast a non-zero weight. This reduces the need for memory storage, transactions as well as computations. We have implemented compact convolution and fully connected layers on Virtex-7 FPGA. The results indicates that compact convolution layers exhibits superior performance and energy efficiency compared to the state-of-the-art SMM and direct convolution. Compact convolution has an average performance improvement of 32.51% and 29.43% in addition to an energy efficiency of 34.14% and 29.58% over SMM and direct convolution. The compact fully connected layer achieved an average performance improvement and energy efficiency of 26.61% and 30.85% over layers without compaction.

Declarations. This work was funded by the MulticoreWare Inc, and IPTIF, IIT Palakkad project No. IPTIF/TD/IP/003.

References

1. Albericio, J., Judd, P., Hetherington, T., Aamodt, T., Jerger, N.E., Moshovos, A.: Cnvlutin: ineffectual-neuron-free deep neural network computing. ACM SIGARCH Comput. Archit. News **44**(3), 1–13 (2016)
2. Capra, M., Bussolino, B., Marchisio, A., Masera, G., Martina, M., Shafique, M.: Hardware and software optimizations for accelerating deep neural networks: survey of current trends, challenges, and the road ahead. IEEE Access **8**, 225134–225180 (2020)
3. Chang, S.E., et al.: Mix and match: a novel fpga-centric deep neural network quantization framework. In: 2021 IEEE International Symposium on High-Performance Computer Architecture (HPCA). pp. 208–220. IEEE (2021)
4. Chen, Y.H., Yang, T.J., Emer, J., Sze, V.: Eyeriss v2: a flexible accelerator for emerging deep neural networks on mobile devices. IEEE J. Emerg. Selected Topics Circuits and Syst. **9**(2), 292–308 (2019)
5. Cheng, Y., Wang, D., Zhou, P., Zhang, T.: A survey of model compression and acceleration for deep neural networks. arXiv preprint arXiv:1710.09282 (2017)
6. Chou, S., Kjolstad, F., Amarasinghe, S.: Format abstraction for sparse tensor algebra compilers. Proc. ACM on Prog. Lang. **2**(OOPSLA), 1–30 (2018)
7. Han, S., et al.: Deep compression and EIE: Efficient inference engine on compressed deep neural network. In: Hot Chips Symposium. pp. 1–6 (2016)
8. Han, S., et al.: Eie: efficient inference engine on compressed deep neural network. ACM SIGARCH Comput. Archit. News **44**(3), 243–254 (2016)
9. Hoefler, T., Alistarh, D., Ben-Nun, T., Dryden, N., Peste, A.: Sparsity in deep learning: pruning and growth for efficient inference and training in neural networks. J. Mach. Learn. Res. **22**(1), 10882–11005 (2021)

10. Ofir, A., Ben-Artzi, G.: Smm-conv: Scalar matrix multiplication with zero packing for accelerated convolution. In: Proceedings of the IEEE/CVF Conference on Computer Vision and Pattern Recognition. pp. 3067–3075 (2022)
11. Parashar, A., et al.: Scnn: an accelerator for compressed-sparse convolutional neural networks. ACM SIGARCH Comput. Archit. News **45**(2), 27–40 (2017)
12. PyTorch: Pruning tutorial. https://pytorch.org/tutorials/intermediate/pruning_tutorial.html, Accessed on 04 July 2023
13. Qasaimeh, M., Zambreno, J., Jones, P.H.: An efficient hardware architecture for sparse convolution using linear feedback shift registers. In: 2021 IEEE 32nd International Conference on Application-specific Systems, Architectures and Processors (ASAP). pp. 250–257. IEEE (2021)
14. Shafique, M., Marchisio, A., Putra, R.V.W., Hanif, M.A.: Towards energy-efficient and secure edge AI: A cross-layer framework ICCAD special session paper. In: 2021 IEEE/ACM International Conference On Computer Aided Design (ICCAD). pp. 1–9. IEEE (2021)
15. Smith, S., Karypis, G.: Tensor-matrix products with a compressed sparse tensor. In: Proceedings of the 5th Workshop on Irregular Applications: Architectures and Algorithms. pp. 1–7 (2015)
16. Stewart, R., Nowlan, A., Bacchus, P., Ducasse, Q., Komendantskaya, E.: Optimising hardware accelerated neural networks with quantisation and a knowledge distillation evolutionary algorithm. Electronics **10**(4), 396 (2021)
17. Sze, V., Chen, Y.H., Yang, T.J., Emer, J.S.: Efficient processing of deep neural networks: A tutorial and survey. Proceedings of the IEEE **105**(12), 2295–2329 (2017)
18. Yuan, Z., et al.: Sticker: A 0.41-62.1 tops/w 8bit neural network processor with multi-sparsity compatible convolution arrays and online tuning acceleration for fully connected layers. In: 2018 IEEE symposium on VLSI circuits. pp. 33–34. IEEE (2018)
19. Zhang, S., et al.: Cambricon-x: An accelerator for sparse neural networks. In: 2016 49th Annual IEEE/ACM International Symposium on Microarchitecture (MICRO). pp. 1–12. IEEE (2016)

Special Session: Near and In-Memory Computing

TAPRE-HBM: Trace-Based Processor Rapid Emulation Using HBM on FPGAs

Johannes Knödtel[1,2]([✉]) [ID], Hector Gerardo Muñoz Hernandez[1] [ID],
Alexander Lehnert[1,2] [ID], Gia Bao Thieu[3] [ID], Sven Gesper[3] [ID],
Guillermo Payá-Vayá[3] [ID], and Marc Reichenbach[2] [ID]

[1] Chair of Computer Engineering, Brandenburg University of Technology
Cottbus-Senftenberg, Cottbus, Germany
hector.munozhernandez@b-tu.de
[2] Institute of Applied Microelectronics and Computer Engineering,
University of Rostock, Rostock, Germany
{johannes.knoedtel,alexander.lehnert,marc.reichenbach}@uni-rostock.de
[3] Chair for Chip Design for Embedded Computing,
Technische Universität Braunschweig, Braunschweig, Germany
{g.thieu,s.gesper,g.paya-vaya}@tu-braunschweig.de

Abstract. The use of High Bandwidth Memory (HBM) is one way to solve the bottleneck of memory bandwidth limitation. Furthermore, the integration of HBM memories in Field Programmable Gate Arrays (FPGA) now also makes it possible to use this memory technology in a wide range of applications and even in embedded systems. Nevertheless, the use of HBM poses major challenges for architecture development. In addition to highly parallel access, high latencies must be hidden. Furthermore, the partitioning of the data and the bus structure play a decisive role. Finally, memory controller implementations are mostly vendor specific making it difficult to predict the exact performance of the memory subsystem. In this paper, we present TAPRE-HBM, an FPGA-based rapid prototyping platform for analyzing computer architectures with HBM memory backends. The goal of this work is to evaluate and assess the impact of particular memory access patterns. As these patterns are an emerging property of the architecture and application, such traces can be created by simulating the target computer architectures which should use the HBM memory subsystem without the need for a specific implementation or integration. Any incurred latency will be revealed by this method, even if only a system-level model exists. Using the FPGA-based rapid prototyping platform, performance predictions can be made and thus it can be determined whether the selected target architecture or software running on the target architecture is suitable for use with HBM memories. The proposed platform is analyzed using a vector processor as an example and present various optimizations to increase the memory bandwidth. Compared to other works, a high number of memory transactions can be simulated on real hardware, with a high memory interface frequency and arbitrary delays between transactions.

F. Palumbo et al. (Eds.): ARC 2023, LNCS 14251, pp. 307–321, 2023.
https://doi.org/10.1007/978-3-031-42921-7_21

1   Introduction

The constant increase in processor performance, due to higher frequencies and a steady increase in core count, has made it clear that memory technologies are struggling to keep up [22]. As a large portion of current applications is moving towards big data and deep learning, the memory bottleneck becomes even more evident, as more data is needed to be processed even faster every time. This means that these applications are limited by the available memory bandwidth. Data is processed faster than it is fetched from memory [13].

One of the most common solutions to the bandwidth limitation is the utilization of 3D-stacked memory dies, which ultimately culminated in the family of HBM technologies [12]. The structure of HBM is composed of a stack of Dynamic Random Access Memory (DRAM) dies interconnected by Through Silicon Vias (TSVs) with a base logic die at the bottom [12]. A key difference between traditional DRAM and HBM is that the latter usually operates at a lower clock frequency, but it compensates this by using wider buses and more channels [5]. This highly parallel architecture brings some complex memory addressing. Xilinx Field Programmable Gate Arrays (FPGAs) tackle this problem with memory controllers that have internal switches that route memory requests to different channels. An example is Xilinx's HBM subsystem [2], which unfortunately is a proprietary closed-source implementation, making its internal functionality unclear for users.

Since the HBM standard was defined in 2013 by the Joint Electron Device Engineering Council (JEDEC) [11], HBM2 was introduced, upgrading the density per slice from 2 GB to 8 GB, and the bandwidth per chip from 128 GB/s to 256 GB/s [12]. HBM3 promises to double the specifications of HBM2, but is not as widespread yet [19].

The second generation of HBM technology, HBM2, has been incorporated to state-of-the-art (SoA) FPGAs, allowing to achieve bandwidths of up to 460 GB/s for a dual-stack memory in highly reconfigurable architectures [1]. This bundle of technologies combines HBMs high bandwidth, with FPGAs which are known for their flexibility and inherent configurability, making a strong case for exciting and novel ways to bridge the memory gap discussed.

Along with HBM-equipped Systems-on-a-Chip (SoCs), there are several applications ported and optimized for HBM accesses, including an implementation for sparse deep neural networks (DNNs) [9] and convolutional neural networks (CNNs) [17]. Memory-bound applications have the largest potential to benefit from HBM thanks to the provided bandwidth. Although there exist studies of improvement potential from ported applications [20] and general overview works [8], the hurdle of optimizing applications for HBM are still high.

The high number of memory channels and the increase in latency in HBM poses a challenge in system design. This means that memory accesses must utilize all channels to maximize bandwidth, and latencies must be hidden via clever hardware design.

Additionally, HBM channels only take care about a dedicated part of the available memory. In many cases, switches are used to allow access from multiple ports. Their usage increases latency even further and creates hard to predict timing behavior [5]. This effect is analogous to the concept of non-uniform memory access. Unfortunately, the tools available to developers are currently not sufficient to properly predict timing behavior without concrete implementation and integration.

All points stated above, i.e. the application and mapping dependency of making use of the large potential HBM performance, create the need for a methodology to rapidly estimate the performance of hardware designs. Current methodologies for predicting memory performance, unfortunately, do not sufficiently address all needs in modern hardware design. Our work provides means of analyzing reduction in memory-bounded delays and thus performance improvements by emulating arbitrary processors trace-based on an HBM-equipped FPGA.

The Near-Memory Computing idea aims to overcome the memory bottleneck by bringing processing and memory close together [8]. FPGAs play an important role in this context, as they combine both flexibility and energy efficient hardware acceleration [8]. The realization of the performance potential, which novel memory technologies such as HBM provide, depends on a non-trivial memory mapping effort [5]. These observations underline the need for a simple way to rapidly evaluate memory access strategies, mappings and patterns. The proposed methodology can fulfill these needs by providing a way to feed arbitrary traces into the HBM interface.

The main contributions of the current work can be summarized as follows:

– Addressing the current state-of-the-art of tools used for HBM simulation and emulation
– Introducing TAPRE-HBM: a TrAce-based Processor Rapid Emulation using HBM on FPGAs
– Presenting a vertical vector processor architecture [21] utilized in this work as a use-case to evaluate the memory traces employed to proof the efficiency of TAPRE-HBM
– Evaluation and discussion of the results using the Alveo U55C board [1] from AMD Xilinx, which justifies the usage of HBM

The rest of the paper is organized as follows: The related work is presented in Sect. 2. Section 3 introduces the architecture of TAPRE-HBM and the methodology it follows to obtain the latency determination based on memory traces. Section 4 is divided into few subsections. First, we present the vertical vector processor architecture that was selected as a use case for TAPRE-HBM. Later, the results of TAPRE-HBM running on an Xilinx Alveo U55C board [1] are evaluated and discussed. Finally, Sect. 6 concludes the work.

2   Related Work

Optimal memory mapping strategies for HBM are not well established yet, making it difficult for hardware designers to decide on one strategy. Simulation

Table 1. Comparison of Memory Simulators

Framework		HBM	Metrics	
Method	Type		Speed	Max. Trace Length
GEM5 [3]	Software	No	300 kHz [23]	not applicable
ramulator [14]	Software	Yes	165 kHz [14]	not applicable
DRAMsim3 [16]	Software	Yes	181 kHz [16]	not applicable
LIME [10]	Hardware	Low	100 MHz [23]	not specified
SoftMC [4]	Hardware	No	100 MHz [23]	8192
MEG [23]	Hardware	Yes	100 MHz [23]	not specified
TAPRE-HBM	Hardware	Yes	250 MHz	65536

approaches help to bridge this knowledge gap, as they enable rapid prototyping of different memory access strategies for various combinations of hardware designs and algorithms and give accurate performance estimations. A fair comparison to classical DRAM and direct memory access (DMA) engines requires cycle-accurate simulations. There are two trace-based cycle-accurate approaches explored in several frameworks.

Frameworks such as GEM5 [3], ramulator [14], or DRAMsim3 [16] simulate memory and the corresponding memory accesses purely in software. This enables simple integration of models and enables compatibility with simulation tools of algorithms and processing hardware. Apart from the low simulation speed, there are several drawbacks of state-of-the-art (SoA) simulators for the simulation of FPGA-based accelerators. As already established, optimal performance of HBM can only be achieved with proper memory access optimization. Such entities need to be modeled and simulated also, increasing the overhead over the accelerator alone. Furthermore, the support for HBM is limited, with support by ramulator and DRAMsim3 but not by GEM5.

Software-based simulation tools have one major drawback when it comes to the evaluation of memory performance of hardware designs targeted at reconfigurable logic devices in a near-memory context. HBM accesses on devices such as the AMD Xilinx Alveo U55C rely on an interconnect structure. Such structures are difficult to model in software, due to their proprietary nature. On top of that, other works propose memory access interleavers, e.g. the MAO [5]. Simulations running directly on the FPGA hardware do not rely on modelling these structures but rather use them directly.

Apart from software-based simulation tools, there are FPGA-based simulators, such as LIME [10], SoftMC [4], and MEG [23]. SoftMC is a framework with support for arbitrary traces targeted at classical DRAM with no support for 3D memory. LIME and MEG, on the other hand, support HBM. While LIME uses DRAM and emulates HBM behavior, MEG uses real HBM on a Xilinx Virtex Ultrascale+ board for processing traces. Both LIME and MEG are built around RISC-V host processors, with MEG focusing on full-stack support and LIME supporting a small accelerator core and trace generation.

The methodology presented in this work, called TAPRE-HBM, lives among LIME, SoftMC, and MEG. It supports cycle-accurate simulation of arbitrary traces on real HBM implemented on a Xilinx U55C board, combining the functionality of SoftMC with the features of MEG. Table 1 shows an overview of key features and performance metrics of the presented tools. TAPRE-HBM does not only outperform any other simulator in terms of frequency, but also features significantly larger instruction memory than e.g. SoftMC. The main difference between TAPRE-HBM and other hardware-based approaches is a focus on hardware level performance metrics, such as attainable clock speed at the memory interface. The trade-off between optimized experimental setup, feature set and raw performance metrics needs to be acknowledged when interpreting this comparison between simulators. Especially software simulators are more convenient, as they do not require specific hardware and can easily be modified.

3   Methodology

In this section, we will describe the principles of our methodology and the hardware background of it.

3.1   Hardware Platform

While the general concept is applicable to most FPGAs equipped with HBM, the platform our implementation is based on is the AMD Xilinx Alveo U55C. Since it is not possible to directly interface the HBM, this section will detail the way the memory is structured on this card.

3D-memory technologies such as HMC and HBM consist of stacked DRAM blocks and offer increased bandwidth compared to traditional DRAM technologies [8]. An HBM stack consists of eight independent memory channels, each divided into two $B = 64$ bit pseudo channels (PC) [6], as depicted in Fig. 1. Every PC has a dedicated channel with an assigned address region of memory [5] by means of through-silicon vias [15]. Xilinx FPGAs feature two HBM channels, resulting in 32 PCs and 8 GB total capacity [5]. Furthermore, Xilinx provides an interconnect that groups 4 PCs to a full crossbar interconnect. Adjacent interconnects are connected with two 64-bit connections in each direction. In total, 32 AXI busses connected to the interconnects are exposed to the FPGA at half the frequency of the HBM and 256-bit each.

3.2   Implementation

TAPRE-HBM emulates memory accesses by feeding a sequence of accesses to the channels of the underlying Advanced eXtensible Interface (AXI) instances. AXI interfaces structure transactions in terms of handshakes on different channels dedicated to different functions. A read transaction, for example, consists of a handshake on the Address Read (AR) channel, to supply the address among other parameters, followed by a handshake on the Read (R) channel, which

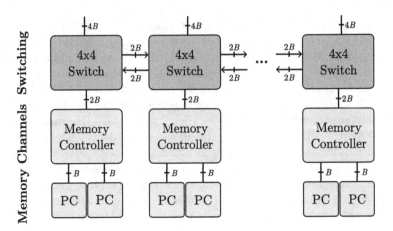

Fig. 1. Overview of Xilinx HBM Switching Implementation Featuring Pseudo Channels (PC) of Bitwidth $B = 64$ bit.

returns the requested data. The sequence of accesses performed by the TAPRE-HBM implementation is based on a user-supplied memory trace. In order to honor the time behavior represented in the traces, the requests are delayed, as they are in the given trace. An example of a read transaction on AXI is given in Fig. 2. As stated above, this transaction consists of two steps:

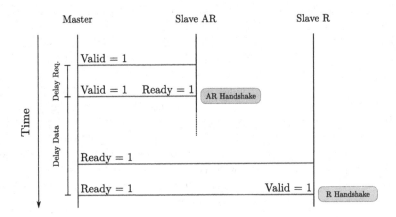

Fig. 2. Sequence of Handshakes for AXI Read Transaction

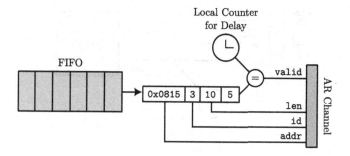

Fig. 3. Schematic of the Delaying FIFO

1. **AR Handshake**: transmission of parameters for the read, such as address and burst length.
2. **R Handshake**: return of the read data.

These handshakes are implemented via a ready/valid interfaces, where the sending side asserts the validity of the data using the valid signal and the receiving side asserts the readiness to receive data via the ready signal. A handshake is complete when both valid and ready signals are asserted.

The handshakes of the Address Read (AR), Address Write (AW), Read (R), and Write (W) channels are recorded. This allows the user to find the two sources of delays that can be measured in this way: The delay incurred by the AR or AW channel not being ready to accept requests and the delay until the read data arrives or the write data is accepted by the interface.

Internally, these features are implemented via lightweight First-In First-Out Queues (FIFOs), with an additional counter for delaying handshakes by masking out the ready and valid signals. Our implementation utilizes UltraRAM blocks as memory for all FIFOs to exploit the abundant memory resources of the used board. A schematic of this delay FIFO can be found in Fig. 3.

The recording of the handshakes is also implemented as FIFOs, as can be seen in Fig. 4. When a handshake occurs, it is recorded with a timestamp and the transaction id. From this data, the delays described above can be reconstructed and analyzed.

The schematics described above are composed as shown in Fig. 5. While TAPRE-HBM is built to only support HBM, the underlying structures could also be utilized to interface other types of memory, as long as it supports the AXI-MM interface.

4   Case Study: Vertical Vector Processor (V²PRO) Architecture

4.1   V²PRO Architecture

Dedicated hardware accelerators are essential for efficient processing of artificial intelligence (AI) algorithms such as neural networks. [21] is developing an AI

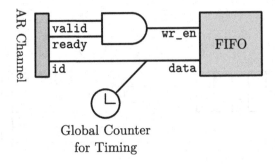

Fig. 4. Schematic of the Handshake Tracing Interface

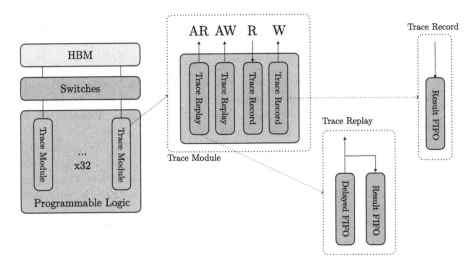

Fig. 5. Hierarchy of TAPER-HBM

accelerator system called V^{2}PRO that uses a massive-parallel vector coprocessor [18] and a custom RISC-V host processor. The V^{2}PRO architecture is based on the concept of vertical vector processing, which processes multidimensional vectors sequentially. It is different from the horizontal vector concept used in SIMD (single instruction multiple data) which is used e.g. in GPUs and can efficiently process complex addressing schemes used in CNNs. The V^{2}PRO achieves high performance by processing multiple vectors in parallel units.

The V^{2}PRO vector processor architecture (shown in Fig. 6) is divided into clusters, each with multiple vector units connected to a single DMA unit. Each vector unit has a local memory, two vector lanes for processing, and a load/store lane for data transfer between the local memory and register files of the vector lanes. The DMAs transfer data between the external memory and the local memory of each vector unit. However, scaling the V^{2}PRO architecture with multiple clusters and multiple vector units per cluster causes a memory bottleneck.

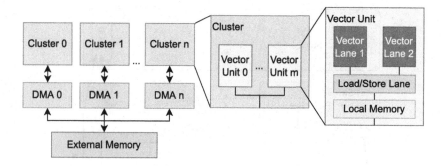

Fig. 6. Overview of the V²PRO Architecture [21]

63 30	29	28 21	20 0
Memory Address	ID	Length	Delay

Fig. 7. Representation of Trace Entries as Input to TAPRE-HBM

This bottleneck arises due to the parallel access of each cluster's DMA to external memory, and due to using a simple single-port memory controller which can only serve one DMA at a time. This bottleneck can either be mitigated by enhancing the DMAs with a multi-port DMA-Cache structure, called DCMA [21], or by using a multi-port memory controller, such as an HBM memory controller, which is evaluated in this work.

In this work, the V²PRO architecture implements 32 clusters and 2 units per cluster, i.e., 32 parallel DMAs, to fully utilize the 32 available channels of the HBM controller. Optimizations concerning the memory hierarchy of the vector processor architecture are out of this work's scope.

4.2   Applications and Trace Generation

For developing, debugging, and profiling applications for the vector processor, an instruction set simulator (ISS) is used [21]. The ISS is written in C++ and allows the cycle-accurate simulation of the V²PRO architecture. The parallel DMAs load or store one- or two-dimensional data using burst transfers. A burst transfer loads or stores multiple 64 bit data words sequentially. The 2D data is accessed using multiple one-dimensional burst transfers. For a given application and vector processor configuration, the ISS simulations can be used, not only to verify the correct execution of the application, but also to extract profiling metrics including traces of the memory transfers.

As an example application, memory traces from the YOLO-Lite CNN, a small CNN with 482 million FLOPS and 2.18 MB of weight data (32 bit) [7], are generated. The entries of traces consist of 64 bit depicted in Fig. 7. TAPRE-HBM uses AXI version 4 (AXI4) as its interface, which allows bursts up to 256

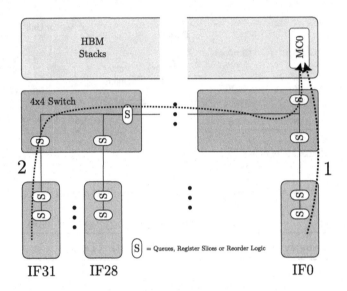

Fig. 8. Paths through the HBM Topology

beats. In order to attach it to the AXI interfaces of the HBM block, which is AXI version 3 (AXI3), an AXI4-to-AXI3 protocol converter is used, which makes long bursts possible in the first place, since AXI3 only provides up to 16 beats per burst.

5   Evaluation

5.1   Analysis of Time-Dependent Behavior

In order to show the capabilities to deeply analyze performance issues in HBM, the memory accesses from the vector processor running the YOLO-Lite example as described above are presented. The time-dependent latency behavior is visualized in Fig. 9. This scatter plot describes the delay from the AR/AW handshake to the last beat in the R/W channel on the Y axis. A kernel density estimation is given at the top of the figure, so that the number of requests of each channel at a point in time can be estimated.

Unfortunately, the logic of the switches is proprietary, but using the available documentation [2] the behavior can be explained by the topology:

1. At the beginning of the YOLO-Lite application, the input image is distributed segment-wise to all local memories of the vector processor. Therefore, all DMAs access the same memory space of the external memory and also the same HBM memory controller interface.
2. Hence, the latency quickly increases on all interfaces. Interface 0 is the closest interface to the data, requested on all interfaces (e.g., Route 1 in Fig. 8). It receives data fairly quickly, as lateral connections in the switches have not

yet forwarded requests to the corresponding memory controller. With more and more traffic coming from the lateral connections, congestion builds up, leading to very high latencies.

3. This affects more distant interfaces more strongly, as they have to pass more queues, increasing latency (e.g., Route 2 in Fig. 8).

4. The latency from AR/AW Handshake to R/W Handshake, starts to taper off with time for two reasons: Firstly, the queues along the route of a request are now filled, delaying the AR/AW handshake, while not increasing the delay from AR/AW handshake to R/W handshake. Secondly, some parts of the system have completed their tasks, decreasing competing traffic on lateral connections, and queues. This results in staircase-like steps in the plot.

5. The number of requests, as can be seen in the density above the scatter plot, is also interesting. It shows, that interfaces closer to the memory controller can issue their requests earlier.

This small case study using the V^2PRO shows the necessity of optimizing the memory access to take advantage of the HBM memory. By using a trace-based methodology, issues can be attributed to channels, transactions or access patterns as an emergent property of the data gathered. The core trade-off of HBM memory compared to traditional DRAM is the increased bandwidth and delay at decreased frequency.

Therefore, performance improvements from using HBM strongly depend on the scheduling of memory accesses. Several recent works propose memory mapping, access reordering or interleaving strategies to reduce memory delays for certain applications. E.g., Holzinger et al. [5] propose a Memory Access Optimizer (MAO) to improve performance for random and some strided patterns. To specifically overcome the problem of accessing data in the same memory space, a cache can optimize our transfers. Another approach is to implement a broadcasting feature to transfer the same data to all DMAs.

In summary, using the results of the latency evaluations of TAPRE-HBM, optimization methods can be precisely developed regarding the processor architecture and its applications. In a second step, the optimized architectures can rapidly be evaluated with TAPRE-HBM again.

5.2 Properties of Implementation

Due to the lightweight architecture of TAPRE-HBM, access to HBM can be simulated with higher clock frequencies and with a longer trace than most SoA methodologies. While the depth of the FIFOs containing the traces is configurable, the system was tested with a set number of configurations, that all meet timing. All 32 interfaces of the HBM on the board, which consist of read and write channels, are connected to FIFOs with 1024 entries in this evaluation. In total, this amounts to 65536 accesses that can be simulated in one execution, outperforming alternatives like SoftMC [4]. Per recorded channel, 4096 entries can be stored in our evaluation configuration. With this setup, our design reaches a clock frequency of 250 MHz, which is exceeds the maximum frequencies of any

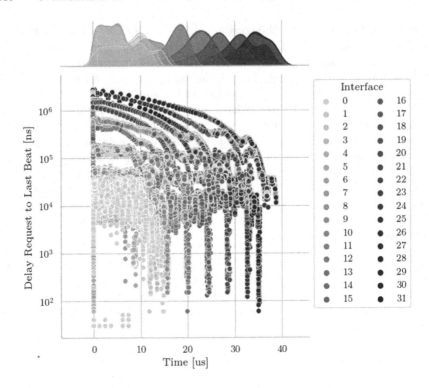

Fig. 9. Latency over Time

other hardware-based framework, as given in Sec. 2. It is important to acknowledge that there are potentially more capable configurations available, although these often involve a trade-off with reduced frequency.

Table 2 shows the resource consumption of the different configurations used in this work. All configurations were implemented with 100 MHz and 250MHz. The Xilinx U55C Alveo board used in our implementation has a total of 1,303,680 Look-up Tables (LUTs), 2,607,360 Flip Flops, 2,016 BRAM blocks, and 960 Ultra RAM (URAM) blocks. The percentages shown in Tab. 2 are relative to the total resources of the U55C Alveo board.

It is worth mentioning that although the operating frequencies of the whole design can change from one implementation to another, the HBM internal memory interface frequency for each stack was set to 900 MHz, which is the maximum frequency for the U55C Alveo board.

Table 2. Resource Consumption of Different Implementations

#Chan.	Freq.	LUTs	Flip Flops	BRAM Blocks	URAM Blocks
4	100 MHz	2.69%	1.99%	0.99%	2.5%
4	250 MHz	2.69%	2.03%	0.99%	2.5%
8	100 MHz	3.66%	2.61%	0.99%	5%
8	250 MHz	3.66%	2.61%	0.99%	5%
16	100 MHz	5.61%	3.86%	0.99%	10%
16	250 MHz	5.61%	3.86%	0.99%	10%
32	100 MHz	9.60%	6.43%	0.99%	20%
32	250 MHz	9.61%	6.43%	0.99%	20%

6   Conclusion

Overcoming the challenges of implementing hardware with HBM support, such as a large number of memory channels and long latencies, poses significant difficulties. Existing memory simulators face limitations in terms of speed, HBM support, trace length, and interface clock frequency, either due to software-based limitations or other factors. To address these challenges, we introduce TAPRE-HBM, which fulfills all the aforementioned requirements. By prioritizing performance and resource efficiency, the implementation of TAPRE-HBM achieves the desired objective of providing the framework for emulation of memory traces for rapid evaluation of HBM performance.

6.1   Future Work

In order to obtain a more realistic dependency between data transfers and processing, the handling of the data synchronization point will be implemented in TAPRE-HBM. DMA data synchronization points, which indicate that, e.g., the V^2PRO architecture waits for all DMA transactions to finish, are already an essential feature of most processor architectures. These synchronization points can be included in the traces as a new feature. Therefore, when reading a data synchronization command in a trace, TAPRE-HBM will wait for every DMA command currently in the FIFO to finish before serving new commands.

Acknowledgement. The authors would like to thank AMD for the provided hardware and software under the Xilinx University Program.

References

1. AMD / Xilinx: Alveo U55C high performance compute card. https://www.xilinx.com/products/boards-and-kits/alveo/u55c.html, Accessed: 15 May 2023
2. AMD / Xilinx: AXI high bandwidth memory controller v1.0, 2021

3. Binkert, N., et al.: The Gem5 simulator. SIGARCH Comput. Archit. News **39**(2), 1–7 (2011). https://doi.org/10.1145/2024716.2024718
4. Hassan, H., et al.: SoftMC: A flexible and practical open-source infrastructure for enabling experimental DRAM studies. In: 2017 IEEE International Symposium on High Performance Computer Architecture (HPCA). pp. 241–252 (2017). https://doi.org/10.1109/HPCA.2017.62
5. Holzinger, P., Reiser, D., Hahn, T., Reichenbach, M.: Fast HBM Access with FPGAs: analysis, architectures, and applications. In: 2021 IEEE International Parallel and Distributed Processing Symposium Workshops (IPDPSW). pp. 152–159. IEEE, Portland, OR, USA (2021). https://doi.org/10.1109/IPDPSW52791.2021.00030
6. Huang, H., et al.: Shuhai: a tool for benchmarking high bandwidth memory on FPGAs. IEEE Trans. Comput. **71**(5), 1133–1144 (2022). https://doi.org/10.1109/TC.2021.3075765
7. Huang, R., Pedoeem, J., Chen, C.: YOLO-LITE: a real-time object Detection algorithm optimized for Non-GPU computers. In: 2018 IEEE International Conference on Big Data (Big Data). pp. 2503–2510 (Dec 2018). https://doi.org/10.1109/BigData.2018.8621865
8. Iskandar, V., Ghany, M.A.A.E., Göhringer, D.: Near-memory computing on FPGAs with 3D-Stacked memories: applications, architectures, and optimizations. ACM Trans. Reconfigurable Technol. Syst. **16**(1), 1–32 (2022). https://doi.org/10.1145/3547658
9. Jain, A.K., Kumar, S., Tripathi, A., Gaitonde, D.: Sparse deep neural network acceleration on HBM-Enabled FPGA platform. In: 2021 IEEE High Performance Extreme Computing Conference (HPEC). pp. 1–7 (2021). DOI: https://doi.org/10.1109/HPEC49654.2021.9622804
10. Jain, A.K., Lloyd, S., Gokhale, M.: Microscope on memory: MPSoC-enabled computer memory system assessments. In: 2018 IEEE 26th Annual International Symposium on Field-Programmable Custom Computing Machines (FCCM). pp. 173–180 (2018). https://doi.org/10.1109/FCCM.2018.00035
11. JEDEC: Standard high bandwidth memory (HBM) DRAM specification. https://www.xilinx.com/products/boards-and-kits/alveo/u55c.html (2015)
12. Jun, H., et al.: HBM (High Bandwidth Memory) DRAM Technology and Architecture. In: 2017 IEEE International Memory Workshop (IMW). pp. 1–4. IEEE, Monterey, CA, USA (2017). https://doi.org/10.1109/IMW.2017.7939084
13. Kim, N.S., Chen, D., Xiong, J., Hwu, W.m.W.: Heterogeneous Computing Meets Near-Memory Acceleration and High-Level Synthesis in the Post-Moore Era. IEEE Micro **37**(4), 10–18 (2017). https://doi.org/10.1109/MM.2017.3211105
14. Kim, Y., Yang, W., Mutlu, O.: Ramulator: a fast and extensible dram simulator. IEEE Comput. Archit. Lett. **15**(1), 45–49 (2016). https://doi.org/10.1109/LCA.2015.2414456
15. Lee, J.C., et al.: High bandwidth memory(HBM) with TSV technique. In: 2016 International SoC Design Conference (ISOCC). pp. 181–182 (2016). https://doi.org/10.1109/ISOCC.2016.7799847
16. Li, S., Yang, Z., Reddy, D., Srivastava, A., Jacob, B.: DRAMsim3: a cycle-accurate, thermal-capable DRAM simulator. IEEE Comput. Archit. Lett. **19**(2), 106–109 (2020). https://doi.org/10.1109/LCA.2020.2973991
17. Nguyen, V.C., Nakashima, Y.: Analysis of fully-pipelined CNN implementation on FPGA and HBM2. In: 2021 Ninth International Symposium on Computing and Networking Workshops (CANDARW). pp. 134–137 (2021). https://doi.org/10.1109/CANDARW53999.2021.00029

18. Nolting, S., Giesemann, F., Hartig, J., Schmider, A., Paya-Vaya, G.: Application-specific soft-core vector processor for advanced driver assistance systems. In: 2017 27th International Conference on Field Programmable Logic and Applications (FPL). pp. 1–2 (Sep 2017). doi:https://doi.org/10.23919/FPL.2017.8056836
19. Samsung: HBM3 Icebolt. https://semiconductor.samsung.com/dram/hbm/hbm3-icebolt/, Accessed 14 May 2023
20. Shi, R., Kara, K., Hagleitner, C., Diamantopoulos, D., Syrivelis, D., Alonso, G.: Exploiting HBM on FPGAs for data processing. ACM Trans. Reconfigurable Technol. Syst. 15(4), 1–27 (2022). https://doi.org/10.1145/3491238
21. Thieu, G.B., et al.: ZuSE Ki-Avf: application-specific AI processor for intelligent sensor signal processing in autonomous driving. In: 2023 Design, Automation & Test in Europe Conference & Exhibition (DATE). pp. 1–6 (2023). https://doi.org/10.23919/DATE56975.2023.10136978
22. Wang, Z., Huang, H., Zhang, J., Alonso, G.: Shuhai: benchmarking High Bandwidth Memory On FPGAS. In: 2020 IEEE 28th Annual International Symposium on Field-Programmable Custom Computing Machines (FCCM). pp. 111–119. IEEE, Fayetteville, AR, USA (2020). https://doi.org/10.1109/FCCM48280.2020.00024
23. Zhang, J., Zha, Y., Beckwith, N., Liu, B., Li, J.: MEG: A RISCV-based system emulation infrastructure for near-data processing using FPGAs and high-bandwidth memory. ACM Trans. Reconfigurable Technol. Syst. 13(4), 1–24 (2020). https://doi.org/10.1145/3409114

An Almost Fully RRAM-Based LUT Design for Reconfigurable Circuits

Philipp Grothe(✉) [iD], Saleh Mulhem [iD], and Mladen Berekovic [iD]

Institute of Computer Engineering (ITI), University of Lübeck,
Ratzeburger Allee 160, 23562 Lübeck, Germany
{ph.grothe,saleh.mulhem,mladen.berekovic}@uni-luebeck.de

Abstract. In the last decade, resistive random-access memory (RRAM) has been used in designing field-programmable gate arrays (FPGAs). The non-volatility of RRAM has made it a promising substitute for the traditional static random-access memory (SRAM) in emerging non-volatile FPGAs. Most use cases for RRAM in these FPGAs are restricted to the utilization in routing infrastructures and as a one-to-one substitute for the SRAM memory cells in building FPGA lookup tables (LUTs). In contrast, other FPGA building blocks remain the same. These approaches do not fully embrace RRAM as an emerging circuit element beyond memory. In this paper, we introduce an almost fully RRAM-based LUT design. Our design approach relies on RRAM implementing arbitrary Boolean logic in disjunctive normal form. The unique properties of RRAM crossbars are utilized to effectively integrate address decoder and memory in a single crossbar structure, reducing the amount of auxiliary CMOS components. The simulation results show that our RRAM-based LUT design exhibits low energy requirements at sub-picojoule consumption for read operations. Furthermore, it can achieve fast operations at more than 2.5 GHz for read accesses. To show the practicality and usability of our design, we also present an example application.

Keywords: Resistive random-access memory · RRAM · FPGA · LUT

1 Introduction

Since 1971 and right after the seminal work of Leon Chua [5], several studies have proposed *resistive random-access memory* (ReRAM or RRAM) as a promising candidate to substitute the conventional memories [24,32]. The advantages of RRAM over conventional memory stem from RRAM consisting of single-device, multi-level memory cells [21], where the devices are arranged in highly compact crossbar arrays [31], and computations can be performed within the memory [19]. These properties fit the trend towards more energy efficient computing [8,29]. Consequently, RRAM has been perceived as a potential successor of *static random-access memory* (SRAM) and flash memory in designing *field programmable gate arrays* (FPGAs). RRAM-based FPGAs are expected to exhibit less area, less delay, and lower power consumption than conventional FPGAs

© The Author(s), under exclusive license to Springer Nature Switzerland AG 2023
F. Palumbo et al. (Eds.): ARC 2023, LNCS 14251, pp. 322–337, 2023.
https://doi.org/10.1007/978-3-031-42921-7_22

such as SRAM-based or flash-based FPGAs [27]. Recent works on RRAM-based FPGA designs show that RRAM-based FPGAs can achieve a high level of performance together with low-level power consumption [25].

The general FPGA architecture includes several programmable blocks, so-called *configurable logic blocks* (CLBs). Each CLB consists of several logic cells. One logic cell includes a *lookup table* (LUT), a flip-flop, and a *multiplexer* (MUX), as shown in Fig. 1a. The LUTs are the basic functional building blocks providing the configurability. The configuration bits are stored in SRAM cells, and the MUX chooses the LUT output based on the input (select bits). This mechanism allows the LUT to implement any Boolean function. Figure 1b shows a 3-to-1 LUT architecture as an example of a conventional SRAM-based LUT, where the configuration bits are stored in SRAM.

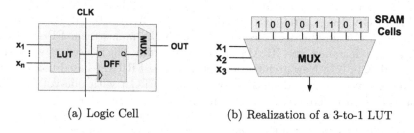

(a) Logic Cell   (b) Realization of a 3-to-1 LUT

Fig. 1. General FPGA Architecture and its Building Blocks

To benefit from the unique properties of RRAM, LUT architectures utilizing RRAM have been proposed [9,27]. However, the recent architectures of RRAM-based LUTs mainly replace the SRAM cells with RRAM ones. This work avoids deploying RRAM only as a one-to-one replacement at the device level in conventional architectures and instead introduces a new design strategy for RRAM-based LUTs. Our contributions can be summarized as follows:

- We introduce a new RRAM-based LUT design. Our design does not follow the mainstream SRAM-based LUT design as it is an almost fully RRAM-based LUT. Supplemental *complementary metal-oxide-semiconductor* (CMOS) logic is deployed at the edge between the analog and digital domain to ensure compatibility of the LUT with conventional CMOS building blocks.
- We analyze our architecture regarding energy, performance, and timing aspects. A full LUT layout in a 45 nm *process design kit* (PDK) is presented to determine the required area for the LUT.

To the best of our knowledge, this work is the first architectural design of its kind.

2   Background and Motivation

This section is divided into three parts: First, reviewing the new designs of a reconfigurable circuit utilizing RRAM; second, discussing recent RRAM-based LUT designs; and third, showing the motivation for our RRAM-based LUT design.

2.1   RRAM-Based Reconfigurable Circuit Designs

In the last decade, several works have introduced RRAM-based hardware elements. The idea is to exploit RRAM properties to substitute CMOS-based technology. RRAM outperforms CMOS by several properties such as high density, non-volatility, fast read speeds, and lower power consumption [22]. For instance, RRAM-based MUXs were designed in [26]. The results show that the RRAM-based MUX reduces the area-delay, and power-delay products by 2.6× and 3.8×, respectively, compared to the purely CMOS-based MUX. In [34], eight different Boolean logic functions were realized by RRAM-based nonvolatile reconfigurable sequential logic. Furthermore, mapping schemes exist that take the approach of mapping individual logic gates into RRAM crossbars, such as IMPLY [16] and MAGIC [17]. The results indicate that RRAM-based reconfigurable logic is a promising step toward non-von Neumann computing architectures.

One FPGA design strategy relies on deploying RRAM-based hardware elements in FPGA designs to be compatible with the mainstream FPGA architectures. For instance, the RRAM-based MUX from [26] is used as a routing FPGA-MUX in [27]. New architectures of hybridized RRAM-based non-volatile SRAM cells were proposed in [2], providing the FPGA with non-volatility. In [7], new RRAM-based programmable interconnects were presented. A similar approach was conducted in [6] to use RRAM for programmable interconnects and stacking them on top of logic blocks. In [23], RRAM-based routing crossbars were also developed. In [20], a non-volatile resistive-change switch together with in-crossbar switches was deployed to build the so-called Via-Switch FPGA. All mentioned works have focused on designing new RRAM-based FPGAs, and the majority have tried combining CMOS- and RRAM-based technologies. Other works have focused on developing RRAM-based logic cells or the RRAM-based LUT.

2.2   RRAM-Based LUT Designs

The mainstream design strategy of LUTs is to replace SRAM cells with RRAM-based ones. An early example is presented in [18], where SRAM is replaced with a pair of differential RRAM cells connected to a conventional MUX. Similarly, in [9], RRAMs are proposed to replace the SRAMs of the LUT, but also an RRAM-based MUX is deployed for routing. Following this work, the LUT design uses RRAM as a direct replacement for the SRAM also utilized in [12]. In [27], the proposed RRAM-based LUT design uses an RRAM-based non-volatile SRAM topology instead of a purely SRAM-based one to achieve non-volatility. In [28], the proposed RRAM-based FPGA uses an SRAM-based MUX and RRAM-based registers to design the LUT. Compared to purely SRAM-based FPGAs, the results show that this RRAM-based FPGA improves up to 8%, 22%, and 16% in area, delay, and power, respectively. In [12], a conventional decoder is combined with resistive storage and dedicated control circuitry to omit external configuration ROM through the non-volatility of RRAM. A novel 2-to-1 RRAM-based LUT was designed in [1,15]. In [4], 1R RRAM cells were deployed to replace SRAM. Both dimensions of the crossbar were used to get a large address space and a small footprint.

A different design strategy of LUTs for almost completely omitting complementary CMOS logic was first introduced in [30]. Two separate mapping schemes are presented, either using the switching of an RRAM cell for the gate function itself or for storing the output of the gate. The specific differences between [30] and our work are discussed at the end of Sect. 3.

Similarly, LUTs constructed from the pure logic mapping schemes mentioned in Subsect. 2.1 (IMPLY, MAGIC) also suffer from the disadvantage that RRAM cells are written during logic evaluation and since the resulting outputs are inputs for other gates, evaluation can not be realized in a single operation.

2.3   Motivation and Paper's Contributions

In a direct comparison with conventional memory, RRAM promises several advantages. Its smaller area requirements already allow for a higher density integration in conventional production, with the perspective of 3D stacking promising even further reduction of the spatial footprint. Among non-volatile memories, it exhibits among the lowest energy requirements and fastest access times. Additionally, even though its endurance is limited, it is on par with other technologies.

How can these unique properties of RRAM be utilized to implement LUTs? Can the amount of necessary CMOS components beyond the memory be significantly reduced through the use of RRAM? This paper is motivated by these questions, and here we try to answer them. The proposed architecture is designed with applications in mind that require infrequent reconfiguration but a high throughput of read accesses. Thus, the energy, delay, and other advantages of RRAM are optimally utilized while avoiding its disadvantages, such as limited endurance, degradation, etc.

3   New RRAM-Based LUT Architecture

The proposed LUT architecture uses an RRAM crossbar to implement the minterms of a Boolean function of its wordline inputs (Fig. 2), and an additional output stage implements a column-wise disjunction and selective inversion (Fig. 3), resulting in the LUT realizing arbitrary Boolean logic in disjunctive normal form. In this regard, the design bares similarities to the architecture of *programmable logic arrays* (PLAs) [13]. Both designs share the advantage that not every possible input combination should point to an explicit memory location. However, the proposed architecture avoids the need for two separate planes as present in PLAs and the resulting long delay.

The scope of this work is limited to the design for LUT evaluation through the reading of the memristive or resistive memory. Programming schemes for general 1R crossbars have been published and are applicable to the crossbar employed in the proposed architecture [14]. No tight integration into the architecture is needed as multiplexing between read and write circuitry is feasible for programming. For the targeted application in FPGAs or general reconfigurable circuits, programming is only necessary during reconfiguration, which is rare compared to read accesses. This also allows for reduced redundancy as programming circuitry can be used to reconfigure multiple LUTs in sequence.

3.1 Solution Space and Crossbar Dimensions

For n inputs, a traditional LUT realizes 2^{2^n} different n-to-1 functions by 2^{2^n} possible configurations. Table 1 illustrates an example of a 2-to-1 LUT, where $n = 2$ results in $2^n = 2^2 = 4$ different input combinations and consequently $2^{2^n} = 2^{2^2} = 16$ distinct functions.

Table 1. 2-to-1 LUT Realizing 16 Logic Functions and their Inverses with an Excerpt of Input and Output Combinations.

A	B	C	Corresponding Function	Inverse Function
0	0	0		
0	1	0	C=0	C=(¬A∧¬B)∨(¬A∧B)
1	0	0		∨(A∧¬B)∨(A∧B)
1	1	0		
0	0	0		
0	1	0	C=A∧B	C=(¬A∧¬B)∨(¬A∧B)
1	0	0		∨(A∧¬B)
1	1	1		
...	...	...	...	...
0	0	1		
0	1	1	C=(¬A∧¬B)∨(¬A∧B)	C=0
1	0	1	∨(A∧¬B)∨(A∧B)	
1	1	1		

To determine the crossbar dimensions required to realize a LUT, one must account for 2^n possible conjunctions in the logic function - one for each possible input combination. Every possible conjunction is represented by a specific column configuration. For the intuitive mapping of one conjunction to one column, this results in a maximum of 2^n columns for the LUT configuration that is always asserted as true. However, for every configuration utilizing l conjunctions, there is an inverse configuration using exactly $n - l$ conjunction that produces inverse outputs for every possible input. Taking advantage of these inverse configurations reduces the number of necessary columns by half at the cost of one configuration bit and a switchable inverter stage controlled by it to get the desired output by inverting it twice. Examples of these inverse functions are listed in Table 1.

The number of rows is derived from the number of inputs. It is doubled to account for the negation of inputs. Instead of adding inverters to the cells in the crossbar, the proposed architecture adds a negated row for each input. This is necessary since an input can be contained in multiple conjunctions negated and non-negated, otherwise resulting in the need for one inverter per input per column. While causing overhead, our approach scales favorably. It doubles the number of RRAM cells which are relatively small and adds n inverters, thereby avoiding the additional need for $n2^n$ inverters as well as one bit of configuration memory for each of them. The resulting crossbar has a size of $2n$ times 2^{n-1} or $n2^n$ cells in total.

3.2 Crossbar Configuration

In the proposed LUT architecture, although the resistive memory cells are capable of achieving multiple analog resistance levels, they are used digitally either in a *low resistance state* (LRS) or a *high resistance state* (HRS). The input levels are digital, swinging between GND and V_{DD}.

Each column implements one of the determined conjunctions as shown in Table 1. The aim is to configure the crossbar in a way that when the input function is to be evaluated as true, the path between active inputs and evaluated outputs consists of only cells in the LRS state - resulting in a path with the least possible resistance. Hence, for each literal that is not negated, the memory cell at the corresponding original wordline is set to the LRS, and for each negated literal, this is done for the cell at the inverted wordline. All other cells in the columns are reset to the HRS. Since a minterm by definition contains every literal exactly once, either non-negated or negated, it is always half of the cells in an active column that are set to the LRS with the other half set to the HRS.

This is illustrated in Fig. 2. The crossbar is configured as a 2-input LUT that is always evaluated as true. This is achieved trough the mapping of all four possible input combinations to one column each. For each conjunction of the desired function, exactly one column is evaluated as true when the respective inputs are applied. A disjunction of all column outputs must be implemented to realize the whole function and the outputs must be made CMOS-compatible.

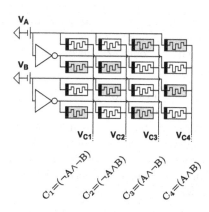

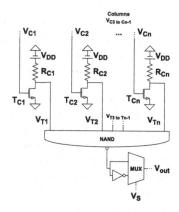

Fig. 2. Crossbar Configuration Equivalent to the Last Function Shown in Table 1 (LRS Shaded Green)

Fig. 3. Supplemental NMOS Transistors and CMOS Logic in the Output Stage

3.3 Output Stage

While the dot product engine capabilities of the RRAM are typically tied to the use of currents as the output quantity, the proposed implementation is based on voltages, as evident by the use of *metal-oxide-semiconductor field-effect transistors* (MOSFETs) in the output stage instead of more complex sense amplifiers. The sneak-path problem typical in 1R crossbars is used to its advantage to get voltage readings at the column outputs. Since the transistor at the column does not sink any current, the current is forced into the inputs set to low. The inverters, as well as the inputs - other LUTs or buffers that are part of routing structures - can sink this current. The interactions within the crossbar are complex, but effectively a voltage divider is constructed from the active cells (those in rows with a high input) in the column that is read and the path of least resistance in the other cells. Figure 4a shows a circuit substitution for the equivalent voltage divider. In the illustrated configuration both inputs are high and the inverters are sinking the current. Both LRS cells in the column are in the path towards the measured node V_{C4} while the HRS cells in the column are in the path towards ground. This results in the bigger voltage drop occurring after V_{C4} and therefore a high column output voltage. This way of utilizing the crossbar effectively avoids the caveats commonly associated with 1R crossbars.

The number of possible output voltages is limited by the constraints applied to the crossbar configuration:

- Every active column has half of its cells set to the LRS and half to the HRS.
- Due to the input inverters, half of the inputs are set to low and half to high.
- No identical columns exist in the same crossbar simultaneously.

Additionally, when considering only the circuit and not the implemented function, the following observations can be made:

- Which column is active has no impact, only the number of active columns.
- Only the combination of input and column configuration is relevant. A single-column configuration with all possible input combinations or vice versa accounts for all observable output states.

Figure 4b shows the simulation of the subset of relevant configurations resulting in the illustrated pattern of voltages. Five discrete bands of voltages can be observed. The deviations within the bands can be attributed to the input combination and the slightly different behavior of the inverted inputs compared to the non-inverted inputs, as well as the number of columns containing LRS cells. The deviation within a single band is not significant. The bands themselves correlate with resistance ratio as illustrated in Fig. 4a, which itself is a result of the logic evaluation of the column:

- **Highest Band:** All active cells in the column are in the LRS.
- **High Band:** The majority of the LRS cells in the column are active cells. At the given crossbar size, this is a ratio of three to one.

- **Middle Band:** The same amount of LRS is in the column as in path to ground. This is true for a column where half of the LRS cells are active. Inactive columns also exhibit voltages in this band.
- **Low Band:** The minority of the LRS cells in the column are active cells.
- **Lowest Band:** All active cells in the column are in the HRS. The path to ground, therefore, contains all LRS cells.

Only the highest band is evaluated as true. The voltages shown in Fig. 4b apply only to the specific implementation, but the pattern is transferable to all implementations of the same architecture. In bigger crossbars more bands with more intermediate states can be observed.

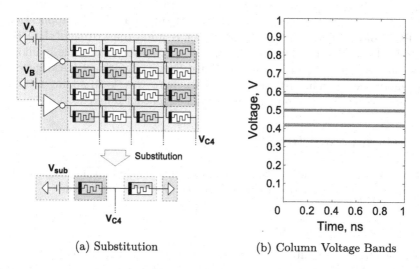

(a) Substitution   (b) Column Voltage Bands

Fig. 4. Voltage Division in Crossbar Illustrated through Substitution Circuit and Resulting Voltage Bands

To implement the threshold, each column is connected to the gate terminal of an *n-channel metal-oxide-semiconductor field-effect transistor* (NMOS). A resistor is added between V_{DD} and the drain terminal as a pull-up. The resistor value is chosen such that the output voltage measured between the resistor and the transistor is pulled down when a sufficiently high voltage is applied to the transistor gate. The suitable value for this resistor also depends on the characteristics of the adjacent transistor. Thus, the output exceeds the threshold of the connected logic gate, resulting in the inverted truth value of the conjunction evaluation. The circuit is shown in the top part of Fig. 3.

To implement the disjunctions of the logic function, only the pre-evaluated conjunctions in the columns are of concern. Since the outputs of the columns are inverted, the OR function of all columns is realized through a NAND gate with one input per column, which are functionally equivalent as per De Morgan's laws. Since the output of the NAND gate operates between GND and VDD, the voltage levels require no further A/D conversion at the LUT output. The NAND gate is a conventional CMOS-based gate. The last substage of the output stage is the inverter stage which is used to select whether or not the output is to be inverted. This is implemented through a single inverter and a 2-input MUX, both conventional designs. The MUX can be omitted if complementary outputs are desired. The selection of the output is then done through the routing.

While similarly motivated and also based on logic implemented in an RRAM crossbar, the main difference between the design presented in [30] and our proposed solution is that we avoid changing the content of the RRAM during LUT evaluation. This design decision is made due to the relatively limited write endurance of RRAM [33]. Every time an RRAM cell is written to, it degrades. A LUT that utilizes only read operations during LUT evaluation can therefore be expected to prolong the lifetime of the RRAM substantially. For application in an FPGA for example, reconfiguration, which requires the writing of the RRAM in the LUTs, is a comparatively rare occurrence. At the same time, millions of reads can happen between reconfigurations. Further, writing RRAM generally takes more energy than just reading it. This energy overhead adding up over a multitude of accesses can potentially make a significant difference.

4   Experimental Results

In this section, we simulate the proposed RRAM-based LUT design and we evaluate it based on several factors such as timing, area and power.

4.1   Experimental Setup

The proposed LUT architecture is evaluated by using a SPICE simulation. While for larger architectures, simulation frameworks that add abstraction are suitable, SPICE offers an unparalleled degree of precision for simulations on the device level. The simulation of the RRAM relies on the following points:

- The simulation of the RRAM is based on a well established, compact Verilog-A model of metal-oxide RRAM devices as described and implemented in [11].
- Device variations are accounted for in simulations of randomly sampled deviations of resistance values compatible with the model.
- The layout of our RRAM crossbar is created by adapting the model layout presented in [10] for RRAM compatible with the 45 nm process.

All other devices are based on a generic 45 nm process library [3]. V_{DD} as well as the voltage levels of all inputs set to high are fixed to 1 V. Under ideal conditions, the RRAM cells exhibit a resistance of 15 kΩ in the LRS and 40 kΩ in the HRS, which are achieved by setting the initial gap to 212 pm and 481.64 pm, respectively. In the context of the employed model, the LRS could be considered to be an intermediate HRS, but it will be referred to as the LRS. The value of R_C and the width of T_C should be tuned for the transistor to switch at the appropriate threshold generating suitable voltages at each column. In Fig. 5

the relationship between transistor width and resistor value is illustrated for the given technology node. Figure 5a shows this relationship for a true positive evaluation (top) and the edge cases where the thresholds are closest (bottom). Higher values (lighter yellow) signify a wider margin for tolerance of deviating resistances in the RRAM crossbar. This is further illustrated in Fig. 5b in which the resistance is swept for a fixed transistor width of 240 nm and a multiplier of ten, and the transistor output voltage V_T is plotted alongside the resulting V_{out} at the end of the output stage.

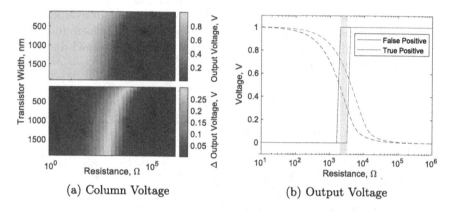

(a) Column Voltage   (b) Output Voltage

Fig. 5. (5a) Top: Switching Characteristics for Transistor Width and Resistor, Bottom: Solution Space between True Positives and False Positives (5b) Column Voltages V_T (dashed) and Output Voltages V_{out} (solid) for True Positive and False Positives against Resistance of R_C (Color figure online)

In the following, the architecture is simulated and evaluated for a 4-to-1 LUT using the described setup.

4.2   Design Stability

RRAM manufactured today is prone to device variations. Different cells within the crossbar may exhibit inter-device variations due to which the same write process causes deviating resistance values. Furthermore, even for the same device slight resistance deviations might be observed after multiple write operations due to intra-device variations. Excessive variations can lead to false evaluations at the column output. This is especially true for the LRS increasing and the HRS decreasing in resistance simultaneously, effectively decreasing the on-off ratio. To ensure correct operation of the LUT under these conditions, device variations must be modeled as part of the simulation.

To reduce the computational requirements when simulating variations of all cells at once, samples of variations based on the utilized model were taken for a single device in the LRS of 15 kΩ and the HRS of 40 kΩ and the distributions are randomly sampled for each cell. Repeating this for each cell over multiple runs covers all expected deviations for the whole crossbar.

The simulation was done for the configurations with the lowest margin for error, corresponding to the closest values in the highest and second-highest voltage band in Fig. 5b. Figure 6 shows the measured voltages after the transistor at the output of the crossbar for all runs. As there is no overlap between the true positives and the true negatives, there is no expected configuration for which no definitive evaluation is possible. Therefore, device variations do not result in incorrect outputs for the chosen LRS and HRS based on the utilized model.

Operating the circuit under worst-case assumptions can generally be avoided by employing a read-and-verify programming scheme. In these schemes, values written to the crossbar are verified by reading out the cell afterward. In case of excessive deviation, the value is written anew. While this introduces time overhead, it is negligible as the verify operation is only performed during the relatively rare reconfiguration phase.

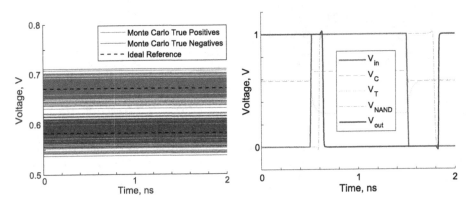

Fig. 6. Output Voltages of Monte Carlo Simulation

Fig. 7. Delay between Input and Output Signals with Intermediate Signals

4.3   Timing Analysis

The delay of the LUT between a change in input signals and the change in the output is caused by capacitances in the circuit. Figure 7 shows the worst-case timing measured in the simulation. The changing input is plotted in blue and the change at the output in red. Intermediate measurements are plotted alongside. A worst-case peak-to-peak rise time of approximately **166 ps** can be observed as well as a fall time of **390 ps**. This results in a theoretical maximum frequency of **2.564 GHz** the LUT can operate at.

An advantage of the proposed architecture is that the timing is mostly invariant. This is due to the number of cells in the LRS and HRS being constant for every active column and the number of active rows also being constant due to the inverters at each input for every possible configuration.

4.4 Area Evaluation

As discussed in Sect. 3.1, the crossbar dimensions are dictated by the number of LUT inputs. In the case of the 4-to-1 LUT, an 8×8 crossbar is required. The layout is shown in Fig. 8. The components are grouped by function and labeled accordingly. The devices are best discernable in the metal layers (blue, red, and green), with their boundaries additionally shaded yellow.

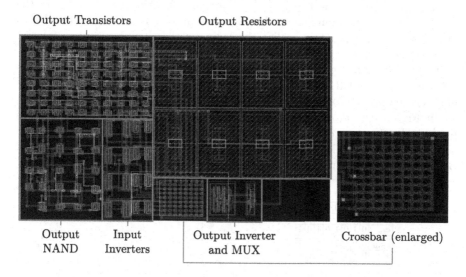

Output Transistors   Output Resistors

Output   Input   Output Inverter   Crossbar (enlarged)
NAND   Inverters   and MUX

Fig. 8. LUT Layout in 45 nm PDK (Color figure online)

As is typical for architectures including RRAM, peripheral circuitry significantly contributes to the overall area consumption. The resistors in the output stage dominate the design area. The design has an overall area of **189 μm^2**. Only 16 μm^2 can be attributed to the RRAM crossbar. The area could be further decreased by optimization across multiple hierarchy levels. For the layout of our design, optimization is only performed on the component level.

4.5 Energy Measurement

In contrast to SRAM-based LUTs, RRAM-based LUTs are non-volatile. Thus, no refresh operation of the memory content is required. This effectively eliminates the static power consumption of the LUT design.

Further, the power consumption in operation depends on the input configuration and the output, which is dependent on the RRAM configuration. The more conjunctions are to be evaluated as true, the higher the power consumption.

The overall power consumption ranges from **0.82 mW** to **1.18 mW**. In combination with the read access time of 390 ps as described in Subsect. 4.3, this results in **0.32 pJ** to **0.46 pJ** of energy consumed per LUT read access. The average is, however, skewed towards lower power consumption due to the correlation with the number of minterms in the implemented function.

5   Case Study: Full Adder Realization Utilizing RRAM-Based LUTs

As a proof-of-concept and for the feasibility and functional correctness of the design, a full adder is implemented using the proposed 4-to-1 LUTs. Two LUTs are employed to separately realize the logic for the summing output (s) and the carry output (carry$_{out}$). Figure 9 shows the mapping and the necessary connections. The mapping in Fig. 9 is shown in a simplified version. Green squares represent a pair of RRAM cells in the LRS and HRS states corresponding to the non-negated input. Conversely, red squares represent the inverted inputs.

In Fig. 10, the inputs and outputs for a simulation of the full adder are plotted, showing the correctness of the logic implementation and, therefore, the feasibility of this application. The top plot shows both outputs, s and carry$_{out}$. Below it, the inputs are plotted for reference.

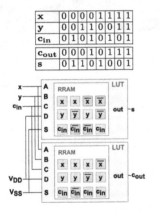

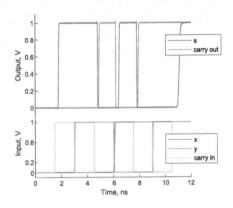

Fig. 9. Full Adder Mapping (Color figure online)

Fig. 10. Adder Behavior and Timing

Larger-scale implementations and benchmarks of the proposed architecture require higher-level frameworks or, preferably, integration into existing synthesis-toolflows and are therefore expected in later follow-up publications.

6   Conclusion

In this paper, an almost fully memristive LUT design was introduced. The proposed LUT architecture relies on an RRAM crossbar to implement the minterms of a Boolean function of its wordline inputs, and an additional output stage implements a column-wise disjunction. This is achieved through a novel mapping scheme for dense crossbars that utilizes the analog properties of the RRAM devices. The proposed RRAM-based LUT can realize all possible n-to-1 Boolean functions.

Further, the proposed RRAM-based LUT architecture was evaluated by using SPICE simulations based on 45 nm technology. The architecture does not suffer from the issues commonly associated with RRAM. The sneak path problem is utilized as part of the mapping technique and the design avoids all write operations during LUT evaluation to prolong the lifetime of the RRAM cells.

Acknowledgments. This work has been supported by DAIS (https://dais-project. eu/), which has received funding from the ECSEL Joint Undertaking (JU) under grant agreement No 101007273. The JU receives support from the European Union's Horizon 2020 research and innovation programme and Sweden, Spain, Portugal, Belgium, Germany, Slovenia, Czech Republic, Netherlands, Denmark, Norway, and Turkey.

References

1. Almurib, H.A., et al.: A memristor-based LUT for FPGAs. In: The 9th IEEE International Conference on Nano/Micro Engineered and Molecular Systems (NEMS), pp. 448–453 (2014)
2. Bazzi, H., et al.: RRAM-based non-volatile SRAM cell architectures for ultra-low-power applications. Analog Integr. Circ. Sig. Process **106**(2), 351–361 (2021)
3. Cadence Design System Inc: GPDK045 - 45nm CMOS 11M/2P generic PDK (2022)
4. Chen, Y.C., et al.: A novel peripheral circuit for RRAM-based LUT. In: 2012 IEEE International Symposium on Circuits and Systems (ISCAS), pp. 1811–1814 (2012)
5. Chua, L.: Memristor-the missing circuit element. IEEE Trans. Circ. Theory **18**(5), 507–519 (1971)
6. Cong, J., Xiao, B.: MRFPGA: a novel FPGA architecture with memristor-based reconfiguration. In: 2011 IEEE/ACM International Symposium on Nanoscale Architectures, pp. 1–8 (2011)
7. Cong, J., Xiao, B.: FPGA-RPI: a novel FPGA architecture with RRAM-based programmable interconnects. IEEE Trans. Very Large Scale Integr. (VLSI) Syst. **22**(4), 864–877 (2014)
8. De Nil, M., et al.: Ultra low power ASIP design for wireless sensor nodes. In: 2007 14th IEEE International Conference on Electronics, Circuits and Systems, pp. 1352–1355. IEEE (2007)
9. Gaillardon, P.E., et al.: GMS: generic memristive structure for non-volatile FPGAS. In: 2012 IEEE/IFIP 20th International Conference on VLSI and System-on-Chip (VLSI-SoC), pp. 94–98. IEEE (2012)
10. Giacomin, E., Gaillardon, P.E.: A resistive random access memory Addon for the NCSU FreePDK 45 nm. IEEE Trans. Nanotechnol. **18**, 68–72 (2018)
11. Guan, X., et al.: A spice compact model of metal oxide resistive switching memory with variations. IEEE Electron Device Lett. **33**(10), 1405–1407 (2012)
12. Guo, Y., et al.: A compact memristor-CMOS hybrid look-up-table design and potential application in FPGA. IEEE Trans. Comput. Aided Des. Integr. Circuits Syst. **36**(12), 2144–2148 (2017)

13. Kambayashi, Y.: Logic design of programmable logic arrays. IEEE Trans. Comput. **28**(09), 609–617 (1979)
14. Kim, K.H., et al.: A functional hybrid memristor crossbar-array/CMOS system for data storage and neuromorphic applications. Nano Lett. **12**(1), 389–395 (2012)
15. Kumar, T.N., et al.: A novel design of a memristor-based look-up table (LUT) for FPGA. In: 2014 IEEE Asia Pacific Conference on Circuits and Systems (APCCAS), pp. 703–706 (2014)
16. Kvatinsky, S., et al.: Memristor-based material implication (IMPLY) logic: design principles and methodologies. IEEE Trans. Very Large Scale Integr. (VLSI) Syst. **22**(10), 2054–2066 (2013)
17. Kvatinsky, S., et al.: Magic-memristor-aided logic. IEEE Trans. Circuits Syst. II Express Briefs **61**(11), 895–899 (2014)
18. Lin, W.P., et al.: A nonvolatile look-up table using ReRAM for reconfigurable logic. In: 2014 IEEE Asian Solid-State Circuits Conference (A-SSCC), pp. 133–136. IEEE (2014)
19. Nguyen, H.A.D., et al.: A classification of memory-centric computing. ACM J. Emerg. Technol. Comput. Syst. (JETC) **16**(2), 1–26 (2020)
20. Ochi, H., et al.: Via-switch FPGA: highly dense mixed-grained reconfigurable architecture with overlay via-switch crossbars. IEEE Trans. Very Large Scale Integr. (VLSI) Syst. **26**(12), 2723–2736 (2018)
21. Pellegrino, L., et al.: Multistate memory devices based on free-standing VO2/TIO2 microstructures driven by joule self-heating. Adv. Mater. **24**(21), 2929–2934 (2012)
22. Rai, S., et al.: A survey of FPGA logic cell designs in the light of emerging technologies. IEEE Access **9**, 91564–91574 (2021)
23. Sampath, M., et al.: Hybrid CMOS-memristor based FPGA architecture. In: 2015 International Conference on VLSI Systems, Architecture, Technology and Applications (VLSI-SATA), pp. 1–6 (2015)
24. Strukov, D.B., et al.: The missing memristor found. Nature **453**(7191), 80–83 (2008)
25. Tang, X., et al.: A high-performance low-power near-VT RRAM-based FPGA. In: 2014 International Conference on Field-Programmable Technology (FPT), pp. 207–214 (2014)
26. Tang, X., et al.: Circuit designs of high-performance and low-power RRAM-based multiplexers based on 4T(ransistor)1R(RAM) programming structure. IEEE Trans. Circuits Syst. I Regul. Pap. **64**(5), 1173–1186 (2017)
27. Tang, X., et al.: Post-P&R performance and power analysis for RRAM-based FPGAS. IEEE J. Emerg. Sel. Topics Circ. Syst. **8**(3), 639–650 (2018)
28. Tang, X., et al.: A RRAM-based FPGA for energy-efficient edge computing. In: 2020 Design, Automation & Test in Europe Conference & Exhibition (DATE), pp. 144-a-144-f (2020)
29. Tsekoura, I., et al.: An evaluation of energy efficient microcontrollers. In: 2014 9th International Symposium on Reconfigurable and Communication-Centric Systems-on-Chip (ReCoSoC), pp. 1–5. IEEE (2014)
30. Xie, L., et al.: Non-volatile look-up table based FPGA implementations. In: 2016 11th International Design & Test Symposium (IDT), pp. 165–170. IEEE (2016)
31. Xing, J., Serb, A., Khiat, A., Berdan, R., Xu, H., Prodromakis, T.: An FPGA-based instrument for EN-Masse RRAM characterization with ns pulsing resolution. IEEE Trans. Circuits Syst. I Regul. Pap. **63**(6), 818–826 (2016)
32. Xu, C., et al.: Design implications of memristor-based RRAM cross-point structures. In: 2011 Design, Automation & Test in Europe, pp. 1–6. IEEE (2011)

33. Zahoor, F., et al.: Resistive random access memory (RRAM): an overview of materials, switching mechanism, performance, multilevel cell (MLC) storage, modeling, and applications. Nanoscale Res. Lett. **15**(1), 1–26 (2020)
34. Zhou, Y.X., et al.: Nonvolatile reconfigurable sequential logic in a HFO 2 resistive random access memory array. Nanoscale **9**(20) (2017)

A Light-Weight Vision Transformer Toward Near Memory Computation on an FPGA

Takeshi Senoo, Ryota Kayanoma, Akira Jinguji, and Hiroki Nakahara[✉]

Tokyo Institute of Technology, Tokyo, Japan
nakahara.h.ad@m.titech.ac.jp

Abstract. Computer Vision AI is making remarkable advances in image recognition, object detection, and segmentation tasks. However, the model size continuously expands, necessitating dedicated hardware acceleration for the real-time processing of these tasks on embedded systems. The Vision Transformer (ViT) is gaining attention as a new approach to replace Convolutional Neural Networks (CNN) in image recognition tasks. However, ViT, while achieving high recognition accuracy, requires a complex structure and many parameters, making it difficult to implement in real time. Near-memory computing allows faster processing by closely placing data processing and memory access together. We are optimizing ViT for near-memory computation. We design a distributed on-chip memory suitable for near-memory computing and a calculation flow that closely integrates with it on an FPGA. This allows us to achieve more real-time image AI processing with higher recognition accuracy. With ImageNet2012 test images, the recognition accuracy of LW-ViT was 78.38% in the Top-1 category and 94.12% in the Top-5 category. Our implementation was 1.6 times faster than an embedded GPU while maintaining the same recognition accuracy. Compared with other FPGA implementations, while achieving a real-time processing time of 29.97 fps for camera images, the recognition accuracy was 6.6–10.2 points higher. Therefore, our implementation is suitable for real-time image recognition with high recognition accuracy.

1 Introduction

1.1 A Vision Transformer (ViT) for Real-Time Computer Vision Systems

Computer Vision AI is making remarkable progress in tasks such as image recognition [9], object detection [17], and segmentation [18], and is being adopted in various embedded systems. However, the model size is steadily increasing, and dedicated hardware acceleration is necessary for the real-time processing of these tasks on embedded systems. Processing Vision AI tasks have performance and power consumption limitations on embedded CPUs and GPUs. Therefore, a dedicated hardware accelerator is required. Hardware dedicated to image AI specializes in fast and efficient processing of image data and execution of complex neural network models. The hardware design dedicated to image AI features high parallel processing, high-bandwidth memory access, and low power consumption. This allows multiple image data to be processed simultaneously and its weights and intermediate results to be efficiently stored and accessed.

F. Palumbo et al. (Eds.): ARC 2023, LNCS 14251, pp. 338–353, 2023.
https://doi.org/10.1007/978-3-031-42921-7_23

Research on FPGA-based Vision AI [22] focuses on developing advanced architectures and optimization techniques. For example, efforts are being made to introduce dedicated matrix operation units [3], quantization techniques [11], sparsity [8], and the use of low-bit operations [5]. This is expected to improve the speed and efficiency of model inference.

Vision Transformer (ViT) [6] is attracting attention as a new approach to replace Convolutional Neural Network(CNN) [14] in image recognition tasks. Using transformer models makes it possible to extract feature representations of image data effectively. ViT has been reported to achieve superior recognition accuracy in image processing tasks compared to conventional CNNs. Further research and application are expected to improve ViT performance and applicability to various image recognition tasks. However, while ViT achieves high recognition accuracy, it requires a complex structure and many parameters, making it difficult to implement in real-time. Therefore, we propose a lightweight ViT and its hardware architecture to achieve real-time image recognition while achieving high recognition accuracy in image recognition tasks.

1.2 Near-Memory Computing for Vision AI Hardware

Near-memory computing is an important method in hardware implementation for deep learning image processing. In near-memory computing, the efficiency of the computation is improved by placing data processing and memory access closely together. This allows for high-speed data processing in image processing tasks. The advantages of near-memory computing are as follows. Firstly, efficient use of memory bandwidth can be mentioned. By performing data processing close to memory, the time for reading and writing data can be reduced, and memory bandwidth can be maximally utilized. In addition, the reduction of data movement is also a major advantage. Data movement is a major factor in energy consumption and delay, but in near-memory computing, data processing and memory access are placed closely together, significantly reducing data movement. As a result, energy efficiency is improved, and high-speed image processing is achieved. However, there are also challenges in the hardware implementation of near-memory computing. Integration with hardware is one such issue. To achieve near-memory computing, it is necessary to integrate the memory system and the computing processing unit closely. Therefore, even in ViT, it is necessary to convert the model for a limited size of on-chip memories and to design hardware.

1.3 Related Works

We summarize several papers on the hardware implementation of image-processing AI that utilizes near-memory computing. Numerous studies have applied Near Memory Computing to FPGAs. Chen et al. [3] proposed an energy-efficient dataflow architecture called Eyeriss for CNNs. It can be implemented on an FPGA, and because each Processing Element (PE) has its local memory, data reuse is optimized, and memory access is significantly reduced. Eyeriss can be interpreted as a type of near-memory computing approach. Chi et al. proposed a new architecture, PRIME, for neural network computation in Resistive Random Access Memory (ReRAM)-based main memory using Processing-in-Memory (PIM) architecture [4]. This architecture can efficiently compute convolutional neural networks (CNNs) while minimizing data movement. Gao et al. proposed TETRIS for efficient acceleration of neural networks utilizing 3D stack memory [7]. It employs near-memory computing within the 3D stack memory to improve spatial scalability. Hsieh et al. proposed MAERI, a scalable and flexible near-memory accelerator [10]. This architecture employs a reconfigurable dataflow architecture optimized for DNN computations, achieving high computational efficiency while minimizing data movement.

These studies provide new approaches to enhance performance and energy efficiency in the hardware implementation of image processing AI by leveraging near-memory computing.

1.4 Proposed Method

We adopt the near-memory computation and leverage the on-chip memory of FPGA as distributed memory to optimize hardware for image AI. We propose a lightweight ViT (Vision Transformer) structure suitable for hardware implementation. The MLP (Multi-Layer Perceptron), which tends to require a large memory size due to its large number of parameters, is converted to a point-wise convolution. Additionally, the Patch Embedding, which results in a complex hardware structure, is replaced with 2D convolution. Furthermore, we introduce fixed-point representation to improve computational efficiency. While adopting dynamic quantization with limited degradation in recognition accuracy, it incurs a latency disadvantage due to the need to compute the maximum value each time. We propose a pseudo-dynamic quantization method that precomputes the maximum value based on the statistical properties of the training dataset. We design a distributed on-chip memory suitable for near-memory computing and an operation flow closely coupled with them on FPGA. It achieves real-time processing while realizing high-precision image AI processing.

1.5 Organization of the Paper

The rest of the paper is organized as follows: Sect. 2 defines the vision transformer (ViT); Sect. 3 proposes the light-weight vision transformer (LW-ViT); Sect. 4 shows the architecture for a near-memory computation; Sect. 5 shows the experimental results; and Sect. 6 concludes the paper.

2 Definition

2.1 Linear Operation (Linear)

Let n be a bit precision, $x_i, y_i, w_i, z_i \in \{0,1\}$ be binary variables, $X = (x_0, x_1, \ldots, x_n)$ be the input, $Y = (y_0, y_1, \ldots, y_n)$ be the internal variable, $W = (w_0, w_1, \ldots, w_n)$ be the weight, f_{act} be the activation function, and $Z = (z_0, z_1, \ldots, z_n)$ be the the output. Note that, in this paper, a capital letter denotes an integer, while a small letter denotes a binary value. Figure 1 shows a circuit for **a linear operation (Linear)**. The following expression shows an operation for the Linear:

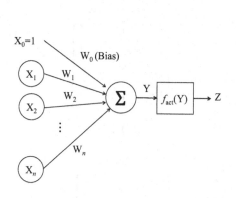

Fig. 1. Multi-layer Perceptron (MLP).

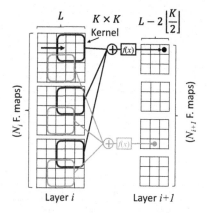

Fig. 2. Convolutional Operation.

$$Y = \sum_{i=0}^{n} W_i X_i,$$

$$Z = f_{act}(Y),$$

where X_0 is a constant one and W_0 denotes **a bias** which corrects the deviation of the given data. Typically, the activation function is realized by a sigmoid, a tanh, a ReLU [15], and so on. In the paper, we use the ReLU function suitable for hardware realization.

2.2 Convolutional Layer

A convolutional deep neural network (CNN) consists of **a 2D convolutional layer, a pooling layer**, and a classification layer. Each layer consists of multiple **feature maps**. First, the feature map reacts to corresponding subdivided training data by 2D convolutional layers with pooling layers to recognize the input image. Then, the classifier selects the appropriate reactions from feature maps. Usually, the classifier is realized by the fully connected neural network. In this paper, for layer i, K_i denotes the kernel size, N_i denotes the number of feature maps, and L_i denotes the feature map size. Figure 2 shows the 2D convolution operation. It computes the output by shifting a $K \times K$ size **kernel**. For (x, y) at the output feature map value $i + 1$, the following MAC (multiply-accumulation) operation is performed:

$$Y_{i+1,x,y} = \sum_{k=0}^{N_i-1} \left(\sum_{m=0}^{K-1} \sum_{n=0}^{K-1} X_{k,x+m,y+n} W_{k,m,n} \right) \quad (1)$$

$$Z_{i+1,x,y} = f_{act}(Y_{i+1,x,y}).$$

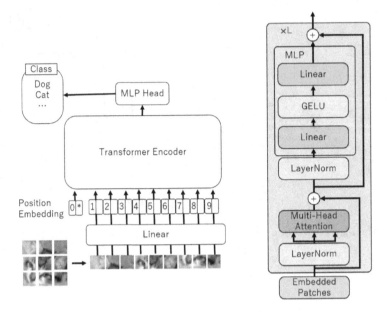

Fig. 3. Vision Transformer (ViT).

In the 2D convolutional operation, Z is mapped to (x, y) at the output feature map $i + 1$. In the fully connected layer, $L_i = 1$ and $K_i = 1$. By inserting the non-linear and low-imaging operations into the convolution layers, we can reduce the number of computations in the convolution layers while obtaining the movement invariance. We call this **a pooling operation**, which can be realized by a simple circuit. In this paper, we implement the average-pooling operation. The computation can be calculated by multiplying a fixed coefficient of 1 divided by the number of pixels to calculate and add the average value. In this paper, calculating the average value of a 2×2 region is equivalent to a convolution operation with a weight of 0.25.

2.3 Vision Transformer

Figure 3 shows the Vision Transformer (ViT). ViT leverages the features of transformer models in image recognition tasks. Transformer models use self-attention mechanisms and positional encoding to extract feature representations of input images. ViT consists of two main components: an encoder and a decoder. The encoder converts input images into feature maps and extracts feature representations using positional encoding and a self-attention mechanism. The decoder takes feature representations from the encoder as input and performs the final class classification. In this section, we will describe in detail the structure of the encoder, the decoder, the self-attention mechanism, and positional encoding. The next chapter will explain how to replace these with structures suitable for inference hardware.

Encoder: Transforms the input image into a feature map and extracts significant features. The encoder consists of multiple layers, including the following elements. It splits the input image into small patches by patching and vectorizes each patch. Patch Embedding applies a linear transformation to the patch vectors to generate feature representations. Positional Encoding encodes the positional information of the patches, providing the model with spatial information. Self-Attention learns the interrelationships between patches, further refining the feature representations. **Decoder:** takes feature representations from the encoder as input and performs the final class classification. The decoder includes components of typical neural networks, such as fully connected layers and softmax functions. Note that we only consider image processing tasks, so the decoder is not subject to implementation. **Self-Attention:** is a central element of transformer models that learn the interrelationships between patches. The self-attention mechanism calculates three vectors: query, key, and value, determining the importance of each patch. This enables the model to focus its attention on important features. **Positional Encoding:** is used to provide the model with the positional information of the patches. Positional encoding generates a vector corresponding to the position of the patch using sine and cosine functions, which are integrated into the feature representation. This allows the model to consider the spatial relationships of the input image.

3 Light-Weight Vision Transformer (LW-ViT)

This chapter will replace ViT with a structure suitable for near-memory hardware.

3.1 Point-Wise Convolution

Point-wise convolution is a Convolutional Neural Network (CNN) type and refers to convolution operations with a kernel size of 1×1. In this operation, independent convolutions are performed for each input channel at each position in the input tensor.

The main advantages of point-wise convolution are as follows:

Dimension Reduction: Point-wise convolution reduces the number of channels in the input tensor. For example, if the number of channels in the input tensor is C and the number of filters in the point-wise convolution is K, the number of channels in the output tensor is K. This can reduce the number of model parameters and computational cost.

Introduction of Nonlinearity: Point-wise convolution can generate nonlinear feature maps as it has different weights for each channel. This makes it easier for the model to learn more complex functions. On the other hand, traditional MLP (Multi-Layer Perceptron) has a more constrained representational capacity as the fully connected layer applies the same weights to all input elements.

Network Flexibility: Point-wise convolution enhances network flexibility by transforming feature maps at specific locations within the model. This allows the model to learn the interactions between channels and combine features. Furthermore, point-wise convolution can be combined with other convolution operations, further improving the model's representational ability.

Improved Computational Efficiency: Point-wise convolution significantly reduces computational cost due to its 1×1 kernel size. Particularly, since the convolution operation does not depend on the spatial dimensions of the input tensor, it is easy to speed up through parallel processing and hardware acceleration.

With these advantages, point-wise convolution has superior features to the MLP structure. Therefore, point-wise convolution is an essential element in image processing and the design of convolutional neural networks.

3.2   Meta Former

Meta-Former [19] aims to apply the features of the transformer model to image recognition tasks. Meta-Former modifies the encoder part of the Vision Transformer to extract image features. Among them, Pool-former is a major component of Meta-Former.

Characteristics of Pool-Former: Pool-former is a pooling mechanism used within the encoder of Meta-Former. While the traditional Vision Transformer extracted feature representations using self-attention, Pool-former adopts a different approach by introducing pooling.

Pooling Mechanism: In Pool-former, instead of self-attention, a combination of convolutional and pooling layers generates feature maps. The pooling layer plays the role of downsampling image features, and the convolutional layer extracts local features. This combination balances preserving information, improving memory efficiency, and the computational efficiency of convolution.

Pool-former has several advantages over traditional ViT:

Improved Memory Efficiency: In Pool-former, by combining convolution and pooling, the dimensions of the feature map are reduced, thereby reducing memory usage.

Improved Computational Efficiency: The combination of pooling and convolutional layers reduces the computation in convolution operations, enabling faster processing.

Model Interpretability: In Pool-former, since pooling and convolution operations are performed, the internal processing of the model becomes more interpretable.

Improved Robustness: Pool-former, by combining convolution and pooling, can extract local features and thus acquire feature representations robust to data variations and noise.

Due to these advantages, Pool-former in Meta-Former exhibits superior performance in improved memory and computational efficiency, increased interpretability, and enhanced robustness compared to traditional Vision Transformer. The memory and computational efficiency improvements make it well-suited for near-memory computing and easily implementable on FPGA architectures with distributed on-chip memory.

3.3   Patch Embedding by Convolution

There are several advantages to replacing the patch embedding mechanism with convolution operations. These advantages are explained below.

Capturing Global Features: The patch embedding mechanism divides an input image into small patches and vectorizes each patch. However, convolution is performed on the entire input image using a filter in convolution operations. This allows you to capture global features directly. By considering a wider range of information than the patch embedding mechanism, feature extraction with a wider field of view is possible.

Improved Computational Efficiency: The patch embedding mechanism performs independent transformations for each input image patch, increasing computation. On the other hand, convolution operations can efficiently extract features by sharing convolution kernels. In particular, convolution operations have improved speed and are suitable for parallel computation and hardware acceleration.

Sharing Spatial Information: The patch embedding mechanism considers positional information by applying positional encoding to each patch. On the other hand, convolution operations can share local information within the range of the convolution kernel. This promotes the sharing of spatial information in feature representations. In particular, convolution operations can efficiently extract these features if similar features exist in close positions within the image.

Improved Generalization Performance: Convolution operations can capture statistical characteristics of image data by using the same filter in different areas of the image. Therefore, it can demonstrate better generalization performance even for images in areas not included in the training data. While the patch embedding mechanism considers positional information through positional encoding, more powerful feature extraction is possible through convolution operations, allowing for constructing models with higher generalization performance.

Thus, by replacing the patch embedding mechanism with convolution operations, you can enjoy benefits such as capturing global features, improving computational efficiency, sharing spatial information, and improving generalization performance.

3.4 Batch Normalization

Layer Normalization (LayerNorm) [1] and Batch Normalization(BatchNorm) [12] are two representative approaches of normalization techniques in neural networks. In this paper, we replace existing LayerNorm with BatchNorm. We discuss the benefits of this.

Reduced Dependence on Mini-batch Size: BatchNorm normalizes using statistics (mean and variance) of each sample in the mini-batch. This shares statistical information for individual samples within a mini-batch, making it less affected by the size of the mini-batch. In contrast, LayerNorm calculates the mean and variance individually for each sample, which may decrease performance when the mini-batch size is small or when the distribution of samples within a mini-batch is different.

Applicability to Sequential Data and Variable Length Inputs: BatchNorm can be applied to sequential data and variable-length inputs as it calculates the mean and variance for each sample in the mini-batch. Since LayerNorm is calculated individually for each sample, its application may be limited when dealing with sequential data or variable length inputs.

Improved Training Speed: BatchNorm improves the convergence speed of learning by using statistical information within the mini-batch. On the other hand, since LayerNorm is calculated individually for each sample, the effect of improving the speed of learning is limited.

Regularization: BatchNorm has a regularization effect on the model by normalizing based on statistical information within the mini-batch. This prevents overfitting and can improve the generalization performance of the model. On the other hand, since LayerNorm is calculated individually for each sample, the regularization effect may be limited.

From these advantages, BatchNorm has superior characteristics to LayerNorm regarding reduced dependence on mini-batch size, applicability to sequential data and variable length inputs, improved learning speed, and regularization effects.

3.5 Pseudo-Dynamic Quantization

We conducted a preliminary study. We trained Pool-former using Training Aware Quantization, but the training did not converge. We analyzed the cause. In ViT, there is a characteristic of updating the values of activation functions by minute amounts during the warm-up period at the beginning of training. We had no choice but to use float32 precision for model training. Therefore, we adopt post-training quantization, which trains with float32 precision and quantizes when porting to hardware.

To efficiently utilize the arithmetic unit, we propose pseudo-dynamic quantization. Let the maximum absolute value of the dynamic range of input X be $|Max(X)|$, and quantize the input value to n bits by truncating the fractional part after multiplying 2^{n-1} by the value normalized to 0.0–1.0 by $|Max(X)|$. Compared to static quantization that directly multiplies by 2^{n-1}, it can efficiently quantize even when the dynamic range is extremely large or small. The dynamic range in the LW-ViT model is wide, and the number of bits is limited, so dynamic quantization is superior. Since the learned weight W is fixed at inference time, the pre-computed value $|Max(W)|$ is used. On the other hand, the maximum value of the input X depends on the input image, so additional computation is required to find the maximum value, which requires additional circuits during hardware implementation and extends the latency. In the LW-ViT model, the calculation results of the encoder part during inference tend to be within a certain range. Therefore, the maximum value of the inference result of the training image is used as a fixed value to substitute and eliminate the maximum value search process. We propose a pseudo-dynamic n-bit quantization as shown below:

$$Y_Q = \frac{2^n}{|Max(X_{i+1})|} ReLU \left(\frac{|Max(X)||Max(W)|}{2^{n-1}2^{n-1}} Z_Q + Bias \right).$$

To obtain the computed value Y_Q after quantization, normalize the result Z_Q of the convolution process with the normalized value of the quantization bit (e.g., 2^{8-1} if $n = 8$), and multiply the maximum values $|Max(X)|$, $|Max(W)|$ of the weight and input value. Then add the bias value and pass it through the activation function (ReLU

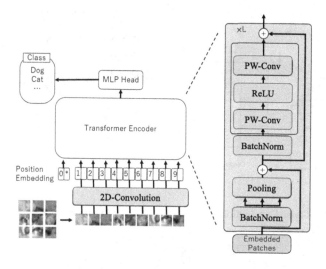

Fig. 4. Light-weight Vision Transformer (LW-ViT).

function in this study). To reduce inter-layer memory communication bandwidth, quantize again. Normalize by the maximum value $|Max(X_{i+1})|$ of the next layer and round off with the quantization bit. Here, we substitute the maximum value of the input value of the target layer $|Max(X)|$ and the maximum value of the next layer $|Max(X_{i+1})|$ with the maximum value of the test image.

3.6 LW-ViT

Figure 4 shows the Vision Transformer (ViT). The LW-ViT we developed performs processing with the Transformer Encoder for each patch and classification with the MLP Head, similar to the overall structure of ViT. It performs 2D-Convolution instead of Patch Embedded. While the Transformer Encoder block of ViT was composed of an Attention and an MLP part, LW-ViT comprises Pooling and Convolution layers. The activation function is replaced with the easy-to-implement ReLU. We use BatchNorm, which is easy to implement on hardware. Therefore, LW-ViT has a structure that is easier to implement on hardware than ViT.

4   Near-Memory Architecture for LW-ViT

LW-ViT simplifies the complex attention structure into a simple pooling layer. In addition, a Convolution layer with shared weights realizes the Linear layer, which holds many parameters. Therefore, LW-ViT only needs to realize convolution operations, pooling operations, and skip connections.

Figure 5 shows point-wise convolution. Each pixel for each channel is grouped into a vector and convolved with learned weights. Therefore, it is compatible with near-memory computation realized by on-chip distributed memory. These operations are

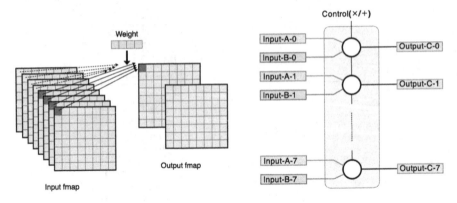

Fig. 5. Point-wise Convolution.   Fig. 6. Vector Operation.

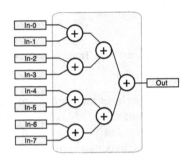

Fig. 7. Adder Tree.

realized by multiplication for each vector element. On the other hand, skip connections perform vector element addition of the calculation result vector of each layer and the input vector. Therefore, a circuit that switches between vector addition and multiplication with a control circuit is efficient in terms of hardware utilization. Figure 6 shows vector operations.

Figure 7 shows an addition tree. In point-wise convolution, the addition of each element is necessary. The addition tree realizes this. By switching these circuits with a control circuit, we can realize each operation of LW-Convolution. Figure 8 shows the Processing element (PE). We switch the configuration for each layer of LW-ViT and perform operations on a vector-by-vector basis.

Figure 9 shows the overall configuration of the circuit. Trained parameters are stored in DDR memory and loaded into the weight buff for each Point-wise operation layer. On the other hand, input images are loaded from the host's DDR memory to Fmap buf and computed rapidly with a distributed near-memory architecture. These are appropriately controlled by the data selection circuits indicated in green in Fig. 9. Because the proposed architecture is simple due to the LW-ViT structure, it can rapidly process LW-ViT by performing parallel operations on parameters and input/output data stored in the on-chip memory on an FPGA.

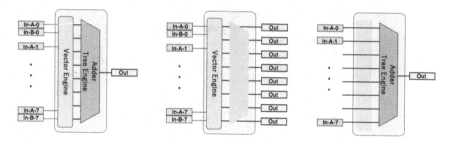

Fig. 8. Processing Element (PE) (left). Vector operation mode (center) and adder tree mode (right).

5 Experimental Results

5.1 Training Results of an LW-ViT

We designed LW-ViT. The detailed structure is shown in Table 1. LW-ViT was trained on the ImageNet2012 1K benchmark dataset. The framework used was PyTorch 1.13.0 [16], and the GPU was NVIDIA A6000. After training for 300 epochs and evaluating with ImageNet2012 test images, the recognition accuracy of LW-ViT was 78.38% in the Top-1 category and 94.12% in the Top-5 category.

5.2 FPGA Implementation

We implemented the proposed LW-ViT on the Xilinx Inc. Zynq UltraScale+ MPSoC ZCU102 evaluation board, which has the Xilinx Zynq UltraScale+ MPSoC FPGA (ZU9EG, 274,080 LUTs, 548,160 FFs, 1,824 18Kb BRAMs, 2,520 DSP48Es). We used the Xilinx Inc. Vitis HLS 2022.2 and Vivado 2022.2 with a timing constraint 200 MHz. Our implementation used 109,644 LUTs, 95,264 FFs, 1,706 18Kb BRAMs, and 1,016 DSP48Es. Also, it satisfied the timing constraint for real-time applications. Since our architecture computed an image with 17.3 msec, the number of frames per second (FPS) was 57.8. We measured the dynamic board power consumption: It was 14.9 W. Thus, the performance per power efficiency was 2.32 (FPS/W).

5.3 Comparison with Other Implementations

Table 2 shows a comparison with other implementations. We compared classification accuracy and inference time (throughput) using the ImageNet2012 image dataset for 1000 classes. The measurement of the execution time was done for each image. The batch size was 1, and the time from when the inference was started with the image stored

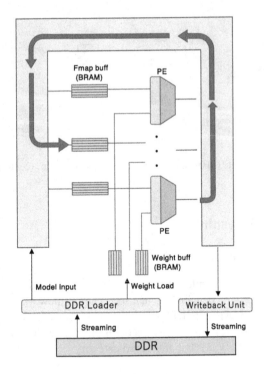

Fig. 9. Overall Architecture.

in the CPU memory to when the inference result was written back to the CPU memory was measured. The GPU used for comparison was Nvidia's Jetson AGX Xavier. Python3.9 and PyTorch1.13.0 were used for inference on the GPU. Our implementation maintained the same recognition accuracy and was 1.6 times faster than the GPU. Compared to other FPGA implementations, it achieved a real-time processing time of 29.97 fps for camera images, while the recognition accuracy was 6.6–10.2 points higher. Therefore, our implementation is suitable for real-time image recognition with high recognition accuracy.

Table 1. Detailed our LW-ViT structure.

Stage	Output Size	Details
Patch Embedding	$16 \times 16 \times 64$	2D-Convolutional Operation
Transformer Encoder Stage 1	$8 \times 8 \times 64$	Transformer Block including: 2×2 Pooling with PW-Conv, ReLU, PW-Conv Four Blocks
Transformer Encoder Stage 2	$4 \times 4 \times 128$	Transformer Block including: 2×2 Pooling with PW-Conv, ReLU, PW-Conv Four Blocks
Transformer Encoder Stage 3	$2 \times 2 \times 256$	Transformer Block including: 2×2 Pooling with PW-Conv, ReLU, PW-Conv Four Blocks
Transformer Encoder Stage 4	$1 \times 1 \times 512$	Transformer Block including: 2×2 Pooling with PW-Conv, ReLU, PW-Conv Four Blocks
Classification Head	1×1000	Fully-connected layer followed by softmax

Table 2. Comparison with embedded platforms with respect to the ImageNet2012 Classification Task (Batch size is 1).

	Platform	Model	Prec	Freq	Top-1 Acc.	Throughput
Ours	ZCU102 (ZU9EG)	LW-ViT	INT8	200 MHz	78.3%	57.8 fps
GPU	Jetson AGX Xavier	LW-ViT	FP16	1.37 GHz	78.9%	35.9 fps
Synetgy [21]	Ultra96 (ZU3EG)	DiracDeltaNet	INT1-4	250 MHz	68.3%	96.5 fps
MobNetV1 [20]	ZCU102 (ZU9EG)	MobileNet	INT8	333 MHz	68.1%	809.8 fps
MobNetV2 [13]	10AX115N4F40E2SG	MobileNetV2	INT16	250 MHz	71.7%	658.0 fps

6 Conclusion

ViT has been attracting attention as a new approach to replace CNN in image recognition tasks. However, it was difficult to implement in real-time due to its complex structure and the large number of parameters required, despite its high recognition accuracy. We proposed a lightweight ViT model designed for near-memory computation. We designed a distributed on-chip memory architecture suitable for near-memory computing on FPGA and an operation flow closely coupled to it, realizing fast and efficient image AI processing. When evaluated with ImageNet2012 test images, the recognition accuracy of LW-ViT was 78.38% in the Top-1 category and 94.12% in the Top-5 category. Our implementation maintained the same recognition accuracy and was 1.6 times faster than the embedded GPU. Compared to other FPGA implementations, it achieved a real-time processing time of 29.97 fps for camera images, while the recognition accuracy was 6.6–10.2 points higher. Therefore, we demonstrated that our implementation is suitable for real-time image recognition and image recognition tasks requiring high recognition accuracy.

Acknowledgments. This research is partly supported by the Grants in Aid for Scientistic Research of JSPS.

References

1. Ba, J.L., Kiros, J.R., Hinton, G.E.: Layer Normalization. arXiv preprint: arXiv:1607.06450 (2016)
2. Chen, Y., et al.: DaDianNao: a machine-learning supercomputer. In: Proceedings of the 47th Annual IEEE/ACM International Symposium on Microarchitecture, pp. 609–622 (2014)
3. Chen, Y.H., Emer, J., Sze, V.: Eyeriss: a spatial architecture for energy-efficient dataflow for convolutional neural networks. In: Proceedings of the 43rd Annual International Symposium on Computer Architecture, pp. 367–379 (2016)
4. Chi, P., et al.: PRIME: a novel processing-in-memory architecture for neural network computation in reram-based main memory. In: Proceedings of the 43rd Annual International Symposium on Computer Architecture, pp. 27–39 (2016)
5. Courbariaux, M., Bengio, Y., David, J.: BinaryConnect: training deep neural networks with binary weights during propagations. In: Proceedings of the 28th International Conference on Neural Information Processing Systems, pp. 3123–3131 (2015)
6. Dosovitskiy, A., et al.: An image is worth 16x16 words: transformers for image recognition at scale. arXiv preprint: arXiv:2010.11929 (2020)
7. Gao, M., Ayers, G., Kozyrakis, C.: TETRIS: scalable and efficient neural network acceleration with 3D memory. In: Proceedings of the Twenty-Second International Conference on Architectural Support for Programming Languages and Operating Systems, pp. 751–764 (2017)
8. Han, S., Pool, J., Tran, J., Dally, W.: Learning both weights and connections for efficient neural networks. In: Proceedings of the 28th International Conference on Neural Information Processing Systems, pp. 1135–1143 (2015)
9. He, K., Zhang, X., Ren, S., Sun, J.: Deep residual learning for image recognition. In: Proceedings of the IEEE Conference on Computer Vision and Pattern Recognition, pp. 770–778 (2016)
10. Hsieh, K., et al.: The Cacti 9.0 manual. In: Proceedings of the 23rd International Conference on Architectural Support for Programming Languages and Operating Systems, pp. 671–684 (2018)
11. Hubara, I., Courbariaux, M., Soudry, D., El-Yaniv, R., Bengio, Y.: Binarized neural networks. In: Proceedings of the 30th International Conference on Neural Information Processing Systems, pp. 4107–4115 (2016)
12. Ioffe, S., Szegedy, C.: Batch normalization: accelerating deep network training by reducing internal covariate shift. In: Proceedings of the 32nd International Conference on Machine Learning, pp. 448–456 (2015)

13. Knapheide, J., Stabernack, B., Kuhnke, M.: A high throughput MobileNetV2 FPGA implementation based on a flexible architecture for depthwise separable convolution. In: Proceedings of the International Conference on Field-Programmable Logic and Applications (FPL), pp. 277–283 (2020)
14. Krizhevsky, A., Sutskever, I., Hinton, G.E.: ImageNet classification with deep convolutional neural networks. In: Proceedings of the 25th International Conference on Neural Information Processing Systems, pp. 1097–1105 (2012)
15. Nair, V., Hinton, G.E.: Hinton, rectified linear units improve restricted Boltzmann machines. In: Proceedings of the 27th International Conference on Machine Learning, pp. 807–814 (2010)
16. Paszke, A., et al.: PyTorch: an imperative style, high-performance deep learning library. In: Advances in Neural Information Processing Systems, vol. 32, pp. 8024–8035 (2019)
17. Ren, S., He, K., Girshick, R., Sun, J.: Faster R-CNN: towards real-time object detection with region proposal networks. In: Proceedings of the IEEE Conference on Computer Vision and Pattern Recognition, pp. 1137–1149 (2016)
18. Ronneberger, O., Fischer, P., Brox, T.: U-Net: convolutional networks for biomedical image segmentation. In: Proceedings of the International Conference on Medical Image Computing and Computer-Assisted Intervention, pp. 234–241 (2015)
19. Yu, W., et al.: MetaFormer is actually what you need for vision (2022). arXiv:2111.11418
20. Wu, D., et al.: A high-performance CNN processor based on FPGA for MobileNets. In: Proceedings of the International Conference on Field Programmable Logic and Applications (FPL), pp. 136–143 (2019)
21. Yang, Y., et al.: Synetgy: algorithm-hardware co-design for ConvNet accelerators on embedded FPGAs. In: Proceedings of the International Symposium on Field-Programmable Gate Arrays (FPGA), pp. 23–32 (2019)
22. Zhang, C., Li, P., Sun, G., Guan, Y., Xiao, B., Cong, J.: Optimizing FPGA-based accelerator design for deep convolutional neural networks. In: Proceedings of the 2015 ACM/SIGDA International Symposium on Field-Programmable Gate Arrays, pp. 161–170 (2015)

PhD Forum Papers

Radiation Tolerant Reconfigurable Hardware Architecture Design Methodology

Eike Trumann[1]([✉])(ID), Gia Bao Thieu[1](ID), Johannes Schmechel[1],
Kirsten Weide-Zaage[2](ID), Katharina Schmidt[3], Dorian Hagenah[3],
and Guillermo Payá Vayá[1](ID)

[1] Chair for Chip Design for Embedded Computing, Technische Universität
Braunschweig, Braunschweig, Germany
{eike.trumann,g.thieu,j.schmechel,g.paya-vaya}@tu-braunschweig.de
[2] RESRI Group, Institute of Microelectronic Systems (IMS), Leibniz Universität
Hannover, Hanover, Germany
kirsten.weide-zaage@ims.uni-hannover.de
[3] Bundeswehr Research Institute for Protective Technologies and CBRN Protection
(WIS), Munster, Germany

Abstract. The purpose of this research topic is to investigate the properties of reconfigurable devices (i.e., FPGA) under a radiation environment to finally propose a new methodology to design and evaluate cost-effective radiation hardening measures for reconfigurable devices. As a first step, the radiation hardness of an existing common off-the-shelf reconfigurable hardware device (FPGA) is investigated with regard to different radiation sources, including fast neutron radiation and gamma radiation. Therefore, an experiment is proposed to evaluate in run-time the changes on the memory configuration logic (e.g., configuration of each LUT, routing switches, connection boxes, DSPs, ...) and memory user logic (e.g., content of each Block RAM, Flip-Flop, Distributed RAM implemented on LUTs, ...). As a result, the chosen FPGA will be modelled in terms of fault probability of each FPGA component for a given radiation environment. These models will be integrated in a new simulation fault injection environment. In a third step, new cost-effective radiation hardening mechanisms, including configuration adjustments, design redundancy, and specialized hardware designs with error detection and correction, will be proposed and evaluated using the previously proposed environment. The proposed radiation hardening mechanisms shall be verified by using real-world radiation sources. The goal is to provide a new methodology for the design of radiation tolerant hardware architecture for FPGA devices.

Keywords: Radiation Hardness · Fault Injection · FPGA

1 Introduction and Motivation

Fault tolerance of embedded processing systems used e.g. in industrial, aerospace, or other mission-critical applications has been a vivid research topic for the last

F. Palumbo et al. (Eds.): ARC 2023, LNCS 14251, pp. 357–360, 2023.
https://doi.org/10.1007/978-3-031-42921-7_24

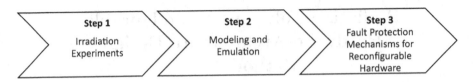

Fig. 1. Overview of the project steps

decades. Especially in aerospace applications and around particle and nuclear physics research facilities, the radiation hardness with respect to different kinds of radiation is of interest [1]. For many of those applications, reconfigurable hardware devices, such as Field Programmable Gate Arrays (FPGAs), are of interest, as they allow a more flexible and cost-effective implementation of hardware designs for low-volume applications. Although dedicated radiation-hardened chips are available on the market, often both the high cost and low performance compared to recent non-radiation-hardened devices hinder widespread usage of those devices for computationally demanding tasks. Therefore, there is a trend of using lower cost commercial off-the-shelf (COTS) components even in harsh environments while implementing additional safeguards against radiation effects [3].

The goal of this PhD research topic is to measure and model the effects of different radiation sources on FPGA devices, and propose and evaluate methods to reduce the risk of radiation effects. A model-based methodology will be proposed and validated though real-world radiation experiments. The proposed methodology should facilitate the usage of cheaper COTS FPGA devices in radiation-prone environments, leading to cost savings as well as increased flexibility in hardware design.

For measurements of irradiation effects in the first project phase, access to a fast neutron source, a gamma radiation burst source, and a cobalt-60 source has been granted. To estimate the effects of these different radiation sources, as a first step, shown in Fig. 1, the radiation influence on a commercial available Xilinx Artix-7 FPGA device was measured and a first statistical fault model is generated, distinguishing both user and configuration memory. The irradiation experiments are described in detail in Sect. 2. On the basis of the statistical observations from those irradiation tests, the error-prone parts can be identified. To allow the development of radiation hardening mechanisms, the statistical model of irradiation effects can be used to build a fault injection simulation environment (see Step 2 and 3 in Fig. 1). Finally, the proposed radiation hardening mechanisms can be validated through real-world experiments using the facilitated radiation sources.

2   First FPGA Irradiation Experiment Results

To investigate the effects of different radiation sources, a common hardware testbed has been developed [6] (see Fig. 2). The testbed consists of eight Arty-A7 35T FPGA evaluation boards, containing Artix-7 FPGA devices. The boards are arranged at different distances (Fig. 3) to the radiation sources to allow statistical modeling of the irradiation influence regarding distance. To detect faults

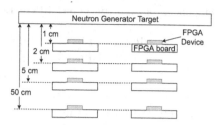

Fig. 2. Experiment setup with FPGA next to neutron generator target [6]

Fig. 3. Overview of the positioning of multiple FPGA boards [6]

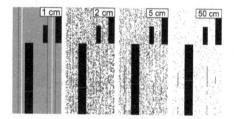

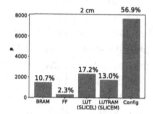

Fig. 4. Heatmap of Radiation Influences on the FPGA Floorplan [6]

Fig. 5. Distribution of Measured Bitflips between Different Kinds of Memory [6]

in user and configuration memory, the FPGA bitstream is read back regularly using the standard JTAG mechanism after writing the memory contents into the bitstream. To detect hard faults (i.e., faults that persist after the end of the irradiation and a reconfiguration of the FPGA), the reference bitstream is also used to completely reconfigure the device periodically every 30 min. Currently, fault errors can be directly detected in Block RAM, flip-flops, look-up-tables, and look-up-table RAM. The occurrence of faults in the configuration memory can be also be detected, but cannot be directly interpreted, and therefore the effect those have on designs running on the device needs further investigation.

This experimental setup was tested and evaluated under 2.45 MeV neutron irradiation [6]. 56,255 errors in the memory contents and no hard faults were detected during 8 h of irradiation. Figure 4 shows the heatmap of the detected errors in the four distances. A random distribution of the errors over the FPGA device can be seen. Figure 5 exemplarily shows the distribution of the errors among the different memory components at 2 cm. The probabilities for a bit error per bit, memory component and neutron fluence was calculated for 2.45 MeV neutron irradiation (Table 1). It can be seen that the flip-flops and LUTRAM are most prone to neutron irradiation. Hence, future fault tolerant hardware architectures must have more protection in the user level.

3   Further Work and Conclusions

Based on the statistical model derived from the irradiation experiments, in the 2nd and 3rd step (shown in Fig. 1), a fault injection simulation framework will

Table 1. Soft-Error Probabilities [%/(Bit·$\frac{neutrons}{cm^2}$)] per Fluence and Bit for the Memory Components of the Arty-A7 35T FPGA Board under 2.45 MeV Neutron Irradiation [6]

BRAM	FF	LUT	LUTRAM	Config. Mem
2.53E−09	1.93E−08	7.55E−09	1.35E−08	3.10E−09

be implemented for the evaluation of new radiation hardening hardware mechanisms. For this, existing fault injection frameworks might be extended to analyze the statistical findings from the irradiation effects. This framework shall allow the injection of faults in both user and configuration memory by simulating the target hardware architecture [2] or directly injecting faults on a target FPGA device via partial reconfiguration [5]. It is worth mentioning that the radiation hardening hardware mechanism should make use of the run-time reconfiguration capabilities of recent FPGA devices, which can be used to detect faults on the user and configuration memory [4]. Using these capabilities, design level mitigations for hard faults shall also be investigated. The implemented fault injection simulation framework together with the proposed radiation hardening mechanisms will be validated by means of real experiments.

Cost and other disadvantages of radiation-hardened devices are a major burden in many use cases. Providing a cost-effective and easy-to-implement solution for radiation concerns might increase the performance of reconfigurable hardware devices in those applications while at the same time reducing development and deployment costs. The statistical model of the radiation effects might be used by other researchers and engineers to propose further radiation hardening mechanisms while saving cost for their own irradiation experiments.

References

1. Autran, J.L., Munteanu, D.: Soft Errors: From Particles to Circuits. CRC Press, Boca Raton (2017)
2. Nowosielski, R., et al.: FLINT: layout-oriented FPGA-based methodology for fault tolerant ASIC design. In: Design, Automation & Test in Europe Conference & Exhibition (DATE), pp. 297–300 (2015). https://doi.org/10.7873/DATE.2015.0278
3. Pellish, J.: Commercial off-the-shelf (COTS) Electronics Reliability for Space Applications. NASA (2018)
4. Reorda, M.S., Sterpone, L., Ullah, A.: An error-detection and self-repairing method for dynamically and partially reconfigurable systems. IEEE Trans. Comput. **66**(6), 1022–1033 (2017). https://doi.org/10.1109/TC.2016.2607749
5. Sterpone, L., Violante, M.: A new partial reconfiguration-based fault-injection system to evaluate SEU effects in SRAM-based FPGAs. IEEE Trans. Nucl. Sci. **54**(4), 965–970 (2007). https://doi.org/10.1109/TNS.2007.904080
6. Thieu, G.B., et al.: A probability soft-error model for a 28-nm SRAM-based FPGA under neutron radiation exposure. In: 24th International Conference on Thermal, Mechanical and Multi-Physics Simulation and Experiments in Microelectronics and Microsystems (EuroSimE) (2023). https://doi.org/10.1109/EuroSimE56861.2023.10100757

A Control Data Acquisition System Architecture for MPSoC-FPGAs in Computed Tomography

Daniele Passaretti$^{(\boxtimes)}$ ⓘ and Thilo Pionteck ⓘ

Otto-von-Guericke University of Magdeburg, Magdeburg, Germany
{daniele.passaretti,thilo.pionteck}@ovgu.de

Abstract. This research topic aims to investigate system models and hardware architectures of Computed Tomography scanners to provide the plug-and-play capability to add new internal components and to process images in real-time to meet requirements for interventional procedures. For this purpose, different medical requirements have been investigated, considering their implications for system and hardware designers. Based on these preliminary results, a new control data acquisition system architecture for MPSoC FPGAs has been proposed. This architecture is designed to control/synchronize all CT components and to collect and process data on-the-fly. A CT architectural model, a configurable dataflow architecture for data acquisition, a mixed-precision image data processing core, and a mechanism to support isolation on MPSoC-FPGAs have been proposed for this scope. Finally, these results were used to assemble an open-interface CT scanner, where the proposed architecture was validated and evaluated in terms of plug-and-play capability, timing, and hardware performance.

Keywords: System-on-Chip · Computer Architecture · Computed Tomography · Cyber-Physical Systems · Data Acquisition Systems

1 Introduction and Motivation

Computed Tomography (CT) is widely used in medical radiology, providing a non-invasive approach to generate 2D/3D images of a patient's internal organs [2]. In order to counteract the growth of tumors, physicians have proposed new image-guided techniques for tumor ablation, opening new challenges for the design of new multimodal imaging devices. These devices have two main challenges: the interoperability of new sensors/actuators and the generation of real-time images. To address these issues and to support researchers and physicians in exploring new medical techniques, Academia has proposed a new open-interface CT that allows the addition of components such as detectors, X-ray tube systems, and other sensors, access to internal component configurations, and exploration of new reconstruction algorithms, for interventional CT (iCT) applications [3].

We investigate the control/synchronization issues of different vendor components and real-time data acquisition and pre-processing in existing CT scanners.

© The Author(s), under exclusive license to Springer Nature Switzerland AG 2023
F. Palumbo et al. (Eds.): ARC 2023, LNCS 14251, pp. 361–365, 2023.
https://doi.org/10.1007/978-3-031-42921-7_25

We have identified their limitations and proposed a hardware/software architecture for MPSoC-FPGAs. The proposed architecture implements a control data acquisition system where components can be added in a plug-and-play fashion, and data is collected and pre-processed on-the-fly, providing the aforementioned functionality to the proposed open-interface CT. The rest of the paper is organized as follows: Sect. 2 introduces the research methodology and contributions. Sect. 3 describes the integration of the proposed architecture on the open-interface CT. Sect. 4 discusses the results and future works of this PhD.

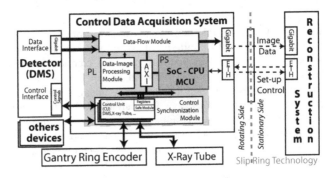

Fig. 1. CT architectural model for the open-interface CT

2   Methodology and Contribution

In the proposed open-interface CT scanner, components can be plugged and controlled in real-time. In the first step, we analyzed and matched medical and hardware design requirements. We identified three main CT scan modes: Axial/Helical, Multi-Modality, and Interventional. Although these modes have different timing and image quality requirements, they can use the same sensors/actuators. Therefore, we have proposed a common CT architectural model shown in Fig. 1, where the Control Data Acquisition System (CDAS) architecture for MPSoC-FPGAs can be configured at runtime to meet the different requirements [6]. While other CT architectural models use a distributed solution for control and data acquisition tasks [1], we defined a centralized solution where each physical component has a corresponding hardware and software unit in the CDAS. This centralized solution simplifies the plugging of new components into the system and enhances the timing issues, meeting the real-time requirements.

2.1   Control Data Acquisition System Architecture

To meet real-time requirements, we classified tasks into three different classes: control/synchronization tasks, data acquisition tasks, and data processing tasks. Then, we divided real-time and non-real-time tasks within each class. Finally, we mapped real-time and non-real-time tasks to the Programmable Logic (PL) and Processing System (PS) of the MPSoC-FPGA, respectively. Tasks of different components are mapped in separate modules to run them in isolated domains [7].

2.2   Configurable Datapath for Data Acquisition

In order to acquire data in real-time, we have proposed a configurable datapath, which is implemented on the PL of the CDAS architecture [8]. At design time, the datapath can be configured for acquiring data from various sensors (e.g., detectors), filtering and merging them before storing in memory or forwarding them to another system. To support multiple independent data streams, each receiver/transceiver gets a system and a reference clock and generates a data clock in relationship with the data rate. All the independent streams are merged in the scheduler stage, where asynchronous FIFOs realize the clock crossing between the receiver, processing, and transmitter domains. In contrast to related works [10], the proposed architecture does not use any external memory to buffer data, exploiting individual pipeline instances for each clock domain. [8]

2.3   Image Processing Core

To improve the reconstruction algorithm, we propose an on-the-fly image processing core implemented in the CDAS architecture [5]. It receives data directly from the Configurable Datapath, processes and sends them back to the Configurable Datapath, which forwards the processed data to the reconstruction system. The Processing Core implements the I0-correction step in a pipelined architecture and can be extended to perform the other pre-processing steps. To enhance the I0 correction, we have proposed a solution that processes raw attenuated data, unlike related work that uses intensity data to perform it.

2.4   Design Space Exploration for Image Processing Architecture

The proposed image processing core enables the exploration of the design space, using as input parameters the different data formats [5]. In fact, we have used it to find which data format between floating-point and fixed-point improves the reconstruction performance, considering the image quality, the time, and the resource utilization in the cost function. We have observed that fixed-point 16 and 32 bits use only LUTs without DSP blocks, improving timing performance [5].

2.5   Isolation Method for MPSoC-FPGA

As mentioned, blocks associated with different components must run in isolated hardware instances. Since isolation mechanisms are provided only for a few MPSoC-FPGAs, we investigate this problem by targeting low-cost devices. We have proposed a new method for supporting isolation that is based on three elements: Protection Domains (PDs), Memory Regions (MRs), and Access Policies (APc) [4]. In addition, we have exploited the AXI-communication, where a Protection Unit (PU) denies/accepts transactions. Each PU is associated with one or more PDs and MRs at design time. At run-time, the APs define the matching between PUs and MRs, denying/accepting transactions of a Master (part of a PD), to a Peripheral or a Memory Address (part of an MR).

3   Realization

The proposed CDAS architecture has been mainly described in SystemVerilog and implemented on the Zynq 7000 SoC ZC706 Evaluation Kit. Data are collected via gigabit transceivers configured with IP blocks. The CDAS hardware architecture runs at different clock speeds: the system clock at 100MHz, transceiver reference clocks at 156MHz, and the processing core at 200MHz. The CDAS software modules are managed by the Petalinux operating system running on the PS. Finally, a PCB board permits to connect CT components to the MPSoC-FPGA.

4   Results and Future Work

We have obtained various results from the explained research contributions [4–8], which comprise our proposed CDAS architecture for MPSoC FPGAs. The overall architecture without processing core introduces a maximum delay of 50 clock cycles and utilizes only 3305 LookUp-Tables (LUTs) and 4390 Flip-Flops (FFs). As reported in Ref. [5], the processing core has different timing and resource utilization based on the selected data format. In the case of iCT, the best format that optimizes delay and resource utilization, keeping image quality, is the 32-bit fixed-point. It introduces a delay of 40 ns and utilizes only 1245 LUTs and 309 FFs. We also observed that the proposed protection unit with 16 PDs and 16 MRs introduces no delay to the AXI transaction and uses only 950 LUTs and 678 FFs of the selected FPGA-MPSoC. In the next steps of our research, we intend to extend the processing core to the other preprocessing steps. In addition, we have planned to start the exploration of new adaptive SoCs [9] that offer hardware accelerators capable of performing the back-projection phase of the reconstruction algorithm.

References

1. AMD-Xilinx: Medical Imaging with CT Scanners and MRI Machines. https://www.xilinx.com/applications/medical/medical-imaging-ct-mri-pet.html
2. Hsieh, J.: Computed Tomography: Principles, Design, Artifacts, and Recent Advances. SPIE press, Bellingham (2003)
3. OVGU: KIDS-CT, Open-Interface-CT (2021). https://www.forschungscampus-stimulate.de/de/services/open-interface-ct/index.html

4. Passaretti, D., Boehm, F., Wilhelm, M., Pionteck, T.: Hardware isolation support for low-cost SoC-FPGAs. In: Schulz, M., Trinitis, C., Papadopoulou, N., Pionteck, T. (eds.) ARCS 2022. Lecture Notes in Computer Science, vol. 13642, pp. 148–163. Springer, Cham (2022). https://doi.org/10.1007/978-3-031-21867-5_10
5. Passaretti, D., Ghosh, M., Abdurahman, S., Egito, M.L., Pionteck, T.: Hardware optimizations of the X-ray pre-processing for interventional computed tomography using the FPGA. Appl. Sci. **12**(11), 5659 (2022)
6. Passaretti, D., Joseph, J.M., Pionteck, T.: Survey on FPGAs in medical radiology applications: challenges, architectures and programming models. In: 2019 International Conference on Field-Programmable Technology (ICFPT) (2019)
7. Passaretti, D., Pionteck, T.: Hardware/software co-design of a control and data acquisition system for computed tomography. In: 2020 9th International Conference on Modern Circuits and Systems Technologies (MOCAST), pp. 1–4. IEEE (2020)
8. Passaretti, D., Pionteck, T.: Configurable pipelined datapath for data acquisition in interventional computed tomography. In: 2021 IEEE 29th Annual International Symposium on Field-Programmable Custom Computing Machines (FCCM) (2021)
9. Vissers, K.: Versal: the Xilinx adaptive compute acceleration platform (ACAP). In: Proceedings of the 2019 ACM/SIGDA (2019)
10. Xie et al.: FPGA implementation of high-speed data acquisition system for high-resolution millimeter wave radar. In: MOCAST 2020 (2020)

Simulation and Modelling for Network-on-Chip Based MPSoC

Julian Haase[1]([⊠])[iD] and Diana Göhringer[1,2][iD]

[1] Chair of Adaptive Dynamic Systems,
Technische Universität Dresden, Dresden, Germany
{Julian.Haase,Diana.Goehringer}@tu-dresden.de
[2] Centre for Tactile Internet with Human-in-the-Loop (CeTI), Technische Universität
Dresden, Dresden, Germany

Abstract. As systems that can adapt their architecture and behavior in response to their environment become increasingly valuable in modern applications, research and development in inherently adaptive embedded systems is gaining momentum. Network-on-Chip based multi-processor architectures are promising for the development of adaptive embedded systems. The aim of this PhD work is to create a comprehensive simulation platform that bridges the gap between simulation and the design of such adaptive systems on real hardware. This paper introduces our proposed platform, presents preliminary results, and highlights upcoming steps and planned future work in this research topic.

Keywords: Simulator · Modelling · Network-on-Chip · SystemC TLM · heterogeneous MPSoC

1 Introduction

The evolution of Very Large-Scale Integration (VLSI) technologies has catalyzed a significant increase in the number of transistors integrated on Systems-on- Chip (SoCs), escalating to billions. Therefore, modern SoCs with a variety of applications could be equipped with numerous Intellectual Property (IP) cores. This massive integration of processing elements (PEs) on a single chip, known as Multiprocessor SoC (MPSoC), offers unprecedented parallel computation power for embedded devices like Field Programmable Gate Arrays (FPGAs), while simultaneously necessitating a scalable communication architecture [1]. The performance of those systems has consequently become heavily reliant of this communication infrastructure. Nowadays, the Network-on-Chip (NoC) architecture has emerged as a promising approach. Owing to its attributes such as low latency, high throughput, and scalability, NoCs appear well-suited to address the demands of modern MPSoCs [1]. However, the Design Space Exploration (DSE) of NoC-based MPSoC architectures is vast and complicated due to their numerous attributes. NoCs encompass a wide range of characteristics such as topology, routing algorithms, flow control, buffer size, virtual channels, and many more. Given this context, the importance of simulating these systems early in the design phase becomes crucial, enabling the development of prototypes that

© The Author(s), under exclusive license to Springer Nature Switzerland AG 2023
F. Palumbo et al. (Eds.): ARC 2023, LNCS 14251, pp. 366–370, 2023.
https://doi.org/10.1007/978-3-031-42921-7_26

can run not only accelerated applications or bare-metal ones (on microprocessors), but also sophisticated operating systems without the need to go to the real hardware. Despite the existence of NoC simulators such as Noxim [2], difficulties remain in accurately but abstractly modelling those heterogeneous MPSoC architectures incorporating with various PEs such as RISC-V Virtual Prototypes (VPs) [3] or hardware accelerators. In addition, security aspects require further research, as there may be non-trusted components in the system due to third party IP cores. Furthermore, there is currently a significant gap in the adequate modelling of reconfiguration for embedded devices, particularly in terms of accurately reflecting the impact of reconfiguration on performance and application in MPSoC architectures. Alternative solutions are necessary to surmount the limitations of existing methodologies, with a particular emphasis on reducing design time and efforts. Such advancements directly enable the accelerated realization of more capable, efficient, and performance-optimized embedded systems. This enhancement in the design process is crucial as it translates into faster time-to-market and the potential to address more complex computational challenges in real-world applications. Hence, the following main objectives can be derived for this PhD thesis. Providing a new *simulation platform* to investigate the performance and security implications under the inclusion of RISC-V VPs in NoC-based MPSoC. This platform should not only improve the understanding of these systems, but also should provide starting points for potential design optimizations. In addition, early design prototyping is intended to close the gap between simulations and real hardware. Establishing robust methodologies for *modelling reconfiguration*, with a focus on Dynamic Partial Reconfiguration (DPR) of FPGA. The modeling process should accurately capture the reconfiguration strategies and their impact on the overall system. This objective is crucial in understanding the implications and benefits of dynamic reconfigurability in NoC-based MPSoC, enabling more versatile and adaptable hardware designs.

2   Overview of Proposed Simulation Platform

The proposed simulation platform, PANACA, comprises three integral components and is based on SystemC-TLM. Firstly, it features a highly configurable NoC simulation that allows for a wide range of network features to be explored [4]. It delivers flexible and precise modeling of network elements with an extensive range of adjustable parameters such as topology, routing algorithm, and flow control. PANACA's in-built simulation and exploration management features facilitate a detailed, automated examination of the expansive design space. Secondly, PANACA also enables the simulation of RISC-V based MPSoCs, allowing for a cohesive analysis of these systems' computational and communication facets [5]. A developed memory-mapped network adapter bridges the RISC-V processors and the NoC, facilitating efficient communication through a unified API. Crucially, this API is designed such that the application using it is compatible with both simulation and hardware without necessitating any code modification. Figure 1 shows how the base platform is extended with the tool flow for RISC-V cores.

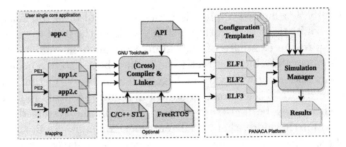

Fig. 1. Overview of the complete tool flow. An application app.c is split into several chunks (app1.c ...) which lead to own files for each RISC-V processing element.

Lastly, the platform incorporates security features through special network adapters, fostering an in-depth understanding of the security implications in NoC-based MPSoC [6]. The communication protocol based on authenticated encryption with recovery mechanisms establish secure end-to-end communication between the NoC nodes. In addition, a selected key agreement approach required for secure communication is implemented. If data is tampered with or deleted during transmission, recovery mechanisms ensure that the corrupted data is retransmitted by the network adapter without the need of interference from the processing element. Together, these components create a comprehensive platform that significantly aids in the design and analysis of complex, secure, and efficient NoC-based MPSoCs.

3   Preliminary Results

The PANACA platform, with its comprehensive modeling capabilities, ensures high simulation performance without compromising the correctness of timing, aided by SystemC TLM Loosely-Timed style. The studies in [4,5] evaluates the simulator's performance using different configurations varying in network size. The simulation runtime in PANACA scales linearly with the increase in network traffic, implying a direct correlation. Notably, larger networks, due to the quadratic growth of nodes in a mesh topology, will witness a more rapid escalation in runtime. The simulation runtime varies from around 1 ms for 4×4 NoC to around 15 ms for 32×32 NoC which has more then 1000 PEs. The study in [6] presents several findings regarding the impact of the proposed recovery mechanism on network traffic in the face of attacks. When more attacks are launched, more flits are injected into the network, which in turn correlates with the acceptance rate. This interaction leads to an inversely proportional relationship between the acceptance rate and the information gain. The latency in cycles is found to increase with a higher number of attackers present in the network, given that more packets may require retransmission for successful forwarding to the PE. Moreover, with a fixed attack probability of 0.1, the introduction of recovery mechanism only increases latency by a moderate range of 10% to a maximum of 30%.

4   Conclusion

This PhD project proposes a simulation platform PANACA that enables the modelling of NoC-based MPSoCs including RISC-V VP cores as PEs. Moreover, the platform incorporates security features through special network adapters, fostering an in-depth understanding of the security implications. The preliminary results indicate a high simulation speed making it useful for early design phase prototyping. Still, further work is necessary to make the proposed PhD work applicable for more application scenarios and architectures. We plan to establish robust methods for modelling reconfiguration, with a focus on DPR of FPGA. The modeling process should accurately capture the reconfiguration strategies and their impact on the overall system. In addition, we plan to verify the platform with a corresponding adaptive hardware platform [7] implemented on Xilinx devices. Some adaptive routing algorithms which tackle failed or attacked links in the network could improve the network robustness. At the evaluation level, we plan to provide more motivating examples and real-world scenarios where we can demonstrate our platform.

Acknowledgement. Funded by the German Research Foundation (DFG, Deutsche Forschungsgemeinschaft) as part of Germany's Excellence Strategy - EXC 2050/1 - Project ID 390696704 - Cluster of Excellence "Centre for Tactile Internet with Human-in-the-Loop" (CeTI) of Technische Universität Dresden.

References

1. Benini, L., Micheli, G.D.: Networks on chips: a new SoC paradigm. Computer **35**(1), 70–78 (2002). https://doi.org/10.1109/2.976921
2. Catania, V., Mineo, A., Monteleone, S., Palesi, M., Patti, D.: Noxim: an open, extensible and cycle-accurate network on chip simulator. In: 2015 IEEE 26th International Conference on Application-specific Systems, Architectures and Processors (ASAP), pp. 162–163 (2015). https://doi.org/10.1109/ASAP.2015.7245728
3. Herdt, V., Große, D., Pieper, P., Drechsler, R.: RISC-V based virtual prototype: an extensible and configurable platform for the system-level. J. Syst. Archit. 109, 1 October 2020. https://doi.org/10.1016/j.sysarc.2020.101756
4. Haase, J., Gros, A., Feichter, M., Göhringer, D.: Panaca: an open-source configurable network-on-chip simulation platform. In: 2022 35th SBC/SBMicro/ IEEE/ACM Symposium on Integrated Circuits and Systems Design (SBCCI), pp. 1–6 (2022). https://doi.org/10.1109/SBCCI55532.2022.9893260
5. Haase, J., Ali, M., Göhringer, D.: Unlocking the potential of RISC-V heterogeneous MPSoCs: a panaca-based approach to simulation and modeling. In: Embedded Computer Systems: Architectures, Modeling, and Simulation, Springer International Publishing (2023)

6. Haase, J., Jaster, S., Franz, E., Göhringer, D.: Secure communication protocol for network-on-chip with authenticated encryption and recovery mechanism. In: 2022 IEEE 33rd International Conference on Application-specific Systems, Architectures and Processors (ASAP), pp. 156–160 (2022). https://doi.org/10.1109/ASAP54787.2022.00033

7. Charaf, N., Haase, J., Kulisch, A., von Elm, C., Göhringer, D.: Rtass: a runtime adaptable and scalable system for network-on-chip-based architectures. In: 26th Euromicro Conference on Digital System Design (DSD) (2023)

A Design-Space Exploration Framework for Application-Specific Machine Learning Targeting Reconfigurable Computing

Safdar Mahmood[1(✉)], Michael Huebner[1], and Marc Reichenbach[1,2]

[1] Chair of Computer Engineering, Brandenburg University of Technology,
Cottbus, Germany
{mahmood,huebner}@b-tu.de, marc.reichenbach@uni-rostock.de
[2] Integrated Systems, The University of Rostock, Rostock, Germany

Abstract. Machine learning has progressed from inaccessible for embedded systems to readily deployable, thanks to efficient training on modern computers. Regrettably, requirements for each specific application which relies on machine learning varies on a case-by-case basis. In each application context, there exists multiple conditions and specifications which call for different design implementations for optimal performance. In addition to that, targeting reconfigurable computing involves further considerations and workarounds such as quantization, pruning, accelerator design, memory usage and energy-efficiency for power-constrained systems. The aim of this Phd Project is to undertake an analysis and investigation of the limitations inherent in application-specific machine learning within the context of reconfigurable computing. Our objective is to investigate in this new dimension and propose a hardware/software framework to facilitate a meticulous design-space exploration, enabling the identification of optimal strategies for achieving an effective and efficient design process by exploiting dynamic reconfiguration.

Keywords: Reconfigurable Computing · Neural Networks · Design Space Exploration · Optimization · Field-Programmable Arrays (FPGAs)

1 Introduction

Deep Convolutional Neural networks implemented on field-programmable gate arrays (FPGAs) have been extensively studied and researched. However, despite the progress made in this area, the potential of runtime reconfiguration for neural networks has yet to be fully exploited. Currently, different implementations of the same application with varying levels of accuracy, its run-time execution latency and energy footprint exist, exhibiting the diverse research opportunity within the field. Moreover, different models with different characteristics can exist for specific use cases within a single application, such as night versus day vision in autonomous driving. These examples, combined with traditional optimization techniques like pruning and quantization etc., highlight the additional

© The Author(s), under exclusive license to Springer Nature Switzerland AG 2023
F. Palumbo et al. (Eds.): ARC 2023, LNCS 14251, pp. 371–374, 2023.
https://doi.org/10.1007/978-3-031-42921-7_27

dimensions of flexibility in machine learning implementations on FPGAs in the context of reconfigurable computing. This Phd project aims to explore this new dimension and envision a hardware/software framework for design space exploration (DSE) that harnesses the potential of run-time reconfiguration.

1.1 Problem Specification

In line with the application scenario which was presented in [2], we consider here the same use-case of detecting improvised land-mines using machine learning techniques, which can eventually be deployed on FPGAs. In this preliminary work [2], it is shown that different off-the-shelf CNN architectures with varying number of parameters exhibit different levels of accuracy, precision and recall. For this particular application, recall as a metric is considerably important. Since recall is calculated as $tp/(tp + fn)$, any number of false negatives (fn) means higher risk of undetected mines, where as false positives (fp) do not pose any risk. This also means a theoretical recall of 100% is desired for minimizing the risk of not detecting a landmine when there is in fact a mine present (False Negatives). In the light of these factors, a model can be trained and evaluated by fixating a metric to a certain value while trying to maximize other related metrics. Some preliminary investigation into training such models based on the simulated [3] land-mines dataset used in [2], yielded following results as presented in Table 1.

Table 1. Top 3 Custom CNNs trained for detecting improvised land-mines using GPR image dataset from [2]

	Parameters	Accuracy	Precision	Recall	$Precision_{at\,Recall=100\%}$
1	316545	90.97%	85.37%	96.55%	81.01%
2	926465	90.65%	87.58%	92.41%	79.23%
3	608833	90.34%	83.14%	98.62%	80.56%

Precision at Recall = 100% ($P_{Recall=100\%}$) represents instances of respective models when recall was capped at 100%. We can see from Table 1 that highest Precision for ($P_{Recall=100\%}$) was at 81.01% for CNN model 1(316k parameters). But the best overall performance is represented by CNN model 3 (608k parameters) with a maximum recall of 98.62%. To minimize the false negatives, these models can be used in several stages. For example, model 1 can be used to filter out images with best precision = 81.01% and subsequently the filtered out images can be run through model 3 with a comparatively similar accuracy of 90.34% and the best general recall of 98.24%. Also, it is to be noted that all these models have different number of parameters which might result in varying execution latency and energy consumption. To accommodate such diverse requirements of an application, we can employ dynamic reconfiguration on FPGAs. This allows us to facilitate the execution of different models on various hardware designs from a range of available configurations. To establish a design workflow for such an application, a comprehensive and intricate exploration of the design space is necessary for optimal results. Therefore, we propose this framework and design space exploration which aims to facilitate the development of FPGA-based hardware that can dynamically adapt to the application's requirements in terms of time, energy, and runtime efficiency, as demanded by its context.

2   Approach and Framework for Design Space Exploration

Problem Identification. The first step in the framework as shown in Fig. 1 is to identify the specific application and its requirements within the given scenario. This involves understanding the unique needs and objectives of the application, such as its desired performance, accuracy, and efficiency for each separate use case. Additionally, it is crucial to consider the constraints and limitations of the scenario in which the application will be deployed.

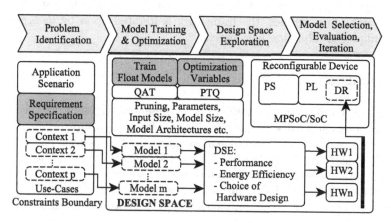

Fig. 1. Design-Space Exploration Framework for Application-Specific Machine Learning targeting Reconfigurable Computing

Model Training and Optimization. During the model training and optimization phase, Quantize Aware Training or Post Training Quantization techniques are applied to train the neural network models. These techniques involve quantizing the model's parameters and activations to lower bitwidth representations. By exploring different bitwidths for quantization, a trade-off between model accuracy and resource utilization can be achieved. At this stage, it is also desired to carefully consider the choice of hardware design, specifically whether to opt for a dataflow-based architecture e.g. FINN [1], a generic deep neural network (DNN) accelerator or a customized architecture based on quantization-adaptable compute units (CUs). Also, in case of post-training quantization (PTQ), accuracy and performance of a set of models might vary drastically as compared to each other based on the bitwidth reduction or calibration during quantization [2].

Design Space Exploration. In the design space exploration phase, a comprehensive analysis based on the previous stage is conducted to identify diverse hardware designs tailored to each specific use case. Evaluation of various models includes metrics like accuracy, precision, recall, energy efficiency, and runtime latency, considering factors as shown in Fig. 1. This assessment determines the most suitable models for different use cases based on performance and resource utilization. Feasibility of dynamic FPGA reconfiguration is also assessed, enabling seamless switching between models for specific use cases or scenarios. This adaptability maximizes efficiency and performance within a given application scenario.

Model Selection, Evaluation and Iteration. In this stage, the optimal models are to be selected by evaluating the results from design space exploration. The requirements and constraints of each use case are to be carefully considered to determine the most suitable models for performing dynamic reconfiguration. For each use case within the given application scenario, the chosen models should align with the desired objectives and constraints provided in first stage. Based on the evaluation outcomes, the framework is iterated upon by incorporating new techniques or adjusting parameters.

3   Conclusion

In this Ph.D. Forum paper, a framework is presented, highlighting the importance of comprehensive design space exploration for application-specific machine learning with multiple use cases to achieve optimal performance. The introduction of dynamic reconfiguration in FPGAs adds a new dimension for analysis and investigation, offering new research possibilities when combined with diverse application requirements. In the future, we also plan to include custom computing architectures which are adaptable to specific use-cases and constraints.

References

1. Blott, M., et al.: FINN-R: an end-to-end deep-learning framework for fast exploration of quantized neural networks. ACM Trans. Reconfig. Technol. Syst. **11**(3) (2018). https://doi.org/10.1145/3242897
2. Mahmood, S., Scharoba, S., Schorlemer, J., Schulz, C., Hubner, M., Reichenbach, M.: Detecting improvised land-mines using deep neural networks on GPR image dataset targeting FPGAs. In: 2022 IEEE Nordic Circuits and Systems Conference, NORCAS 2022 - Proceedings (2022). https://doi.org/10.1109/NorCAS57515.2022. 9934735
3. Schorlemer, J., Jebramcik, J., Baer, C., Rolfes, I., Schulz, C.: A statistical FDFD simulator for the generation of labeled training data sets in the context of humanitarian demining using GPR. In: 2022 IEEE MTT-S International Conference on Numerical Electromagnetic and Multiphysics Modeling and Optimization, NEMO 2022, pp. 1–3 (2022). https://doi.org/10.1109/NEMO51452.2022.10038521

Author Index

F. Palumbo et al. (Eds.): ARC 2023, LNCS 14251, pp. 375–376, 2023.
https://doi.org/10.1007/978-3-031-42921-7

Printed in the United States
by Baker & Taylor Publisher Services